Moral Controversies in American Politics

Moral Controversies in American Politics

Third Edition

Raymond Tatalovich and Byron W. Daynes, Editors

With a Foreword by Theodore J. Lowi

M.E.Sharpe

Armonk, New York
London, England

Library of Congress Cataloging-in-Publication Data

Moral controversies in American politics / edited by Raymond Tatalovich and Byron W.
Daynes.—3rd ed.
    p. cm.
   Includes index.
   ISBN 0-7656-1420-0 (hardcover : alk. paper). ISBN 0-7656-1421-9 (pbk. : alk. paper)
 1. Public policy (Law)—United States. 2. United States—Social policy—Case studies.
3. Social norms—Case studies. 4. Civil rights—United States—Case studies. 5. Social
values—United States—Case studies. I. Tatalovich, Raymond. II. Daynes, Byron W.

KF450.P8M67 2004
320.6'0973—dc22

2004022387

Printed in the United States of America

The paper used in this publication meets the minimum requirements of
American National Standard for Information Sciences
Permanence of Paper for Printed Library Materials,
ANSI Z 39.48-1984.

♾

| BM (c) | 10 | 9 | 8 | 7 | 6 | 5 | 4 | 3 | 2 | 1 |
| BM (p) | 10 | 9 | 8 | 7 | 6 | 5 | 4 | 3 | 2 | 1 |

To our mentor,
Theodore J. Lowi,

who inspires us
as his teachings continue to guide us

R.T.
B.W.D.

Contents

Tables

Foreword

New Dimensions in Policy and Politics

Theodore J. Lowi

Public policy can be defined simply as an officially expressed intention backed by a sanction. Although synonymous with law, rule, statute, edict, and regulation, public policy is the term of preference today probably because it conveys more of an impression of flexibility and compassion than the other terms. But citizens, especially students and practitioners of political science, should always be aware that *policy* and *police* have common origins. Both come from "polis" and "polity," which refer to the political community itself and to the "monopoly of legal coercion" by which government itself has been defined. Consequently, all public policies must be understood as coercive. They may be motivated by the best and most beneficent of intentions, and they may be implemented with utmost care for justice and mercy, but that makes them no less coercive.

There are multitudes of public policies because there are multitudes of social arrangements and conduct that people feel ought to be controlled by coercive means if public order is to be maintained and people are to be able to pursue their private satisfactions in peace. Consequently, some kind of categorization is necessary if meaningful policy analysis is to take place. If the editors and authors of this volume had a particular reason for inviting me to participate in their important project by writing this foreword, it was probably because I was young and foolish enough back in the 1960s to attempt to provide a categorization of public policies and, somewhat later, to describe the logic underlying the categories. If there had been a second reason for involving me it was probably because they found the scheme uncomfortable as well as useful.

In brief, I began the categorization with a simple question: If all policies are coercive, is it possible that we can develop a meaningful, small set of policy categories by asking a prior question of jurisprudence: How many kinds of coercion are there? Leaving aside the fine points of definition, I identified four logically distinguishable ways that government can coerce, and I then attempted to demonstrate, with some degree of acceptance in the field, that each of these types of coercion underlies a type of identifiable public policy. The source of each type of policy was, therefore, so close to state power itself that each, I reasoned, should be located in history and that each would, over time, tend to develop its own distinctive political structure. I was attempting to turn political science on its head (or back on its feet) by arguing that "policy causes politics."

The four categories were given the most appropriate names I could contrive at the time: Distributive Policy, Regulatory Policy, Redistributive Policy, and Constituent Policy. (Figure 1 is the fourfold formulation.) Lately I have grown accustomed to a modification of the names of the categories in order to emphasize the intimacy of the historical association between the type of policy and the type of politics that tends to be associated with it: The Distributive (or Patronage) State, the Regulatory State, the Redistributive (or Welfare) State, and the State within the state.

During the very decade (roughly 1964–1974) that these categories were being developed, the national government was going through a virtual second New Deal. There was an explosion of new regulatory and welfare programs. Although most of these new policies fit comfortably enough into the fourfold scheme, there *was* something new about many of them that was not being captured by the scheme. Every scheme of categorization (of anything) sacrifices informational detail and nuance in order to gain analytic power, but is there a point where the sacrifice is too great? Students of these 1960s and 1970s policies referred to them as "new regulation," "social policy," and "social regulation" in order to convey an emerging sense that there is indeed something about these policies that does not fit comfortably into existing categories. Tatalovich, Daynes, and associates do a valiant job of trying to catch the meaning of the "new" and the "social" and why these policies somehow do not fit into any preexisting scheme. In the opinion of these authors, the only way to preserve the fourfold scheme is to add, in effect, a fifth category, which they call "social regulatory policy."

There is no need to take issue directly with the definition of this fifth category. I will try instead to *subsume* it. I recognized at the outset that

Figure 1   **Types of Coercion, Types of Policy, and Types of Politics**
Applicability of Coercion
(Works through)

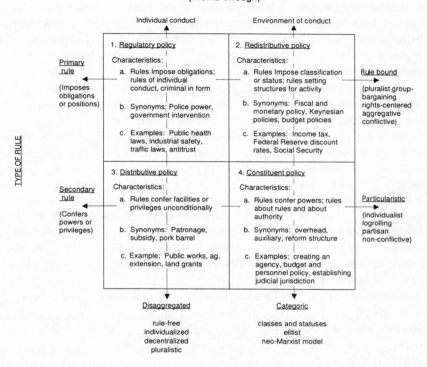

Individual conduct   Environment of conduct

	1. Regulatory policy	2. Redistributive policy
Primary rule (Imposes obligations or positions)	Characteristics: a. Rules Impose obligations; rules of individual conduct, criminal in form b. Synonyms: Police power, government intervention c. Examples: Public health laws, industrial safety, traffic laws, antitrust	Characteristics: a. Rules Impose classification or status; rules setting structures for activity b. Synonyms: Fiscal and monetary policy, Keynesian policies, budget policies c. Examples: Income tax, Federal Reserve discount rates, Social Security

Rule bound
(pluralist group-bargaining
rights-centered
aggregative
conflictive)

	3. Distributive policy	4. Constituent policy
Secondary rule (Confers powers or privileges)	Characteristics: a. Rules confer facilities or privileges unconditionally b. Synonyms: Patronage, subsidy, pork barrel c. Example: Public works, ag. extension, land grants	Characteristics: a. Rules confer powers; rules about rules and about authority b. Synonyms: overhead, auxiliary, reform structure c. Examples: creating an agency, budget and personnel policy, establishing judicial jurisdiction

Particularistic
(individualist
logrolling
partisan
non-conflictive)

TYPE OF RULE

Disaggregated   Categoric

rule-free   classes and statuses
individualized   elitist
decentralized   neo-Marxist model
pluralistic

there is something special about the cases being dealt with in this book. They are cases of regulatory policy in my terms; if they do not seem to fit comfortably it is because the *politics* of the "new" or "social" regulation looks a lot more like what is to be expected with the politics of redistributive policy. The authors discover in their cases that the observed political behavior is more ideological, more moral, more directly derived from fundamental values, more intense, less utilitarian, more polarized, and less prone to compromise.

However, while granting these authors their empirical findings, I resisted creating a new category to fit the findings until all ways of maintaining the fourfold scheme have been exhausted. This position is one part ego but at least four parts bona fide concern not to destroy the simplicity and, more importantly, the logic of the scheme. For one cannot solve the problem by merely adding a new category. Addition of a category weakens the logic altogether. The fifth category will not work entirely until its logic has been worked out and until a probable sixth is coupled with it to give the new scheme a reasonable symmetry.

In the spirit of trying to preserve the fourfold scheme and at the same time trying to give the new findings their due, I will try an alternative. Some people will agree with me that it is a way to preserve the fourfold scheme. Others will say that I am being too accommodating and will destroy the fourfold scheme by turning it not merely into a six or eightfold scheme, but what appears (as in Figure 4, p. xix) to be a twelvefold scheme. Either way, the effort will enhance and dramatize the value of the case materials presented in this volume.

For several years, at least through three editions of this book, I have shared with these authors a concern for how to make sense of the "new politics" of the public-interest groups on the left and the right in the United States and in Europe. Although these groups seem to be seeking policies that could be categorized as (largely) regulatory or redistributive, they refused to join what most of us would consider mainstream political processes, insisting instead on trying to convert political issues into moral polarities, claims into rights, legislation into litigation, grays into blacks and whites, and campaigns into causes and crusades. If there is confusion among analysts about all this, it is because there is an obvious, age-old fact that we have all been overlooking: that for every type of mainstream politics there is a *radical politics*. Policies can remain the same; types of policies can also remain the same—regulatory, or redistributive, or whatever. Just as some mainstream strategies will pay off and some will not (giving each policy type its political distinctiveness) so will radicalization as a strategy sometimes pay off and sometimes will not pay off. When it does pay off, there is likely to be an intensification of all the political elements without necessarily transforming the patterns altogether; and, to repeat, the policy at issue can remain in the same category even as its politics are being radicalized.

Figure 2, a first step toward a new scheme, is an attempt to define radical in relation to mainstream in politics. The *Oxford English Dictionary* defines radical as "of or pertaining to a root or roots." That is the meaning in mathematics and the origin of the term in politics. It is associated with extremes precisely because people who insist on getting to the root of things are likely to express themselves intensely, rejecting the rules and procedures designed to produce compromise—in other words, rejecting mainstream or ordinary politics. However, as soon as the two dimensions, radical and mainstream, are put side by side it becomes obvious that they are not a simple dichotomy because it is in the nature of radical politics to be so much more ideological that radicalism is at least dichotomous within itself. (I say "at least" because a full-scale analysis of radicalism would require more distinctions than the simple two needed here.) Ideology is not absent in mainstream politics, but lower intensity permits mainstream politicians to practice their skill, which is to obtain practical consensus on goals

Figure 2   **Public Philosophy: Mainstream and Radical Politics**

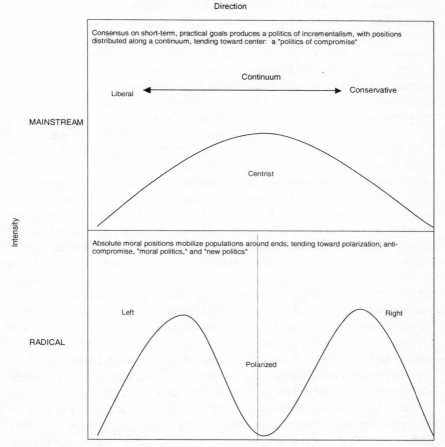

Direction

Consensus on short-term, practical goals produces a politics of incrementalism, with positions distributed along a continuum, tending toward center: a "politics of compromise"

Continuum

Liberal ← → Conservative

MAINSTREAM

Centrist

Intensity

Absolute moral positions mobilize populations around ends; tending toward polarization; anti-compromise, "moral politics," and "new politics"

Left   Right

RADICAL

Polarized

and to reduce differences to a point where political conflict becomes political competition, strategy becomes tactic, and compromise is possible
because the stakes are incremental. To the radical, mainstream means
trivialization, and that is absolutely true. Figure 2 attempts to capture this
evaluation for the mainstream by placing relevant ideologies on a continuum,
with the concentration of positions toward the center, where the frontier
between left and right is very fuzzy.

This is precisely where radicalism differs most: What is a rather fuzzy frontier for the mainstream is a formalized border between radicals of the left and
the right. Intensity of commitment demands an underlying logic, and logic
demands some degree of consistency, reinforced by a conscious affiliation.
Positions are distributed accordingly, in what can best be illustrated in Figure 2

as a bimodal distribution. So consistently is radical politics polarized that this distribution has to be maintained in any diagrammatic analysis. (This is why in Figure 4 we go from four mainstream to eight radical categories.)

Figure 3 moves the analysis one step further by attempting to specify the general substantive orientations of the two dimensions. The basic four policy categories are maintained (across the top and extending through both Mainstream and Radical dimensions). The cells contain brief descriptions of the general political orientation for each of the eight resulting patterns. In this diagram, the left-right direction of ideology is disregarded for the sake of simplicity, based on the assumption that even radicals can, in the words of Carl Friedrich, "agree on what to disagree about." A word of explanation is needed mainly for the concepts in boldface. These were the best available words to connote the general orientation; the prose in each box is an effort to spell that out. Note, for example, the distinction between ERROR and SIN; this is an antinomy, which is intended to suggest how differently the two types view the same regulatory issue. The mainstream approach to regulation is as close to instrumental as human beings can get. Mainstream political actors avoid taking a moral posture toward the conduct to be regulated; conduct is to be regulated only because *it is injurious in its consequences.* Though privately the mainstreamer may consider prostitution immoral, the mainstream public position would be that prostitution should be regulated as to its potential for disease or its association with drugs and abduction. The radical would define the conduct moralistically; that is, for the radical, conduct is to be regulated because *it is good or bad in itself.* From the radical left, prostitution is a sinful product of a sinful economic system; for the radical right it is a sinful expression of bad character. But radicals take a moral posture toward it while mainstreamers can take it as a conduct in need of modification. Regulation is itself a mainstream word, coming from the French, régle (rule), so that réglementation means "to impose rules upon" or to regularize. From the radical, moralistic standpoint, regulation is for wishy-washy liberals. If "bad conduct" is bad enough to warrant the attention of the state, the objective of radical regulation is complete elimination of the conduct.

There is no need to treat the three remaining categories too extensively, since the phenomenon of concern in this book is regulation. Suffice it to say that the boldface concepts in each of the categories were also selected as antinomies that distinguish most clearly between mainstream and radical discourse, with radicals of both sides agreeing with each other on what to disagree about. Thus, even on something as commonplace as distributive policy (patronage), radicals can be quite moralistic: Railroads should be public corporations because capitalism is bad; museums should be built because art is good. In contrast, for mainstreamers, the whole point of resorting to patronage

Figure 3   **How Policy Problems are Defined in Mainstream Politics**

	Regulative (Policy toward conduct)	Distributive (Policy toward facilities)	Redistributive (Policy toward status)	Constituent (Policy toward structure)
MAINSTREAM	Control the *consequences* of conduct, consequences defined in purely instrumental terms. Orientation of the discourse is:	Goals defined instrumentally or denotatively, without a governing rule. Orientation of the discourse is:	Class and status relations are specified but redistributive effect minimized by spreading benefits upward and obligations downward. Exclusiveness softened with equities. Orientation of discourse is:	A process definition of the Constitution and rights; a representation definition of government; the good administrator is neutral, obedient to elected officials; decision by competition. Orientation of discourse is:
	ERROR	UTILITY	ENTITLEMENT	ACCOUNTABILITY
RADICAL	Control of conduct as good or bad *in itself*, consequences defined in moral absolutes; stress particularly on bad conduct. The orientation of discourse is:	Goals defined in terms of consequences but moral consequences, such as improvement of character (right) or defense against capitalism (left). The orientation of discourse is:	Class and status relations are exclusive, imbedded in absolutes that transcend policy. Property rights (right) and welfare rights (left); social definitions of rights (left), individualist definitions of rights (right). Orientation of discourse is:	A substantive definition of the Constitution. Good government is commitment to a substantive definition of justice. The good administrator is committed to the program (left) or to good moral character (right). The orientation of discourse is:
	SIN	CIVIC VIRTUE	RIGHTS	COMMITMENT

policy is its UTILITY, its complete amorality; patronage policy is a way to displace conflict, not confront it. For redistributive policy, the near antinomy between ENTITLEMENT and RIGHTS should be close to self-evident. Description in the boxes might help marginally. The constituent policy categories may cause a bit more of a problem, but that need not be a burden for us here. The best way to think about this category is through the history of American approaches to the "good administrator." For the Founders, the ideal of the good administrator was virtually the philosopher king, an elite of talent, experience, judgment, and morality. Beginning with Andrew Jackson, the ideal of a good administrator was the "common man." This was demeaned as the "spoils system," but it was more accurately termed "rotation in office." As Andrew Jackson put it, "the duties of all public offices are, or at least admit of being made, so plain and simple that men of intelligence may readily qualify themselves for their performance." Jackson's standard was, later in the nineteenth century, replaced with skill—later called "meritocracy." That has changed in various ways in the past century, but the ideal of the good administrator has remained an instrumental one. Nowadays, the conservative view excepts the instrumental but would subordinate to character. On the left, the question of skill is subordinated to loyalty to the program.

We can now turn to Figure 4, the main point and purpose of this enterprise. Figure 4 combines features of Figures 1–3 and joins them to actual policy issues. The antimonies from Figure 3 are repeated in boldface to evoke (without enough space to be explicit) a sense of the political patterns to be expected.

Figure 4 is a variation on an earlier effort to make sense of environmental policies, which are so rich in "new politics."[1] Although one-quarter of the figure (Regulatory) is relevant to the cases in this volume, the full, fourfold presentation in the figure is provided in hopes of making a productive linkage to the findings of this book and in hopes of putting these findings in an inherently comparative context.

I like this figure, as revised, not merely because it might preserve my scheme. It confirms my own confidence that policy categorization (not necessarily mine) will in the long run be the route to the new political theory because it arises out of some fundamental political truths: (1) that there are inherent limits to the ways a state can control society, no matter how powerful that state may be; (2) that each of these ways is so fundamental that each way has enough of a history and a regularity to become in itself a kind of regime; and (3) that every regime tends to produce a politics consonant with itself. This particular effort has perhaps added a fourth truth: that political leaders can transform politics through radicalization, by adding a moral dimension to the policy discourse. Radicalizing the policy (i.e., adding the

Figure 4 Policies and Politics in Two Dimensions

POLICY TYPE

DIMENSION OF POLITICS	1 Regulatory	2 Distributive	3 Redistributive	4 Constituent
MAINSTREAM	**ERROR** Standards of conduct Economic sector regulation Regulation to maintain competition Regulatory taxes Licensing to enforce standards	**UTILITY** Public works Defense installations and stockpiling R & D Sales of public property or access to it Unconditional licensing	**ENTITLEMENT** "Social costs" Income taxation Economic policy through the tax system ("tax expenditure") Social Security Monetary policies	**ACCOUNTABILITY** "Causal theory" Liberal, value-free education Policies restricting state action Administrative reform for neutral, scientific decisionmaking

RADICAL

	SIN		**CIVIC VIRTUE**		**RIGHTS**		**MORAL GOVERNMENT**	
	Left	Right	Left	Right	Left	Right	Left	Right
	Right to results of regulation (suits to force regulation)	Right to public order and self-defense	Public ownership of essential service	Public works for private market	Progressive income taxation exclusively	Sales taxes and other regressive taxes exclusively	"Class theory"	"Obligation theory"
	Cost-oblivious economic regulation	Regulation for moral guidance	Displacement of corporate power	Subsidies to industry for the public good	Antiwealth taxes (estate, luxuries, etc.)	Punitive taxes ("sin" taxes to discourage alcohol, tobacco, etc.)	Socialization education	Moral education
	Affirmative action	Victimless crimes	Planning for national use of resources		Welfare as a right	Welfare as a moral lesson	Bill of Rights (complete nationalization)	State rights
	Capitalism as morally suspect	Capitalism as a moral good	Convert distributive to redistributive	Convert distributive to moral regulation			Participatory democracy (judicially enforced)	Republicanism ("rightly understood")
							Programmatic administrator	Good administrator
							Party executive	Commander-in-chief executive

moral dimension) will almost certainly change the political patterns, but even radicalized political patterns will still vary according to the particular policy category (regime) in question.

Since Tatalovich, Daynes, and associates have concentrated on the regulatory category, I will hold my elaboration of this now two-dimensional scheme to the regulatory quadrant alone. But this should not mask the fact that if we had cases here of radicalized policies in, say, the redistributive category, the political pattern, though radicalized, would probably differ from the pattern observed in the radicalized regulatory cases.

Virtually all regulatory policy, as we know it from the familiar economic regulatory programs of the national government, approaches conduct in an almost purely instrumental way. It arises largely out of concern for conduct deemed good or bad *only in its consequences*. (See Figure 4, upper left corner.) The very term *regulation* or *regulatory policy*, as suggested above, became the term of choice by lawyers, economists, and policymakers because the goal of most of these policies is not so much to eliminate the conduct in question but to reduce it, channel it, or otherwise constrain it so that the conduct might persist but with fewer of the injuries (or in some instances, more of the benefits) attributed to it. But there is another whole reality of regulatory policies, and those policies are concerned with conduct *deemed good or bad in itself* (lower left corner in figure). The first type, instrumental regulation, will be abbreviated as C_1. The second, moral regulation, will be referred to as C_2. Most C_2 regulation in the United States has escaped the recent attention of most political scientists (until this volume) because it has been the province of state government. Examples include the criminal law, all the sex and morality laws, some family and most divorce laws, the basic compulsory education laws, and the fundamental property laws. The intrinsic moral orientation of this kind of policy accounts also for the fact that state politics in the nineteenth century (when most of these policies were being enacted as a matter of positive, statute law) was far more radical, often violent, than the politics of regulation at the national level. Note well that the descriptions of state politics will reveal that they were dominated far less by political parties and far more by interest groups and social movements. Some of those interest groups engaged in mainstream politics—lobbying, bargaining, and compromise within the party structure. But groups engaged in "direct-action politics," "single-issue politics," and "social movement politics" to a far greater extent than the pattern normally experienced at the national level.

"Marriage policy" provides a very good contemporary case study of the radical political consequences of adding moral (C_2) considerations to mainstream political discourse. Marriage as such has nothing to do with morality or religion. Marriage is a civil contract, therefore a civil union that any couple can enter into by going together to their county courthouse or town or city hall, getting the forms from the county, town, or city clerk, and filling out the forms with personal information. The clerk then stamps and signs. Then (using New York as a common example) the marriage must be "solemnized" by a "public officer," as specified by law. That officer can be a magistrate or a clergyman, as defined by law. These are equal and interchangeable "marriage officers," and "no particular form or ceremony is required. . . ."[2]

A *wedding* can of course be performed by clergy, with any elaborate ceremonies and sacred texts associated with that particular religion. But it would not be a legal *marriage* unless one of those robed figures were a certified "marriage officer" indistinguishable legally from any other magistrate as provided by law. Americans are the most religiously observant people in all of the democracies of the world, so that it is not surprising that so many Americans are unable to imagine marriage without the participation and the blessing of the appropriately costumed representatives of the faith shared by the bride and groom. Insecurity often shadows a marriage of mixed religions, especially if the two faiths are a good distance apart. Purely civil marriages "at city hall" without the participation of clergy have been considered incomplete, to such an extent that civil marriages are quite frequently followed by a "church wedding." This is especially true for youngsters who elope and later seek the blessing or acceptance of one or both sets of parents by a second marriage in an agreed-upon church. Nevertheless, it is the civil marriage that is genuine; the follow-up church wedding is purely symbolic.

Moral regulations by the dozens apply to married persons, but only as part of the population at large and not as an intrinsic part of marriage. Marriage in fact frees the married couple to engage in certain kinds of conduct that, until recent years, was a crime for unmarried persons to engage in. In fact, there still exists in the morality laws of many states, albeit rarely implemented, provisions that make it a crime for any two persons to engage in *any* sexual act other than fornication in the missionary position between two persons of opposite sex who are married. The more "heinous" sexual acts, such as incest or sodomy or rape or seduction of a minor by an adult are not marriage morality laws at all but are moral regulations that apply across the board, as crimes committed by any persons, married or not. And certain types of persons are forbidden by law on moral grounds to marry. At present, one cannot be married to more than one person at a time. ("At present" has to be added because bigamy rules can change from generation to generation.) At present, one person cannot marry another if there is to close a blood relation between the two. (As with bigamy, the rules of incest vary from time to time.) And until the late 1960s, it was a crime in some states for a Caucasian to marry a person of a different race.[3] None of this is pertinent to marriage as such.

In fact, most of the moral/religious (C_2) content of marriage policy has been not about marriage at all but about the end of marriage: divorce. And this makes marriage as a case study all the more interesting, because there has been a dramatic secular decline in the moral content of divorce policy during the past fifty or more years, to such a degree that we can safely generalize that "no-fault divorce" now prevails throughout the nation, and no-fault divorce has *taken virtually all of the morality out of the institution of marriage.*

Thus, in the memory of most living Americans, the terms of discourse in matters of marriage policy, including divorce, has been instrumental, mainstream. That is, until gay and lesbian couples came forward to demand "equal protection of the laws." Then quite suddenly the policy discourse regarding marriage became once again infused with morality, and marriage politics became radicalized. From the standpoint of state law, nothing at all had to be changed in order to permit state-qualified "marriage officers" to marry couples of the same sex. New York law provides simply that "marriage is a civil contract." And it refers to couples seeking marriage as "parties." To be even-handed, and politically correct, the provision refers to "him or her" and "he and she," but nowhere does the law provide that one contracting party has to be a "he" and the other has to be a "she." Thus, nothing has to be changed in law to marry a couple comprised of two "hes" or two "shes," as long as the couple follows the simple procedures of filling out the application and solemnizing the agreement with a magistrate, plus one or more witnesses.

Same sex marriage became an issue through the efforts of those who favor or oppose same sex marriage on moral grounds, which led to the movement toward return to a general definition of marriage as a moral matter. The immediate effect was once again the removal of marriage policy out of mainstream politics. At the state level it removed the issue out of political parties and legislatures into the judiciary (typical of radicalizing policy in the United States). Meanwhile it also nationalized the issue, contributing especially to the re-invigoration of religious and other conservative movements toward the more general effort to restore morality to the marriage contract and to other areas of conduct, toward C_2. There had for a long time been a virtual wall of separation between church and state, with the church monopoly of *weddings* remaining unthreatened while legal *marriage* remained secular, civil. This was going to change.

During the last two decades of the twentieth century, the Republican Party was moving rightward under the influence of a morality grounded religious movement, combined with a secular right wing which shared much of the moral domestic agenda and added to it a morally grounded foreign policy. So influential was this joining together of two or three political movements within the Republican Party that it drew the Democrats rightward as well.

Signs of this moralization of national politics are to be seen by the bipartisan enactment of new and very tough Crime Control Act provisions under Bill Clinton. Other signs were the revival of moral stigmatizing of the poor in the 1996 welfare reform and, more relevant here, the Defense of Marriage Act, which was the first effort ever to establish a national standard of marriage, and in this case to establish a national standard that only a marriage between two persons of the opposite sex would be recognized as a legal marriage. This produced a presidentially supported proposal for a constitutional amendment prohibiting the states from enacting legislation that recognizes as legal the marriage between two persons of the same sex. In fact the decision goes still further by barring the Massachusetts legislature from enacting provisions for "civil union" in which spouses (of whatever gender) would have "all the same benefits, protections, rights and responsibilities under law as are granted to spouses in a marriage."

Paul Starr, a liberal writing in a staunchly liberal journal, *The American Prospect*, observed in exasperation—but in a manner fully confirming the transformative effect that (moral) policy causes (radical) politics:

> The [liberal] Massachusetts judges and religious conservatives are joined in a kind of antagonistic cooperation. They agree that constitutional law ought to settle the question of same-sex marriage and are forcing Americans to deal with the issue in those terms. But the case for leaving controversies to politics and legislation, rather than fixing them in constitutional principle, is especially strong where public sentiment is fluid and highly charged. Legislation allows for negotiations among elected representatives; *a legislative compromise may be incremental*, the losing side is more likely to accept the outcome, and the result may be more stable and legitimate in the eyes of the public.[4]

These examples merely anticipate innumerable examples in the chapters to come, in which all the cases are examples of the policy-to-politics connection that ought to be a prime focus of political science. But there is the normative issue beyond these observations and patterns: It is lodged in Starr's observation and confirms misgivings I have carried around for a very long time but did not manage to express until my 1995–1996 book, *The End of the Republican Era*[5]: *Morality in politics is antagonistic to mainstream, ordinary politics, in particular to party politics.* Republicans led—and Democrats followed—with a vast expansion of the moral definition of policy issues; and as they did that, they seriously weakened their own institution, party government. Deradicalization—by removal of moral definitions from marriage, civil rights, product and employee liability, single motherhood, child dependency, contraception, abortion, and so forth—contributed to the revival of a two-party system in state after state, reversing a pattern that had prevailed between 1896 and the 1950s: That pattern was a one-party Democratic South and an almost equally one-party Republican North. It was treated by many, including most political scientists, as a two-party system when it was in fact two *one-party* systems that looked sort of like a two-party system if one limited one's vision *to Congress.*

With the revival of moral discourse in politics in the 1980s and 1990s, we can perceive definite signs of a return, a decline toward one-partyism. The two-party system today seems stronger; but that is a false signal. Although Congress today looks more like the disciplined parties of the era around 1900—comparable to the British House of Commons—the present level of party unity comes much less from party discipline and much more from member consensus arising out of stable one-party states based on moral consensus. And this is being virtually institutionalized by unprecedented bipartisan abuse of the power of parties in the state legislatures to redistrict by radical gerrymandering congressional and state representative districts following each decennial census. Redistricting has always been one of the more cynical aspects of party politics. State party leaders often collaborate (conspire?) to redistrict in a way that strengthens the position of incumbents in both parties. More recently, state party leaders under the Voting Rights Act have also collaborated to draw district lines to increase the number of minority representatives to Congress and to state legislatures—even when that produces a net increase in white conservative Republicans. But now both parties show no need to collaborate: Each uses its hold on the state legislatures to create safe seats for their own party—making their state a *legislated* one-party system.

Radicalism has its place in a democracy. So does morality. Many of the major advancements in governing and in civil rights and civil liberties have been made only by social movements whose moral fervor overwhelms vested interests and inertia. But there can be "too much of a good thing," in every sense of that old phrase. This is all worth pondering as we read through the fascinating and enlightening contributions in this volume: How does moral politics influence public policy?

Introduction

Social Regulations and the Policy Process

Raymond Tatalovich and Byron W. Daynes

In a now classic article, Theodore J. Lowi argued that government enacts three different types of public policy: distributive policy (government subsidies), regulatory policy (government controls on business), and redistributive policy (government welfare programs).[1] Although he later added a fourth type, constituent policy,[2] Lowi was primarily concerned about *economic* policies and did not address the policies that erupt from moral conflicts until he penned the forward to the first edition of this work in 1988. The term *regulation,* as Lowi employed it, is generally associated with government controls on businesses, from the auto industry to the stock market, that stimulate or restrict competition, protect the consumer and worker, and ensure a stable legal environment for economic transactions.

Moral conflicts are unlike economic disputes. While economic conservatives would defend free markets against liberal demands for government restraint of competition, battles over morality policy often find conservatives defending the normative status quo whereas liberals are more likely to accommodate changes in social values. As a consequence, moral conservatives want individual freedoms subordinated to community norms, whereas liberals defend personal liberties from the majority. With social regulations, therefore, what is being regulated is not an economic transaction but a social relationship. Changing social relationships may give rise to demands from citizens that legal authority be used to affirm the traditional normative order, or modify it, or sanction entirely new standards of behavior. In sum, we offer this working definition of social regulatory policy: *the exercise of legal authority to affirm, modify, or replace community values, moral practices, and norms of interpersonal conduct.*

The first scholar to extend Lowi's policy framework to other countries was T. Alexander Smith, who took notice that morally charged "emotive-symbolic" policies were fundamentally unlike Lowi's economic disputes.[3] In 2003 Smith joined with Raymond Tatalovich to write a comprehensive assessment of the morality policy process in the Western democracies, especially in the United States, Canada, United Kingdom, Germany, and France.[4] Smith and Tatalovich bolstered our thesis that "status" politics lies at the heart of moral conflicts. It was Max Weber who compared status groups, defined as "communities based upon the sharing of similar claims to social honor and prestige," to social classes that have "similar economic capacity to command scarce resources and life chances."[5] Studies have linked status anxieties to many social issues, including the Women's Christian Temperance Union, antiobscenity campaigns, opposition to the equal rights amendment for women, anti-immigrant "nativist" outbursts, battles over secularism in public school curricula, and support for reestablishing public school prayer.[6]

In previous editions we hypothesized the impact of moral conflicts on the American political system in the form of fourteen propositions. In this volume we provide brief explanations of these fourteen propositions to guide readers through these nine case studies. At the end of each case study, the author(s) briefly summarize whether each hypothesis is supported or unsupported by the evidence. *The "Summary of Propositions" in each chapter is included to encourage the reader to consider what specific arguments, events, and historical developments would support, or contradict, each hypothesis.*

Proposition 1a: Single-issue groups are the lobbies that most increase public awareness and the political significance of social regulatory policy.

Groups that Theodore J. Lowi would expect to become mobilized over distributive policy (beneficiaries), economic regulations (trade associations), and redistributive policy ("peak" associations) would typically not be engaged in contentious social regulations, because most interest groups are created to defend the economic interests of their memberships, not to champion moral crusades. Because principle and altruism are the key motivating forces behind moral conflicts, though interest sometimes come into play, grassroots activism surfaces in the form of single-issue advocacy. Single-issue groups are the preferred organizational strategy for defenders of the traditional moral order.

Proposition 1b: Single-issue groups promote absolutist positions on social regulatory policy that polarize the debate between nonnegotiable, moral alternatives.

Moral conflicts pose challenges to our system of government. The conflicts over abolition and Prohibition rocked the nation to its philosophical foundations, and, looking ahead, moral conflicts may become endemic in the postmaterialist society of the twenty-first century. This attribute brings a disruptive influence to normal political discourse and consensus building because, as the foreword by Theodore J. Lowi explains, moral discourse is polarizing. True, values and religion are sources of moral conflicts, but political ideology and "rights" rhetoric can have similar effects. Demanding one's rights—real or imagined—is *the* rationale for abortion, same-sex marriage, and gun ownership.

Proposition 2a: Courts promote legal change in social regulatory policy by asserting individual rights and liberties against traditional social values.

The degree to which personal behavior ought to be regulated is a public consideration that is weighed against the individual's desire to be free from government interference. How society defines this balance is the essence of social regulatory policy. Judicial activism respecting social norms began with the school desegregation ruling in *Brown v. Board of Education,* 347 U.S. 483 (1954); since then, the high court's concern for civil liberties and minority rights has displaced its earlier focus on economic disputes. The legal quandary is that litigants argue that certain persons are being denied liberties in real situations, while the state tries to argue that long-term, indirect dangers will confront society if deviant social behavior is permitted. Given this choice, judges tend to side with the plaintiffs.

Proposition 2b: Federal courts have expanded the opportunities for using litigation to change social regulatory policy outside the normal political process.

Because state laws enforce moral codes, the primary legal approach to nationalize moral conflict is to challenge those statutes in federal courts. Where discrimination is alleged, the equal protection clause may be used to challenge the constitutionality of state laws, but the due process clause allows more opportunities for raising constitutional challenges. The doctrine of incorporation—applying provisions in the Bill of Rights to the fifty states—is not found in the first ten amendments or elsewhere in the Constitution, nor was incorporation the original intent of the Framers who designed the Constitution. Rather, this jurisprudence evolved after the Supreme Court began to broadly interpret the Fourteenth Amendment, which prohibits any state from denying its citizens their "life, *liberty*, or property" (emphasis added) without "due process of law." Because incorporation doctrine is judge-made law that is not grounded in the language of the Constitution, this activist jurisprudence has inspired a strong dissent among conservatives. Whether the conservative critique is valid or not, the mere allegation that incorporation is illegitimate intensifies the political controversy over judicial activism with respect to moral conflicts.

Proposition 3a: Presidents generally do not exert decisive leadership to change social regulatory policy, although they may make symbolic gestures.

We hypothesize symbolic leadership from the White House. Presidential leadership would be largely rhetorical given the obvious political constraints. How aggressively would any president promote legalized abortions, pornography, or racial quotas? How often would a president disparage religion, oppose the death penalty, or glorify same-sex marriage? Whenever presidents do become involved, however, their activities are colored by partisanship.

Proposition 3b: Republicans exploit social regulatory policy to mobilize conservative voters, whereas Democrats are constrained not to abandon liberalism.

The optimal strategy for a Democrat is to equivocate and say little in order not to offend public opinion or alienate the party's liberal wing. Republicans, on the other hand, can be outspoken because the preferences of their rank and file are often compatible with the views of the general electorate. The beginning of the social agenda in modern presidential politics dates from the 1968 campaign of Richard Nixon.

Proposition 4a: Congress usually opposes the federal judiciary and aligns itself with the state legislatures on social regulatory policy.

Since plaintiffs utilize the federal courts to challenge state morality policy, we hypothesize that Congress typically would side with the states. Activists who seek judicial redress do so precisely because the political branches are not sympathetic to the plight of individuals or groups who deviate from the norms of society. It would be counterintuitive to argue that, when faced with a highly charged moral conflict, Congress would find common ground with an unelected Supreme Court rather than the state legislatures.

Proposition 4b: Electoral pressures encourage Congress to represent traditional values in social regulatory policy.

The fundamental reason why Congress sides with state legislatures on social regulations is that political forces constrain the popularly elected branches. Many observers of the morality policy process, including T. Alexander Smith, argue that political elites are risk-adverse when faced with highly visible moral conflicts, therefore preferring to avoid the issue, but ultimately they have to address those concerns. Whenever the citizenry is aroused, public opinion weighs heavily on congressional deliberations.

Proposition 5a: Public opinion is often conservative, sometimes moderate, and rarely liberal, but always less intense with respect to social regulations than the ideology of those who favor social change.

Since we argue that moral conflicts are grounded in status politics, a *reverse* class dynamic operates. Generally speaking, lower socioeconomic-status people are more liberal on economic issues than more affluent groups, but upper socioeconomic-status groups are more tolerant of diverse lifestyles and supportive of civil rights than less affluent Americans. Lipset once labeled this pattern "working class authoritarianism."[7]

Proposition 5b: Legal changes in social regulations that make major revisions in community norms will be resisted by the public, especially any target populations.

When major revisions in community norms are mandated by law, notably the judiciary, public opinion may not readily accept them. Moreover, the perceived legitimacy of official acts has implications for the consensus-building process and compliance with the law, because a population subgroup with intense feelings about social regulations that target it will probably resist complying, although the cooperation of that targeted group may be needed for effective implementation of the new regulations. How willing are Catholic hospitals and physicians to perform abortions? What are the odds that gun owners (let alone criminals) will register their firearms?

Proposition 6a: Agencies of the federal government usually have limited jurisdiction over social regulatory policy.

Although enactment of the Civil Rights Acts of 1964, 1965, and 1968 increased the regulatory role of federal agencies in civil rights enforcement, in many aspects of social regulation the impact of the federal bureaucracy is marginal compared to the role of states and localities. In some cases, there is no federal law to enforce. Even when there is federal legislation, the agencies may lack the personnel and resources to implement social regulations given the magnitude of the enforcement problem. Or federal agencies may simply lack the political will to do the job, meaning that federal vigilance may vary according to external political pressures. The administrative arena is a microcosm of the legislative arena of power.

Proposition 6b: The ability of federal agencies to implement social regulations depends on the liberal versus conservative pressures exerted by Congress, the presidency, the judiciary, supportive groups, and regulated interests.

The administrative arena is circumscribed by these institutional actors, especially the courts, since groups may litigate to ensure rigorous enforcement of statutory law and judicial decrees.[8] The interplay of the left and right political forces defines the vigor with which social regulations are enforced by the bureaucracy. Which party controls the White House will affect political appointments to key agencies and which interest groups influence the choice of those appointees. The majority party in the House of Representatives and/or the Senate has a voice in deciding the level of appropriations that flow to an agency. Organizations that support federal enforcement are politically weaker, usually, than those interests being regulated.

Proposition 7a: Federalism is important to social regulatory policy because historically the states had jurisdiction over most of these issues.

The movement since the 1930s toward economic regulation of capitalism by the federal government did *not* displace the state governments because previously the states had intervened little in the marketplace. But social regulations historically involved a pervasive role by state and local governments long before federal intervention began. The "police powers" under the Tenth Amendment ensure that subnational governments will be more than equal partners in the federal relationship. In numerous ways, the states safeguard public order, safety, health, and moral character. It is the individual state that decides whether gambling is a vice to be discouraged or a virtue to be exploited through state lotteries and how the age of adulthood is defined for the purposes of alcoholic consumption, driving, or reading sexual materials. Most states enacted blue laws to regulate Sunday sales, and the majority still refuse to legalize marijuana use and prostitution. The list of morality policies regulated by states goes on and on.

Proposition 7b: The enforcement of social regulatory policy often depends on the compliance of state and local officials as well as on decision makers in the private sector.

No federal law is easy to implement, but there are unique problems with social regulations. One complication is the sheer number of persons affected by social regulations. Prohibitions on elementary and secondary schools, for example, involve tens of thousands of local school districts; regulations on hiring and firing affect hundreds of thousands of employers; some controls affect millions of individual Americans. More fundamentally, because building consensus on volatile morality policies is more difficult to achieve, noncompliance can pose a serious problem for implementation. This issue can be especially troublesome when the federal judiciary decrees new social regulations. The fact that the Supreme Court promulgates a law, as the issue of abortion so vividly illustrates, does not automatically bring the matter to a close. Even a constitutional amendment is no assurance that controversy will end. The classic example of social regulatory policy at the federal level was the ratification of the Eighteenth Amendment—Prohibition—in 1920, although the illegal manufacture, sale, and consumption of alcoholic beverages was not halted. In 1933, on the eve of the New Deal, three-fourths of the states ratified the Twenty-first Amendment to repeal Prohibition and to refederalize policy on alcoholic consumption by allowing the states to regain their authority to legalize as well as regulate and tax the consumption of alcoholic beverages.

The debate over Prohibition, according to policy analyst Kenneth J. Meier, began as a "two-sided" morality policy (the "drys" who abstained versus the "wets" who drank) but evolved, following the repeal of Prohibition by the Twenty-first Amendment, into a "one-sided" morality policy in which, today, "one 'acceptable' position" predominates among policy elites and the citizenry.[9] Our nine case studies are all "two-sided" moral conflicts that seemingly will persist until they simply become irrelevant with the passage of time. Only at that juncture will a de facto settlement in public opinion be achieved—when the normative order, law, and social regulatory policy are once again mutually reinforcing.

Moral Controversies in American Politics

1

Abortion

Pro-Choice versus Pro-Life

Ruth Ann Strickland

Near the thirtieth anniversary of the watershed decision of *Roe v. Wade,* Norma McCorvey, the original plaintiff in the case, announced that she would petition the Supreme Court to reopen *Roe.* Based on changes in law and technology since 1973, McCorvey sought to have *Roe* overturned. Also, since the 1973 ruling, eight of the nine original *Roe* justices have died or retired. The abortion question is far from settled, and *Roe v. Wade* could be significantly modified or even overruled if President George W. Bush, a self-proclaimed pro-life advocate, gets the opportunity to appoint one or more new justices to the high court. The abortion wars continue in Congress, the state legislatures, and state courts between clashing pro-choice and pro-life advocacy groups. *Roe* leaves behind many unanswered questions: When does life begin? and When should the fetus be given the chance to develop and thrive? It pushes society to ponder reproductive privacy, the degree of bodily integrity guaranteed to women, and the extent to which abortion is an individual right. The abortion issue divides people into seemingly irreconcilable camps— those who sponsor family values and the rights of the unborn versus those who champion women's individual rights and choice.

Before her appointment to the Supreme Court, Ruth Bader Ginsburg argued that *Roe* stymied the political process that already was moving in a reformist direction and significantly prolonged the abortion controversy by making consensus less likely.[1] The framing of abortion as a right may have undercut the emerging consensus that favored abortions for therapeutic or medical purposes. There is no doubt that the trimester formula in the *Roe* ruling opened the door to the viability issue and intensified the moral debate over when a fetus becomes a person who, therefore, deserves due-process guarantees. Because the issue has been framed in the United States, unlike Europe where the issue is considered a public health concern, as a question of a woman's right to bodily integrity and privacy versus a fetus's right to life, common ground and compromise in the political arena have been almost impossible to attain.

Historical Evolution of the Abortion Issue

Abortion was not considered an offense under Roman law or Catholic canon law, and throughout most of the 1800s there were no national legal restrictions on obtaining an abortion in the first few months of pregnancy. The standard of quickening (or the first notice of fetal movement by a pregnant woman) was used to determine whether abortion was permitted in any given case. English common law throughout most of the nineteenth century did not recognize fetal rights in criminal prosecutions until quickening.[2] The quickening standard became controversial in 1821 when Connecticut—a predominantly Catholic state—enacted the first statute making abortion illegal after quickening. Missouri (1825), Illinois (1827), and New York (1828) followed suit, but the New York law was unique in its "therapeutic" qualification, legalizing abortions necessary to save a mother's life. Sixteen more states adopted restrictive abortion laws between 1830 and 1849, mostly making abortion a crime after quickening. Maine's law made any method of abortion a crime except if the mother's life was in danger.[3] During the period between 1840 and 1870, estimates hold that there was one abortion for every five to six live births. Abortion was a highly visible, frequently performed, commercial procedure from 1800 through 1870.[4]

A chilly climate toward the abortion procedure was created during the mid-nineteenth century by the medical community, which mobilized to oppose abortion on moral grounds and fears that abortions were not being performed safely.[5] The American Medical Association (AMA) lobbied against abortions obtained without a physician's designation that the abortion was "therapeutic."[6] Dr. Horatio Storer, an obstetrician and gynecologist who led a movement to criminalize all abortions, eventually persuaded the AMA to pass a resolution in 1859 that urged state legislatures to forbid all abortions. As a consequence, most abortions were outlawed in most states during the Civil War period.[7] Abortions were permitted only if, in the opinion of the physician, a woman's life was at stake. Ten states required the concurring opinion of a second physician.[8]

In 1873 Congress passed the Comstock Act, which aided and abetted the antiabortion agitation. This antiobscenity law also included a ban on the transportation through the mails of any drug, medicine, or object that could be used for abortion or contraceptive purposes and a prohibition on mailing advertisements of such items.[9] In effect, the Comstock Act stifled dissemination of information and discussions about birth control or abortion.

The historical record is important to the modern abortion controversy, especially the rationales offered for why antiabortion restrictions emerged. According to pro-choice advocates and some feminists, declining birth rates, especially among native white Protestants as compared to immigrant Catholics, was a major concern. According to this argument, the passage of antiabortion laws arose in part out of a nineteenth-century desire to promote homemaking as a vocation by increasing the birth rate among middle-class women and to decrease it among the lower class. This perspective is supported by estimates that by 1900 it was unwed lower-class women or immigrant wives who sought and obtained abortions, not married, middle-class, Protestant women.[10]

Another perspective is that abortions were banned in order to save women from themselves, because early surgical abortion procedures exposed women to risks and possibly death. In 1828, for example, one estimate of the death rate from sepsis after abortion surgery was greater than 30 percent. Still another perspective held that antiabortion laws came about due to the public's and the medical community's disgust at the commercial spectacle and large profits earned from performing abortions.[11] A pro-life argument, which emerged in the twentieth century, argued for protecting not only the mother but the fetus, holding that under the Fourteenth Amendment the unborn had due-process rights.[12]

Once federal and state antiabortion laws were in place, a period of quietude reigned from 1900 through 1950, at least on the surface of the American social and political landscape. Data on illegally obtained abortions during this period suggest that women continued to obtain abortions at roughly the same rate, despite the newly enacted restrictions.[13] By the 1950s, hospitals had established abortion committees to process requests for abortions and to designate whether, in the judgment of the physician, the abortion was necessary to save the mother's life.[14] In 1955 Planned Parenthood sponsored a conference on abortion, promising to keep the event "quiet," and for the first time since the criminalization of abortion, physicians and other professionals attending the conference called for legislative reforms that would make "therapeutic" abortion a matter between patient and physician.[15] In 1959, one year after the Planned Parenthood conference proceedings were published, the American Law Institute (ALI), alarmed by illegal abortions in unsanitary conditions and back-alley deaths, proposed legalized abortions when the physical or mental health of the mother was at stake or when the child would be born with serious physical or mental defects.

The case of Sherry Finkbine in 1962 further highlighted the problems with existing antiabortion laws. A mother of four, Finkbine chose to have an abortion after learning that the drug thalidomide, which she had taken early in her pregnancy, caused gross birth defects. She petitioned an Arizona hospital to provide her an abortion (the hospital had routinely allowed such abortions in the past under a liberal interpretation of Arizona's abortion statute) but, when her story made the headlines in newspapers across the country, the local prosecutor threatened the assisting physician with arrest, and subsequently the hospital canceled the surgery. (Finkbine eventually obtained the abortion abroad.) Also in 1962, in Grove, Oklahoma, Dr. W.J. Bryan Henrie was convicted of a crime—performing abortions—and was sentenced to two years in jail. After serving his sentence, Dr. Henrie began a solo campaign to liberalize abortion laws.[16]

In the mid-1960s Lawrence Lader, who authored a book on family planning advocate Margaret Sanger, started pushing for abortion law reform. Two pro-choice groups—the Association for the Study of Abortion (New York–based) and the Parents' Aid Society—were created in 1964. Patricia Maginnis, founder of the San Francisco–based Society for Humane Abortion, in 1965 advocated repeal of all abortion restrictions in order to give women rather than physicians control over the abortion decision. Maginnis also established an underground operation that reportedly sent thousands of women seeking abortions to Mexico, Japan, Sweden, and other less hostile environments.[17]

In 1968 the National Association for the Repeal of Abortion Laws was formed (originally known as the New York Abortion Rights Action League and one year later it became the National Abortion Rights Action League, or NARAL). In the late 1960s the liberalization movement began to develop a national base of support. The National Organization for Women (NOW) in 1967 adopted a plank demanding the right of women to control their reproductive capacities and, therefore, seeking repeal of restrictions on access to abortion. In 1968 the American Civil Liberties Union (ACLU) also called for the repeal of all criminal abortion laws, and the Planned Parenthood Federation reversed its earlier position and endorsed abortion rights in 1969.

The liberalization movement resulted in eighteen states reforming their original antiabortion statutes. In 1966 Mississippi added rape as another therapeutic exception. In 1967 Colorado was the first state to adopt the American Law Institute guidelines proposed in 1959. North Carolina and California adopted the ALI model shortly thereafter, and by 1972 fourteen other states had liberalized their abortion laws. Alaska, New York, Washington, and

Hawaii went beyond therapeutics and codified abortion as an elective procedure. Instead of arguing for a woman's right to bodily integrity or a right to privacy, the early reformers justified abortion reforms on health grounds (saving the life or preserving the mental or physical health of the mother).[18]

Roe v. Wade, 410 U.S. 113 (1973), galvanized the pro-life movement. The National Right to Life Committee was founded in Detroit in June 1973, and the National Conference of Catholic Bishops (NCCB) issued a statement that any Catholic involved in any phase of abortion would be excommunicated. The NCCB also supported a constitutional amendment to outlaw abortion. To promote that objective, the U.S. Catholic Conference funded and created the National Committee for a Human Life Amendment.[19] Following *Roe,* pro-life organizations sprang up in every state, and every year since, on January 22, the anniversary of *Roe,* pro-life groups march on the U.S. Capitol steps, carrying signs and making speeches.

Judiciary

When the Supreme Court in *Griswold v. Connecticut,* 381 U.S. 479 (1965), struck down that state's law banning the sale of birth control information and devices, it ruled that a "right to privacy" could be inferred from a penumbra of several guarantees found in the Bill of Rights. The right to privacy, therefore, was created implicitly by the First Amendment freedom of association provision, the Third Amendment ban on forced quartering of soldiers in private dwellings, the Fourth Amendment protection from unreasonable searches and seizures, the Fifth Amendment prohibition of coerced confessions, and the Ninth Amendment guarantee that rights not specifically mentioned in the Constitution might still exist.

The first abortion ruling by a federal district court occurred in the 1969 case of *United States v. Vuitch* (305 F. Supp. 1032 D.D.C.). Judge Gerhard Gesell found the therapeutic exception phrase void for vagueness and held that the state had no compelling interest in regulating abortions. However, Judge Gesell urged the government to appeal his decision, which it did. In 1971 *United States v. Vuitch* (402 U.S. 62), the first abortion decision of the U.S. Supreme Court, upheld the District of Columbia's abortion statute, clarifying that a mother's life and health included not only her physical well-being but also her psychological well-being; the Court, however, declined to pronounce that abortion was a fundamental right.[20]

Roe v. Wade

The central question in *Roe* was the constitutionality of the 1857 Texas statute that criminalized abortion except to save a woman's life. Justice Harry

Blackmun, writing for the majority, declared the statute unconstitutional and ruled that the right to privacy encompassed a woman's decision to end her pregnancy—in effect establishing a constitutional right to abortion. Blackmun devised a trimester formula that would be used to balance these competing interests. In the first trimester (three months) of pregnancy, the abortion decision is left to the medical judgment of the woman's attending physician in consultation with the patient. In the second trimester, the state may regulate the abortion procedure in the interest of the mother's health. During the third trimester, when fetal viability is an issue, the state may regulate or even prohibit abortions to protect the life of a fetus and, therefore, may allow abortions only when necessary to protect the life or health of the mother.[21] *Roe* struck down forty-six state laws and superseded the repeal laws in the other four states. By issuing this sweeping decision, the Supreme Court provoked a national debate that forever changed political discourse about this issue. It mobilized the right-to-life movement, temporarily lulled pro-choice proponents into a false state of security, and shifted the locus of abortion policy to Washington, D.C. By the 1980s all three branches of government would be embroiled in the issue.[22]

From Roe to Webster (1973–1989)

Including *Roe,* nineteen abortion cases reached the Supreme Court through 1989.[23] With the exception of four rulings that allowed governments to ban public funding and use of public facilities for abortions—*Beal v. Doe* (1977), *Maher v. Roe* (1977), *Poelker v. Doe* (1977), and *Harris v. McRae* (1980)—the Court has conceded very little to pro-life interests. The fundamental underpinnings of *Roe* remain intact.

City of Akron v. Akron Center for Reproductive Health, 462 U.S. 416 (1983), involved the most restrictive city ordinance of any municipality in the nation. This ordinance mandated that all second- and third-trimester abortions be performed in a hospital, that unmarried minors under age fifteen obtain parental consent or a court order before obtaining an abortion, that physicians give all patients antiabortion information including the point that "the unborn child is a human life from the moment of conception," that patients must wait twenty-four hours after this lecture before obtaining an abortion, and that physicians must dispose of fetal tissue and remains in an unspecified "humane and sanitary manner." By a 6–3 vote the high court struck down all these provisions, holding that no city or state regulation could "interfere with physician-patient consultation or with the woman's choice between abortion and childbirth." In particular, the requirement that second- and third-trimester abortions be performed in hospitals was held to be an unreasonable infringement on a woman's right to an abortion, placing undue hardships and costs on her.[24]

The Court in *Thornburgh v. American College of Obstetricians and Gynecologists,* 476 U.S. 747 (1986), voted 5–4 to strike down a Pennsylvania statute that required physicians to give patients antiabortion information including pictures of fetuses at various stages of development, to publicly identify the attending physician and provide information about the woman obtaining an abortion, to use a degree of care necessary to preserve the life and health of any unborn child in a postviability abortion that would favor the life of the fetus at a risk to the mother's health, and to require a second physician in postviability abortions except in a medical emergency.[25]

However, some restrictions on abortions have been allowed. The Court has ruled that under certain circumstances a state may require a minor woman to get parental permission or give parental notification before obtaining an abortion (*Bellotti v. Baird [I],* 428 U.S. 132 [1976]; *H.L. v. Matheson,* 450 U.S. 398 [1981]; *Planned Parenthood Association of Kansas City, Mo. v. Ashcroft,* 462 U.S. 416 [1983]). Also upheld are restrictions on public funding for abortions at both the state and federal levels when there was no threat to the health or life of the mother (*Poelker v. Doe,* 432 U.S. 519 [1977]; *Harris v. McRae,* 448 U.S. 297 [1980]). The Court also affirmed requirements that a second physician be present during a postviability abortion and that physicians perform second-trimester abortions in a licensed hospital, which includes outpatient hospitals (*Planned Parenthood Association of Kansas City, Mo. v. Ashcroft,* 462 U.S. 416 [1983]).

The pivotal case of *Webster v. Reproductive Health Services,* 492 U.S. 490 (1989), gave pro-life activists hope that the Rehnquist Court might reverse *Roe.* An abortion clinic challenged a Missouri statute that banned the performance of abortions in public institutions, even when the woman paid for her abortion. This restrictive law also included a preamble that declared that life begins at conception, a regulation that required physicians to conduct viability tests prior to performing abortions, a two-parent notification requirement for minors with a procedure for judicial waiver, a forty-eight-hour waiting period for minors, and a prohibition on public funding of abortion counseling. By upholding the viability testing and the prohibition on the use of public facilities or public personnel in the performance of abortions, the Court moved away from its "strict scrutiny" standard and toward Justice O'Connor's "unduly burdensome" standard, which she had articulated in *Akron* and *Thornburgh.* For the first time since 1973, only a minority of justices—four—voted to reaffirm *Roe,* and Justice Antonin Scalia, who wrote a concurrence, still argued that *Roe* should be overturned.

From Webster to Madsen (1989–1994)

Webster, by sending a signal to state governments that the reconstituted Supreme Court would consider abortion restrictions that did not strictly meet controlling judicial precedents, refederalized abortion. In only a short period of time (July 1989 to July 1990), 351 abortion bills were introduced in state legislatures.[26] *Webster* energized pro-life advocates while pro-choice proponents feared its repercussions.[27]

Both *Hodgson v. Minnesota,* 497 U.S. 417 (1990), and *Ohio v. Akron Center for Reproductive Health,* 497 U.S. 417 (1990), dealt primarily with the issue of a parental notification requirement for minors. By votes of 5–4 and 6–3 respectively, the Court upheld parental notification requirements as long as a procedure for judicial waiver existed. By 1989, thirty-one states had passed legislation requiring teenagers under age eighteen to either notify their parents before getting an abortion or obtain parental consent. These decisions validated the movement in the states toward parental involvement in a minor's abortion decision, and the later case of *Planned Parenthood of Southeastern Pennsylvania v. Casey,* 505 U.S. 833 (1992), which upheld a one-parent consent requirement for minors with a judicial bypass, gave further legitimacy to state parental involvement regulations. As of May 1996, twenty-eight states enforced these mandatory parental involvement laws. In 1997 the Supreme Court upheld a Montana law that required an unmarried minor to notify one parent forty-eight hours before having an abortion, although a judge could grant a waiver if convinced that the minor is mature enough to make the decision on her own or if notification would harm her best interests.[28]

In 1991 the Court entered another abortion dispute. The Reagan administration imposed a gag rule that banned any discussion of abortion in federally funded family planning clinics, even if a woman's health or life was at stake. President George H.W. Bush instructed Solicitor General Kenneth Starr to defend the gag rule, which was being challenged by a physician and a clinic that received federal money. Abortion clinics receive Title X money and millions of women depend on these clinics for health care and family planning information. But in another 5–4 vote, this time intermingled with the issue of free speech, the Supreme Court upheld the gag rule, arguing that congressional intent on whether or note to allow such funding was vague.

In 1992 *Casey* presented another possible challenge to *Roe.* The disputed Pennsylvania Abortion Control Act placed additional restrictions on abortions, including a mandatory twenty-four-hour waiting period, parental consent, spousal notification, an informed consent provision, and reporting and public disclosure requirements. Although the Rehnquist Court reaffirmed the central holding in *Roe,* by upholding all the provisions *except* spousal notifi-cation, it explicitly overruled the *Akron* and *Thornburgh* decisions and aban-doned "strict scrutiny" in favor of the less stringent "undue burden" standard of judicial review.

Pro-lifers who blockaded entrances to abortion clinics (so-called abortion rescues) and engaged in threatened or actual violence led pro-choice advo-cates to strike back with federal lawsuits and injunctions, claiming that those tactics violated the civil rights of women who try to obtain abortions.[29] A coalition of pro-choice groups—NOW, Planned Parenthood of Metropolitan Washington, and several Virginia abortion clinics—filed suit under the Ku Klux Klan Act of 1871 and 42 U.S.C. Sec. 1985(3), which was enacted to prevent conspiratorial efforts to deny any group its civil rights. In *Bray v. Alexandria Women's Health Clinic,* 506 U.S. 616 (1993), the plaintiffs ar-gued that the KKK Act should be used to stop clinic blockades by Operation Rescue and the Bray family. Under the KKK Act, however, plaintiffs had to show that the defendants acted with "class-based, invidiously discriminatory animus." In its 5–4 decision, the Supreme Court held that the act did not protect women from pro-life health clinic blockades and, further, that the pro-life blockades did not constitute sex-based discrimination.[30]

Pro-choice activists turned to another statute in hopes of curtailing clinic blockades—the Racketeer Influenced and Corrupt Organizations (RICO) Act of 1970. In *National Organization for Women v. Scheidler,* 510 U.S. 249 (1994), NOW and two women's health care centers argued that the defen-dants (a coalition of antiabortion groups called Pro-Life Action Network, and Joseph Scheidler) had conspired to engage in illegal activities (including intimidation, bombings, vandalism, and other violent acts) aimed at putting the abortion providers out of business, in violation of RICO. The defendants contended that Congress intended RICO to apply only to profit-seeking ven-tures and that application of RICO to protest activities would violate the defendants' First Amendment rights. A unanimous Supreme Court rejected the defendants' claims and allowed NOW and the group of women's health centers to pursue civil suits against the clinic blockaders under RICO.[31]

Madsen v. Women's Health Center, 114 S.Ct. 2516 (1994), further limited the activities of antiabortion protesters. Specifically, *Madsen* addressed a state judge's injunction that prohibited antiabortion protesters from blocking or obstructing access to an abortion clinic in Melbourne, Florida; congregating, picketing, or demonstrating within thirty-six feet of the property line of the clinic, approaching within a 300-foot radius of the clinic any person seek-ing its services or its staff; physically abusing, harassing, or crowding per-sons trying to leave the clinic; and threatening any clinic personnel.[32] The Court's 5–4 decision upheld parts of the Florida injunction, including the thirty-six-foot buffer zone and prohibitions on noise by antiabortion protest-ers that was disruptive and could be heard by clinic patients during hours when surgical procedures were performed. Justices Kennedy, Thomas, and Scalia vigorously dissented, arguing that "the judicial creation of a 36-foot zone in which only a particular group, which has broken no law, can not exercise its rights of speech, assembly, and association, and the judicial en-actment of a noise prohibition, applicable to that group and that group alone, are profoundly at odds with our First Amendment precedents and traditions."[33]

Twenty-six major abortion cases reached the Supreme Court between 1972 and 1994, of which twenty-four were split decisions and seven were decided on 5–4 votes. These splintered decisions indicate a lack of consensus on the high court about abortion policy as well as reflecting changes in the Court's composition. Vacancies enabled Presidents Reagan and Bush to mold its membership to be more sympathetic to the pro-life agenda. Reagan's first opportunity arose in 1981 when Sandra Day O'Connor, who had a pro-life reputation, replaced Justice Potter Stewart (who had voted with the majority in *Roe*). In Reagan's second term, Chief Justice Warren Burger retired and Associate Justice William H. Rehnquist was nominated to replace him. To fill Rehnquist's seat, Reagan nominated a conservative Roman Catholic, U.S. Court of Appeals Judge Antonin Scalia.[34] In 1988 Reagan replaced Justice Lewis Powell with Anthony M. Kennedy, and in 1990 President George H.W. Bush was able to appoint David Souter to replace William Brennan—a core supporter of abortion rights. Although Souter refused to comment on his abortion views during his confirmation hearing, pro-choice advocates avidly opposed his appointment, but he was easily confirmed. When Justice Thurgood Marshall, another reliable pro-choice vote, resigned during the 1990–1991 term of the high court, President Bush nominated Clarence Thomas, an Afri-can-American conservative with decidedly pro-life views.

With the election of a pro-choice president—Bill Clinton—in 1992, the prospects of overturning *Roe* dimmed. When Justice Byron White (who dis-sented in *Roe*) retired in 1993, he was replaced by Ruth Bader Ginsburg. Ginsburg specifically stated in her confirmation hearings that the right to privacy was central to a woman's dignity and that abortion was a decision a woman should make for herself. Stephen Breyer—another Clinton appointee —ascended to the Court in 1994, upon Justice Harry Blackmun's retirement, and took a judicially restrained position. When Senator Strom Thurmond (R-SC) of the Judiciary Committee asked Breyer about the constitutional status of abor-tion rights, Breyer responded, "That's the law." The March 4, 2004, release of the late Justice Harry A. Blackmun's papers revealed that the 1992 *Casey* decision was much closer than anyone had realized. Justice Blackmun indi-cated that Justice Kennedy initially voted with the anti-*Roe* conservatives but later changed his vote when Chief Justice Rehnquist began circulating what Kennedy thought would be the majority decision to finally overturn *Roe.* So even with the election of a pro-choice president, *Roe* was threatened.[35]

Although the Rehnquist Court was decidedly more conservative than the Warren Court and demonstrated a willingness to modify *Roe,* the subsequent Clinton appointments to the Supreme Court have stymied efforts to significantly reverse abortion rights. But a splintered Court may be the wave of the future. Note that a 5–4 pro-life majority upheld abortion restrictions in the 1989 *Webster* case while a 5–4 pro-choice majority placed restrictions on antiabortion protesters in the 1994 *Madsen* case.

From Cheffer to Stenberg (1995–2000)

In 1994 Congress passed the Freedom of Access to Clinic Entrances Act (FACE), prohibiting the obstruction of access to reproductive health services. As the first freestanding federal legislation designed to guarantee a woman's access to abortion services, it sparked further controversy and litigation over buffer zones. In July 1995 the Supreme Court let stand the lower court ruling in *Cheffer v. Reno,* 55 F.3d 1517 (11th Cir. 1995), stating that Congress had the authority to enact FACE under the commerce clause of the Constitution. In another follow-up to *Madsen, Schenck v. Pro-Choice Network of Western New York,* 519 U.S. 357 (1997), found the Court voting 8–1 to uphold other restrictions against antiabortion protesters. The Court upheld a fifteen-foot zone around entrances to clinics, protecting patients and clinic staff from protester interference, but the majority refused to uphold a "floating buffer zone" that extended that zone to areas not in the immediate vicinity of the entrance. The majority ruled that these floating buffer zones would impose an undue burden on the protestors' and sidewalk counselors' free speech rights and were not necessary to protect relevant governmental interests.[36] In the *Hill v. Colorado* case, 530 U.S. 703 (2000), the Supreme Court similarly upheld a state law requiring pro-life demonstrators to remain at least eight feet away from anyone entering or leaving medical facilities. The combination of these rulings indicates the precarious attempt to balance the privacy rights of clinic patients and staff against the free speech rights of antiabortion protestors.

A more direct challenge to abortion rights emerged in the form of state bans on "D and X" (dilate and extract) operations, or late-term abortions. In *Stenberg v. Carhart,* 530 U.S. 914 (2000), Justice Breyer, writing for the 5–4 majority, said that the Nebraska ban on so-called partial-birth abortions violated *Roe* and *Casey* by not specifying an exception to preserve the health of the woman and for imposing an undue burden on a woman's ability to seek a safe abortion. In this one ruling, the high court struck down thirty state laws that banned the procedure.[37] The Supreme Court, although clearly capable of producing a pro-choice majority, is viewed as vulnerable by many pro-choice advocacy groups.[38] Given the pro-life agenda of President George W. Bush, his reelection would afford him the opportunity to make two or three decisive appointments to the Supreme Court. If so, then the balance of ideology on the Court could shift dramatically and, once again, redefine the scope of abortion rights (Table 1.1).

Public Opinion

Since 1965 opinion polling on abortion has been frequent. The National Opinion Research Center (NORC) has asked a set of questions about whether a woman should be able to obtain abortion under six different circumstances. From 1965 to 1973, support for access to abortion in all categories grew, but with substantially more approval for abortions when a woman's health is at stake, when the pregnancy resulted from rape, or when the baby might be born with a serious defect. Support leveled off in the mid- to late 1970s and declined slightly during the 1980s, yet by the 1990s the trend reversed and support picked up again slightly.[39] Support of abortion for any reason rose to 39 percent by 1982, fell to 37 percent in 1988, and peaked in 1990 at 42 percent (Table 1.2).

Some polls are framed bimodally and ask: "In general, do you favor or oppose the U.S. Supreme Court decision making abortions up to three months of pregnancy legal?" In 1969 40 percent of those interviewed favored abortion while 50 percent were opposed. Eighteen years later, a Gallup poll, with virtually the same question, found that 45 percent said yes and 45 percent said no. By 1989, at the time of the *Webster* ruling, 56 percent favored *Roe* and 42 percent opposed it (Table 1.3). A January 2003 poll asked "[w]ould you describe yourself as being more pro-choice—supporting a woman's right to have an abortion—or more pro-life—protecting the rights of the unborn children?" Forty-nine percent characterized themselves as more pro-choice and 45 percent saw themselves as more pro-life. Support for abortion rights increases when people are asked whether they favor the Supreme Court ruling that women have the right to an abortion during the first trimester of their pregnancy. When phrased this way, 55 percent of the respondents favor *Roe* and 40 percent oppose it.[40]

When respondents are given specific abortion scenarios to consider, support for abortion varies according to circumstances (Table 1.4). Public opinion trends between 1995 and 2000 did not bode well for aspects of the pro-life agenda, especially when traumatic reasons were given for obtaining

Table 1.1

Votes on Key Abortion Cases: Impact of Changes in the Makeup of the Supreme Court

Justices	1973 *Roe*		1983 *Akron*		1986 *Thornburgh*		1989 *Webster*		1994 *Madsen*		2000 *Stenberg*	
	PC	PL	PC	PL	PC	PL	PC	PL	PC	PL	PC	PL
Burger	X		X			X	—	—	—	—	—	—
Brennan	X		X		X		X		—	—	—	—
Marshall	X		X		X		X		—	—	—	—
Stewart	X		—	—	—	—	—	—	—	—	—	—
Blackmun	X		X		X		X		X		—	—
Powell	X		X		X		—	—	—	—	—	—
Douglas	X		—	—	—	—	—	—	—	—	—	—
Stevens	—	—	X		X		X		X		X	
Rehnquist		X		X		X		X	X			X
White		X		X		X		X	—	—	—	—
O'Connor	—	—		X		X		X	X		X	
Scalia	—	—	—	—	—	—		X		X		X
Kennedy	—	—	—	—	—	—		X		X		X
Souter	—	—	—	—	—	—	—	—	X		X	
Thomas	—	—	—	—	—	—	—	—		X		X
Ginsburg	—	—	—	—	—	—	—	—	X		X	
Breyer	—	—	—	—	—	—	—	—	—	—	X	

Note: PC = pro-choice vote; PL = pro-life vote; dash indicates that this justice was not on the Court to render a decision. Also note that starting with the *Thornburgh* case in 1986, votes on landmark cases have been split 5–4.

15

Table 1.2

Public Support for Abortion Under Certain Circumstances (percentage of respondents)

	Mother's health	Rape	Fetal defect	Low income	Unmarried	No more children	Any reason
1965	71	56	55	21	18	15	—
1972	83	74	74	46	41	38	—
1973	91	81	82	52	47	46	—
1974	90	83	84	52	48	45	—
1975	88	80	90	51	46	44	—
1976	89	80	82	50	48	45	—
1977	88	80	83	52	47	44	36
1978	88	80	80	45	39	40	32
1980	88	80	80	50	46	45	39
1982	89	83	81	50	47	46	39
1984	87	77	77	44	43	41	37
1985	87	78	76	42	40	39	36
1987	85	85	77	43	40	40	38
1988	89	81	78	42	40	40	37
1990	89	81	78	45	43	43	42
1996	92	77	54	32	—	—	—

Sources: National Opinion Research Center (NORC) data; General Social Surveys; Gallup Report, February 1989. Selected years of data are reported in Raymond Tatalovich, *The Politics of Abortion in the United States and Canada: A Comparative Study* (Armonk, NY: M.E. Sharpe, 1997), p. 112. Data for 1996 was drawn from the *Gallup Poll Monthly*, August 1996, p. 32.

Table 1.3

Bimodal Distribution of Public Opinion on Abortion (in percent)

Year	Favor	Oppose	No opinion/not sure
1969	40	50	10
1972	46	45	9
1973	52	41	7
1974	47	44	9
1976	60	31	9
1981	56	41	3
1985	50	47	3
1986	45	45	10
1989	56	42	2

Sources: Gallup Reports, 1969, 1972, 1974, and 1986; Harris Poll, 1989. Question asked: "In general, do you favor or oppose the U.S. Supreme Court decision making abortions up to three months of pregnancy legal?"

an abortion. The following percentages of respondents (averaged across the period from 1995 to 2000) approved of abortion for these reasons: 89 percent when a mother's health was at risk, 80 percent in cases of severe fetal defect, and 82 percent in cases involving pregnancies that are the result of rape. Support falls significantly when socioeconomic reasons are cited: 44 percent when the family is too poor to support another child, 43 percent when the mother is single and prefers not to marry, and 43 percent when a married woman is pregnant but the couple does not desire additional children.[41]

Other opinion polls raise alarm within the pro-choice camp, especially when the public seems willing to narrow access to abortions. In late 2002 respondents were asked about specific abortion restrictions. Seventy-eight percent favored requiring the woman seeking an abortion to wait twenty-four hours. On laws requiring doctors to inform patients about alternatives to abortion, 88 percent were in favor. On whether women under the age of eighteen should have to obtain parental consent before obtaining an abortion, 73 percent favored such laws, and when asked whether they favored making it illegal to perform the late-term abortion procedure in the last six months of a pregnancy except to save the mother's life, 70 percent would outlaw the procedure.[42] A 2003 Gallup/CNN/*USA Today* survey asked Americans about such abortion restrictions and the results were similar. But this poll also asked whether Americans support a constitutional amendment to ban abortions in all circumstances except when necessary to save the life of the mother. This more extreme proposal was supported by only 38 percent but opposed by 59 percent.[43]

Table 1.4

Multimodal Distribution of Opinion on Legal Conditions for Abortion
(percentage of respondents)

	Legal under any circumstances	Legal under certain circumstances	Legal under all circumstances
1975	21	54	22
1977	22	55	19
1979	22	54	19
1980	25	53	18
1981	23	52	21
1983	23	58	16
1988	24	57	17
1989	28	51	17
1990	31	53	12
1991	33	50	33
1992	33	51	33
1993	32	51	32
1994	33	51	13
1995	31	53	12
1996	25	58	15

Source: Gallup Reports as reported in Neil Nevitte, William P. Brandon, and Lori Davis, "The American Abortion Controversy: Lessons from Cross-National Evidence," *Politics and the Life Sciences* 12 (February 1993), p. 21. The 1993 data are from *Gallup Poll Monthly* (April 1993), p. 38, and the 1994–1996 data are from *Gallup Poll Monthly* (August 1996), p. 31.

The 2004 Zogby International Values Poll reveals two distinct Americas— the Red States (that voted for George W. Bush in 2000) and the Blue States (that supported Al Gore). As evidence of a culture war,[44] only 31 percent of Red State voters favor abortion whereas 42 percent of voters in the Blue States do. On whether abortion destroys a human life and constitutes manslaughter, 59 percent of Red State voters as compared to 46 percent of Blue State voters believe this is true. A quarter century after *Roe,* abortion still divides the United States.

Interest Groups

The debate over abortion, a decades-long struggle, is characterized by the rhetoric of war.[45] The *Roe* decision did not bring about a truce; it simply redefined the rules of engagement. The abortion debate in the twenty-first century is still largely defined by the pro-life and pro-choice advocates rather than by public opinion.

The Pro-Choice Coalition

Consisting of a loose coalition of women's groups, health care associations, local abortion reform and repeal groups, population movement activists, religious denominations, and traditional liberal groups, the movement was overawed by the sweeping rulings in *Roe* and *Doe*. Before becoming powerful or even well organized, the pro-choice movement paradoxically had already won one of its most coveted victories.[46] Prior to 1973, local single-issue groups (for example, the Association for the Study of Abortion and the Abortion Rights Association of Illinois) dominated the movement. Eventually, however, single-issue groups combined with multi-issue organizations to create the National Association for the Repeal of Abortion Laws. Support from established organizations such as Planned Parenthood and the American Civil Liberties Union was crucial, since these larger groups possessed badly needed institutional expertise on how to lobby Congress. After the *Roe* decision, liberal Protestant churches (such as the Presbyterian and United Methodist churches), Reform Jewish synagogues, and a splinter group of Catholics joined the pro-choice cause. In 1973, the Religious Coalition for Reproductive Choice (formerly known as the Religious Coalition for Abortion Rights) was formed largely in response to efforts aimed at overturning *Roe v. Wade* by constitutional amendment. The coalition is an alliance of national religious organizations from major faiths with affiliates around the country, including Clergy for Choice Network, Spiritual Youth for Reproductive Freedom, and the Black Church Initiative. Catholics for a Free Choice (CFFC), also formed in 1973, supports family planning and abortion, debunking the myth that all Catholics follow the bishops unquestioningly. CFFC originally just wanted recognition for pro-choice Catholics but in the 1970s and 1980s focused on lobbying for reproductive freedom and generating a feminist movement infused with religion.

The American Civil Liberties Union and the National Organization for Women have taken a leadership role in defending abortion rights. The Reproductive Freedom Unit of the ACLU, founded in 1973, makes protection of the right to privacy and reproductive choice its primary purpose. NOW first called for abortion rights in 1967, but the *Webster* ruling caused a rejuvenation of activity by women's groups, including the 1990 Freedom Caravan for Women's Lives state-by-state campaign to bring in volunteers and promote pro-choice candidates in the 1990 elections. A spin-off organization of NOW, the Feminist Majority Foundation, is a multi-issue organization generally oriented toward getting women into positions of power. It seeks to end various abortion restrictions, such as parental notification, and spearheads the National Clinic Defense Project, which seeks to protect abortion and family planning clinics from antiabortion activities. Both NOW and the Feminist Majority Foundation sponsor marches in Washington, D.C., evaluate recent judicial decisions on reproductive rights, and campaign to protect the future of *Roe.*[47]

Medical interest groups also have gotten involved. The American College of Obstetricians and Gynecologists (ACOG) supports legal, safe, accessible, and publicly funded abortions. The Planned Parenthood Federation of America runs pro-choice television ads. Medical Students for Choice, founded in 1995, encourages medical students to become abortion providers.[48] The National Abortion Federation (NAF), founded in 1977, is an association of abortion providers that issues fact sheets and collects data on incidents of violence and disruption against abortion providers.

Founded in 1969, NARAL Pro-Choice America is the premier pro-choice, single-issue national organization. With a grassroots network of over thirty-five state affiliates and half a million members nationwide, it is also the largest organization devoted entirely to defending abortion rights. It files amicus curiae briefs regularly in abortion rights cases and monitors the status of state and federal restrictions. In 1993, the O'Leary/Kamber Reports ranked NARAL among the top three most effective lobbying groups on Capitol Hill.[49] NARAL has done much to professionalize the pro-choice movement by hiring staff, using paid political consultants, engaging in polling, and employing technologies, such as focus groups, normally used by political parties.[50]

The pro-choice coalition generally has viewed the federal judiciary as an ally in the battle to protect reproductive freedom. A study of federal district court abortion cases decided between 1973 and 1990 reveals that involvement of pro-choice interest groups increases the probability that the judges will enter a pro-choice decision. Pro-choice litigation is dominated by civil liberties groups, especially the ACLU and Planned Parenthood, and they have a much higher success rate than other organizational litigants in federal district courts. Civil liberties groups prevailed in 87 percent of the cases in which they participated and Planned Parenthood won 82 percent of its cases.[51]

The central pro-choice argument is that decisions about abortion should be a private matter between physician and patient. Women should be allowed to terminate an unwanted pregnancy without external interference, not because abortion is desirable but because it is important to their privacy. Pro-choice advocates accuse their opponents of trying to substitute the judgment of clergy or governmental officials for that of women and their physicians. Pro-choice feminists go further in making the container or vessel argument, which dismisses the claim that an embryo is a person. Putting fetal rights before those of the woman who carries the fetus makes the woman a second-class citizen, and to elevate the fetus to independent personhood is to ignore the interdependency between mother and fetus. Not only is the fetus a part of her body, not a mere inhabitant ready to come out and survive under any conditions, but the fetus also can affect her health. Thus, when the rights of the fetus are elevated above the mother's rights, a woman may be asked to sacrifice her health and well-being for the survival or well-being of another.

The Pro-Life Lobby

Pro-life groups are more single-issue-oriented, focusing almost entirely on abortion, than the pro-choice coalition, which has garnered the support of more multi-issue interest groups.[52] Unlike the pro-choice coalition, which has been led by secular interests, the Roman Catholic Church spearheaded the right-to-life movement and used the National Conference of Catholic Bishops (NCCB) to organize the National Right to Life Committee (NRLC). The Mormon Church and Southern Baptists also consistently oppose abortion. Christian evangelicals were first mobilized by the Christian Action Council, founded by Billy Graham in 1975, and by Dr. C. Everett Koop, who was later appointed surgeon general by President Reagan. By 1978 the Moral Majority (consisting primarily of Christian evangelicals under the leadership of Jerry Falwell) poured money into congressional races and distributed family ratings on members of Congress. One of Falwell's top goals was a constitutional amendment banning abortion.

In 1989 the Moral Majority closed down due to declining revenues, but it was quickly replaced by the Christian Coalition, led by televangelist Pat Robertson, who used his *700 Club* viewership to further the Christian Coalition's political goals as well as his own presidential aspirations. The Christian Coalition's political savvy became crystal clear at the 1992 and 1996 Republican National Conventions, when the coalition weighed in on the abortion issue and prevented pro-choice Republicans from moderating the antiabortion plank. Now dubbed the Christian Coalition of America, one of its primary missions is to protect "innocent human life." Among the victories in 2004 that members cite is the partial-birth abortion ban enacted by Congress as well as their success in zeroing-out abortion family planning funding.[53]

Medical pro-life groups have also surfaced. The American Association of Pro Life Obstetricians and Gynecologists (AAPLOG), established in 1973 by Dr. Matthew J. Bulfin, tries to persuade colleagues to oppose abortion. Doctors for Life, founded in 1978, represents physicians who believe that human life begins at conception and who refuse to participate in performing abortions or euthanasia. The first nonsectarian pro-life organization was founded in 1971 as the Americans United for Life Legal Defense Fund. It engages in vigorous educational campaigns, in addition to providing legal defense counsel to the parties in litigation and providing testimony in support of pro-life legislation. It also drafts model state legislation with numerous abortion restrictions and authors amicus curiae briefs before the Supreme Court and lower federal courts.[54] The largest and best-known pro-life organization is the National Right to Life Committee (NRLC). With over 3,000 local chapters, it plays a leading role in lobbying state legislatures to pass restrictive abortion laws. Affiliated groups of the NRLC include the National Right to Life PAC (formed to elect pro-lifers to public office), American Victims of Abortion, Black Americans for Life, and National Teens for Life.

Frustrated by the slow changes that resulted from traditional NRLC lobbying efforts and the steady rate of abortions, new militant antiabortion groups emerged in the late 1970s and mid-1980s. Operation Save America (once called Operation Rescue National), the Pro-Life Action League (PLAL), and the Prolife Nonviolent Action Project (PNAP) began abortion rescues in which protesters sing, pray, and create human blockades that allow pro-life counselors the opportunity to dissuade women from entering the clinics or obtaining abortions. Modeling their actions on civil disobedience, over 29,000 pro-life advocates were arrested between 1987 and 1991. These pro-life extremists believe that the only tactic to end abortions is to force abortion providers out of business. Operation Save America calls on all Christians to end the child-killing.[55]

By 1994 the radical pro-life activists called the killing of doctors and staff who provided abortion services justifiable homicide. One year later, disgruntled Operation Rescue members splintered and formed the American Coalition of Life Activists, which, along with the Defenders of the Defenders of Life, targeted for violence and intimidation well-known physicians who performed abortions. The highly publicized murders of Michael Griffin, David Gunn, George Tiller, John Britton, James Barrett, Shannon Lowney, Barnett Slepian, and Leanne Nichols by anti-abortion zealots created a backlash against the pro-life movement, prompting legislative and judicial action.[56] As of 2004 the pro-life movement has not completely recovered from that public relations debacle, apart from the pro-choice success in establishing buffer zones at abortion clinics.

Pro-life advocates believe that the life of a baby begins long before birth. A new human being is growing in the womb from the moment of fertilization, and they support their belief that the fetus is a human life with medical facts. At six weeks there are brain waves; at ten to eleven weeks the fetus is sensitive to touch; one nineteen-week baby born prematurely survived. This proves, they believe, that the fetus is a living being.[57] By comparing abortion to genocide and slavery, pro-life advocates depict abortion as a threat to basic American values. If abortions continue, they believe, it will lead to an anchorless, godless society with no family values.[58] Abortions not only subvert the sanctity of life but inflict psychological pain on antiabortionists who are horrified by the death of unborn children, disgusted by acts that their religion regards as mortal sins, or fearful that legal abortion will reduce the numbers, significance, and influence of their racial group.[59]

From the Extremes to Common Ground

Only a small number of intense activists on each side of the abortion debate are organized. Twenty-two percent of pro-life advocates view abortion as critical to their vote, while only 12 percent of pro-choice voters feel this strongly about the abortion issue. Still, 34 percent of those committed pro-lifers intended to vote for Bill Clinton in 1996, a pro-choice candidate, while 15 percent of committed pro-choice advocates indicated they would support pro-life candidate Bob Dole.[60] In a study of California abortion activists, pro-life activists were likely to be politically inexperienced and were predominantly women homemakers (63 percent). In contrast, 94 percent of female pro-choice activists worked outside the home.[61] Pro-life activists, then, had more time for letter writing, picketing, and other grassroots activities.[62] This demographic difference gives pro-life advocates a grassroots mobilization advantage.

There are attempts to find common ground in the contentious abortion debate. The Common Ground Network for Life and Choice, founded in 1989, set up local groups in Cleveland, Buffalo, Denver, Washington, and Baltimore to promote dialogue on this most divisive issue. The founders of the organization—Mary Jacksteit, a Benedictine nun who opposes abortion, and Adrianne Kaufmann, a lawyer and labor arbitrator who supports abortion rights—apply their experiences to promote a dialogue process based on common ground. The organizers are not trying to reach a middle position on abortion but rather focus on activities that could reduce the need for abortions. Areas of common interest include more emphasis on adoption, reduction of pregnancy among teenagers, and an end to violence against abortion clinics and providers. Since its inception, the Common Ground Network has operated in some twenty cities, convening one-day dialogue workshops and facilitating consensus-building processes. It has 2,000 members. Other groups, notably the Public Conversations Project, try to facilitate civil conversations on emotional topics like abortion. Since its founding in 1989, the participants have held dialogues that help them develop ways to facilitate effective communications between pro-life and pro-choice advocates. Such talks represent a modest beginning, but public opinion polls since 1965 indicate that this direction is where the majority of Americans would like the abortion debate to go.

Presidency

Abortion has been a partisan issue dividing Democrats and Republicans since 1976, when their party platforms began to take opposing positions. The Democratic Party is captured by pro-choice interests and the Republican Party is controlled by pro-life interests when the party planks are written on abortion. Before *Roe,* President Nixon in 1971 asserted that abortion on demand as a method of population control was unacceptable and that the unborn also have rights. His Democratic presidential opponent, George McGovern, countered that abortion was a private matter between a woman and her physician. After *Roe,* abortion became a more salient issue, and in 1976 it played a more prominent role in presidential politics. Although both Gerald Ford and Jimmy Carter preferred to ignore the issue, repeated questions on the campaign trail forced them to address it. Both gave fence-straddling responses, with Ford opposing abortion on demand and favoring state government control of the procedure but also recognizing the need for abortions in exceptional cases. Carter, a born-again Christian, personally opposed abortion and federal funding for abortions but also opposed any constitutional amendment to overturn *Roe.* The 1976 party platforms reflected the tentative steps each party was taking toward polarization. The Democratic Party acknowledged the divisive religious and ethical nature of the issue but opposed any effort to overturn *Roe.* The Republican Party endorsed a position on abortion that valued human life and supported the efforts of those who sought a constitutional amendment to protect the unborn. These murky responses were not very satisfying to the pro-life or pro-choice advocates.[63]

During the Carter administration, an ambivalent attitude toward abortion prevailed as President Carter tried to placate the pro-choice and pro-life sides. He made no attempt to reverse *Roe* but did oppose federal funding of abortion, thus alienating both sides of the abortion dispute. Carter was challenged by Senator Edward Kennedy (D-MA), a pro-choice advocate, in the 1980 primaries. Ronald Reagan, on the other hand, aggressively supported the antiabortion position by taking a hard-line pro-life stance. The party platforms diverged more sharply in 1980, with the Democrats supporting *Roe* and rejecting any constitutional amendment to restrict or overturn it and the Republicans favoring a constitutional amendment to protect the unborn as well as restrictions on federal funding of abortion. By 1984 the parties were absolutely polarized. The GOP platform recognized for the first time that the unborn have a fundamental right to life while the Democrats recognized reproductive freedom as a fundamental human right.[64]

Reagan transformed the abortion debate. His administration tried to reverse *Roe,* recruited pro-life judges for the federal bench, and imposed restrictive regulations on the availability of abortions. Although Reagan promoted the pro-life agenda, some observers argue that his rhetoric did not match his actions. Abortion was not a priority item early in the Reagan presidency and only later, in his second term, did Reagan issue the gag rule on abortion counseling and limit funding for abortion clinics.[65] Reagan's successor, George H.W. Bush, was initially pro-choice but during his 1988 election bid followed Reagan by calling for the criminalization of abortion. Michael Dukakis, his Democratic opponent, defended abortion rights. The party platforms in 1988 were diametrically opposed on the abortion issue.[66] After Bush defeated Dukakis, he continued the Reagan administration policies. Bush looked to the federal courts for more abortion restrictions, and his Justice Department filed an amicus curiae brief in *Webster* asking that *Roe* be overturned. In 1990, however, after President Bush delivered a message to antiabortion protesters on the anniversary of *Roe*, his press secretary told reporters that Bush's views were personal and based on his conscience but that the GOP was big enough to accommodate varying points of view. Lee Atwater, then Republican national chairman, expressed a similar sentiment when he, in a speech to the Republican National Committee, stressed his commitment to an umbrella party that would allow both sides of the abortion issue to coexist within the Republican Party.[67]

In 1992 George Bush faced Bill Clinton, who stressed his moderate "New" Democrat values. In 1992, in contrast to 1976, 1980, and 1984, all the Democratic presidential contenders were pro-choice. Clinton and Gore carefully controlled their convention, even going so far as to prevent pro-life Governor Robert Casey (D-PA) from making an antiabortion speech to the convention. The Democratic platform backed *Roe* and supported the right to choose regardless of ability to pay. The Republican national convention, although well orchestrated, was inundated with the remarks from favorites of the Christian Coalition and the extreme right wing of the party. The GOP platform of 1992 adamantly opposed abortion and reaffirmed support for a human life amendment.

When Clinton sought reelection in 1996, he was opposed by Republican Bob Dole, who faced a field of several primary challengers for the nomination. Ironically, in 1974 Dole had used the abortion issue to defeat Dr. William Roy in a narrow reelection victory to his congressional seat. Confronted by abortion again in a 1996 presidential primary debate, Dole flip-flopped, at first saying he opposed all abortions and later saying he supported abortions in certain circumstances such as rape, incest, or if the life of the mother was endangered by carrying the pregnancy to term.[68] Once again a pro-choice president was elected to office. But Clinton faced GOP majorities in both houses of Congress, which shifted the legislative branch toward pro-life interests.

In 2000 a pro-life president was elected to office. During the 2000 presidential campaign, George W. Bush avidly courted pro-life forces while simultaneously sidestepping the abortion issue. Using a strategy called the Texas Three-Step, he gave lip service to an abortion ban when addressing groups like the Christian Coalition (one step) but, when interviewed on *Meet the Press,* stated that the nation was not ready for a constitutional amendment banning abortions (two step) and, finally, he publicly envisioned a "world free of abortions" and supported banning the partial-birth abortion procedure, teaching abstinence, promoting adoption, allowing parental notification laws, and eliminating taxpayer funding of abortions (three step).[69] Cleverly Bush articulated a seemingly nonthreatening, moderate pro-life agenda.

Bureaucracy

Whereas Bill Clinton issued five executive orders in 1993 overturning anti-abortion initiatives that had been in force during the Reagan and Bush administrations (for example, Clinton lifted the gag rule prohibiting professionals at Title X clinics from counseling women about abortion services, lifted the ban on RU-486 and fetal tissue research, and allowed U.S. aid to international family planning programs, including those engaged in abortion counseling), George W. Bush in 2001 hailed a new day for a pro-life agenda and vowed to modify or reverse some of Clinton's executive orders.[70] On the twenty-eighth anniversary of *Roe v. Wade,* President George W. Bush acted to reverse the Clinton administration policy on aid for international family planning groups. On his first full day of work in the Oval Office, Bush issued an executive order denying federal funding to overseas groups that provide abortion counseling or otherwise assist women in obtaining abortion services. This decision reinstated restrictions supported by Presidents Ronald Reagan and George H.W. Bush by placing restrictions on the $425 million in aid set aside for overseas family planning.[71] In June 2001, the Center for Reproductive Law and Policy—a privately funded abortion rights group—sued the Bush administration, arguing that the rule affected over 400 organizations, that the "global gag rule" violated free speech and political association, and that it restricted what these overseas counseling agencies could do with their own money.[72]

In reaction to Clinton's executive order that lifted the ban on the marketing of RU-486 (a drug that blocks the hormone needed for the fertilized egg, or embryo, to thrive in the uterus), President Bush's newly appointed secretary of health and human services, Tommy G. Thompson, announced that he would conduct a new review of the safety of RU-486. RU-486, also known as mifepristone, is the first alternative to surgical abortion approved in the United States.[73] Because the Clinton administration rules were issued late in Clinton's second term and had not yet been implemented, the door was open for a new review.[74] Bush also appointed Dr. W. David Hager, a controversial pro-life obstetrician/gynecologist who advocates Bible reading and prayer for women suffering from premenstrual syndrome and who ardently opposes mifepristone, to head the Federal Drug Administration Reproductive Health Drugs Advisory Committee. In another administrative action, President Bush ruled that the Hyde Amendment applies to funding RU-486 in the Medicaid program.[75] (The Hyde Amendment, a rider to the annual Labor/Health and Human Services [CHHS] appropriations bill, prevents Medicaid and any other federal funding from those departments from funding abortions.) Controversial for over fifteen years, RU-486 is once again in play in the political arena.

In a 2001 national address, President Bush stated that he would permit federal tax funding of stem cell research from human embryos but added that research would be limited to stem cells already extracted and that the government would not sanction the destruction of new embryos. Bush viewed this policy as a viable compromise, allowing researchers to explore the possible cures for human disease that could result from stem cell research without crossing "a fundamental moral line" that would result in the destruction of human embryos.[76] On January 20, 2002, Bush proclaimed "National Security of Human Life Day": "On September 11, we saw clearly that evil exists in the world, and that it does not value life. Now we are engaged in a fight against evil and tyranny to preserve and protect life." Pro-choice advocates believed that this wording was a veiled attempt to liken abortion to terrorism. In late 2002 the Bush administration issued regulations that made fetuses eligible for health care coverage under the state Children's Health Insurance Program (CHIP), viewed by NOW and other pro-choice organizations as an effort to elevate the legal status of fetuses over that of women. The Bush administration also supported the Reagan administration policy that bans American women who serve abroad in the armed forces from obtaining abortions at overseas military hospitals.[77] President Bush signed into law the Partial-Birth Abortion Ban Act, which President Clinton had twice vetoed, the Born-Alive Infants Protection Act, and the Abortion Non-Discrimination Act.[78]

Congress

Once the *Roe* decision was announced, Congress became the logical flash point for pro-life interest groups. Significant attempts to legislate abortion policy began in 1973, with nearly 10 percent of congressional representatives sponsoring or cosponsoring antiabortion legislation or constitutional amendments. By 1976 more than fifty different varieties of pro-life constitutional amendments had been introduced in Congress, but none were passed.[79] One success story for the pro-lifers was the Hyde Amendment. Originally it allowed use of Medicaid funds for abortions only if the pregnant woman's life was endangered, but legal challenges held up its implementation for a few years during which Medicaid abortions were funded also in cases of rape and incest. But in 1981 the Hyde Amendment returned to its original language of permitting abortions only to save the woman's life, and this policy did not change for another thirteen years, until 1994, when the 103rd Congress reenacted coverage for cases of rape and incest.[80] Legislative riders to bills prohibited the use of funds in programs in which abortion is a method of family planning (Family Planning Services and Population Act of 1970), prevented judges or public officials from ordering recipients of federal funds to perform abortions (Health Program Extension Act of 1973), and barred Legal Aid lawyers from giving legal assistance on how to obtain nontherapeutic abortions (Legal Services Corporation Act of 1974). An avalanche of restrictions was also attached to appropriations bills to ban the government from paying for abortions except to save the mother's life, including abortion services at military hospitals, federal funding for abortions in the District of Columbia (and extending even to the use of the District's own funds), and federal health benefits to pay for abortions.[81]

Studies of congressional voting on abortion bills indicate that ideology, not party, is the most important predictor of congressional votes.[82] When a partisanship variable is used that combines party affiliation with ideology, the more partisan and liberal Democratic senators vote pro-choice while the more partisan and conservative Republican senators vote pro-life.[83] Evidence from the 101st and 102nd Congresses (through 1991) indicated a slight shift in favor of a pro-choice legislative strategy. Of the seventeen key House votes on abortion in these two Congresses, pro-life forces won only six (or 35 percent) of the roll call votes.[84] Pro-choice forces in the 1990s, although still playing defense, in warding off the most restrictive bills, have taken the offensive by introducing such pro-choice legislation as the 1991 Freedom of Choice Act (which did not pass) and the 1993 Freedom of Access to Clinic Entrances Act (FACE), which was enacted. Passed by large margins in the House and the Senate, FACE was supported by pro-life and pro-choice legislators. FACE, prompted by violence directed against women's health centers and abortion providers across the country, criminalized blockades of reproductive health facilities as well as the use of force or threats of force against those using the facilities. This measure, signed by President Clinton in May 1994, has proved to be a deterrent. Data show that, under FACE, violent incidents directed at abortion providers decreased from 3,429 in 1993 to 1,815 in 1995.[85]

Pro-life members of Congress struck back in 1995 and 1996 with two legislative proposals to ban the partial-birth (late-term) abortion procedure and to prohibit abortion information on the Internet or online services. In 1995 the House of Representatives voted to ban a specific late-term abortion procedure, which the bill's sponsors call partial-birth abortion, but later that year the Senate passed the House bill with an amendment to allow the procedure if the pregnant woman's life was endangered.[86] The bill would have subjected a physician who violates the late-term ban to possible fines, civil suits, and/or a maximum of two years' imprisonment. Because the final version did not permit the procedure if the woman's life was endangered, it was vetoed by President Clinton in April 1996.

A less emotional issue was raised in 1996 by Representative Henry J. Hyde (R-IL), a longtime abortion opponent who successfully buried a little-noticed provision in the Telecommunications Act of 1996. This proviso criminalized the use of interactive computer systems to provide or receive information about abortion. First Amendment proponents and abortion rights groups challenged the measure in court, where a United States attorney told federal district judge Charles P. Sifton that the Justice Department considered the bill unconstitutional and not enforceable. The judge held that it was unnecessary to issue an injunction restraining implementation of the measure until actual harm to speech was incurred.[87]

In 1997 Senate Minority Leader Tom Daschle (D-SD) proposed compromise language that would prohibit most abortions after the fetus reached viability except if a woman's life was endangered or she faced grievous injury to her health. Clinton signaled his support for this bill but it was defeated in a floor vote.[88] Pro-life supporters were given some help in May 1997 when the American Medical Association (AMA) endorsed a ban on a specific partial-birth abortion procedure called dilation and extraction (D&E). The new measure protected doctors from prosecution if they intended to deliver a baby but were forced to use D&E to protect the woman's life. The American College of Obstetricians and Gynecologists, however, opposed the ban, arguing that it allows legislators to make decisions best left to medical professionals. This bill passed both houses of Congress with no exception other than saving the woman's life,[89] but was vetoed by President Clinton because it contained no exception to preserve the *health* of the woman.[90]

During 1999, as in the past years, pro-life forces were stronger than pro-choice forces in the House of Representatives, whereas the Senate was a political battleground, only narrowly passing a nonbinding resolution by 51–47 to endorse *Roe v. Wade.* By 1999 the GOP chairs of most key House committees were pro-life, and over 85 percent of Republican representatives voted pro-life compared to the 14 percent to 31 percent of Democrats who voted pro-life. In the Senate, similarly, 85 percent of Republicans voted pro-life while only 4 percent of Democrats did. Pro-life victories in 1999 included restrictions on funding abortion counseling overseas and limiting funds for abortions in federal prison except where necessary to save the life of the pregnant woman.[91]

Pro-life forces were unable to make significant inroads in the 106th session of Congress leading up to the 2000 elections. The House passed a partial-birth abortion ban, again, to go on record as opposing the procedure before the Supreme Court rendered its opinion in *Stenberg v. Carhart.* The House passed two bills in 1999—the Child Custody Protection Act (designed to impose a nationwide parental notification law) and the Unborn Victims of Violence Act (which criminalized harm to the "unborn child" from the moment of conception). In September 2000 the House passed the Born-Alive Infants Protection Act, stipulating that all infants born alive be treated as persons under federal law. The Senate delayed action on these bills but eventually support the Born-Alive Infants Protection Act.[92]

After eight years of the Clinton-Gore administration, pro-life forces in 2001 had high hopes with the election of a pro-life president and Republican majorities in the House and Senate. One of President George W. Bush's first executive orders reinstated the Mexico City Policy (imposing limits on overseas groups that provide abortion counseling or services to women). A bipartisan group of fifty representatives and fifteen senators organized to overturn it. Arguing that the policy reversal would undermine many clinics that provide essential reproductive health services abroad, thus causing more unwanted pregnancies, the group introduced legislation to repeal it, but failed.[93] In 2001 the House also rejected efforts to allow use of federal funds to perform abortions in federal prisons and to overturn the prohibition on the use of taxpayer monies to fund abortions at military facilities overseas.

In 2002 the 107th Congress continued backing restrictions on abortion access for women who depend on federal assistance for their health care, including Medicaid and Medicare clients, U.S. servicewomen and their dependents overseas, and women in federal prison. For the fifth time the House of Representatives passed the partial-birth abortion ban and, in addition, was especially proactive in its support of the pro-life agenda by passing the Child Custody Protection Act and supporting legislation that allowed health care companies to impose a gag rule on agencies providing abortion services and counseling. In the 108th Congress, only 142 fully pro-choice members were elected to the House and 33 more were elected to the Senate. Since pro-life supporters gained ascendancy in the House and Senate in 1994, Congress has voted on reproductive health issues 148 times and the pro-choice groups lost all but twenty-five of those votes.[94]

By far the most heralded pro-life victory came in 2003 with the passage of the Partial-Birth Abortion Ban Act. After an eight-year struggle and two vetoes by President Clinton, lobbying begun by the National Right to Life Committee in 1995 came to fruition. Even though this legislation allows the late-term procedure to save a woman's life, it has no exception for health or medical necessity. Three pro-choice groups—the American Civil Liberties Union, Planned Parenthood, and the Center for Reproductive Rights—have filed lawsuits challenging the ban as unconstitutional.[95]

Federalism

Between 1973 and 1989, the states enacted nineteen types of antiabortion regulations, including conscience clauses (35 states), postviability requirements (29), postviability standards of care (29), abortion funding limits (25), fetal tissue experimentation bans (23), parental notification (18), informed consent (17), parental consent (17), second-trimester hospitalization requirements (17), insurance restrictions that allow for maternity benefits but exclude abortion (10), spousal notification (7), and a requirement that women be notified that the fetus experiences pain in second-trimester abortions (1).[96]

The *Webster* ruling refederalized abortion policy back to the states, and between 1989 and 1992 new abortion restrictions were generated. Premier among these were efforts to ban "birth control" abortions (all abortions, opponents say, except those necessary to save the pregnant woman's life or in cases of rape, incest, or gross fetal abnormality).[97] By the end of 1991, nine states had passed new restrictions on abortion. Michigan, Nebraska, and South Carolina, which had already enacted parental notification requirements for minors seeking abortions prior to *Webster,* added the necessary judicial bypass provision. Mississippi, North Dakota, and Ohio required a waiting period and passed right-to-know statutes, the latter requiring a discussion between physician (or provider) and patient of alternatives to abortion and the dangers of the procedure before it could be performed. Louisiana and Utah enacted the most restrictive laws, modeled on the centerpiece of the post-*Webster* antiabortion movement, namely a ban on birth control abortions. Given impetus by the 1992 *Casey* decision, the eleven states of Idaho, Kansas, Louisiana, Mississippi, Nebraska, North Dakota, Ohio, Pennsylvania,

South Carolina, South Dakota, and Utah enacted mandatory waiting periods. On the pro-choice side, Connecticut, Maryland, Nevada, and Washington passed liberalizing abortion laws that, in essence, wrote *Roe* into state law.

In the six years from 1990 to 1996, twelve more states passed bans on abortion after the fetus is viable; the viability time period, when specified, varied from twenty to twenty-four weeks. Of the forty-one states that have postviability bans, twelve require that a second physician be present at a postviability abortion to give medical attention to the fetus. From 1993 through 1995, six more states passed right-to-know or informed consent statutes, with a total of thirty states requiring this regulation by 1996. By June 1996 thirty-seven states mandated parental consent or notice for abortion. Though declared unconstitutional in some states, the laws are enforced today in at least thirty states. Federal law since 1994 requires all states to pay for life-saving abortions or abortions that resulted from rape or incest, and only fifteen states go further by publicly funding abortions for low-income women on the same terms as other pregnancy-related health services.[98] In 1995 and 1996, thirty-two anti-choice state laws were enacted as compared to sixteen laws in 1993 and 1994. Pro-choice advocates have been alarmed because a majority of state legislatures have indicated a willingness to restrict abortion beyond the limits put forward in *Roe*.[99]

Following the lead of pro-life forces in Congress, state legislators also have proposed bans on partial-birth abortions. By May 1997 forty states had taken up this issue[100] and, as of February 2004, partial-birth bans in five states have provisos protecting the woman's life and health that meet the requirements of *Stenberg v. Carhart*. Twenty-six other states have partial-birth bans that do not meet Supreme Court requirements, of which eighteen are being blocked by the courts and eight remain unchallenged.[101]

By the thirtieth anniversary of *Roe,* states were continuing to enact abortion restrictions. Seventeen states have gag rules banning certain organizations that receive state funds from counseling or referring women to abortion services. Nine states have unenforceable laws requiring spousal consent before a married woman may obtain an abortion. Forty-four states require that only physicians may perform abortions.[102] As of 2004, ten states allow production of "Choose Life" license plates; five of them permit donation of the proceeds to pro-life organizations and crisis pregnancy centers. Twenty-seven states still require mandatory counseling, and twenty-one states impose a waiting period between counseling and the abortion procedure. The number of states with parental involvement restrictions has risen, with thirty-three now requiring some parental involvement in a minor's decision to abort. Since the 1994 passage of the Freedom of Access to Clinic Entrances Act, twelve states and the District of Columbia have adopted laws to protect abortion providers, such as prohibitions on blocking the entrances to facilities, buffer zones, and other antiharassment measures. Four states allow private insurance coverage of abortion only if the woman's life is endangered by carrying the pregnancy to term, and forty-five states allow certain health care providers to refuse to provide contraceptive services and reproductive health care on religious or moral grounds.[103]

State restrictions on abortion are likely to continue. Not only is the populace generally supportive of more restrictions on availability of the abortion but so are state legislatures. Studies indicate that states with strong pro-life legislatures and avid pro-life governors enact more restrictions than states with pro-choice legislatures and governors.[104] Support for abortion restrictiveness in the states was found to depend more on political factors, like the dominance of conservatism in the post-*Webster* era, than socioeconomic conditions. On whether abortion restrictions have had an impact, finally, Maureen Oakley finds that abortion regulations affect abortion rates but do not necessarily prevent women from seeking abortions, although they raise the costs of doing so.[105]

Summary of Propositions

1a (single-issue groups): Supported, because both pro-choice and pro-life single-issue groups predominate, but especially among pro-life activists.

1b (absolutist politics): Supported, because pro-life and pro-choice arguments are almost diametrically opposed and they fundamentally disagree about what the core issues in the abortion debate are.

2a (judicial activism): Supported, because *Roe v. Wade,* other rulings by the federal judiciary have defined the boundaries of abortion rights and permissible restrictions.

2b (incorporation): Supported, because *Roe v. Wade* nullified the anti-abortion laws of forty-six states.

3a (presidential symbolism): Unsupported, because Reagan, Clinton, and George H.W. Bush took executive actions that went beyond rhetoric or symbolism.

3b (partisan presidents): Supported, because since 1980, Republican presidents have displayed their pro-life sympathies and Democratic presidents have defended the pro-choice agenda.

4a (Congress and states): Supported, because in 1973, when the abortion laws of the District of Columbia and the vast majority of states did not authorize first-trimester abortions, and in the years since, much would depend upon whether the courts opposed an abortion restriction enacted by the Congress and states (bans on late-term abortions, for example).

4b (Congress and elections): Supported, because pro-life constituencies are represented by pro-life legislators and pro-choice constituencies are represented by pro-choice legislators at both the federal and state levels.

5a (opinion and ideology): Unsupported, because generally public opinion is moderate relative to the pro-choice and pro-life positions.

5b (law and society): Supported, because extremely committed pro-life advocates do not accept legalized abortion and resort to direct action and illegal forms of protest.

6a (marginal agencies): Supported, because the federal role in the implementation of abortion policy is very limited.

6b (agency pressures): Supported, because the implementation of abortion policy can shift toward a pro-choice or pro-life position depending upon micromanagement by Congress and the partisan composition of the executive branch.

7a (federalism): Supported, because states had complete jurisdiction over abortions prior to *Roe*.

7b (compliance): Supported, because the states continue to impose regulations on the availability of abortion services that often pose challenges to *Roe v. Wade*.

For Further Insight Into the Abortion Debate

Abortion Rally: March for Life. VHS tape, one videocassette. West Lafayette, IN: C-SPAN Archives, 2000. Pro-life advocates present their viewpoints at the twenty-seventh annual March for Life, voicing their opposition to *Roe* and calling for an end to legalized abortion.

Arroyo, Raymond. *Town Hall Meeting—A Pro-Life Summit: 30 Years After Roe vs. Wade*. VHS tape, one videocassette. Birmingham, AL: Eternal World Television, 2003. This film provides an overview of the status of the contemporary pro-life movement, providing input from ethicists, lawyers, and grassroots activists.

Cronkite, Walter, and Eric Sevareid. *Abortion and the Law*. DVD video, one videodisc. Princeton, NJ: Films for the Humanities and Sciences, 2003. In examining the legal, moral, social, and psychological aspects of abortion in the United States, this documentary presents diametrically opposed stances from clergymen, lawyers, and physicians.

Feminist Majority Foundation. *Never Go Back*. VHS tape, one videocassette. Arlington, VA: Feminist Majority Foundation, 2002. This film examines the threat that pending Supreme Court retirements will pose to accessible, legal abortion in the United States and examines strategies to prevent the overturn of *Roe*.

Mohler, R. Albert, Richard D. Land, David McIntosh; Terry Schlossberg, and Russell Moore. *Roe vs. Wade Thirty Years Later*. VHS tape, one videocassette. Louisville, KY: Carl F.H. Henry Institute for Evangelical Engagement, 2003. Focusing on the pro-life movement and abortion legislation in the United States, this film offers an evangelical perspective on abortion politics.

Shlain, Tiffany, Maya Draisin, Xandra Castleton, and Jennifer Steinman. *Life, Liberty and the Pursuit of Happiness.* VHS tape, one videocassette. San Francisco: Video Project, 2002. Updating the 1950s version with the same title, this film employs political and social satire to examine reproductive freedom for women. Celebrating *Roe v. Wade*, it explores what could happen if choice is taken away.

Voices of Choice: Physicians Who Provided Abortions Before Roe v. Wade. VHS tape, one videocassette. New York: Physicians for Reproductive Choice and Health, 2003. With oral histories of twenty-two physicians and others who provided abortion services before *Roe,* this multimedia project provides insights from another era.

http://abortionfacts.com. The Web site of Abortionfacts.com, though presenting itself as a "just the facts" information source, actually addresses the history of abortion with loaded language such as "abortion survivors" and "abortionists speak," quickly dispelling the appearance of objectivity. It is a pro-life information source.

www.agi-usa.org. This is the Web site of the Alan Guttmacher Institute, whose mission is to protect reproductive choices and to provide data and policy analysis on reproductive health issues.

www.democratsforlife.org. This is the Web site of Democrats for Life of America, which expresses a dissenting pro-life viewpoint within the Democratic Party and offers updates on state and federal law as well as activities of pro-life Democrats in the news.

www.kff.org. The Web site for the Henry J. Kaiser Family Foundation, a research organization providing health care quality assessments and improvement information, deals extensively with access to abortion services.

www.lifenews.com. This is the Web site of LifeNews.COM, a pro-life group that examines national, state, and local news on abortion politics and issues.

www.naral.org. This Web site of National Abortion Rights Action League Pro-Choice America offers an annual, state-by-state report on abortion restrictions and up-to-date analysis of case law and abortion issues.

www.now.org/issues/abortion. This Web site of the National Organization for Women offers fact sheets on reproductive rights and updates on the organization's stands and pro-choice activities.

www.nrlc.org. The Web site of the National Right to Life Committee offers congressional updates and other news on abortion-related issues and politics from a pro-life perspective.

www.pro-choice.org. The Web site of the National Abortion Federation provides information on violence and intimidation tactics used at abortion clinics.

www.rcrc.org. The Web site of the Religious Coalition for Reproductive Choice puts forth a pro-faith, pro-family, pro-choice perspective.

www.religioustolerance.org. The Web site of Religious Tolerance.org is produced by an interfaith group that consists of staff with diverse beliefs, both pro-life and pro-choice perspectives, on abortion.

www.roevwade.org. The Web site of RoevWade.org depicts abortions as hurting women physically and psychologically and seeks overturn of *Roe v. Wade*.

http://speakout.com/activism/abortion. This Web site of SpeakOut.com provides both pro-choice and pro-life on-line and up-to-date news, including policy analysis, on abortion.

2

Affirmative Action

Minority Rights or Reverse Discrimination?

Gary C. Bryner

Affirmative action is a tremendously important issue in American politics for at least two reasons. First, it is a symbolic and highly visible reminder of the enduring problem of race and the challenges that face America in dealing with its history of discrimination and inequality. Second, affirmative action is one package of policies aimed at improving the economic and social opportunities for African-Americans (as well as other people of color and women). More remains to be done to ensure that all Americans enjoy real equality of opportunity.

The controversy over affirmative action threatens the progress already made during the past half-century of civil rights. The rancorous debate highlights significant differences between how blacks and whites view political, economic, and social policy in the United States. The rancor threatens the viability of affirmative action as a means to achieving a color-blind society and equal opportunity for all. But its proponents argue that racial discrimination continues to be such a pervasive problem that nondiscriminatory or color-blind standards are not enough and that we must support more aggressive efforts under affirmative action to end discrimination and overcome its effects.

Equal employment opportunity, generally understood, means that decisions about the selection, promotion, termination, and treatment of individuals in employment must be free of considerations of race, color, national origin, religion, and sex. Equal employment opportunity is based on nondiscrimination—that biased considerations are unconstitutional and morally unacceptable. Affirmative action is defined here, following the U.S. Civil Rights Commission, as having three components. First, it is remedial: affirmative action denotes efforts that take race, sex, and national origin into account for the purpose of remedying discrimination and its effects. Second, affirmative action seeks ultimately to bring about equal opportunity: affirmative action assumes that "race, sex or national origin [must be considered] in order to eliminate considerations of race, sex and national origin," that "because of the duration, intensity, scope and intransigence of the discrimination women and minority groups experience, affirmative action plans are needed to assure equal employment opportunity."[1] Third, affirmative action specifies what racial groups are to be considered part of the "protected class" covered by its policies.

In practice, there is no agreement on the definition of affirmative action. The term represents a range of public policies along a continuum from outreach and recruitment of candidates, remedial efforts to "make whole" victims of past discrimination, racial diversity as one of several factors in making decisions, flexible goals for increasing the percentage of blacks in certain positions, devices such as separate admission tracks or contract set-asides that treat minority and white candidates differently in order to increase minorities' participation rates, and numerical quotas. There is little controversy over the outliers, because almost everyone favors outreach programs but opposes quotas. Nor is there controversy about which groups should benefit. Under Title IV of the 1964 Civil Rights Act, the primary equal employment opportunity statute, minority groups include blacks, Hispanics, Asian or Pacific islanders, and Native Americans and Alaskan natives. Under public works legislation that sets aside 10 percent of funds for minority-run enterprises, groups included are "blacks, Spanish-speaking persons, Orientals, Native Americans, Eskimos, and Aleuts." Federal agencies with policy responsibility in this area define protected groups as blacks (all racial groups of Africa except North Africa), Hispanics (Mexicans, Puerto Ricans, Cubans, Central or South Americans, and members of other Spanish cultures), Asian/Pacific Islanders (from the Far East, Southeast Asia, the Indian subcontinent, and Pacific Islands), and Native Americans (original people of North America who maintain their tribal identity).

A more fundamental debate involves how to conceptualize affirmative action. Some people view affirmative action in terms of equality of results, not equality of opportunity, or the redistribution of employment opportunities to mirror the distribution of groups in society. Opponents call affirmative action "reverse discrimination" (racial discrimination against whites), though others who emphasize "preferential treatment" view affirmative action either as a moral imperative to remedy past discrimination or as a social evil that perpetuates race consciousness and injustice.[2] Those who reject affirmative action, including some blacks, see it undermining the self-respect of the intended beneficiaries and denigrating the progress and advancement achieved by blacks.[3] Proponents counterargue that affirmative action has increased the percentage of minority students in selective colleges, so any movement away from affirmative action—to, say, granting preference only to persons from low-income families—would be likely to produce a decline in racial diversity. Yet that viewpoint would probably provoke this rebuttal: "While discrimination for most blacks is an unfortunate fact of life, it is no longer . . . the central fact of life."[4] These competing aspects of affirmative action underlie the differences in the evolution of public policies by government decision makers.

Federalism

After World War II, some states enacted laws and programs to protect the civil rights of blacks. New York was the first state to use the term *affirmative action* in providing for remedies to victims of employment discrimination. A 1964 study by the U.S. Department of Labor (done in response to the passage of Title VII of the Civil Rights Act) determined that twenty-four states had fair-employment laws that prohibited private employers from discriminating on the basis of race, color, creed, and national origin in decisions relating to hiring or discharging employees, wages, and other conditions of employment. Moreover, twenty-two of those state laws were essentially compatible with the provisions of the Civil Rights Act.[5] However, none were located in the South. Title VII of the 1964 Civil Rights Act encouraged states to enact and implement their own fair employment laws and assumed that most of Title VII would be enforced by state agencies. In 1965 the Equal Employment Opportunity Commission (EEOC) allowed agencies in some twenty-two states to begin enforcing the federal law. Clearly, Title VII was aimed at the southern states without laws protecting blacks from discrimination.

As support for affirmative action began to unravel politically and legally in the 1990s, opponents promoted popular initiatives to end affirmative action in several states, including California, Colorado, Florida, Illinois, Oregon, and Washington. The University of California Board of Regents also voted in 1995 to end the use of race as a factor in applications and to review outreach programs. Guidelines in 1995 for pursuing ethnic and racial diversity required schools to admit 50 percent of their applicants solely on academic achievement, with the other half to be evaluated according to "special circumstances" such as whether the applicant has shown unusual persistence and determination, needs to work, is from an educationally or socially disadvantaged background, or comes from a difficult family situation. Critics argued that evaluating which applicants were disadvantaged would be burdensome and imprecise, but the regents rejected their appeals to reinstate the traditional affirmative action program. In early 1996 the Board of Regents voted to delay the implementation of the new admissions program until spring 1998.[6]

The most visible anti–affirmative action efforts were ballot initiatives and legislative proposals to end the practice in state and local governments. Ten states considered legislation or ballot initiatives in 1995 to abolish affirmative action, but none was enacted, and by early 1996 ballot initiatives to end affirmative action had been proposed in six states and another seventeen state legislatures were considering similar bills.[7] But most attention focused on California, where two professors started a petition drive to roll back affirmative action because it had been transformed from voluntary outreach to a system of quotas and mandates. Proposition 209, the California Civil Rights Initiative, provided that the state of California "shall not discriminate against or grant preferential treatment to any individual or group on the basis of race, sex, color, ethnicity, or national origin in the operation of public employment, public education or public contracting."[8] However, the movement was faltering by the end of 1995, when Governor Pete Wilson suggested that Ward Connerly, a black Sacramento businessleader who as a member of the Board of Regents had led the fight for ending affirmative action in California universities, take over the drive.[9] Connerly's organizational and fund-raising abilities paid off. The Republican National Committee took over the signature-gathering process, and the measure qualified for the ballot in February after Governor Wilson turned in the final batch of petitions.[10] Some one hundred groups had joined a coalition opposing the initiative, including the YWCA, the National Organization for Women, the NAACP Legal Defense and Education Fund, the Feminist Majority, and the Mexican American League. Students from a hundred colleges across the nation spent their summers working in California to oppose the measure.[11] Proponents of the initiative spent an estimated $6 million, including $2.5 million donated by the Republican Party. The opposition, Stop Prop 209, raised about $2.5 million.[12] California voters passed Proposition 209 in November 1996 by a 54 to 46 percent margin to amend Article 1 of the state constitution as follows:

> The state shall not discriminate against, or grant preferential treatment to, any individual or group on the basis of race, sex, color, ethnicity, or national origin in the operation of public employment, public education, or public contracting . . .

Nothing in this section shall be interpreted as prohibiting bona fide qualifications based on sex which are reasonably necessary to the normal operation of public employment, public education, or public contracting.

Critics immediately filed lawsuits challenging the initiative, but they were
unsuccessful in overturning the measure.[13] In 2002 Ward Connerly began
promoting a companion proposition to prohibit California governments from
asking residents to specify their race on government forms.[14] That Connerly
initiative was rejected by the voters in 2003. Washington in 1998 became the
second state to abolish state-based affirmative action when it passed a proposition similar to California's Proposition 209, and two years later the Florida
legislature enacted a law that banned the consideration of race as a factor in
college admissions.[15]

Congress

As the nonviolent civil rights protests and demonstrations by ad hoc groups
of students and community activists in the late 1950s were transformed into
violent confrontations in the early 1960s, civil rights groups and political
activists, trade unions, civil liberties associations, and religious leaders joined
together in a broad-based social movement to lobby Congress and the Kennedy
Administration for decisive action.[16] This outpouring of support for civil
rights, combined with lobbying and political activities under the umbrella of
the Leadership Conference on Civil Rights (founded in 1949 to coordinate
such efforts), resulted in significant civil rights planks in the platforms of
both parties in 1960.[17]

President John Kennedy did not actively pursue civil rights legislation
until 1963, and his hesitation has been attributed to concerns that opposition
by southern chairs of key committees would help defeat other New Frontier
programs. Legislative initiatives resulted from the recommendations of the
Civil Rights Commission, established in 1957. Its 1961 report recommended
that Congress create a new agency similar to the President's Committee on
Equal Employment Opportunity or empower that agency to enforce nondiscrimination in all employment decisions where federal funds or contracts
were involved. Unions would be prohibited from discriminatory practices in
accepting or discharging members or in segregating them. Congress also
was encouraged to ensure access to job training programs for minority groups
and access to vocational education and apprenticeship opportunities for teenagers. In 1963 the commission recommended that fair employment legislation be extended to employment practices within interstate commerce and
that all employment funded through federal grants, loans, and other spending take place in a nondiscriminatory manner.[18]

The Civil Rights Act of 1964

By mid-1963 debate in Congress focused on the public accommodations provisions because public attention had been generated by the sit-ins and demonstrations directed at restaurants and hotel operators who refused to serve black customers. No bill was enacted before Kennedy's assassination. President Johnson, five days after Kennedy's death, addressed Congress to urge passage of this civil rights bill: "No memorial oration or eulogy could more eloquently honor President Kennedy's memory than the earliest possible passage of the civil rights bill for which he fought so long."[19] The assassination was perhaps more responsible than anything for the passage of the bill at that time. Although Johnson likely saw it as an opportunity to extend his constituency, he had no record on civil rights and some civil rights leaders believed Johnson had been unsupportive of their earlier legislative efforts.[20]

The House bill passed in 1964 was rejected as too extreme by Republican leaders, who then negotiated with both parties' leaders and Justice Department officials to eventually soften the legislation enough to forge bipartisan support and to overcome southern opposition. There was particular opposition to the sections on equal employment opportunity and access to public accommodations, both of which were amended. The amendment prohibiting discrimination on the basis of sex would become the most important change; contrary to the strategy of its sponsor, who hoped the proposal would generate opposition to the whole package, the amendment including sexual discrimination passed and generated additional support for the entire bill.

In the Senate, legislative action was blocked by a filibuster, conducted by eighteen southern Democrats and one southern Republican, that featured a twenty-four-hour-long speech by then Democrat Strom Thurmond of South Carolina. Southern opposition focused mainly on the provisions that allowed a cutoff of federal funds for discriminatory practices and that established a fair practices commission. Republicans wanted concessions on two other provisions—access to public accommodations and fair employment practices—and ultimately the negotiators agreed to provisions that permitted government suits only for egregious cases of discrimination (where there was a clear "pattern or practice" of discriminatory behavior), that required the administrative agency created to enforce the law to seek *voluntary* compliance with the law, and that permitted individuals to sue in federal courts for redress. The filibuster was ended on June 10, whereupon southerners then offered numerous amendments that were soundly defeated. However, northern Democrats grew weary and decided not to propose strengthening amendments as they originally planned. The House of Representatives, agreeing not to tamper with the fragile Senate compromise, passed the bill.[21]

Title VII of the Civil Rights Act of 1964, which targeted fair employment practices, contained five major provisions. First, it prohibited hiring, firing, disciplinary, and other employment and union practices on the basis of race, color, religion, national origin, and sex. Second, coverage was extended to employees and union members in organizations with more than twenty-five individuals. (The act later was amended to reach organizations with fifteen or more members.) Third, there were exemptions for individuals who need security clearances for government employment, for individuals hired for educational responsibilities by educational institutions or for religious activities by religious groups, for employees whose particular religion, national origin, or sex were bona fide occupational qualifications, and for Native Americans hired on or near reservations. Fourth, Title VII created an independent Equal Employment Opportunity Commission (EEOC) with the authority to investigate claims brought by aggrieved individuals, to attempt negotiated resolutions, and to provide technical assistance to employers and unions seeking to comply with the law. The attorney general was empowered to bring suits for widespread (pattern or practice) discrimination, and individuals also could bring suit should EEOC conciliatory efforts fail. Finally, Title VII defined as permissible seniority systems, merit systems, tests used in application procedures, and different standards of compensation or work responsibilities as long as these practices were not used with the intent to discriminate.

Section 703(j) of Title VII, added in order to blunt criticisms that the law would require hiring quotas, prohibited "preferential treatment to any individual or group . . . on account of an imbalance which may exist with respect to the total or percentage of persons of any race, color, religion, sex, or national origin employed . . . in any comparison with the total number or percentage in any community, state, section or other area or in the available workforce in any community." Its sponsors argued that the law "does not require an employer to achieve any sort of racial balance in his workforce by giving preferential treatment to any individual or group." "What the bill does," one explained, "is to simply make it an illegal practice to use race as a factor in denying employment."[22]

Once Title VII was enacted, its supporters began pressing to strengthen the EEOC. Legislation was introduced in 1965 to give the EEOC authority to bring charges against employers who discriminated, to issue cease-and-desist orders in order to end prohibited practices, and to order employers to hire or reinstate victims of discrimination. This proposal won broad bipartisan support in the House but, in the Senate, faced opposition from southern Democrats allied with other senators who voiced the fears of business lobbyists about increased governmental intervention in their decision making. The proposal was defeated.[23]

Equal Employment Opportunity Act of 1972

In late 1971 legislation amending Title VII cleared a Senate committee. This bill granted the EEOC cease-and-desist powers, but the Nixon administration opposed any transfer of power from the Justice and Labor Departments to the EEOC, whereas the NAACP, the Commission on Civil Rights, and the AFL-CIO backed the transfer. Opposition was led by Senators Sam Ervin (D-NC) and James Allen (D-AL), who argued that such authority would render the EEOC "prosecutor, judge and jury" and would prevent employers from enjoying the rights of due process. Ervin and Allen favored the Nixon administration proposal to empower the EEOC to bring suits against violators of Title VII provisions, but three times the Senate narrowly voted to reject the Ervin-Allen alternative. Then Senator Allen threatened a filibuster to block any final vote on the amendments, whereupon its supporters, after failing to garner sufficient votes to invoke cloture and prevent the filibuster, agreed to compromise. The court-enforcement alternative was passed by the Senate along with other points of controversy—bringing state and local government employees under Title VII, expanding coverage to firms with fifteen or more employees, and maintaining the power to bring pattern or practice suits by the attorney general rather than by the EEOC.

In the House, organized labor favored the transfer of power to the EEOC as a strategy to weaken the Labor Department and the Philadelphia Plan developed by the department to increase minority employment in the construction industry in that city. The labor–civil rights coalition had re-formed to lobby for the revisions but split over the transfer. House and Senate conferees eventually accepted most of the Senate provisions but authorized the EEOC to bring pattern or practice suits against employers, brought employees of educational institutions under coverage (they were exempted from the 1964 Act), and created the Equal Employment Opportunity Coordinating Council to facilitate cooperation among the EEOC, the Office of Federal Contracts Compliance (OFCC), and other federal agencies.

The Equal Employment Opportunity Act of 1972 was a defeat for civil rights groups, whose major goal was to empower the EEOC to issue cease-and-desist orders against discriminatory employment practices. One civil rights leader described the act as a "slap in the face, but not a knockout punch" for the civil rights movement.[24] The tortuous history of the 1972 amendments showed that Congress was quite willing to rely on the federal courts as the primary agent for implementing equal employment opportunity. For southern members of Congress, it seemed an attractive alternative since federal judges resided in the communities where they presided and, in addition, were screened and approved by senior senators before being nominated by the president. For nonsouthern legislators, federal bureaucrats free from local prejudices were viewed as more vigilant enforcers of the law, but federal judges provided some degree of independence and were preferable to relying on state and local authorities. Congress also deferred to the federal judiciary to define the substantive provisions of Title VII. In a detailed analysis of the 1964 Act and its 1972 amendments, the legislative sponsors claimed that "in any area where the new law does not address itself, or in any areas where a specific contrary intention is not indicated, it was assumed that the present case law as developed by the courts would continue to govern the applicability and construction of Title VII."[25]

Congressional debate over the 1972 amendments included a claim, unchallenged by proponents of affirmative action, that "to hire a negro solely because he is a negro is racial discrimination just as much as a white only policy. Both forms of discrimination are prohibited by Title VII." Moreover the Senate rejected an amendment that would have prohibited federal agencies from requiring employers to practice reverse discrimination by hiring applicants of a particular race or sex in order to reach a quota.[26] In 1978 Congress amended Title VII to reverse the Supreme Court decision in *General Electric v. Gilbert,* 429 U.S. 125 (1976), where the high court had ruled that an employer's exclusion of pregnancy benefits from a disability plan was not gender-based discrimination but was motivated only by economic considerations. Women's, labor, and civil rights groups were very critical of this decision and began lobbying Congress, but the issue became mired in a debate over abortions. In the end, Title VII thus was amended (92 Stat. 2076) to read that all pregnancy-based distinctions are to be considered gender-based discrimination, that pregnancy is to be treated the same way as any other temporary disability in employee benefit programs, and that employers could exempt abortions from coverage for medical payments unless necessary to save the life of the pregnant woman.

In legislation since the 1970s, Congress also began requiring affirmative action by federal agencies with respect to employing veterans and by state agencies receiving federal funds with respect to employing and promoting disabled persons. The Public Works Employment Act of 1977 required 10 percent of federal grants to state and local governments for public works be directed to "minority business enterprises," namely businesses owned and controlled by U.S. citizens from these groups—blacks, Spanish-speaking persons, Orientals, Indians, Eskimos, and Aleuts.

Civil Rights Act of 1991

Changes in the membership of the Supreme Court coupled with strong opposition to preferential treatment in employment decisions, admission to professional programs, and granting of government contracts in the Reagan and Bush administrations converged in the mid- to late 1980s to produce Supreme Court cases rulings that either narrowly interpreted civil rights laws or appeared to reverse past decisions. In particular, seven decisions issued in 1989 provoked demands on Capitol Hill for legislation to overturn these holdings: *Patterson v. McLean Credit Union,* 491 U.S. 164 (1989); *Wards Cove Packing Co. v. Antonio,* 490 U.S. 642 (1989); *Price Waterhouse v. Hopkins,* 490 U.S. 228 (1989); *Lorance v. AT&T Technologies, Inc.,* 490 U.S. 900 (1989); *Martin v. Wilks,* 490 U.S. 755 (1989); *Jett v. Dallas Independent School District,* 491 U.S. 701 (1989); and *Independent Federation of Flight Attendants v. Zipes,* 491 U.S. 754 (1989).

The Civil Rights Act of 1990 passed the House and Senate but a threatened veto, and the lack of votes in either chamber to override President George H.W. Bush, led to intense negotiations by the conference committee to salvage the bill. One compromise, designed to win administration support, put a cap of $150,000 on any punitive damages sought by victims of intentional discrimination. Under 42 U.S.C. § 981, unlimited punitive damages can be awarded to victims of intentional racial discrimination, but the original 1990 legislation extended damage claims to other kinds of discrimination. Business groups opposed expanding their potential liability. Moreover, the Bush administration argued that another provision, requiring that employment decisions producing a disparate impact on women and minorities be justified by a strict showing of "business necessity," would encourage employers to establish quotas to ensure that such disparate impacts do not occur. But negotiations failed: the Civil Rights Act of 1990 was passed with broad, bipartisan support, but was vetoed by President Bush as being a "quota" bill. The veto override attempt failed by one vote in the Senate.[27]

Congress and the White House continued negotiations into 1991, but both sides resisted until other political developments forced a breakthrough. The victory of former Ku Klux Klan leader David Duke in the Louisiana GOP gubernatorial primary and the Senate hearings for Supreme Court nominee Clarence Thomas, who was accused of sexual harassment while head of the EEOC, apparently moved the Bush administration to drop its opposition. Legislation passed Congress on November 7, 1991, and was signed by President Bush on November 21 (105 Stat. 1071). The four objectives of the 1991 act are (1) to provide appropriate remedies for intentional discrimination and unlawful harassment in the workplace, (2) to codify the concepts of "business necessity" and "job-related" enunciated by the Supreme Court in *Griggs v. Duke Power Co.,* 401 U.S. 424 (1971), and other rulings prior to *Wards Cove Packing Company,* (3) to provide statutory guidelines for the adjudication of disparate-impact suits under Title VII, and (4) to repudiate recent

Supreme Court decisions by expanding the scope of civil rights coverage to provide adequate protection for victims of discrimination.

In a typical disparate-treatment case, the burden of proof falls on the plaintiff to show that there is a prima facie case of different treatment. The employer may explain why the decision rested on nondiscriminatory grounds, to which the plaintiff must then show that the rationale is a mere pretext and that the employer actually intended to discriminate. In some cases, however, plaintiffs may show that employment decisions were based on a combination of lawful *and* unlawful motives. In *Price Waterhouse v. Hopkins*, the high court ruled that these "mixed motives" cases were to proceed differently. Initially the plaintiff has a higher burden of showing that the employer *intended* to discriminate and, once that is established, the burden then shifts to the employer to show, by a preponderance of the evidence, that the same decision would have been made absent the discriminatory motivation. The Court held that an employment decision partly motivated by prejudice was not a violation of Title VII because the employer showed that the same decision would have been made absent the discriminatory factor.

The 1991 act overturned *Price Waterhouse* by amending section 703 of the 1964 Civil Rights Act to clarify the prohibition against impermissible consideration of race, color, religion, sex, or national origin in employment practices. A complaining party need only show that "race, color, religion, sex, or national origin was a motivating factor for any employment practice, even though other factors also motivated the practice." Once shown, the court "may grant declaratory relief, injunctive relief . . . and attorney's fees and costs demonstrated to be directly attributable only to the pursuit of a claim under section 703(m) [but] shall not award damages or issue an order requiring any admission, reinstatement, hiring, promotion, or payment" (Section 107 of the Civil Rights Act of 1991).

The Supreme Court has regularly given civil rights laws restrictive holdings during the past fifteen years, only to see those decisions reversed by Congress. In every instance, Congress has broadened the coverage or reach of the civil rights statutes.[28] By enacting these statutes, Congress reaffirmed its original legislative purpose rather than enacting new law. The new GOP-controlled Congress elected in 1994, however, took a much different approach to affirmative action.

The Republican Congress

In 1995 Majority Party Leader Robert Dole (R-KS) and Representative Charles T. Canady (R-FL) cosponsored a repeal of all race and gender preferences.[29] Senator Phil Gramm (R-TX), to popularize his campaign for the GOP nomination, tried to attach riders prohibiting minority set-aside programs to appropriations bills but was blocked by a coalition of moderate Republicans and Democrats. Efforts in the Senate to end affirmative action dissipated as Senator Dole hesitated about whether to champion the issue and the Clinton administration stated its opposition to the bill.[30] House Speaker Newt Gingrich (R-GA) blocked any consideration of legislation repealing affirmation action until Republicans could pass "empowerment" legislation to help minorities and the poor. In early 1996 Congressman Canady began promoting his measure, and the Dole-Canady bill gained approval from the House Judiciary Committee's Constitution Subcommittee.[31] Its purpose, according to Canady, was to "prohibit the Federal Government from intentionally discriminating against, or granting a preference to, any person or group based in whole or in part on race, color, national origin or sex, in three specific areas—Federal contracting, Federal employment, and the administration of other federally-conducted programs." The bill also would prevent the federal government from "requiring or encouraging Federal contractors to discriminate or grant preferences based on race or sex" but permitted affirmative action programs such as outreach and recruitment efforts that sought to increase the pool of women and minority candidates, as long as "at the decision stage, all applicants are judged in a nondiscriminatory manner—that is, without regard to their race or sex."[32] One reason for resistance to anti-affirmative-action legislation was big business, because many corporations not only were afraid of offending women and minorities but also were not inclined to dismantle their own affirmative action programs. Thus, the rollback movement went nowhere in 1995 or since. An additional obstacle was the opposition of the Clinton administration.[33]

Judiciary

The Supreme Court has played a major role in grappling with important issues related to the implementation of Title VII. First, the Court provided criteria for determining when discrimination has occurred. Second, the Court defined appropriate remedies once discrimination had been demonstrated. Third, the Court interpreted actions of employers pursuant to Title VII and indicated which employees, employers, and employment practices were exempt from coverage.

Proving Employment Discrimination

Title VII specified prohibited employment practices, including limiting, classifying, or segregating applicants or employees on the basis of race, color, religion, sex, or national origin in making hiring decisions, determining compensation and other conditions of employment, or discharging employees. Two kinds of discriminatory employment practices became apparent: those that treated *individual* employees differently and those that resulted in disparate impacts among different employee *groups*. Regarding the first, between 1973 and 1981 the Supreme Court tried to define the burden of proof required in proving disparate treatment. In *McDonnell Douglas Corp. v. Green,* 411 U.S. 792 (1973), the Court ruled that the employee who claims to be a victim of discrimination must first show that "(i) he belongs to a racial minority; (ii) that he applied and was qualified for a job for which the employer was seeking applicants; (iii) that, despite his qualifications, he was rejected; and (iv) that, after his rejection, the position remained open and the employer continued to seek applicants from persons of [the employee's] qualifications." If these conditions are met, the burden then shifts to the employer to "articulate some legitimate, nondiscriminatory reason for the employee's rejection." Finally, the employee then could seek to show that the employer's justification was merely a "pretext for discrimination."

The *McDonnell Douglas* decision resulted in lower courts grappling with the question of how extensive the burden of proof had to be—what the Court meant by "articulate" (rather than "prove") and whether "one" or "some" legitimate reasons were sufficient defense. In *Furnco Construction Corp. v. Waters,* 438 U.S. 567 (1978), the Supreme Court, in trying to provide additional guidance for resolving these questions, concluded that "in the absence of any other explanation it is more likely than not that those actions were bottomed on impermissible considerations." Furthermore, the employer then should be allowed "some latitude to introduce evidence which bears on his motive" for his actions. In *Board of Trustees of Keene State College v. Sweeney,* 439 U.S. 295 (1978), the high court ruled that lower courts requiring employers to rebut prima facie cases of discrimination by "articulating some legitimate, nondiscriminatory reason" and "proving absence of discriminatory motive" had erred because the former standard was sufficient. However, the lower federal courts still continued to render conflicting decisions, thus forcing the Court to try again. *Texas Department of Community Affairs v. Burdine,* 450 U.S. 248 (1981), addressed the nature of the proof required of employers charged with a prima facie case of discrimination. The decision of a lower court, which imposed the requirement that employers "prove by a preponderance of the evidence the existence of nondiscriminatory reasons" for taking the actions in question, was rejected by the high court; an employer so charged "bears only the burden of explaining clearly the action."

The determination of whether employment decisions have resulted in a disproportionate impact on minorities or women also raises issues about burden of proof. In *Griggs v. Duke Power*, 401 U.S. 424 (1971), the Supreme Court ruled that employment practices resulting in an adverse impact on minority applicants were illegal. At issue was the employer's use of a general intelligence test and the requirement of a high school diploma in determining promotions from one division of the Duke Power Company to another. Black employees, prevented from transferring to other divisions and the higher-paying jobs within those divisions, brought suit, but the court of appeals upheld the use of the test because the court found no intent to discriminate. The Supreme Court disagreed, arguing that "good intent or absence of discriminatory intent does not redeem employment procedures or testing measures that operate as 'built-in headwinds' for minority groups and are unrelated to measuring job capability." The justices argued that Title VII authorized the use of "any professionally developed ability test" except those that were "designed, intended or used to discriminate because of race" (Section 703[h]). Because members of minority groups failed to qualify for employment positions at a greater rate than nonminority applicants as a result of employer selection devices, the burden of proof then fell upon the employer to show that the selection devices were reasonably related to job performance and were not intended to discriminate against minorities. If the employer could demonstrate that tests were job-related, then the burden shifted back to the plaintiff to show that other selection devices or tests would be just as useful in choosing qualified employees without producing the disparate impact.

Proving that tests and other selection devices measure job-related skills is a very difficult and expensive procedure, which caused some employers to initiate their own hiring or promotion quotas in order to avoid the cost of validating selection devices and to protect themselves against litigation. Critics of the *Griggs* ruling call it inconsistent with legislative intent, because sponsors of Title VII emphasized that an *intent* to discriminate was to be determinative: "Inadvertent or accidental discrimination will not violate the Title. . . . It means simply that the respondent must not have intended to discriminate."[34] The Supreme Court refined its *Griggs* position in *International Brotherhood of Teamsters v. U.S.*, 431 U.S. 324 (1977), ruling that statistical disparity alone was insufficient proof of discrimination and that it must be accompanied by other evidence.

Remedies for Employment Discrimination

In providing for remedies once discrimination is established, the Supreme Court adopted a more conservative stance relative to congressional intent. In *Albemarle v. Moody*, 422 U.S. 405 (1975), the Court ruled that once discriminatory activity was proven, back pay should generally be awarded in order to "make whole" victims of illegal behavior. Retroactive seniority also was upheld in *Franks v. Bowman Transportation Co.*, 424 U.S. 747 (1976). Both these decisions were justified as being consistent with the power of the courts under Title VII to grant equitable relief, and specifically to award back pay, but Title VII indicates that such remedies can be awarded only "if the court finds that the [employer] has intentionally engaged in or is intentionally engaging in an unlawful employment practice" (Section 706[g]).

In *Memphis Fire Department v. Stotts*, 104 S.Ct. 2576 (1984), the Supreme Court maintained that "bona fide" seniority systems could not be undermined to protect the jobs of minorities who, as the last hired, were the first to be fired or laid off by cities or other employers suffering from financial constraints. That ruling was reinforced in *Wygant v. Jackson Board of Education*, 476 U.S. 267 (1986), which reaffirmed that race-conscious actions must meet three conditions: there must be a "compelling state interest" that requires a response, the action taken must be "narrowly tailored," and there must be evidence of prior discrimination.

The Responsibilities of Employers

The third issue for judicial determination is the extent of employer responsibility under Title VII. In *United States v. Weber*, 433 U.S. 193 (1979), the Supreme Court upheld an affirmative action plan embodied in a collective bargaining agreement that reserved 50 percent of the openings in a training program for black employees. A nonminority employee challenged the agreement as a violation of Title VII's prohibition against preferential treatment (Section 703[j]), but the plan was upheld for three reasons. First, although Section 703 prohibited government from requiring preferential treatment in response to a racial imbalance, the section did not interdict a voluntary effort. Second, the plan was temporary and was "not intended to maintain a racial balance but simply to eliminate a manifest racial imbalance." Third, the plan did not "unnecessarily trample the interests of white employees," nor did it "require the discharge of white workers and their replacement with new black hirees."

In various cases the high court has provided hints of what would and would not be acceptable interpretations of affirmative action. *Fullilove v. Klutznick*, 448 U.S. 448 (1980), upheld a 1977 federal works program enacted by Congress that set aside 10 percent of the provided funds for "minority business enterprises." The Court concluded that Congress need not act in a "wholly color-blind fashion" in remedying discrimination but that such actions could be justified only under the broad remedial powers of Congress. In *United Jewish Organization v. Carey*, 443 U.S. 144 (1978), a case involving the redrawing of voting district lines, the Court ruled that the state legislature could consider the impact of redistricting on racial groups even though there had been no finding of discrimination in previous redistricting decisions. In *Regents of the University of California v. Bakke,* 438 U.S. 265 (1978), the Court rejected a medical school admission policy that set aside sixteen admissions for minority applicants. In 1995, however, a federal court of appeals struck down the University of Texas Law School's affirmative action program, which was based on the *Bakke* ruling, because it violated the constitutional rights of nonminority applicants.[35]

In *Local 28 of the Sheet Metal Workers' International Association v. EEOC,* 478 U.S. 421 (1986), the Court held that race-conscious relief as a remedy for past discrimination need not be limited to actual victims of discrimination. A lower court's imposition of a goal of 29.23 percent for black membership in the union was upheld by the Supreme Court as a narrowly tailored and reasonable response to a "history of egregious violations" of Title VII. The remedy was temporary, did not "unnecessarily trample the interests of white employees," was consistent with congressional intent, and was not invoked "simply to create a racially balanced work force." In *Local Number 93, International Association of Firefighters v. City of Cleveland,* 478 U.S. 501 (1986), the Court upheld a consent decree adopted by a lower court that required a fixed number of goals for the promotion of minority employees. The city of Cleveland had negotiated with an organization of black and Hispanic firefighters a set of promotion goals that was submitted to a federal court as a proposed consent decree. The court approved the decree in 1983, over the objections of the union. The Supreme Court found that, even though the plan benefited individuals who were not actual victims of discrimination, Congress had intended to encourage voluntary agreements between unions and employers to end discriminatory practices. Consent decrees were characterized by the Court as essentially voluntary, thus exempting them from congressional restrictions on judicially imposed remedies for Title VII violations.

In 1987 the Supreme Court ruled in *U.S. v. Paradise,* 480 U.S. 149 (1987), a case involving discrimination in the Alabama highway patrol, that federal courts may impose promotion quotas to increase the percentage of qualified minority employees to their level in the relevant labor force, given a long history of discrimination and resistance to court orders. *Johnson v. Transportation Agency,* 480 U.S. 616 (1987), also held that female employees who possessed the requisite qualifications for promotion could be given preferential treatment where there was an "obvious imbalance" of men and women. Even absent legal findings of past discrimination, the Court sanctioned preferential treatment that was a "moderate, flexible, case-by-case approach to effecting a gradual improvement in the representation of minorities and women in the Agency's work force."

Yet the Court also imposed hurdles on governments undertaking affirmative action programs. One case was *City of Richmond v. Croson,* 488 U.S. 469 (1989), which held that lower courts should apply "strict scrutiny" in assessing all race-based classifications devised by state and local governments. Richmond had required prime contractors for city construction projects to subcontract at least 30 percent of their contracts to minority-owned businesses. The Court struck down the plan because the city failed to show a history of discrimination that compelled a remedial effort. General allegations of past discrimination in the construction industry were insufficient. In *Metro Broadcasting Inc. v. FCC,* 497 U.S. 547 (1990), the Court applied an intermediate standard of judicial scrutiny to the Federal Communications Commission policy of favoring minority ownership of radio and television broadcast stations. While the goal of "promoting programming diversity" was an "important" government interest and the agency's specific efforts were "substantially related" to achieving that goal, the high court attached "overriding significance" to the fact that the program had been mandated by Congress. In *Adarand Constructors, Inc. v. Pena,* 115 S.Ct. 2097 (1995), on the other hand, the Court applied a strict scrutiny standard to argue that any racial classification by a governmental body, regardless of the race of those burdened or benefited, must involve "narrowly tailored measures that further compelling governmental interests." Thus it rejected minority set-aside programs in federal highway grants. The case was brought by the owner of a company that was a low bidder for guardrails on a federally funded highway project but that lost the bid to a Hispanic-owned company.

In two highly publicized cases in 2003, the Supreme Court reaffirmed its position on affirmative action in higher education. *Gratz v. Bollinger* (02–516) nullified the University of Michigan undergraduate affirmative action program as unconstitutional but, in a companion case, *Grutter v. Bollinger* (02–241) upheld the affirmative action program of the University of Michigan law school. In both cases, the majority ruled that the Court should give strict scrutiny to practices that use racial classifications but that seeking a diverse student body was a compelling governmental interest. The Court rejected the undergraduate program that automatically awarded twenty points (one-fifth of the total points needed to gain admission) to underrepresented minority applicants because, under that scheme, race was a decisive factor for virtually every minority applicant. Therefore the university failed to give individualized consideration to each student applying for admission and its approach was not narrowly tailored to achieve the stated goal of educational diversity. The law school admission scheme, the goal of which was to enroll a critical mass of minority students, was a flexible system and not an unconstitutional quota.

Presidency

The earliest federal programs to encourage fair employment practices originated in the executive branch. In the 1940s and 1950s there was political pressure by black leaders for governmental action, but presidents from Franklin Roosevelt to John Kennedy offered only regulation of the employment practices of federal contractors. This limited response was politically noncontroversial and also consistent with general expectations that federal funds should not be used to subsidize discriminatory actions. President Roosevelt issued Executive Orders 8802, 9001, and 9346, the first in a series of important presidential initiatives on equal employment opportunity. Under the orders, defense contractors were prohibited from discrimination in hiring and other employment practices on the basis of race, color, creed, or national origin. The Fair Employment Practices Committee (FEPC) was created to monitor compliance.[36] President Truman also issued a series of executive orders that transferred responsibility for FEPC activities to the Defense Department, granted authority to other agencies that contracted for defense-related goods and services to require nondiscrimination in the employment decisions of their contractors, and created the Committee on Government Contract Compliance to monitor compliance with the government's fair employment policy and to study the effectiveness of previous efforts.[37] President Eisenhower issued an executive order in 1953 that established the President's Committee on Government Contracts and, for the first time, extended nondiscrimination requirements to all companies that contracted with the federal government. One year later, a second Eisenhower order extended coverage to subcontractors.[38]

It was not until the Kennedy administration, however, that the executive branch began to consider taking a more aggressive role. Two months after he took office, President Kennedy issued Executive Order 10925, which continued to require fair employment practices of contractors with federal agencies and created the President's Committee on Equal Employment Opportunity. Chaired by Vice President Lyndon Johnson, the committee was given jurisdiction over all complaints of discriminatory behavior by contractors, was empowered to conduct compliance reviews and to require that contractors supply hiring data and other employment records, and was authorized to cancel existing contracts and debar firms violating the executive order from future contracts.[39] For the first time, there was a general acceptance of the power of federal agencies to cancel contracts if companies engaged in

unfair employment practices. Of more importance, however, was the requirement that all contracts include the following clause: "The contractor will
take affirmative action to ensure that applicants are employed, and that employees are treated during employment without regard to their race, creed,
color or national origin" (Part III, Section 301 [1]).

One of the most important affirmative action efforts of the federal government was Executive Order 11246 by Lyndon Johnson in 1965, which delegated to the secretary of labor authority to issue regulations implementing
the order. The rules that were subsequently issued included the requirement
that construction contractors and subcontractors who received federal contracts must comply with goals and timetables for female and minority employees in job categories where both groups had been "underutilized" in the
past. Discrimination on the basis of sex was added in 1967 to the list of
prohibited practices.[40]

The Ford administration was roundly criticized by civil rights groups, with
black leaders attacking budget cuts in health, education, and welfare programs, the lack of initiatives to combat black unemployment, and a general
attitude of "benign neglect" of the concerns of blacks.[41] The Carter administration came into office with a strong commitment to civil rights. In 1978
Carter consolidated the powers and responsibilities of the EEOC and the
Office of Federal Contracts Compliance Programs (OFCCP), and the Justice
Department vigorously advocated affirmative action in the Supreme Court
cases it litigated and where it filed briefs.[42]

The Reagan administration reversed many of the Carter administration
enforcement initiatives, ordered industry-wide targeting to be dropped, and
directed the EEOC to concentrate on cases in which it could readily prove
discrimination. The administration also joined in litigation to overturn decisions by federal courts and state and local governments that imposed hiring
and promotion goals. In 1984, after *Memphis Fire Department v. Stotts,* Assistant Attorney General Reynolds proclaimed that the "era of racial quotas
has run its course" and that EEOC and OFCCP officials no longer would
require employers to develop numerical hiring goals in order to increase
minority employment.[43] However, two 1986 Supreme Court decisions upholding hiring goals dampened those efforts. The Reagan Justice Department had proposed that Executive Order 11246 be rewritten to prohibit the
use of hiring and promotion goals, but that change was never made.

During the first two years of the Clinton administration, White House and
executive branch officials debated what its position should be. In a 1995
address, Clinton largely defended affirmative action and argued that the country should "mend it, don't end it." Clinton appealed to whites, even though
he argued that they were still guilty of discrimination, and he appealed to

blacks, even though he said that the problems facing blacks cannot all be blamed on white America. But President Clinton made little subsequent effort to build support for affirmative action.[44] Later in 1995, the Clinton administration ended a $1 billion Defense Department minority contract set-aside program, the only step taken by the federal government to reduce affirmative action.[45] The program was being challenged by a Minneapolis-based builder, McCrossan Construction Company, who argued in federal court that huge percentages of construction work in some areas were reserved for minority contractors. The Defense Department, applying the strict scrutiny test that the Supreme Court had ordered in 1995, concluded that the program was not narrowly tailored to satisfy a compelling state interest.[46]

In 1996 the Clinton administration suspended for three years all government contract set-aside programs for women- and minority-owned companies but allowed agencies to give preference to these companies on a case-by-case basis. The decision was an attempt to find middle ground by eliminating the kind of affirmative action that the administration felt was closest to quotas. The administration's new guidelines for affirmative action set as a goal the awarding of 5 percent of federal contracts to minority-owned firms. That goal had been unanimously approved by both houses of Congress in 1994 while the Democrats still controlled Congress. Agencies were first required to take racially neutral steps such as outreach in recruitment. They were to commission "disparity studies" to define the available pool of women and minority contractors, determine how large that pool would be if no demonstrable discrimination had occurred, and then use those studies to set goals for the percentage of women and minority contractors each agency should have. The further the agency was from the goal, the more preferential treatment it could engage in, culminating in set-asides for only the most egregious situations.[47] Some $12 billion in annual federal procurement decisions were affected by the guidelines.[48]

In 1996 the Clinton Justice Department issued a memorandum to federal agencies that argued, in response to the 1995 *Adarand* holding, that the "application of strict scrutiny should not require major modifications in the way federal agencies have been properly implementing affirmative action policies" but, to protect themselves against reverse discrimination lawsuits, agencies should be able to show a "compelling" need for race-based policies. That showing could come through "historical evidence" of agency discrimination, "statistical evidence" of underrepresentation of minorities in job categories, or "operational needs" such as having a diverse workforce. No absolute preference would be given on the basis of race, but race could be one of several factors involved in hiring decisions.[49]

The administration of George W. Bush has opposed affirmative action, but that policy has not been a high priority. In the two University of Michigan affirmative action cases decided by the Supreme Court in 2003, the Bush administration recommended that both the undergraduate and law school admissions programs be struck down, but nevertheless claimed a victory in the split decision. Said President Bush after the case was announced, "today's decisions seek a careful balance between the goal of campus diversity and the fundamental principle of equal treatment under the law."[50]

Bureaucracy

The evolution of employment policy has occurred within the partnership of the courts, the Equal Employment Opportunity Commission, the Office of Federal Contracts Compliance (later retitled the Office of Federal Contracts Compliance Programs), and the president. Much of the current controversy regarding equal employment opportunity can be traced to actions taken by the OFCC during this time. The director of OFCC in 1967, Edward C. Sylvester Jr., explained that "in a general way, affirmative action is anything that you have to do to get results. But this does not necessarily include preferential treatment. The key word here is 'results.' . . . Affirmative action is really designed to get employees to apply the same kind of imagination and ingenuity that they apply to any other phase of their operation."[51]

The OFCC issued regulations in 1968 that, for the first time, required all contractors with fifty or more employees and contracts of at least $50,000 to have a written affirmative action plan.[52] The OFCC eventually issued additional regulations, known as Order No. 4, that provided instructions for contractors in complying with Executive Order 11246. These guidelines became the basis for almost all subsequent efforts related to affirmative action. Order No. 4 defined an affirmative action program as a "set of specific and result-oriented procedures to which a contractor commits himself to apply every good-faith effort. The objective of those procedures plus such efforts is equal employment opportunity."[53] The key components of an affirmative action plan were to include an "analysis of areas within which the contractor is deficient in the utilization of minority groups, and further, goals and time-tables to which the contractor's good-faith efforts must be directed to correct the deficiencies and thus to achieve prompt and full utilization of minorities at all levels and in all segments of his work force where deficiencies exist."[54] The OFCC was careful to insist that preferential treatment of any kind was not required; rather, the order required action "necessary to assure that all persons receive equal employment opportunity."

During this period, the OFCC also shifted from a policy of encouraging voluntary compliance with fair employment practices to enforcement activities, including debarment of contractors. In 1969, for the first time, contracting agencies began reporting to Congress that they had canceled or suspended contracts with contractors who failed to comply with EEO requirements and that some contractors had been debarred from future contracts.

The first area of contracting activity to be targeted was the construction industry. Concerned about past discriminatory practices that restricted minority membership in the construction trades, the OFCC instituted a program of goals and timetables for increasing minority employment in the construction industry, named the Philadelphia Plan after the city where it was first put into effect. It empowered the OFCC to set hiring quotas for minority workers that would be applied to federal contractors bidding for jobs in the Philadelphia area. The Department of Labor established goals for the employment of minority ironworkers, plumbers and pipe fitters, and electrical and other workers that would have increased black employment in these crafts from less than 5 percent to between 19 and 26 percent by 1973.[55]

The Nixon administration defended the Philadelphia Plan against its congressional critics, who in 1969 tried to prohibit any appropriations to enforce the requirement that contractors meet minority employment goals. The White House urged the defeat of the appropriations bill, calling the Philadelphia Plan "the most important civil rights issue in a long, long time."[56] Attorney General John Mitchell argued that "it is now well recognized in judicial opinions that the obligation of nondiscrimination . . . does not require, and in some circumstances may not permit obliviousness or indifference to the racial consequences of alternative courses of action which involve the application of outwardly neutral criteria."[57] The Labor Department similarly claimed that enforcement efforts could not rest on findings of discriminatory intent, because evidence for such motivations was so difficult to uncover. Statistical disparity as evidence of discrimination was an extremely important development

> grounded on the common-sense proposition that the underrepresentation of minority and women in any area of economic or professional enterprise is an indication that discrimination may exist. . . . Apparently rational arguments can mask discriminatory behavior and even neutral efforts can unintentionally cause discriminatory results. In such circumstances, the best available means for detecting the possible presence of discriminatory processes is to examine their statutory outcome.[58]

The most important factor in this policy shift was the difficulty in measuring progress in gaining compliance, but a related difficulty was the weakness of data to demonstrate progress in achieving policy objectives. The number of suspended contracts or debarred contractors became convenient indicators of policy effectiveness even though there was no clear correlation between such figures and increased opportunities for minorities. Finally, it should be noted here that the OFCC rather than the EEOC was primarily responsible for these affirmative action initiatives. For much of the late 1960s and early 1970s, the EEOC spent much time trying to get organized, and during its first three years of operation one or two of the five commissioner slots were vacant for more than half the time. There was no chairperson for four months in 1966 and there was a high turnover because the first five commissioners were appointed for terms of five, four, three, two, and one year to assure a future distribution of appointments.[59]

From its conception, the EEOC has been described as understaffed, underfunded, and weak. The number of complaints filed grew from 60,000 in 1990 to 92,000 in 1995, but the number of staff actually fell during those years from 2,853 to 2,183. Also the backlog of cases waiting to be addressed grew from 40,000 to nearly 100,000. Some increase in its caseload was due to new cases filed under the Americans with Disability Act of 1992. As the backlog grew, the agency filed fewer cases. In FY 1990 it filed 643 individual and class action cases; in FY 1996, only 160.[60] Other federal agencies filed 95 job bias cases, of which less than 25 percent were class action suits. Private law firms now handle about 98 percent of the job discrimination cases filed. In 1991 private firms filed 8,140 job discrimination cases as compared to 19,059 in 1995.[61] An EEOC investigator handled an average of 123 cases in 1995, more than double the average of 55 cases in 1990. The backlog forces thousands of complainants to wait before they can take their case to court, because the EEOC must first dismiss, settle, pursue, or pass the case before the courts hear it.[62]

By the late 1990s, the EEOC was resolving more cases each year than new ones received. For example, in 2002 the agency received 29,910 complaints but resolved some 33,200 cases. Of that total, 56 percent were dismissed because the agency could find no reasonable cause to conclude that discrimination had occurred, 19 percent were settled with outcomes favorable to the charging parties, 15 percent were closed for administrative reasons such as failure of the party making the charge to comply with procedural requirements or the outcome of litigation that resolved the issue; and 9 percent were resolved by settlements between the charging party, the employer or union, and the EEOC.[63]

The agency now known as the Office of Federal Contracts Compliance Programs (OFCCP) enforces the nondiscrimination and affirmative action requirements imposed on government contractors under executive orders through compliance reviews and by responding to complaints. In FY 1994,

OFCCP conducted 4,000 compliance reviews and investigated more than 800 complaints. When problems are found, the agency works with the contractor to form a conciliation agreement that may include back pay, job offers, seniority credit, promotions, or "other make-whole remedies to those who have been discriminated." If there is evidence of underutilization of minority and women contractors, the agreement may include outreach and other recruitment efforts and other affirmative action efforts. If conciliation agreements fail to solve the problem, the case may be turned over to the Labor Department for administrative hearings that can terminate in loss of contracts and disbarment from future awards. The OFCCP was responsible for overseeing more than $161 billion in 176,000 contracts to 192,500 companies in FY 1993. According to 1995 congressional testimony, OFCCP does not require contractors to hire or promote women or minorities on the basis of race or sex but only requires "outreach and other efforts to broaden the pool of qualified applicants to include groups previously excluded"; in addition, an employer "is never required to hire a person who does not have the qualifications needed to perform the job successfully." Goals are neither a "ceiling or a floor for the employment of particular groups."[64] The Small Business Administration's (SBA) minority set-aside program has also come under fire for helping companies that are not disadvantaged.[65]

Interest Groups

In the early 1970s, when affirmative action programs became firmly entrenched in the federal bureaucracy and the courts, opposition from interest groups began to mount. This development caused a deep split among former allies in the civil rights movement. Organized labor now was divided over affirmative action; affirmative action was rejected by virtually all major Jewish groups;[66] and further opposition came from organizations representing "white ethnic" voters who believed that they, too, suffered from discrimination. This pattern of group conflict was best illustrated by the 1978 case of *Bakke* that addressed the constitutionality of medical school quotas. Some 116 organizations submitted amicus briefs in this case, and the most important division was between groups representing blacks, Spanish-speaking persons, Asians, and Native Americans versus organizations speaking for the Jewish community and "white ethnic" nationalities. Religious and ethnic minorities do not benefit from affirmative action programs even though religion is mentioned along with race, color, and sex in the 1964 Civil Rights Act. Although no single-issue group filed an amicus brief, racial and ethnic groups within multi-interest organizations from legal, health/medical, and academic sectors were mobilized—for example, the

American Indian Bar Association, the Puerto Rican Legal Defense and Education Fund, the Hellenic Bar Association of Illinois, and the black National Medical Association.

The 2003 University of Michigan cases were also the focus of group litigation. Dozens of public and private universities submitted amicus briefs supporting the University of Michigan, in addition to corporations, some two dozen retired senior military officers and former commandants of the military service academies, and civil rights groups. The Center for Civil Rights represented the plaintiffs in those cases, white male and female students who had been denied admission, and other groups such as the Center for Equal Opportunity and the National Association of Scholars also supported the plaintiffs' case.[67]

Public Opinion

Surveys point to three conclusions about public opinion and equal employment opportunity. First, there has been a gradual shift during the past two decades toward more racial tolerance among both northern and southern whites. In one study, Smith and Sheatsley, using a racial tolerance index,[68] found a significant improvement in public attitudes concerning employment opportunity between 1942 and 1972. When asked, "Do you think Negroes/ Blacks should have as good a chance as white people to get any kind of job, or do you think white people should have the first chance at any kind of job?" 42 percent favored equal treatment in 1942 as compared to 83 percent in 1963, and 96 percent by 1972.

Some polls show only limited support for affirmative action as remedial policy: 85 percent of those surveyed in one poll were opposed "to preferential hiring and promotion of blacks" and a majority of white respondents said it "is not the government's business" to redress cases where blacks have not received "fair treatment in jobs." Opposition to affirmative action and opposition to welfare often go hand in hand because "[r]acial resentment," one study concluded, is the "most potent force in white public opinion today."[69] Eighty percent of respondents in public opinion polls typically agree with statements that the government should fight discrimination, promote equal opportunity, and treat everyone fairly. When asked if they support affirmative action, usually 40 to 50 percent agree. But when asked if they favor special treatment or preferences for blacks, only about a third agree, and when the word *quotas* is used, support falls to about 20 percent. An early 1995 *Los Angeles Times* poll, for example, asked respondents for their views on affirmative action: 39 percent said such programs "go too far," 32 percent said they are "adequate now," and 23 percent said they "don't go far enough." When asked if Congress should ban "preferential treatment in hiring," 73 percent agreed.[70] For fifteen years, opinion polls have shown strong opposition to preferential hiring and race-based college admissions.[71] After reviewing these survey data, Lipset and Schneider concluded:

> Policies favoring quotas and numerical goals for integration . . . violate traditional conceptions of the meaning of equality of opportunity. Americans will accept the argument that race and sex are disadvantages deserving of compensation. . . . They will go along with special compensation up to the point where it is felt that resources have been roughly equalized and the initial terms of competition are once again fair. But the data show that every attempt to introduce any form of absolute preference . . . meets with stiff and determined resistance from the vast majority of Americans.[72]

Opposition to affirmative action among white males seemed to peak in the mid-1990s, according to a *Wall Street Journal*/NBC News poll. In 1991, 44 percent of white men said they opposed affirmative action whereas 67 percent were opposed in 1995, but only 52 percent were against affirmative action by late 1996. The decline in opposition may have resulted from Supreme Court decisions that made it more difficult to defend affirmative action programs. A 1995 Associated Press poll similarly found that 16 percent of its respondents favored affirmative action programs that set quotas, 47 percent favored affirmative action programs without quotas, and 28 percent opposed all affirmative action. Gallup polls conducted in 2001 reported that:

- 58 percent of respondents said they favored affirmative action programs for minorities and women for job hiring in the workplace, 36 percent were opposed;
- 56 percent favored affirmative action programs for admission to colleges and universities, 39 percent were opposed;
- 34 percent said we need to keep affirmative action programs the same, 27 percent favored increasing them and 30 percent favored decreasing them.[73]

The Pew Research Center reported in 2003 that Americans by a 2–1 margin favor "programs designed to increase the number of blacks and minority students" but disapprove by a 3–1 margin "giving [minorities] preferential treatment."[74]

Much like the Supreme Court and presidents, the public supports affirmative action but not quotas or numerical preferential treatment. More support for affirmative action came from business executives who developed such programs in response to OFCCP regulations on contractors. The public affairs director of *Time,* for example, indicated that its affirmative action efforts "didn't change when Reagan came to power" and that efforts "have redoubled in the last four years."[75] An executive of Mountain Bell stated that its minority and female workforce was a "gold mine" for good managers, but had it not been for hiring goals imposed on the company by a court decree, Mountain Bell would not have made such efforts on its own.[76]

Affirmative action has been used by Republicans for three decades to try to splinter the Democratic base of women, minorities, and working-class white males. This strategy was successful in the 1972 presidential election and much more so in appealing to the "Reagan Democrats." It continued into the 1990s, when GOP presidential primary candidate Pat Buchanan appealed to "angry white males" by making affirmative action and opposition to illegal immigration central planks of his platform.[77] Bob Dole and Jack Kemp, who had supported affirmative action earlier in their congressional careers, reversed position when they ran as Republican presidential and vice presidential nominees in 1996.[78] Republicans have largely been successful in achieving their goal of splintering the Democratic Party. What was once a policy with bipartisan support and a united Democratic Party has come to pit unions against minority advocates and to alienate Jewish and white ethnic groups.

Summary of Propositions

1a (single-issue groups): Unsupported, because the primary groups on both sides are characterized by their racial, religious, ethnic, or sexual attributes.

1a (absolutist politics): Supported, because the debate over racial quotas as "reverse discrimination" is a zero-sum conflict, with one side as much opposed as the other side is in favor.

2a (judicial activism): Supported, because Congress deferred to the federal judicial to implement Title VII regarding non-discrimination in employment.

2b (incorporation): Unsupported, because this jurisprudence involves the Equal Protection Clause of the Fourteenth Amendment.

3a (presidential symbolism): Supportive, because presidential leadership rarely goes beyond speech making.

3b (partisan presidents): Supported, because generally Republicans have exploited affirmative action as a wedge issue to attract working-class Democrats, whereas Democrats cannot defend the elimination of affirmative action programs.

4a (Congress and states): Unsupported, because most states had equal opportunity laws prior to the 1964 Civil Rights Act and the federal courts were encouraged by Congress to enforce Title VII provisions.

4b (Congress and elections): Supported, insofar as Congress and state legislators (with the exception of the South) suffered no electoral liability when voting for equal opportunity legislation.

5a (opinion and ideology): Supported, because public opinion differentiates between affirmative action as outreach programs, which the majority favors, and racial quotas, which most Americans oppose.

5b (law and society): Supported, to the degree that there has been much resistance to affirmative action programs that involve quotas or preferential treatment. Unions criticized the Philadelphia Plan, and continuing "reverse discrimination" lawsuits into 2003 showed that white plaintiffs were not accepting of race-based affirmative action programs.

6a (marginal agencies): Unsupported, because the enforcement efforts of the EEOC and the OFCCP are at the core of federal equal employment opportunity policies.

6b (agency pressures): Supported, because EEOC and OFCCP efforts are influenced by the scope of presidential oversight, the adequacy of budgets and staff provided by Congress, the private complainants, and the response by business.

7a (federalism): Unsupported, because affirmative action involves policy debate and political conflict at both the state and federal levels of government.

7b (compliance): Supported, because the magnitude of equal employment opportunity enforcement depends heavily on voluntary compliance by the private sector.

For Further Insight Into the Affirmative Action Debate

Carter, Stephen L. *Reflections of an Affirmative Action Baby.* New York: Basic Books, 1991. Personal account of affirmative action.

Eyes on the Prize. Available for purchase at pricegrabber.com; a PBS documentary film series on the civil rights movement.

Mills, Nicolaus. *Debating Affirmative Action: Race, Gender, Ethnicity, and the Politics of Inclusion.* New York: Delta, 1994. Series of essays debating affirmative action.

Steele, Shelby. *The Content of Our Character.* New York: HarperPerennial, 1991.
    Personal account of affirmative action.
http://aad.english.ucsb.edu. Affirmative Action and Diversity Project.
www.affirmativeaction.org. American Association for Affirmative Action.
www.libraries.colorado.edu/ps/gov/us/affact.htm. U.S. government information on
    affirmative action and civil rights.
www.nationalcenter.org/AA.html. Affirmative Action Information Center.
www.personal.umich.edu/~eandersn/biblio.htm. Resources page for teachers.

3

Animal Rights

Subordinate or Equal Species?

Stephanie A. Slocum-Schaffer

In 1975 Peter Singer published his seminal book, *Animal Liberation,* which begins with the following introduction: "This book is about the tyranny of human over nonhuman animals. This tyranny has caused and today is still causing an amount of pain and suffering that can only be compared with that which resulted from the centuries of tyranny by white humans over black humans. The struggle against this tyranny is a struggle as important as any of the moral and social issues that have been fought over in recent years."[1] The publication of *Animal Liberation*—which articulates this moral case and then enumerates a long list of cruel animal experiments followed by horrifying descriptions of factory farming—thus gave birth to a new morality policy and a new political movement. That movement claims that "animals, like humans, have inherent value that must be respected" and that "speciesism [the bias that humans are superior to nonhuman animals] is no more morally defensible than racism, sexism, or other forms of discrimination that arbitrarily exclude some humans from the scope of moral concern."[2]

At the heart of the debate over animal rights is the distinction between humans and other animals. Is there a substantial difference between human and nonhuman animals? If animals are not substantially different from humans, then should they not have recognized rights? Science, particularly evolutionary biology, has inflamed this controversy by violating the long assumed distinction between humans and the animal world. While religious people like creationists have struggled to maintain this distinction, believing that humans were created in God's image and are therefore different from other animals, animal rightists have taken biologists literally, claiming that there are no true differences.[3] The answer to this key question about the distinction between humans and other animals is thus deeply influenced by one's religious beliefs, cultural relationships, and personal values. Animal rights, in other words, remains more an issue of belief than of fact or evidence, meaning that "[o]pposing world views, concepts of identity, ideas of community, are all at stake. The animal rights controversy is about the treatment of animals, but it is also about our definition of ourselves and of a moral society. For this reason, it cannot be easily resolved"[4] and, moreover, is characterized by high levels of public engagement and conflict.

Interest Groups

Animal Liberation quickly became a call to arms for those interested in animal welfare and animal rights, profoundly influencing many and mobilizing some to action. One who was spurred to action was Henry Spira, a burly man in his fifties who was increasingly concerned about the way in which humans treated animals.[5] Spira's activism was the catalyst for what Smith and Tatalovich call a "triggering event," a dramatic incident that can ignite a full-blown social movement and boost an issue onto the policy agenda. Triggering events do more than pinpoint one issue; they "frame" an entire array of injustices that prompt political activists to demand a fundamental re-ordering of the social hierarchy.[6] The triggering event for the animal rights movement was a highly publicized assault on the American Museum of Natural History in Manhattan for the experiments it was conducting on cats. Beginning in 1959, the museum, with funding from the National Institutes of Health (NIH), had been experimenting on cats in order to observe their sexual performance, including removing some parts of the brain, cutting nerves in the penis, and disabling the sense of smell.[7] Spira saw the experiments as ideal candidates for shocking the public and raising awareness about the mistreatment of animals. He rallied the members of several local animal protection groups to help organize a protest; wrote a series of articles attacking the experiments as cruel and ethically unacceptable; organized a letter-writing campaign against NIH, Congress, and the museum; and spearheaded several demonstrations. In the end, Spira's efforts to attract media attention were successful and the museum ended the experiments.[8]

The campaign against the museum was one of the first expressions of the new "animal rights" sentiments in action, and its victory was just the beginning.[9] Spira proceeded to organize more protests, including a May 1980 demonstration against Revlon for its use of rabbits in product safety tests that resulted in Revlon's providing $750,000 for research on alternative tests. More importantly, new single-issue interest groups concerned with animal "rights" began to emerge and to rejuvenate the older animal welfare movement with new goals: to reform or abolish institutional uses of animals for food, testing, dress, entertainment, and research.[10] Since the late 1970s, these animal rights groups have increased in size and number ranging from fundamentalist and direct action groups, such as the Animal Liberation Front (ALF), to militant and activists groups, like People for the Ethical Treatment of Animals (PETA), to those who work within the legal system to promote animal liberation, such as the Animal Legal Defense Fund (ALDF).

PETA has been one of the movement's most visible and successful groups, in part because the public learned about animal research through investigative work conducted by PETA, work that succeeded in gaining the first conviction of a researcher for cruelty in U.S. history.[11] The publicity from the case helped PETA to launch the movement's first successful direct mail campaign (a tactic borrowed from environmental groups). Its membership then grew rapidly throughout the 1980s, from 8,000 members in 1984 to 300,000 in 1990. By 2003, PETA boasted more than 750,000 members,[12] an expansion that reflects the growth of the entire movement during this time period. By the end of the 1990s there were several hundred animal rights groups and several thousand animal welfare groups.[13]

The rise of a movement concerned with animal "rights" was a dramatic shift away from the politics of animal welfare that had dominated for more than two decades. The first societies to prevent cruelty to animals in the United States originated in the 1860s, were descended directly from British organizations, and were created by privileged elites who wished to protect animals from excessive cruelty. The United States experienced an expansion of this animal welfare movement during the 1950s with the founding of such organizations as the Humane Society of the United States (HSUS). HSUS and other 1950s humane groups broadened the animal welfare agenda by bringing forth concerns about animal research, trapping, the protection of wildlife, slaughterhouse practices, and the problems of pet overpopulation and abandonment.[14] The animal rights movement of the late 1970s, by contrast, went well beyond animal welfare to the fundamental question of animal rights. It was driven by the simple moral position that nonhuman animals are similar enough to humans to deserve moral consideration. If moral consideration is granted, then clearly animals deserve to live dignified lives and should be treated as ends, not as means.[15] This moral position and the language of rights—bolstered by a wider, more diffuse movement in the 1960s and 1970s that condemned the "instrumentalist" and exploitive attitudes of

American institutions[16]—shifted the debate and the politics of the animal welfare issue to a stance based on fundamental values and moral demands. "Rights—whether of patients, women, fetuses, or animals—are accepted as a moral trump card that cannot be disputed. Justified in terms of tradition, nature, or fundamental moral principles, rights are considered non-negotiable. Protestors compare animal rights to human rights, and the charge of 'speciesism' takes its place alongside racism and sexism."[17] There is no better example of how morality can "radicalize" politics, as Theodore Lowi argues,[18] than the animal rights crusade.

The radicalization of the animal welfare issue has had a profound impact. It has exploded Americans' awareness about animal rights, renewed concern about animal treatment and welfare, and generated a powerful social movement.[19] In June 1990, for example, 30,000 to 75,000 people marched in Washington, D.C., for animal rights.[20] That same year 10 to 15 million Americans sent money to animal protection groups. Animal rights issues made the cover of *Newsweek,* were examined in news programs such as *48 Hours,* and have been portrayed favorably in comic strips like *Doonesbury.*[21] Public support for scientific research using animals has declined, even when the research produces information about human health.[22] Indeed, the use of animals for product safety testing has declined precipitously, with many companies ending the practice entirely. Vegetarianism and veganism also are on the rise,[23] and there is now a market for "animal loving Barbie" and for sandals made of faux leather and suede. The animal rights campaign against fur is perhaps the best example of how single-issue advocacy can increase the political saliency of a cause. The campaign against fur was organized and highly publicized, with celebrities, including model Pamela Anderson, actor Kim Basinger, game-show host Bob Barker, and comedian Bill Maher, openly denouncing fur. One consequence is that the American fur industry has suffered a steep decline in demand for its products.[24]

Framing the issue of animal welfare around rights rhetoric has yielded an absolutist position that polarizes the debate. Jasper and Nelkin argue that the movement for animal rights is akin to a moral crusade, with activists working to incite anger in like-minded citizens by employing emotional appeals, dramatic publicity stunts, and "sometimes shrill, self-righteous, and uncompromising" language.[25] Indeed, leaders of the movement use morally loaded language, casting opponents as evil and refusing to negotiate with those who disagree.[26] In fact, animal rights groups soon learned that compromise and negotiation were not effective without public attention and media coverage, both of which are more easily obtained with dramatic events and photographs. As Jasper and Nelkin observe, animal rights groups "discovered that demonizing opponents and exaggerating evils are effective ways to energize supporters and hold their commitment. To mobilize time and money, protest movements must rely on those who feel most strongly about an issue—precisely those most likely to be moral extremists. For them, denunciation of their opponents becomes more satisfying than efforts to communicate."[27]

On the other side of this debate are a variety of groups that defend scientific research, including Coalition for Animals and Animal Research, the American Medical Association's Council for the Defense of Medical Research, Incurably Ill for Animal Research (iiFAR), the National Association for Biomedical Research (which represents 350 of the largest U.S. research institutions), and the Foundation for Biomedical Research (FBR). This countermovement, like the animal rights movement, is also "strident and dismissive" in its tone because, in this battle over public opinion, "scientists are increasingly trying to match the moral strategies of their adversaries."[28] In response to animal rightists' attacks on animal research, scientists argue that freedom of inquiry and the right to academic freedom are being threatened. Professional societies responded to a decision by Cornell University to withdraw support for a faculty researcher who used animal subjects, for example, by declaring that the university's decision violated academic freedom. And like animal rights groups, FBR—a national-level group that publicizes the medical results of animal research and lobbies state and federal legislatures—does not hesitate to use well-known personalities and celebrities (such as Stephen Hawking) and to resort to emotional appeals. Where animal rightists display horrifying photographs of adorable animals being tortured, FBR displays sympathetic medical patients including children, being aided by animal research.[29] Even the fur industry uses the rhetoric of liberty to defend itself. "The decision to wear fur is a personal one. We support the freedom of individuals to buy and wear fur. This freedom is not just a fur industry issue—it's everybody's issue."[30]

There are three basic varieties of animal rights groups—large "welfarist" groups that accept most current uses of animals but seek to minimize their suffering and pain (for example, the Humane Society of the United States), "pragmatist" groups that believe animals deserve moral consideration (as articulated by Peter Singer), and extreme "fundamentalist" groups that demand the immediate abolition of all use of animals on the grounds that they have inviolable rights (for example, ALF).[31] Although the radical tactics of the fundamentalist groups (break-ins, animal liberations, and property destruction) threaten to undermine and split the animal rights movement, the more extreme groups are growing in size and wealth.

Like zealots in the pro-life movement, some animal rights fundamentalists feel a moral obligation to take direct action, even if that means breaking the law, to save innocent beings from suffering and death. They claim that the violation of property laws is justified to stop violence against living beings.[32] For example, the Animal Liberation Front, which the FBI's counterterrorism division has been tracking, has engaged in hundreds of break-ins to liberate animals.[33] Further, the number of illegal actions perpetrated by fundamentalist animal rights groups like the ALF has increased over time. According to the NIH, there were no break-ins reported at NIH-supported labs between 1978 and 1983 but ten in 1984 alone. From 1983 to 1987, animal rights protesters caused an estimated $4.5 million in damages just in the state of California,[34] and several high-profile, respected scientists—such as Michael Podell of Ohio State University—have decided to abandon their research programs because of harassment from animal rights activists. In 2002 a report from the Southern Poverty Law Center's Intelligence Project detailed the increasingly violent tendencies of U.S. animal rights activists— from firebombings to letters booby-trapped with razor blades. One example in 2003 involved the Animal Liberation Brigade, which claimed responsibility for the bombing of a California-based biotechnology firm, sparking yet another terror investigation by the FBI.[35]

Federalism

The first animal anticruelty law in the United States was enacted by the Puritans of the Massachusetts Bay Colony in 1641. Ever since, the states have been the primary actors in regulating the treatment of animals. By 1921 all states had some type of animal anticruelty law on the books.[36] Today all fifty states and U.S. territories have anticruelty statutes and most also acknowledge that animals have certain rights—to nourishment and adequate living conditions, to protection from abandonment, to protection from poisoning, and to humane transportation. However, prosecutions under these laws are generally rare and the penalties minor. Most modern anticruelty statutes also exempt farm animals and animals used for scientific experimentation.[37] In fact, most of the state laws directed at animal experimentation before the 1960s were known as "procurement laws," statutes that forced municipal pounds and animal shelters that received tax funds to surrender dogs and cats for experimentation. They were not motivated by concern for the well-being of animals but rather were intended to ensure that the scientific demand for research animals was met while deterring pet theft. Although animal welfare societies fought against these laws, they were typically overpowered by the more influential research community. It was not until the 1970s that some states began to repeal their procurement laws, although a number of states still retain such laws.[38]

State governments also had—and continue to have—profound influence in the animal rights debate by their regulation of hunting, fishing, and trapping. State fish and game commissions set hunting seasons, place limits on catches, sell licenses, and manage animal populations. The number of animals killed under the auspices of these state agencies each year is more than 100 million birds and 50 million mammals, and animal rights activists blame state governments for encouraging hunting through their management of animal populations and their regulation activities.[39] The Fund for Animals has led several groups in attacking Florida's sponsorship of a deer hunt for children under fifteen years old, for example, and the Committee to Abolish Sport Hunting has been fighting efforts to open state parks to hunting for more than fifteen years. Hunters, on the other hand, have been active in lobbying state legislatures to protect their interests, and forty-one states have passed laws to prevent the harassment of hunters on state-owned land. Even so, these laws are rarely enforced in stopping animal advocates from pursuing hunters into the woods, and several of the laws have been tested in court and found unconstitutional.[40] Recently, the hunting lobby has tried to enshrine "the right to hunt" in state constitutions. It has been successful in six states and is actively pursuing constitutional change in at least thirteen more.[41]

Even more upsetting to animal rightists is the activity they term "canned hunting," or hunting on guaranteed-kill ranches. Such ranches offer hunters a guaranteed kill, an abundance of well-fed animals (often exotic or unusual game), year-round open season, and the opportunity to use a gun, bow and arrow, or spear. Animal rights advocates argue that these hunts are slaughter rather than hunting because the animals, bred and raised in captivity, are mostly tame and because the ranches are fenced and allow them no chance of escape. Outraged by the practice and its growing popularity, animal rightists have lobbied hard to pass state legislation that would ban canned hunting. At least eleven states have banned canned hunting, and in April 1999 the Oregon Department of Fish and Wildlife adopted a regulation that effectively prevents the practice.[42] In November 2000, a voter initiative passed in Montana that banned new game farms and ended the practice of hunting on such private preserves. Animal activists continue to lobby at the state and federal levels to put a stop to the practice,[43] but in several states—notably Texas—public support for such measures is very low. Ranch-hunting in Texas, a tradition that dates from the 1930s, is an estimated $100-million-a-year business.[44]

Unlike hunting, trapping has fewer defenders. Although fewer animals are killed in trapping (around 15 million each year), it is associated with both the fur trade and with the steel leg-hold trap. These traps have provided animal protectionists with much to attack. The pain inflicted by the trap is apparently excruciating; many animals break their teeth or gnaw off their own limbs attempting to escape the traps; and unintended animals like pets often get caught. In response to persistent lobbying by animal welfare and animal rights groups, at least twenty-five states have passed trapping legislation. New Jersey has banned steel leg-hold traps, Florida has banned all traps made of steel, and Massachusetts has prohibited leg-hold traps set on dry land. Many states require trappers to check traps every twenty-four hours so that animals do not suffer long,[45] though a few states have no checking requirements at all.

With respect to processing animals for food, the federal Humane Slaughter Act of 1958 regulated the treatment of animals before slaughter only for packers who sold their meat to the government. Other meat packers were subjected to various state laws already in place in twenty-eight states.[46] Today most states have enacted some type of humane slaughtering laws and have charged state governmental authorities with enforcement.[47] States also regulate the treatment of animals for entertainment. While horse racing is legal in most jurisdictions (as is betting on the outcome of such races), dog fighting is illegal in all states and is considered a felony in some.[48] Also, bullfighting is banned in every state and gamecock fighting is prohibited in forty-four states, although enforcement is lax enough that the "sport" of cock-fighting is still commonplace in many areas.[49] Given the difficulty of prosecuting many of these state laws and the fact that protection of animals is typically not a high priority for local officials, animal protection laws are often not properly enforced.

The states have primary jurisdiction not only in legislative action but also through popular referenda. One analysis of state referenda dealing with morality policy for the period 1980–2000 shows that 29 of the 166 referenda (a little over 17 percent) were concerned with animal rights (typically regulating trapping and hunting) and that the animal rights position prevailed almost 60 percent of the time.[50] And that trend continued into 2002, when three states placed animal rights ballot measures before the voters. Oklahoma voters approved an initiative outlawing cockfighting while voters in Florida supported a ban on the use of gestation crates (narrow metal crates that prevent movement) for pregnant pigs, but an Arkansas initiative to raise penalties for cruelty to animals from a misdemeanor to a felony failed. Observers expect that the success in Florida will generate a nationwide movement to ban gestation crates and more future ballot measures on that issue.[51]

Finally, there is a federal-state partnership even where federal statutes exist. The states have a role to play in the protection of endangered species, an aspect of animal rights policy dominated by the federal Endangered Species Act. This state rule is illustrated by the proposal in 2004 to lift federal protections for the gray wolf; the federal government asked the states of

Montana, Idaho, and Wyoming to draw up plans for monitoring and maintaining the wolf population so that, once the federal government is ready to withdraw, the states will once again have nearly complete control to regulate gray wolves. Or consider the enforcement problem in the controversy over water in Klamath Falls, Oregon, during the summer of 2001. The federal government's decision to cut off irrigation water in a year of record drought in order to protect the endangered suckerfish created a tremendous outcry among struggling farmers. On at least three different occasions, local residents broke the law by reopening the flow of irrigation water, and each time local authorities refused to intervene—the sheriff would not arrest the lawbreakers, the prosecutor would not prosecute, and the local irrigation district ignored the situation. Local officials would not even act to turn the water off again.[52]

Congress

The Constitution does not mention animals and, as noted, the primary legal authority over the use, control, and treatment of animals rests with state governments. However, these laws are ineffective in many circumstances, are often difficult to prosecute, and typically are not fully enforced. In addition, most state laws do not apply to animals used in research, and numerous animal activities—such as the interstate shipment of stolen pets—have a multistate focus that makes one state's efforts to control a problem difficult. National legislation, therefore, has been sought to augment and strengthen state laws on the use and treatment of animals.

Before the 1950s, animal welfare groups were concerned mostly about protecting animals from excessive cruelty. The expansion of such groups in the 1950s—along with an expanded agenda that included concerns about the treatment of animals in research settings, slaughterhouse practices, trapping, wildlife protection, and the overbreeding of pets—led to increased legislative activism at the federal level.[53] The first manifestation of this increased activism was the Humane Slaughter Act of 1958, which was finally signed into law only after the cruel practices of slaughterhouses were brought to the public's attention by animal welfare groups. These practices—including boiling live animals, beating them with iron sledgehammers, subjecting them to electric shock, or knifing them and allowing them to die slowly—were recounted in extensive congressional hearings at which testimony was taken from representatives of humane societies nationwide. Several investigations and studies of slaughterhouse practices were also conducted.[54] The new law required slaughterhouses to stun animals prior to killing them. Poultry and kosher-killed animals were excluded under the law, however, and it pertained only to meat packers who sold their meat to the government.[55] In a later effort to strengthen the enforcement of the Humane Slaughter Act, the Federal Humane Slaughter Act of 1978 was introduced and passed, empowering federal meat inspectors to withhold inspecting the meat of any plants that employed inhumane practices. The 1978 act also banned the importation of any meat slaughtered in an inhumane manner.[56]

Addressing the question of the treatment of animals in research laboratories, the laboratory Animal Welfare Act (AWA), setting the first standards for the treatment of laboratory animals, was finally passed in 1966 after a series of failed bills. Its purposes were simple: to ensure that animals used in research were provided humane care and treatment and, even more important to most Americans, to prevent the sale and use of stolen pets in research activities. The 1966 act was amended in 1970 to enlarge the number of protected animals (although farm animals are still excluded from protection) and again in 1976 to specifically target the treatment of animals during transportation. The act was amended again in 1985 and 1990, further expanding the scope of the law and requiring the use of appropriate anesthetics and tranquilizers. The 1985 amendments—the Improved Standards for Laboratory Animals Act—established an information service in the National Agricultural Library to assist in preventing unintended duplication of experiments, finding alternatives to the use of animals in experiments, and instructing scientists in humane animal care practices. The amendments further required that each registered research facility appoint an Institutional Animal Care and Use Committee to oversee animal care and use.[57] Despite these expansions of the AWA, however, there is "a general consensus that the statute has failed to fulfill its potential in fostering the humane treatment of animals."[58]

This failure, in fact, has motivated fundamentalist groups to increase the number and intensity of their attacks on research facilities that use animals. The violent tactics of animal rights militants led to the passage of the Animal Enterprise Protection Act of 1992, which created felony penalties for causing more than $10,000 damage to a lab or animal commercial enterprise. While it appears that acts of vandalism declined abruptly in response to the act, enforcement of the act has been minimal and violence, harassment, and vandalism are again on the rise.[59]

Recently, two laws designed to augment the protection of laboratory animals won passage thanks to strong pressure from animal rights activists operating within the traditional boundaries of the political system. The ICCVAM Authorization Act established the Interagency Coordinating Committee on the Validation of Alternative Methods, which reviews alternatives to animal tests and recommends changes in testing procedures to the appropriate federal agencies. The Chimpanzee Health Improvement, Maintenance, and Protection Act establishes a system of sanctuaries for government-owned chimpanzees who are ready to be "retired" from federally sponsored research.[60] However, it is noteworthy that neither of these recent laws, nor the Humane Slaughter Act or the laboratory Animal Welfare Act, addressed the issue of animal "rights" per se. Congress legislated only against excessive cruelty or neglect rather than to prevent animal experimentation and the slaughter of nonhuman animals.[61] Indeed, the laboratory Animal Welfare Act still allows animals to be used for any purpose that is deemed necessary to an experiment, no matter how painful or strange.[62]

Congressional actions that seemed to move closer to protecting animal rights were the National Environmental Policy Act of 1969 (NEPA), the Endangered Species Act of 1973 (ESA), and the Marine Mammal Protection Act of 1972 (MMPA). The National Environmental Policy Act required the preparation of environmental impact reports before large federal construction projects could begin. The law also gave legal standing to citizens who wanted to sue for its enforcement, with the result that animal rights activists could sue on behalf of wildlife even if they were not themselves affected.[63] In no time animal activists were suing to delay the construction of new animal laboratories because the environmental impact statements were not in proper order, and the ALDF was able to halt California's annual mountain lion hunt for several seasons on the grounds that environmental assessments had not considered factors like the loss of lion habitats.[64] In 2002 several animal conservation groups brought a suit against the U.S. government, challenging the government's approval of a quota for whale hunting by the Makah Indian Tribe in Washington State. The court of appeals held that the failure of the government to prepare an environmental impact statement before approving the quota violated NEPA.

By the late 1960s, concern was spreading rapidly in the United States about the decline of species around the world. In fact, species and habitat endangerment and extinction were, and continue to be, one of the most urgent environmental problems facing society. Habitat extinction was a particular focus of concern because species cannot live without their supporting environment, and the leading cause of species endangerment and extinction is loss of habitat (which is primarily caused by the activities of mankind). Although species extinction is a natural occurrence, extinction rates had increased dramatically and, according to some estimates, hundreds of thousands of species were headed for extinction.[65] A growing environmental movement —coupled with widespread public concern about species extinction—forced Congress to action. The Endangered Species Act was passed in 1973 by an overwhelming 355–4 margin in the House and 92–0 in the Senate, replacing 1966 and 1969 laws that provided for the listing of endangered species but gave little meaningful protection.

The purpose of the ESA was to "conserve the ecosystems upon which threatened or endangered species depend" and to conserve and recover listed species. Under the law, species could be listed as either "endangered" (in danger of becoming extinct throughout all or a significant portion of their range) or "threatened" (likely to become endangered within the foreseeable future). All species of animals and plants, with the exception of pest insects, were eligible for listing. Like NEPA, furthermore, ESA allowed animal rights activists to sue on behalf of endangered species to protect those animals and their habitats. Since the 1973 Act was passed, several major construction projects have been blocked because they endangered unique species[66] and eighteen domestic species have been "de-listed," as their populations have increased. Seven species have become extinct. By 2004, 516 U.S. species of animals were listed, 744 U.S. species of plants were listed, and 450 U.S. species had their habitats designated as protected.

Along with generalized concern about the decline of species worldwide came particularized worry about populations of marine mammals that seemed fragile, especially whales and dolphins. The blue whale population was reduced to only about twenty known animals by 1965, hundreds of thousands of dolphins were being killed yearly by tuna fishermen, and sea otters were virtually extinct because of aggressive fur trading. In 1971 all the great whales were placed on the U.S. Endangered Species List and a campaign began to enact greater protections for all marine mammals. After lengthy hearings and debate, the Marine Mammal Protection Act was passed in 1972 (later amended in 1981 and 1988). The law set forth a moratorium on the hunting, capturing, and killing of marine mammals, conferred jurisdiction over whales, dolphins, sea lions, and seals to the secretary of commerce, and gave jurisdiction over polar bears, manatees, sea otters, and walruses to the secretary of the interior. However, the tuna industry was given a two-year exemption from the act, allowing the incidental killing of dolphins to continue while the industry developed equipment to prevent such killings. But no changes were made by the tuna industry, and the incidental dolphin killings continued even after the expiration of the two-year exemption period. Animal and environmental groups sued the Department of Commerce for enforcement under the MMPA. After a number of hearings, the activists won quotas on the number of incidental dolphin killings that were allowable.[67]

The ESA and the MMPA were enacted in response to widespread public concern about the state of the environment and the fate of animals on the brink of permanent extinction. Even when there is public support for animal protection goals and active lobbying by animal rights groups, however, Congress often has difficulty taking action. The best example of this is the failure of Congress, despite several attempts, to end the pain and suffering inflicted by steel leg-hold traps; even with 125 cosponsors, a 1983 bill prohibiting trade in furs from animals captured in steel leg-hold traps failed to pass. Such national organizations as the National Trappers Association and the American Fur Resources Institute lobbied to block the legislation.[68] Thus, although steel leg-hold traps have been banned by over sixty countries and there is considerable public distaste about their cruelty, there has been no successful effort by Congress to end their use.[69]

Despite the birth of the animal rights movement and the rhetorical shift from concerns about animal welfare to demands for animal rights, Congress has been unwilling or unable to move beyond traditional policies with respect to the animal rights debate. Although animal rights activists demand an end to animal experimentation, a ban on the use of animals for entertainment, and the abolition of factory farming, Congress has acted only to ensure the "humane" treatment of animals that are to be experimented upon or slaughtered, and legislative exemptions in these acts mean that animal welfare laws do not interfere with the conduct of experiments or the business of meatpacking. Even when Congress takes steps to protect the interests of some wild animals through the Endangered Species Act and the Marine Mammal Protection Act, as Peter Carruthers explains, the motivation behind such laws is "that rare species of animals and rain forests are worth preserving for their importance to *us,* not because they have moral significance, or moral rights, in their own right."[70]

Judiciary

The animal rights movement has employed both the language of "rights" and the strategy of going to the courts. Jasper and Nelkin argue, for example, that many animal activists have seized upon the language of rights to make their case that animals are yet another oppressed group.[71] Indeed, it is not at all unusual to find animal rightists comparing their cause to the 1960s struggle of black Americans to win civil rights, and animal activists consider the "courts strategy" of that movement to be a successful model that should be imitated. Despite efforts to change animal protection policy through the assertion of legal rights, however, the courts have not been sympathetic.

Under the law, animals are the *property* of persons and, as property, "cannot have rights or duties or be bound by or recognize rules."[72] The status of animals as property severely limits the legal protections that they can enjoy. Says Francione: "As a general matter, as long as a particular animal use is considered legitimate, then anything that facilitates that usage will be deemed under the law as 'necessary.'"[73] Therefore, some animal activists have concluded that there is little point in looking to the courts for relief: "If the law regarding animals is to change, it is necessary to eradicate the property status of nonhumans. But it is folly to look to the legal system as playing a leading role in any such change. The principles of common law and the process of common-law adjudication, both of which protect property interests, are scarcely candidates for effecting basic change."[74]

On the other hand, some members of the legal profession have begun to actively fight for the legal recognition of animal rights. These lawyers have created a new field of animal law with goals that go beyond protection under weak anticruelty laws, instead filing novel lawsuits and producing new legal scholarship to try to "chip away at a fundamental principle of American law that animals are property and have no rights."[75] Animal law course offerings in the curricula of such prestigious law schools as Harvard and Georgetown suggest that this legal approach to animal rights may be gaining some legitimacy, and animal lawyers have also scored a few legal victories. In civil cases involving veterinary malpractice or pet deaths, some lawyers have won verdicts and settlements of $15,000 or more, and in other cases, lawyers have won damage awards for loss of companionship or for emotional distress when a pet is killed. In 2000 Tennessee became the first state to pass a statute that allows damages up to $4,000 for emotional distress from the loss of a pet.[76] Furthermore, animal lawyers have had increasing success in battling the euthanasia orders that routinely occur when dogs bite people.[77]

However, certain obstacles hinder the ability of courts to be the agents of fundamental change in animal rights policy. For one, the courts often hold that animals (and other third parties) do not have standing to seek redress or assistance, particularly when filing claims under the Animal Welfare Act. In the early 1980s, for example, PETA and the International Primate Protection League launched a campaign to ensure that seventeen monkeys that were rescued from a research laboratory would be sent to an animal rights sanctuary. Besides holding demonstrations at NIH, PETA sued the agency for custody of the animals, but the U.S. Fourth Circuit Court rejected its suit in 1986, ruling that animal rights groups have no right to speak for animals. Even after several of the monkeys were sent to the San Diego Zoo and the rest to a primate center in Louisiana, PETA continued to demand "custody" of the animals, arguing that the monkeys should be "treated like minors, available for custody."[78] After nearly a decade of protest, PETA finally lost its suit in 1990,[79] setting a precedent that third parties could not sue researchers under the AWA for violations of the act.[80] Furthermore, the courts have ruled in a series of cases that individual animals do not have standing or the right to sue for their own protection. The most famous of these suits, *Citizens to End Animal Suffering and Exploitation v. The New England Aquarium* (1993), involved a dolphin named Kama. Kama was found not to have standing to challenge his transfer to the Naval Oceans Systems Center under the Marine Mammal Protection Act.[81]

The Supreme Court sent an even clearer signal about the "rights" of animals in two other cases. In *Diamond v. Chakrabarty* (1980), the high court asserted that patent protection may exist for "anything under the sun" so long as it is created by humans. The ruling permitted genetically engineered animals—such as the "GloFish," a zebra fish that glows in rooms lit with ultraviolet or black light—to be patentable subject matter in the United States. In *Church of the Lukumi Babalu Aye, Inc. v. City of Hialeah* (1993), the Supreme Court upheld the rights of a religious sect called the Santerians, rather than the city of Hialeah, Florida, which argued that the Santerians' practice of animal sacrifice violated its animal cruelty statutes. The Court ruled that the city could not prohibit the Santerians' animal sacrifice because such a ban violated their First Amendment right to the free exercise of their religion.[82]

Even in cases that appear to support animal rights—as when courts support student refusals to dissect animals in science classes—a closer reading shows that the courts act to protect the rights of the students rather than the rights of animals. Those lawsuits generally are grounded in the constitutional right to freedom of religion, and the students must show that the animal experimentation is required by a governmental actor (a public school), that there is no compelling state interest in requiring the student to engage in animal experimentation, and that the student's refusal is based on a sincere religious belief and not simply a morally based objection.[83] Believing that animals are sentient beings that deserve moral consideration—the position of most animal rightists—is not enough to win a reprieve.

The courts come closest to protecting the interests of animals in cases filed under the National Environmental Policy Act and, especially, the Endangered Species and the Marine Mammal Protection Acts. Even though more than 10 billion animals are killed a year in the United States for food consumption and around 50 million are used in laboratory experiments and for entertainment, animal rightists have found it much easier to force the protection of small groups of wild animals. Specific species of wild animals—unlike domesticated pets, farm animals, or laboratory animals—can be protected by going to the courts under the ESA and the MMPA because these federal laws provide third parties with the standing needed to sue for enforcement. So strict was the ESA initially that in *Tennessee Valley Authority v. Hill* (1978), the U.S. Supreme Court halted the construction of the Tellico Dam to protect the habitat of a single species—a tiny fish called the snail darter. In *Animal Welfare Institute v. Kreps* (1977), a federal district court held that animal activists (in this case, the Animal Welfare Institute) did have standing to bring suit and that the government's decision to waive the ban on importing baby sealskins from South Africa was a violation of the MMPA. Similarly, in 2003, the Federal District Court of Arizona acted to protect the habitat of the Mexican spotted owl (*Strix occidentalis lucida*) in *Center for Biological Diversity v. Norton.* The lawsuit arose when the U.S. Fish and Wildlife Service (USFWS) attempted to designate only about 30 percent of the critical habitat originally proposed for the Mexican spotted owl. The court found that the USFWS's application of the ESA was unlawful since the existence of other habitat protections does not relieve the agency from designating critical habitat.

All these cases found the federal courts protecting wild animals even though those judicial rulings harmed many people and imposed substantial economic costs. In *Tennessee Valley Authority,* for example, the Supreme Court halted the dam's construction even though $53 million had already been spent on the project. Rather than illustrating raw judicial power, however, judicial activism in these cases was made possible by acts of Congress, not because the courts have carved out new "rights" for animals outside of the normal political process. In *Hawaiian Crow ('Alala) v. Lujan,* for example, a federal district court ruled that the *'Alala,* an endangered species of bird, did not have standing on its own to sue under the ESA—it needed a person to do that.[84]

Presidency

The concept of animal rights is so far outside the political mainstream that neither presidents nor parties have needed to address the issue in any systematic way. However, the treatment of animals—and particularly wild animals— has garnered more political attention. Senator Robert Dole (R-KS) was the main sponsor of the 1985 amendments to the Animal Welfare Act, for example, a result of the intense lobbying of animal welfare groups and Dole's stature as a likely GOP presidential candidate. Conflicts over the Endangered Species Act have engendered even more political activity because the ESA has great potential to affect the use of private property. In reacting to the Supreme Court's ruling in *Tennessee Valley Authority v. Hill,* for example, Congress eventually directed that the dam be completed and, over angry objections, President Jimmy Carter signed the legislation "with regret" in 1979.[85]

Another high-profile ESA dispute was the 1990 listing of the northern spotted owl as endangered, which resulted in millions of acres of Pacific Northwest forests becoming protected habitat (see *Robertson v. Seattle Audubon Society*). The timber industry was angry over the loss of millions of acres of timberland, labor unions feared the loss of jobs, and building and real estate interests argued that there would be severe economic harm in their industries. President George H.W. Bush responded by proclaiming that it was "time to make people more important than owls," though his gesture was more symbolic than substantive.[86] A similar scenario intruded upon the presidential campaign of 2000 when the Clinton administration delayed a decision on the breaching (removal) of four major Snake River dams, a move that would have protected the endangered wild salmon. The issue was politically charged in the Pacific Northwest because the dams interrupt the migratory paths of several endangered species of fish but also generate enormous amounts of electricity. Governor George W. Bush of Texas, the presumptive GOP presidential nominee at the time, quickly declared his opposition to any breaching of the dams. Vice President Al Gore, the presumed Democratic presidential nominee and self-declared environmentalist, refused to comment directly on the issue. The decision to delay thus insulated Gore from criticism on both sides, though Gore later released a statement saying that "if sufficient progress toward recovery is not being made, we may then have no choice but to pursue options such as dam breaching. But we must first exhaust all reasonable alternatives."[87]

While symbolic gestures have thus been the staple of presidential politics on the endangered species issue, congressional Republicans have been willing to target the ESA as a means to appease conservatives while Democrats have defended the law as much as possible. Congress has not reauthorized the ESA since 1988 but, instead, provides funding for the law on a year-to-year basis, with critics and backers sparring over funding levels and the future of this legislation. Since the Republican Party took control of Congress in 1995, its members have been engaged in a campaign to rewrite the law—"the federal law that conservatives most love to hate."[88] One congressional opponent is Representative Richard W. Pombo (R-CA), a rancher, who was given the task of rewriting the law in 1995. In 2003 Pombo was promoted over more senior Republicans to chair the House Resources Committee. Although Pombo has said that he has given up trying to recast the ESA as a whole, he is attacking the law bit by bit, beginning with a plan to add "sound science" provisions and then moving on to tackle how critical habitats are designated. Pombo contends that the ESA infringes on the rights of farmers and homeowners and produces more lawsuits and property disputes than protection for wildlife. Most Democrats seem to be just as determined on the other side, however, with the House Resources Committee's ranking Democrat saying, "I think we can build an effective coalition that will block any wholesale revamping of the law itself."[89]

Bureaucracy

The issue of habitat designation surfaces at the forefront of political conflict over the Endangered Species Act. Although a clear mission of the 1973 law was to protect endangered species by protecting their habitat, the U.S. Fish and Wildlife Service only seriously began to designate critical habitat in 2000. Before that time, the USFWS made the determination of critical habitat designations a lower priority than identifying which species were endangered. When environmental groups began filing suits to force critical habitat designations, the agency, finding itself on the losing side of several court battles, was forced to respond. Its designation of 1.2 million acres around Tucson, Arizona, in November 2002 is an example of how politicized the critical habitat issue can become. Although the administration of President George W. Bush had been outspoken in calling the designations counterproductive, the administration was forced by a federal court order to designate the areas around Tucson as habitat critical to the protection of eighteen endangered pygmy owls. Of course, that critical habitat designation imposed serious obstacles to economic development in the fast-growing Tucson area, so developers fought back. And, as has been the pattern with other ESA disputes, Republicans (including the Bush administration) actively supported the developers and business interests while Democrats sided with environmentalists and anti-growth advocates. Craig Mason, the assistant secretary of the Interior charged with this responsibility in the Bush administration, remarked. "Rationally speaking, the costs of critical habitat designation add virtually nothing to the protection of the species. It sucks up a lot of the resources of the Fish and Wildlife Service, and it causes a lot of social and economic upheaval, and the benefits to the species is virtually nonexistent, so it just doesn't make any sense." On the other side of the issue, advocates call the critical habitat provisions vital in setting aside areas necessary for a species' recovery as well as its protection.[90]

When federal agencies do have responsibility for some aspect of animal rights policy, they often find themselves at the mercy of conflicting political winds and pressures from other actors. In cases under the Animal Welfare Act, for example, the U.S. Department of Agriculture (USDA) has been buffeted with directives from Congress, courts, presidents, and interest groups. The most recent chapter in that story concerns a 1994 suit brought by a zoo visitor against the USDA, challenging its regulations concerning treatment of nonhuman primates on the grounds that conditions of confinement did not assure "the psychological well being of primates." In 1998, the U.S. Court of Appeals for the District of Columbia gave the zoo visitor legal standing to sue the government to try to force it to issue regulations assuring chimpanzees "companionship" through group living arrangements.[91] In 2000, however, another federal court of appeals ruled that the regulations were valid and that animal welfare organizations did not have standing to raise the procedural inquiry (see *ALDF v. Glickman*).

Not only the courts but Congress can act to constrain bureaucratic discretion. One example was the 1990s controversy over the USDA's power to regulate the transportation, purchase, sale, housing, care, handling, and treatment of animals under the Animal Welfare Act. Specifically, the conflict was over a 1972 USDA policy that exempted mice, rats, and birds (which account for 95 percent of all experimental animals) from regulations under the AWA. In 1994 several animal rights groups, including the Animal Legal Defense Fund, won a federal court ruling that the USDA's exclusion of rats, mice, and birds was "strained and unlikely."[92] However, an appeals court made that decision moot after ruling that the animal rightists had no legal standing to sue since they could not demonstrate that their members were directly harmed by the regulations.[93] After several more court battles, the USDA signed a pact with animal rights groups, agreeing to draft new caging and care rules. Outraged biomedical groups argued that the new regulations would drain millions of dollars away from research accounts. With pressure from these biomedical groups, Congress delayed the rules after Senator Thad Cochran (R-MS) blocked the USDA rule through a legislative rider added to an agricultural appropriations bill. A year later, Congress reversed itself again, when Democrats took control of the Senate, and the USDA was ordered once more to begin writing the regulations, though the agency was still barred from finalizing any rules for more than a year. Months later, in 2002, Senator Jesse Helms (R-NC) added yet another amendment to a huge agriculture bill, excluding rats, mice, and birds from AWA coverage.[94] Despite the pitched political battle by individuals and interest groups on both sides, the Helms amendment did become law, declaring congressional intent to be that rats, mice, and birds were not protected under the Animal Welfare Act.[95]

Although the USDA found itself in the middle of the AWA controversy, bureaucratic agencies of the federal government generally have quite limited jurisdiction over animal protection policy, mainly because the states continue to exercise most of the power over this policy area. Besides the USDA's responsibility for AWA enforcement, the Marine Mammal Protection Act confers jurisdiction over whales, dolphins, sea lions, and seals to the Department of Commerce. As well, the USFWS, within the Department of the Interior, has the stated mission of conserving, protecting, and enhancing fish and wildlife and their habitats for the continuing benefit of the American people. The USFWS is thus primarily responsible for migratory birds, endangered species, certain marine mammals, the National Wildlife Refuge System, wetlands, conserving habitat, and controlling environmental contaminants.[96] In carrying out its responsibilities under the Endangered Species Act, the USFWS maintains a list of those species determined to be threatened or endangered; once an animal or plant is listed, all protective measures authorized by the law are applied. The USFWS also oversees some hunting activities, though animal activists argue that the agency is heavily influenced by hunting interests. The federal government spends more than $500 million a year to support hunting and, according to animal activists, most of the money is used to artificially increase the number of game animals available for hunters to kill.[97]

Public Opinion

The public is generally supportive of the animal welfare and protection aims of the animal rights movement. A 1994 poll showed that 65 percent of respondents reported having a very favorable or mostly favorable view of the animal rights movement,[98] and 67 percent of respondents in a 1995 Associated Press poll agreed (strongly or somewhat) that an animal's right to live free of suffering should be just as important as a person's right to live free of suffering.[99] According to that same poll, 59 percent believe it is always wrong to kill an animal for its fur, 51 percent believe it is always wrong to hunt an animal for sport, and 46 percent say it is never right to use animals to test cosmetics. More recently, 62 percent of respondents to a 2003 Gallup poll would go so far as passing stricter laws to regulate the treatment of farm animals, and 71 percent said that they believe animals are entitled to some protections from harm and exploitation. In that same poll, however, just 25 percent of the respondents believed that animals deserve the same rights as people.

These poll results demonstrate that once the issue of animal "rights" is raised, public support drops dramatically. Indeed, those favoring fundamental change have learned that reforms that go beyond requiring "humane" treatment of animals are too extreme for most Americans. Questions about the use of animals in scientific research have been extremely controversial and demonstrate this point well. The public, although ambivalent about science, sees a link between animal research and improved public health. When human interests are directly pitted against animal interests, the public is unwilling to go along with what is viewed as extreme animal rights views.[100] Depending on the wording of the question, anywhere from 50 percent to 80 percent of the American public expresses support for animal research.[101] This level of support constitutes a decline of roughly 10 to 20 percent from fifty years ago, when the first national poll on the topic found an 84 percent approval rate for "the use of live animals in medical teaching and research."[102] This decline may be attributed to a change in the degree of confidence that the public has that laboratory animals are treated humanely. In 1948, three-quarters of the American public believed that medical schools treated laboratory animals as well as individual owners would; by 1989, however, only 33 percent of the public thought that animals used in medical and pharmaceutical research were treated humanely.[103]

The degree of public support for research involving animals also varies dramatically with the circumstances. While a 1989 national opinion poll commissioned by *Parents* magazine found that 58 percent of respondents felt that it was acceptable to use animals for medical research, the same poll found that support increased to 78 percent if animal research was "the only way we could find a cure for AIDS."[104] Support for animal experimentation, similarly, is highest when the animal is a rodent or seen as being very dissimilar from humans but lowest when the animal is a dog or cat, both common household pets, or a great ape.[105] Public support also fluctuates depending on the amount of pain the research entails for the animal.[106] Even with these variations, however, polls consistently suggest that animal research is supported by a large majority of the public and that calls for the abolition of animal research are far more radical than the viewpoint expressed by most Americans. Seventy percent of respondents in the 1995 Associated Press poll, for example, believed that the use of animals to test medical treatments is always right or right under some circumstances, and 71 percent of respondents in a Research America poll agreed that the use of animals in medical research is necessary for progress in medicine.[107]

An even harder case for the animal rights position involves the use of animals for human consumption. While "pragmatist" animal rightists have garnered some mainstream support in opposition to the steel leg-hold traps that produce fur and the cruel treatment of animals in factory farms, the fundamentalist position—calling for an abolition of all commercial use of animals—has failed miserably. The fundamentalist position would mean an end to cheeseburgers and leather belts, thus requiring drastic changes in the consumption habits of millions of people. When 92 percent of respondents in a national poll report eating meat, poultry, or fish frequently (71 percent) or occasionally (21 percent), it is clear that the position of animal rightists is much more intense than that of the public at large.[108] As Jeanne Williams argues:

> Since we live in an era of liberation movements, when one group after another has tried to claim the moral attention of the world, it is not surprising to find a mass movement that makes similar claims on behalf of animals, utilizing the same ethical arguments that previous groups have used. Still, the idea that legal rights can be extended to animals continues to strike many people as excessive, and the movement, despite its vigorous growth over the past two decades, has found it difficult to sway public opinion, except on a handful of popular issues such as the wearing of fur.[109]

Extreme tactics—from break-ins and property destruction to animal liberations and personal attacks on scientists—also separate animal rightists from the general public. Only 7 percent of respondents in a 1990 nationwide survey said that they agreed with the animal rights agenda and strategies.[110] For mainstream America, even absolutist rhetoric can significantly diminish the credibility of the movement as a whole:

> The fundamentalist impulse of the movement, its absolutist and uncompromising position, runs the risk of going too far, losing contact with the very sentiments that inspired its rapid growth. . . . And potential supporters of animal rights are especially alienated when activists deny moral distinctions between human and animal life by rhetorically comparing Holocaust victims to chickens, or Downs Syndrome children to chimps.[111]

Sometimes even nonfundamentalist groups like PETA make the mistake of pushing too hard, as when PETA in 2002 claimed that feeding meat, milk, and eggs to children constituted child abuse.[112]

The key to understanding animal rights policy making is found in one simple truth: even though humans and chimps share 99.4 percent of DNA, most Americans believe not only that humans are substantially different from nonhuman animals, but that humans are superior. Whenever the interests of humans come into conflict with the interests or even the lives of animals, therefore, there is little public support for the notion of animal rights. Fishermen have been known to kill endangered or protected species such as the brown pelican or sea lion pups because they will go after baited hooks,[113] and towns such as Auburn, New York, have conducted crow-shooting tournaments because the birds leave their droppings on sidewalks, cars, and park benches.[114] The city council of West Hollywood, California, has even proposed a ban on the declawing of cats—an apparently extremely painful and radical surgery that is the equivalent of removing everything from the bottom knuckle to the end of the finger, including muscle, tendon and bone—even though people do not like cats clawing up their sofas.[115] Probably Mayor Rudolph Giuliani of New York City summed up popular sentiments best when in the summer of 2000 he criticized environmentalists for blocking the city from spraying pesticides to battle West Nile virus: "The reality is that danger to human life is more important than birds, fish and insects."[116]

Summary of Propositions

1a (single-issue groups): Supported, because animal rights organizations are all single-issue groups.

1b (absolutist politics): Supported, with respect to the fundamentalist animal rights groups, but less so with the pragmatist variety or with the traditional animal welfare organizations who are more willing to compromise for limited goals.

2a (judicial activism): Unsupported, because federal courts mainly interpret federal statutes and monitor federal implementation rather than displace the political branches with judicial policy directives.

2b (incorporation): Unsupported, because federal courts have not recognized animals as having legal rights.

3a (presidential symbolism): Supported, because presidents and presidential candidates make few, if any, statements about animal rights.

3b (partisan presidents): Unsupported, although one might hypothesize that Democratic presidents are more sympathetic to environmentalism, which includes endangered species legislation, than Republicans.

4a (Congress and states): Unsupported, because Congress enacted the animal protection statutes that federal courts litigate and, moreover, most states also have enacted animal welfare laws.

4b (Congress and elections): Supported, because Congress has taken steps only to protect endangered species (and only as a result of public pressure), not to enact the more radical position of animal rights.

5a (opinion and ideology): Supported, because public opinion is liberal in supporting many animal protection measures but does not subscribe to the radical animal rights agenda.

5b (law and society): Supported, because targeted populations are unwilling to accept decisions that weigh animal welfare as being more important than human welfare.

6a (federal agencies): Supported, because only three federal agencies play any role in enforcing animal protection laws.

6b (federal implementation): Supported, because any controversial decision by a federal agency will be subjected to cross-pressures from outside political forces on both sides.

7a (federalism): Supported, because states are the primary governmental jurisdictions to regulate animal welfare.

7b (compliance): Supported, to the degree that federal-state-local cooperation is involved in the administration of certain federal laws—for example, designating natural habitats for endangered species.

For Further Insight Into the Animal Rights Debate

Free, Ann Cottrell, ed., *Animals, Nature and Albert Schweitzer*. Washington, DC: The Flying Fox Press, 1982. Relies on the writings of Nobel Prize–winning doctor

Albert Schweitzer to explore the paradoxes of the man-animal-nature relationship and Dr. Schweitzer's "reverence for life."

Morris, Desmond. *The Animal Contract: An Impassioned and Rational Guide to Sharing the Planet and Saving our Common World*. New York: Warner Books, 1990. Argues that humans have betrayed their fellow species in the quest for progress and urges an "Animal Bill of Rights."

People for the Ethical Treatment of Animals. *Unnecessary Fuss*. Edited videotapes stolen from a laboratory where researchers, studying severe head injuries in baboons, are portrayed bantering and joking about injured animals who do not appear to be fully anesthetized.

Planet of the Apes. Director: Franklin J. Schaffner, Twentieth Century Fox, 1968. This movie illustrates how anthropomorphism is a common theme in popular culture, as humans and animals (in this case, apes) exchange roles.

Singer, Peter. *Animal Liberation: A New Ethics for Our Treatment of Animals*. New York: Avon Books, 1975. This book was the catalyst for the emergence of the animal rights movement.

www.animallaw.info. This Web site for the Animal Legal and Historical Center of Michigan State University, DCL College of Law, contains legal materials from all governmental levels in the United States, foreign national law, international documents, and *The Animal Law Review*.

www.nabr.org. Web site for the National Association for Biomedical Research, dedicated solely to advocacy for the humane use of animals in medical research, provides the group's philosophy as well as information on lab animal issues and services for members.

www.peta-online.org. Web site for PETA provides its philosophy, action alerts, current animal rights campaigns, vegetarian recipes, and links to other relevant sites.

Death Penalty

Just Punishment or Legalized Homicide?

Brent S. Steel and Mary Ann E. Steger

In August 1982, the bodies of three strangled and sexually assaulted women were found south of Seattle, Washington, near the banks of the Green River. The discovery of these bodies led to a task force to hunt for the "Green River Killer." Almost twenty years later, on November 5, 2003, a fifty-four-year-old truck painter named Gary Ridgway pleaded guilty to murdering these three women and an additional forty-five women over a sixteen-year period. By committing these forty-eight murders, Ridgway became the worst serial killer in the history of the United States. When asked why he killed the women, many of whom were prostitutes, Ridgway responded: "I hate most prostitutes. I did not want to pay them for sex. . . . I also picked prostitutes as victims because they were easy to pick up, without being noticed. I knew they would not be reported missing right away, and might never be reported missing." Ridgway also commented that he targeted prostitutes "because I thought I could kill as many as I wanted without getting caught."[1] Although Ridgway was convicted in a state with the death penalty (that is, Washington), he will not be put to death because of a plea agreement between defense attorneys and prosecutors requiring him to plead guilty to the forty-eight murders and to help locate the bodies of four of his victims. Ridgway was sentenced to forty-eight consecutive life sentences in prison without any chance of release and a $480,000 fine ($10,000 for each women he admitted to killing).

Is this plea agreement a just outcome for the nation's most prolific serial killer? Or should Ridgway have received the ultimate punishment and be put to death? Although no one can deny the horrific nature of these crimes, there are deep differences in opinion evident in this country concerning the use of the death penalty in such cases. Supporters of the death penalty, such as conservative commentator Allan Bormel, have criticized this plea agreement as follows: "What message are we sending to murderers and potential murderers? You can rape and kill as many as you want and if caught just withhold information—dangling a tantalizing morsel—and a deal is yours. You can take life, but your life will be spared so law enforcement can clear some unsolved cases."[2]

Opponents of the death penalty, such as Judge David Nicols in Washington State, offer a very different perspective: "My purpose is not to criticize the process, which brought Ridgway to his guilty pleas. It is rather to exhort the citizens of Washington to accept the reality that the death penalty as a response to any criminal behavior no longer has validity and should be repealed, because it is impossible to administer with justice and fairness . . . with its repeal, we would stop its inequitable application, the unconscionable costs associated with its administration, and endless appeals."[3]

The use of the death penalty in the criminal justice system remains quite controversial. As illustrated above, some people argue that putting the convicted criminal to death is justified by the heinous nature of the crime and is morally defensible. Opponents argue with equal force that no crime justifies the taking of a life by the state and that the process is fraught with potential error and inequitable application. The conflict surrounding capital punishment is framed by differing interpretations of the rights that are in question. One interpretation is that society and the victims of crimes deserve to receive a sentence of death when the legal system has determined that the nature of the crime committed demands such a sentence. Critics argue that justice is never served by imposing a sentence of death on persons convicted of serious crimes because such a sentence violates the moral principle of universal human dignity.

Debating the Causes of Crime

The debate over the rightness or wrongness of capital punishment is fueled by a profound disagreement about the causes of crime. The "sociogenic" school focuses on the environment and places primary responsibility for crime on society.[4] Poverty, lack of education, high unemployment, unstable homes, the absence of affection, and improper socialization into social norms are cited as causes of crime. The sociogenic approach reflects a liberal political ideology.

The "psychogenic" school is a psychological approach that considers the individual's propensity and inducement to commit crime.[5] That propensity is determined by the individual's ability to conceptualize right and wrong, to manage impulses, to take risks and anticipate their future consequences. Inducement refers to situational factors, such as access and opportunity, that act as incentives to crime. According to this view, the individual is responsible for his or her behavior because a choice is made whether to commit a crime. This view underlies conservative thought and explains why the view's advocates favor severe penalties (such as capital punishment) thought to deter individuals from making the wrong choices. A third approach is the "biogenic" or "sociobiological" explanation. This view is less common among criminologists but has been popularized by political scientist James Q. Wilson. This school relates criminal behavior to such biological phenomena as brain tumors, endocrine abnormalities, neurological dysfunctions from prenatal and postnatal experiences, and chromosomal abnormalities.[6] Preventive crime policies would entail the development of appropriate screening and other diagnostic tests for persons suspected of such physical or mental disorders.

Those who believe in the sociogenic school are less likely to be supporters of the death penalty than those who adhere to either the psychogenic or biogenic schools of thought. They do not view the individual as primarily responsible for his or her criminal behavior and, therefore, do not see a death sentence as an effective deterrent to capital offenses. Instead, they tend to favor a civil libertarian approach that emphasizes the rights of individuals accused of crimes. Those who view criminal behavior as a matter of individual choice (the psychogenic school), in contrast, are likely to see capital punishment as an effective deterrent, because individuals decide whether or not to commit a crime by calculating the degree of risk involved in the commission of a crime versus the prospect of being caught and punished. The psychogenic school supports law-and-order policies that protect the public order by imposing swift, severe punishments on those who commit capital offenses. Those adhering to the biogenic school may or may not view capital punishment as a deterrent to crime, but they nonetheless may feel that capital punishment is the appropriate punishment for individuals who cannot be cured of their criminal predispositions. The primary emphasis would be on preventive policies that identify those who are biologically predisposed to commit gruesome crimes before they do so.

Death Penalty in the United States

The death penalty has been used in the United States for centuries. There were 162 executions performed by local authorities in the 1600s, and in the

1700s the number of executions rose to 1,391. The number remained quite high, reaching 1,005 during the 1880s, 1,280 executions in the first decade of the twentieth century, and 1,289 during the 1920s.[7] Executions continued to increase through the 1930s, with a one-year high of 199 executions occurring in 1935. There were over 100 executions a year through the decade of the 1950s.[8] In the decade of the 1960s, the constitutionality of the death penalty became an issue, and most executions stopped after 1967 pending the outcome of various legal challenges to capital punishment. From 1930 to the end of 1970, however, "there were 3,859 executions under state or federal authority (and another few hundred under military authority)," and "forty-two of fifty U.S. states had a death penalty statute at some time and executed at least one offender."[9]

One Supreme Court case that directly affected the nationwide death penalty moratorium was *Furman v. Georgia* 408 U.S. 238 (1972). Ruling that some states had capital punishment statutes that were unconstitutional, the Court's written opinion provided guidelines for revising these statutes. At that time, 645 convicted criminals were on death row. But just four years later, the Supreme Court cleared the way for the renewal of capital punishment executions in *Gregg v. Georgia* 428 U.S. 153 (1976) and its companion cases, by ruling that the newly revised death penalty statutes were now constitutional. Executions resumed in January 1977.

From January 1977 until September 1990, 140 individuals were executed in the United States. While that number of executions was low, still larger numbers of felons had been sentenced to death. As of September 1990 "there were 2,393 persons on state death rows, ranging from a high of 324 in Texas to 2 in Connecticut, New Mexico, and Wyoming."[10] In 2002, 71 murderers were executed in the United States and another 3,557 were living on state death rows across the nation.[11] This striking disparity between the number of felons sentenced to death and the number executed is a major issue in the debate over capital punishment. Supporters of the death penalty argue that the number and length of postconviction appeals remove the possibility that capital offenders will be swiftly punished (so that their executions will serve as a deterrent) or punished at all. Opponents see postconviction appeals as important last chances to protect the rights of convicted felons, especially when there is some question whether constitutional protections were provided for these felons in their trials.

There are several types of appeals available in death penalty cases, including the direct appeal to the state supreme court, the petition for certiorari to the U.S. Supreme Court (a request for the case to be heard by the Supreme Court based on issues raised in the direct appeal), and habeas corpus appeals, which raise issues that go beyond the trial record, including "newly discovered evidence, fairness of the capital trial, impartiality of the jury, tainted evidence, incompetence of defense counsel, and prosecutorial misconduct."[12] It is very difficult, however, for a prisoner to get a habeas corpus claim considered and even more difficult to secure relief, because prisoners must meticulously follow all the procedural barriers.[13]

The Equal Justice Initiative of Alabama, an organization that litigates on behalf of death row prisoners, believes that death row appeals are extremely important to protect the rights of capital offenders. It reports that 70 percent of the death sentences imposed between 1976 and 1982 were reversed by federal courts due to "fundamental constitutional violations."[14] The federal courts corrected the constitutional errors committed in capital cases tried in state courts. In the 1980s, however, the Supreme Court started to restrict postconviction reviews and to relieve federal courts of the burden of ensuring that fairness prevailed in the growing number of state death penalty cases. This trend led a spokesperson for the Equal Justice Initiative to say:

> In the past ten years the Rehnquist Court has clearly tired of the idealistic expectations raised in the seventies. The decade has seen a strengthening of the inverted notion that due process, equal protection of the law and reliability in criminal case adjudications are not nearly as important as finality when a state wants to execute someone. . . . The consequence of the Court's continuing retreat in capital jurisprudence has been a modern death penalty that is no more predictable, fairly applied or nondiscriminatory than the death penalty the Court stuck down in *Furman* almost twenty-five years ago.[15]

A disturbing fact about capital punishment in the United States is that African-Americans are overrepresented among the inmates on death rows across the nation. Although African-Americans constitute only 13 percent of the total population of the United States, 44 percent of the prisoners living under sentences of death in 2002 were black, 54 percent were white, and another 2 percent were self-identified as American Indian, Asian, or Hispanic (the majority of the Hispanic prisoner population is included in the categories "black" and "white").[16] Of the 885 prisoners who were executed between 1977 and December 5, 2003, 57 percent were white, 35 percent were black, 7 percent were Hispanic, and 2 percent were listed as "other" (Native American, Alaskan Native, Asian, and Pacific Islander).[17] The implications of these disparities are summarized by the U.S. General Accounting Office: "In 82 percent of the studies [reviewed], race was found to influence the likelihood of being charged with capital murder or receiving the death penalty, i.e., those who murdered whites were found more likely to be sentenced to death than those who murdered blacks."[18]

Public Opinion

Public opinion on capital punishment is affected by beliefs about the causes of crime. For law-and-order proponents, the death penalty is a favored public policy because it is seen as a curb on violent crimes and a just punishment (an eye for an eye). This emphasis is expressed by those who look to the Bible, notably the Old Testament, to justify their position. For those individuals who have a law-and-order perspective, a sentence of death for serious offenses is an appropriate, necessary, and morally justified criminal penalty. Those holding civil libertarian beliefs, on the other hand, tend to argue that government has the moral responsibility to protect human dignity. These civil libertarians are more likely to favor government policies that extend and protect the rights of those accused of capital offenses so that the accused have every opportunity to prove their innocence and escape the death penalty.

Deterrence and Revenge as Justifications

There has been substantial support in the United States during the past forty years for the death penalty, and the percentage in favor of capital punishment is quite high (Table 4.1). In 1953 just over two-thirds of the American public favored the death penalty for murder. This figure declined by 1965 to only 45 percent. Support for the death penalty increased through the 1970s and 1980s, with 72 percent of Americans in 1985 saying that they were in favor. The Gallup Poll of 2003 found 71 percent expressing support for capital punishment, a 9 percent drop in support from the 80 percent reported in 1994.

Gallup found major differences in support for the death penalty when controlling for race, gender, partisanship, and ideology. Whites, men, Republicans, and conservatives were much more supportive than blacks, women, Democrats, and liberals. There were also slight geographical differences, with support highest in the South and West followed by the Midwest and the East. Sociological research suggests four factors that increase public support for the death penalty. Data from the 1974–1998 General Social Survey found that "residents of areas with higher homicide rates, a larger percentage of blacks, and a more conservative political climate are significantly more likely to support the death penalty."[19]

While most of the populace support the death penalty, many also believe that it is often unfairly applied. A 2001 Gallup poll found that 65 percent of the respondents agreed that a poor person is more likely than a person of average or above average income to receive the death penalty for the same crime. Also, 50 percent believed that a black person is more likely than a white person to receive the death penalty for the same crime.[20] A 2001 Harris

Table 4.1

Public Support for the Death Penalty for a Person Convicted of Murder

Year	Favor	Oppose	Depends/ no opinion
2003	71	26	3
1995	77	13	10
1994	80	16	4
1991	76	18	6
1988	79	16	5
1985	72	20	8
1981	66	25	9
1978	62	27	11
1976	66	26	8
1972	57	32	11
1971	49	40	11
1969	51	40	9
1967	54	38	8
1965	45	43	12
1960	53	36	11
1957	47	34	18
1953	68	25	7
1936	61	39	NA

Sources: Gallup Poll Monthly, no. 357 (June 1995); *The Gallup Poll: Public Opinion 1995* (Wilmington, DE: Scholarly Resources, 1996). Question: "Are you in favor of the death penalty for a person convicted of murder?"

poll found that 94 percent of Americans believe that innocent people are sometimes convicted of murder and only 42 percent believe the death penalty deters crime, the lowest level recorded by Harris over the past twenty-five years.[21] As with other national polls, however, the Harris poll found quite strong support for the death penalty even though the public is aware that capital punishment may not be "fairly" applied across society.

There is evidence that this support would decline dramatically if life imprisonment without any possibility of parole were a certainty for murderers. A Gallup poll in 2000 showed that, when given the option of life imprisonment without the possibility of parole, the percentage of Americans favoring the death penalty drops to 52 percent.[22] Support for the death penalty drops dramatically when the murderers are children. A 2003 poll by the Pew Research Center for People and the Press found that 35 percent of respondents supported the death penalty for murderers under eighteen years of age, while 58 percent were opposed.[23]

When pollsters ask people who favor the death penalty for their reasons, the most common answer is revenge—an "eye for an eye" (Table 4.2). In a

Table 4.2

Reasons for Favoring the Death Penalty Among the U.S. Public, Gallup Polls 1985, 1991, and 2003 (in percent)

	1985	1991	2003
Revenge: an "eye for an eye"	30	50	37
Acts as a deterrent	22	13	11
Murderers deserve punishment	18	NA	13
Costly to keep murderers in prison	11	13	11
Keeps murderers from killing again	9	19	7
Removes potential risk to community	7	NA	NA
Judicial system is too lenient	NA	3	NA
All others	13	11	31
No opinion	2	2	2

Sources: Gallup Poll Monthly, no. 357 (June 1995); *The Gallup Poll: Public Opinion 1995* (Wilmington, DE: Scholarly Resources, 1996). Question asked of those who favored the death penalty: "Why do you favor the death penalty for persons convicted of murder?" *The Gallup Organization: Jeffrey M. Jones*, "Understanding Americans' Support for the Death Penalty), 2003 (www.gallup.com). Question: "Why do you favor the death penalty for persons convicted of murder?" (Open-ended.)

Note: Totals add to more than 100 percent due to multiple responses.

2003 Gallup poll, 37 percent of the public said that their primary reason for supporting capital punishment was revenge, a decline from 50 percent in 1991 yet higher than the 30 percent reported in 1985. Revenge as justification for capital punishment was given some legitimacy by the Supreme Court. Justice Potter Stewart, writing in *Gregg v. Georgia* 428 U.S. 153 (1976), stated that "capital punishment is an expression of society's moral outrage at particularly offensive conduct." Justice Stewart went on to say, "Retribution is no longer the dominant objective of the criminal law . . . but neither is it a forbidden objective nor one inconsistent with our respect for the dignity of men." In this case, Justice Stewart wrote the majority opinion, which condoned the use of capital punishment as retribution when grievous crimes were involved.

Impact of Economic Considerations

Opponents of the death penalty may ask how much is vengeance worth? It costs several million taxpayer dollars to ensure that those convicted of capital offenses are put to death. Capital trials are complex, time-consuming, and more costly than other types of criminal trials during each stage of the legal process—pretrial, jury selection, trial proceedings, and appeals proceedings. A competently conducted capital trial is preceded by a thorough criminal investigation that takes three to five times longer than those conducted in noncapital cases. Additional costs are incurred when the investigation uses forensic scientists, polygraphers, mental health professionals, and medical experts. Pretrial motions in capital cases are usually numerous and complex, and these cases typically involve the filing of two to six times as many motions as noncapital cases. For example, it is estimated that the plea for life imprisonment by Gary Ridgway, the "Green River Killer" saved the local county $16 million of projected court costs (on top of $10.9 million it spent investigating, prosecuting, and defending him).[24] There are those among the general public who would prefer to spend the tremendous sums of money needed each year in capital cases on programs designed to prevent or reduce crime. Thus opponents of the death penalty might raise a related question: "By focusing on punishing a few individual offenders, are we merely diverting attention and resources away from fundamental structural reforms that address the causes of violent crime?"[25]

Judiciary

The *Furman* case established guidelines for redrafting state statutes on capital punishment. The revised state statutes were expected to (1) have the support of a substantial majority of the people in the state; (2) provide statutory guidance and direction so that the decision to use the death penalty would not be made by jury or judge arbitrarily or capriciously; and (3) apply only to the most severe crimes and not to those crimes where the sentence of death would be grossly disproportionate and excessive punishment. The majority in *Furman* held that capital punishment was not "cruel and unusual in and of itself" but that the arbitrary manner in which it was being implemented by the states did constitute cruel and unusual punishment. *Furman* invalidated the death penalty statutes of the federal government and forty-one states, but most of the states involved rewrote their policy on capital punishment and followed the Supreme Court's direction in doing so. In July 1976 the Court reinstated the constitutionality of the capital punishment statutes it reviewed in the case of *Gregg v. Georgia*. The majority opinion stated that the new statutes contained "objective standards to guide, regularize, and make rationally reviewable" the process by which the death penalty was imposed, and these state policies became the model for the many states that rewrote and enacted their death penalty statutes.

Procedural Justice for Those Convicted of Capital Offenses

Because the Eighth Amendment to the Constitution forbids "cruel and unusual punishments," capital punishment has been prohibited for some crimes such as rape (*Coker v. Georgia* 433 U.S. 584 [1977]). In several cases the Court has imposed limits on the use of capital punishment. For crimes such as premeditated murder where suitable appeal rights have been observed, the Court permits states to administer the death penalty in pursuit of justice (*Gregg v. Georgia*). The Court has further ruled that persons who participate in robberies in which a killing occurs may not be put to death if they themselves did not kill or intend to kill the victim of the crime (*Edmund v. Florida* 458 U.S. 782 [1982]).

The 1986–1987 term of the U.S. Supreme Court represented the inauguration of the Rehnquist era of the high court. One major ruling issued by the Rehnquist Court in 1987 involved a challenge to Georgia's death penalty law on the grounds that statistical evidence showed that killers of white victims received death sentences more frequently than did killers of black victims. In *McCleskey v. Kemp*, 107 S. Ct. 1756 (1987), the Supreme Court turned back that legal challenge in a close 5–4 vote, arguing that statistics showing race-related disparities in the imposition of the death penalty were not enough to sustain constitutional challenges to existing capital punishment laws. When applying the death penalty to juveniles, the Supreme Court had previously decided that the emotional and mental state of the juvenile offenders must be taken into consideration (*Eddings v. Oklahoma* 455 U.S. 584 [1977]). But in 1989 the high court allowed states to execute the mentally retarded and youth who were sixteen years of age when they committed their crimes. The majority opinion in both cases reasoned that the age and mental factors did not "establish the degree of national consensus that this Court has previously thought sufficient to label a particular punishment cruel and unusual."[26]

The Supreme Court under Chief Justice Warren Burger also began chipping away at the number and length of appeals by death row inmates. Prior to the 1980s, lawyers for a death row inmate might initiate numerous postconviction appeals, and each appeal would result in a stay of execution while the petition was pending. Each time an inmate was within hours of being executed, a new appeal would be filed, with the hope that another stay of execution would be granted. The case of Anthony Antone illustrates the delay produced by postconviction appeals. In 1982 this inmate came within twelve hours of being put to death in Florida when a federal court halted his execution after appeals were filed. Two years later the Court refused to block Antone's execution, and he was electrocuted in January 1984.[27] Signaling a new direction, in 1983 the Supreme Court, allowing the state of Florida to execute Robert Sullivan, stated that "[t]here must come an end to the process of consideration and reconsideration."[28] In announcing this decision, Chief Justice Burger indicated that the Court's patience with postconviction appeals had run out when he accused Sullivan's lawyer of making "a sporting contest" of the criminal justice system.

In 1988 newly appointed Chief Justice William H. Rehnquist named former Justice Lewis F. Powell Jr. to head a committee of judges to study the process by which death penalty sentences were reviewed on appeal. In a speech to the American Bar Association convention, Powell reported that only about a hundred executions had been carried out since the Supreme Court had upheld the constitutionality of the death penalty and that the numerous appeals were the reason that so many death sentences were prevented from being carried out.[29] Postconviction appeals were still contentious eight years later, when the Supreme Court agreed to decide the constitutionality of the Anti-Terrorism and Effective Death Penalty Act of 1996 only nine days after the legislation was signed by President Bill Clinton. It enacted significant restrictions on the right of death row inmates to seek review of their convictions in federal courts and imposed "new high standards, tight time limits, and stringent restrictions on successive appeals."[30]

Other 1996 rulings held that indigent inmates on death row do not have a constitutional right to a lawyer in a second round of appeals in state courts and that capital punishment in the military was constitutional. The first ruling meant that poor death row inmates would not be able to effectively challenge their death sentences through multiple appeals. Since the appeals process results in the death sentence being set aside in as many as two-thirds of these cases, this ruling may increase the number of executions in the future.[31] At issue in the second case was the separation of powers between the judiciary and the presidency. In 1984 President Ronald Reagan had issued an executive order bringing the death penalty provisions of the Uniform Code of Military Justice into conformance with the Supreme Court's *Furman* guidelines for capital punishment statutes.[32] In June 1996 the Court validated Reagan's executive order, meaning that the eight military executions that were pending could go forward.

Two recent cases affect the process and application of the death penalty. In 2002 the high court ruled in *Ring v. Arizona* (No. 01–488) that it is unconstitutional to have a judge, rather than a jury, decide the critical sentencing issues in a death penalty case. Nine states had previously allowed judges to decide whether to impose the death penalty after a guilty verdict by a jury. In 2003 the Supreme Court reversed the death sentence of a Maryland man on the basis of an inadequate defense by his trial attorneys (*Wiggins v. Smith*, No. 02–311). Defendants in Maryland are allowed to include a "social history" report on the background and circumstances of each defendant. Since no such report was prepared, Justice Sandra Day O'Connor, writing for the court, commented that "[a]ny reasonably competent attorney would have realized that pursuing such leads was necessary to making an informed choice among possible defenses, particularly given the apparent absence of aggravating factors from Wiggins's background." The Court concluded that the defendant's attorneys failed to provide him effective counsel and therefore violated his Sixth Amendment rights.

Federalism

States with capital punishment are characterized by a law-and-order perspective, which was apparent in the aftermath of the *Furman* decision. As a result of that ruling, thirty-five states tightened the statutes under which the death penalty would be inflicted. Ten states, including North Carolina, Louisiana, and Oklahoma, met the *Furman* objections by requiring mandatory death sentences for specified offenses, while other states, including Georgia, Florida, and Texas, wrote guided-discretion statutes that allowed the courts to decide whether the death penalty was fair in light of sentences for similar offenses. But *Gregg v. Georgia* and its companion cases rejected the mandatory death penalty statutes of Louisiana and North Carolina while upholding the guided-discretion statutes of Florida, Georgia, and Texas. The justices in the majority agreed that the Georgia law (and the Texas and Florida laws) did not "wantonly and freakishly impose the death sentence; it is always circumscribed by the legislative guidelines."[33] The actions of those thirty-five state legislatures in response to *Furman* evidently influenced some justices, one being Justice Potter Stewart, who in *Gregg* referred to "society's endorsement of the death penalty for murder" and further noted that "a heavy burden rests on those who would attack the judgment of the representatives of the people."

Governors' Actions

Governors opposed to capital punishment can exercise their power to commute the death sentences of inmates on death row. A dramatic example occurred in New Mexico in 1986, when Governor Toney Anaya commuted the death sentences of all five men awaiting execution. He reportedly said that the death penalty was "inhumane, immoral and anti-God."[34] Governor Anaya was ending his four-year term and, during his tenure, had stayed all pending executions. Governor-elect Garrey Carruthers had campaigned on this issue and promised to reinstate the death penalty as soon as he took office. This episode clearly illustrates the moral debate over capital punishment. Anaya believed the policy was immoral; Carruthers retorted that capital punishment was legal in New Mexico and, as governor, he was duty-bound to uphold the law.[35]

A similar conflict occurred in New York State, when the state legislature voted in 1989 to override Governor Mario Cuomo's veto of legislation to reinstate the death penalty. Previously the state legislature had voted to reinstate capital punishment thirteen times in the years since the nationwide moratorium was lifted, but the state's governors—first Hugh L. Carey and then Cuomo—had always vetoed the bills. Opponents of capital punishment supported Cuomo's position, which he explained in an opinion piece published in the *New York Times* just before the override attempt:

> History teaches us that if New York does so [reinstates the death penalty], two things will ultimately prove true. Men and women—mostly poor men who are minority members—will be put to death. History also teaches that while most will be guilty, at least some of the people executed in the name of the people of New York will turn out to be innocent. We have buried such "mistakes" before. If we go back to death, we will again.[36]

New York did not reinstate the death penalty until 1996, during the term of Governor George E. Pataki, who strongly supported the policy. In early 1996, Governor Pataki made extraordinary use of his executive power by removing Bronx District Attorney Robert T. Johnson from a murder case against an ex-convict accused of killing a police officer, because the prosecutor previously had stated that he was opposed to capital punishment. Pataki explained his extraordinary action this way:

> What is in this case clear to me is that the District Attorney, because of his deeply held convictions in this case, was not able to apply the law fairly. . . . The murder of a police officer is an extraordinary act. It threatens the rule of law. It threatens the lives of all of us. It is now subject to the death penalty.[37]

States usually have a well-financed and well-organized bureaucracy to assist the prosecution in capital offense cases. No such bureaucracy exists to support the defense in too many states, including Florida and Georgia. In 1985 Jim Smith, the Florida attorney general, appeared before the Florida Senate Judiciary Committee to argue for funding to hire the lawyers to defend inmates facing execution. Earlier that year, the Florida Supreme Court granted stays of execution to two death row inmates who did not have legal counsel, arguing that an inmate's right to due process was violated if the person was executed without a lawyer. David Von Drehle, in his study of death row inmates in Florida, reported that the state government faced the following dilemma:

> There would be no executions without defense lawyers, and there were no
> more defense lawyers. Florida voters demanded executions—so Florida
> politicians were going to have to solve the lawyer shortage. . . . To please
> pro-death penalty voters, Florida officials were forced to find anti-death
> penalty lawyers. The death penalty was turning out to be a whole lot more
> complicated than anyone had anticipated.[38]

Smith's plea was credible because he was a strong advocate of capital punishment and proposed spending "perhaps a million dollars or more a year
trying to put men into the chair."[39] Smith was granted $800,000 to hire full-
time lawyers, investigators, and secretarial help so that death row inmates
without lawyers for their appeals after the state review could gain representation. The bill quickly cleared the Florida legislature and was signed into
law in June 1985, creating a new state agency—the Office of Capital Collat-
eral Representative (CCR).[40]

On first glance, the CCR might be considered a due process–civil libertarian agency, but this was not why it was funded by the state legislature. The
rationale that persuaded the legislators clearly reflected law-and-order thinking. Smith warned the senators that, if they did not fund the agency and
provide lawyers for death row inmates, capital punishment would end in
Florida. He noted that Florida had executed eight men in 1984 and specu-
lated that this figure might double in 1985 if the CCR was in place. As Smith
put it: "The people of this state want capital punishment and I think we ought
to provide the resources to make it happen."[41] Smith's argument was effective because Floridians and their elected state and local officials strongly
supported the death penalty. Florida was a national record-holder in the numbers of executions and inmates on death row.

Georgia is another state with disproportionate numbers of executions and
inmates on death row. Georgia also generously funds the prosecution in capital
cases and underfunds the defense. In 1996 Human Rights Watch reported
that there was no statewide, independent public defender system in Georgia.
Providing defense lawyers for poor defendants is the responsibility of county
government, and most counties simply appoint lawyers from the local bar
association who are in private practice. According to Human Rights Watch,
this leads to the following situation:

> The lawyers appointed may not want the cases, may receive little compen-
> sation for the time and expense of handling them, may lack any interest in
> criminal law, and may not have the skill to defend those accused of crime.
> . . . The lawyer defending the indigent accused in a capital case may not
> have any investigative and expert assistance to prepare for trial and present

a defense. As a result, the poor are often represented by inexperienced lawyers who view their responsibilities as unwanted burdens, have no inclination to help their clients, and have no incentive to develop criminal trial skills."[42]

To improve this situation, Georgia has established the Multi-County Defender office, which was placed within the Georgia Indigent Defense Council. The Multi-County Defender office was to provide specialists to serve as defense counsel in capital cases, but the office has been consistently underfunded. There are "usually over one hundred capital cases pending pretrial in Georgia at any one time," yet the office has not had the resources to hire more than four attorneys.[43] The U.S. Supreme Court's ruling in *Gideon v. Wainwright*, 372 U.S. 335 (1963), requires all states to provide counsel to indigent defendants—including those accused of capital offenses—up through their direct appeals to the highest state court. But there is no constitutional right to legal representation in postconviction cases beyond appeal to the highest state court. Georgia provides neither a statutory right to counsel in capital postconviction cases nor state compensation for representation. Poor defendants must rely on volunteer lawyers if they are available.

Probably the most dramatic event concerning the death penalty involved Illinois. Illinois reinstated the death penalty in 1977, and over the next twenty-two years twelve men were executed while thirteen others were freed from death row based on evidence that they were wrongly convicted. For that reason as well as heightened media attention, Governor George Ryan imposed a moratorium on executions and denounced his state's "shameful record of convicting innocent people and putting them on death row."[44] Ryan then appointed a commission to investigate the Illinois justice system. The commission produced a report indicating many problems, including coerced confessions and evidence based purely on the testimony of jailhouse snitches. These problems led Ryan to comment: "I'm concerned about the whole criminal code we have in Illinois. There is without question a lot of people sitting in prisons today that didn't commit the crimes they are there for." Governor Ryan subsequently commuted the sentences of 157 inmates on Illinois's death row on January 31, 1999. While there is much speculation about why Ryan commuted those sentences—including allegations that he was deflecting public scrutiny from federal investigations of corruption during his tenure as secretary of state—he was widely criticized by the law enforcement community and conservatives and praised by death penalty opponents, including Nelson Mandela of South Africa.

The Illinois moratorium was followed by Maryland, where Governor Parris Glendening in 2002 imposed a moratorium on the death penalty pending a study of potential racial bias in its application. Other states, including Arizona, Connecticut, Delaware, Nebraska, North Carolina, Pennsylvania, Tennessee, and Virginia, also undertook studies, and several states passed legislation prohibiting the execution of mentally retarded defendants (e.g., Arizona, Connecticut, Delaware, Florida, Idaho, Illinois, Missouri, Nevada, Utah, Virginia). Recently Indiana enacted a prohibition on the execution of juveniles, which brings the total number of states prohibiting such executions to sixteen.

Some states without moratoriums are questioning the manner in which inmates are executed, an issue that came to a head with the execution in Florida of Pedro L. Medina on March 26, 1997. Medina was executed by electrocution, and when the power was turned on, the leather mask that he was wearing burst into flames, which lasted for several seconds. A reporter wrote that "the unexpected spectacle left many among the two dozen witnesses visibly shaken . . . but the state doctor in attendance said he thought the death had been instantaneous and painless."[45] Lawton Chiles, the governor, said, "I have not thought it was cruel and unusual punishment. . . . If [the state's seventy-four-year-old electric chair is] not working properly or can't work properly we'll have to see what we can do."[46] Arguing that Florida's form of execution violated the prohibition on cruel and unusual punishment, death penalty opponents also maintained that problematic executions were not all that unusual when lethal injection, a supposedly humane method, was used.

Comparing the Death Penalty Across States

Relatively few death row inmates were executed after the death penalty was renewed, but many more prisoners live on death rows under the sentence of death. By 1983 the number of prisoners on death row, mostly in Florida, Texas, and Georgia, was 1,050, and more than 40 percent of these felons were black.[47] By December 2003 the number of inmates on death row rose to 3,557, and there have been 885 prisoners executed since the nationwide moratorium was lifted in 1976 (34 percent of those executed were black). The states with the most executions are geographically located in the Southeast of the United States, whereas the states that have not executed prisoners or have no death penalty are mainly located in the Midwest and New England (Table 4.3). Population seems a minor factor since the two largest states, Texas and California, only execute approximately 3 percent of prisoners on death row while some small states, such as Oklahoma have many more executions than larger states, for example Illinois. Most states that reinstated the death penalty did so during the late 1970s, but Kansas and New York did not do so until the 1990s. States use a number of means of execution, including

Table 4.3

State Executions in Death Penalty States as of April, 2003

State	Number of people executed since 1976	Death penalty reinstated in
Texas	300	1974
Virginia	87	1975
Missouri	60	1975
Oklahoma	59	1973
Florida	55	1972
Georgia	32	1973
South Carolina	28	1974
Louisiana	27	1973
Alabama	26	1976
Arkansas	24	1973
North Carolina	23	1977
Arizona	22	1973
Delaware	13	1974
Illinois	12	1974
California	10	1977
Nevada	9	1973
Mississippi	6	1974
Utah	6	1973
Ohio	6	1974
Washington	4	1975
Pennsylvania	3	1974
Nebraska	3	1973
Maryland	3	1975
Kentucky	2	1975
Montana	2	1974
Oregon	2	1978
Colorado	1	1975
New Mexico	1	1979
Wyoming	1	1977
Tennessee	1	1974
Kansas	0	1994
New York	0	1995
South Dakota	0	1979
Indiana	0	1973
New Jersey	0	1982
New Hampshire	0	1991
Connecticut	0	1973

Source: "Capital Punishment Statistics," Bureau of Justice Statistics, U.S. Department of Justice. www.ojp.usdoj.gov/bjs

electrocution, the gas chamber, lethal injection, hanging, and a firing squad, and many states include multiple forms of execution in their state statutes.

Generally the states pursue a law-and-order, high-efficiency approach to crime and punishment. Mandatory minimum sentencing laws requiring prison sentences for certain serious offenses are quite common, and a number of states are using determinate sentencing and elimination of parole in order to "toughen up punishments." Such actions proceed from law-and-order assumptions that the punishment should fit the crime and that persons convicted of serious crimes must not get off easy through release on parole. In terms of efficiency, however, most states are now looking for alternatives to imprisonment because imprisonment is expensive, given federal standards for human incarceration. Some states are experimenting with such programs as community-based corrections and expanded work-release opportunities. Not all state politicians fit the stereotype of being "unenlightened about justice policy and advocating a narrow law-and-order posture," as indicated by a study of Illinois legislators. It concluded that they were

> quite diverse in their criminal justice ideology . . . [though manifesting] a pronounced conservative strain in their thinking, trumpeting the importance of crime control and advocating stiff prison terms aimed at effecting deterrence, incapacitation, and retribution. Yet they also evidenced an affinity for elements of the traditional liberal agenda. . . . [by agreeing] that crime has causes rooted in social inequality . . . that rehabilitation is an important goal . . . that prisons should be reasonably humane, and that community corrections is an idea worth exploring.[48]

American Indians and the Death Penalty

Until 1883 Indians arrested for the murder of another Indian were under the sole jurisdiction of tribal governments if the murder took place in Indian country (the reservation lands under the control of the many American Indian nations within the boundaries of the United States). American Indian felons were not, at that time, turned over to the jurisdiction of the U.S. federal courts. This principle was affirmed by the U.S. Supreme Court in 1883 in the case *Ex Parte Crow Dog*, 109 U.S. 556, which acknowledged the exclusive criminal jurisdiction of American Indian tribes over Indian people as an integral component of tribal sovereignty. Two years later, the U.S. Congress passed the Major Crimes Act of 1885, which extended federal jurisdiction to cases occurring in Indian country that involved certain major crimes (e.g., murder, rape, manslaughter, kidnapping, and assault with a dangerous weapon) in which American Indians were both the perpetrators and the victims.

A year later, the 1885 act was challenged as an unconstitutional infringement on tribal sovereignty, but the Supreme Court rejected that argument. Some legal scholars argue that sentencing American Indian felons to death by federal courts is inconsistent with the principle that a person has a right to a trial by a jury of one's peers, in addition to the fact that the death penalty is considered repugnant and barbaric by many Indian peoples. That ruling was ironic because enactment of the 1885 act was viewed as a tool for bringing the law of "civilized" society to tribal nations, who were assumed to be lacking in both law and governance.[49] In 1994 the Crimes and Criminal Procedures title of the U.S. Criminal Code was amended to include the following special provisions for Indian country:

> Notwithstanding sections 1152 and 1153, no person subject to the criminal jurisdiction of an Indian tribal government shall be subject to a capital sentence under this chapter for any offense the Federal jurisdiction for which is predicated solely on Indian country . . . and which has occurred within the boundaries of Indian country, unless the governing body of the tribe has elected that this chapter have effect over land and persons subject to its criminal jurisdiction.[50]

This 1994 provision now allows the tribal governments to determine the criminal jurisdiction in capital cases involving Indian people and crimes committed within lands recognized as Indian country.

Interest Groups

The interest groups most prominent in trying to influence the policy debate over capital punishment can be categorized as (1) professional groups, whose members implement the policy, and (2) secondary groups, whose members are extremely interested but are not involved in its implementation. Professional groups include the International Association of Chiefs of Police, the Fraternal Order of Police, the State Patrol and Probation Officers' Association, the National Sheriffs' Association, the National Association of Attorneys General, the National Legal Aid and Defender Association, the American Bar Association, and similar professional associations representing key actors in the criminal justice process. Secondary groups that focus on the moral dimensions of capital punishment are more likely to capture the public's attention. One important way they attempt to influence public policy is through amicus curiae (friends of the court) briefs, which these groups utilize to introduce new points of law, provide expertise, or add jurisprudential arguments to cases on the Supreme Court docket. Twenty-one of the fifty-two cases involving the rights of the accused and convicted accepted by the Supreme Court in its important 1967–1968 term were brought by the National Association for the Advancement of Colored People, the American Civil Liberties Union (ACLU), and the American Jewish Congress. Such amicus activity by groups promoting civil liberties and due process led to the formation of an opposing organization—Americans for Effective Law Enforcement—that provides expert amicus supporting capital punishment and strong law enforcement.

Professional Groups

The U.S. system of adversary justice gives rise to a tripartite division of labor—prosecutors, defense counsel, and judges—within the criminal justice system.[51] Judges bear responsibility for managing conflict and must be impartial, fair, and detached from the issues dividing the defense and the prosecution. The professional success and career interests of defense attorneys are tied directly to the interests of the accused, whereas prosecutors tend to identify closely with the law enforcement community because their success depends mightily upon the ability of police to secure damning evidence of the commission of a crime. Thus, these actors align themselves differently on capital punishment, because each actor has a stake in maintaining a legal culture that emphasizes professionalism and appropriate procedures. Stuart Scheingold argues that professionals in the criminal justice system divide ideologically along the same lines as do other citizens, but the former's legal training and organizational responsibilities tend to complicate their values.[52] Criminal professionals who think in liberal legal terms (primarily defense attorneys and some judges) will attempt to maximize the rights of defendants in order to protect them from all forms of coercion, and due-process liberals tend to choose the least onerous and most humane sentences and back away from sentences of death. Moderate conservatives, whom Scheingold expects to find represented among judges and prosecutors, are likely to be comfortable with policies that emphasize either deterrence or retribution. Both are consistent with predetermined sentences based on the seriousness of the crime and the offenders' records. Punitive conservatives who favor heavy sentences that create fear in the hearts of would-be offenders tend to be found in police departments, with some found in the ranks of judges and prosecutors.

The American Bar Association (ABA) is the foremost national organization representing attorneys, with high status, effective organization, and skilled leadership. The ABA often takes public stands on criminal justice issues, as when its representatives give testimony at congressional hearings on proposals to reform the U.S. Criminal Code. The ABA also is involved in the nomination processes for federal judges and promotes legal reform in states. Members of the ABA consider themselves somewhat above the political fray, as impartial experts aiding elected decision makers to achieve worthy goals.

The ABA perspective is legalism, which places the association on the high plane of "a government of laws rather than of men" in the eyes of many governmental officials and much of the U.S. public. The ABA does not take a position either for or against capital punishment, but in line with its foundation of legalism the ABA does have policies that are related to the due process rights of felons in death penalty cases.

The ABA House of Delegates, its policy-making body, has long-standing policies supporting the appointment of competent counsel in capital cases; preserving, enhancing, and streamlining the appeals process (habeas corpus review); and eliminating discrimination in capital sentencing on the basis of the race of either the victim or the defendant.[53] The ABA also opposes the execution of mentally retarded persons and those who were eighteen years of age or younger when they committed their crimes. In 1997 the House of Delegates approved a moratorium on executions that would last until jurisdictions implemented policies to ensure that death penalty cases were administered fairly and according to due process principles:

> Resolved, That the American Bar Association calls upon each jurisdiction that imposes capital punishment not to carry out the death penalty until the jurisdiction implements policies and procedures that are consistent with . . . longstanding American Bar Association policies intended to (1) ensure that death penalty cases are administered fairly and impartially, in accordance with due process, and (2) minimize the risk that innocent persons may be executed.[54]

Secondary Groups

There are a number of single-issue organizations that focus on abolishing the death penalty. The National Coalition to Abolish the Death Penalty links individuals and organizations at the national, state, and local levels, acting as a clearinghouse for information sharing and the development of campaigns organized to fight the death penalty.[55] The Southern Coalition on Jails and Prisons, a single-issue group, desires a freeze on all executions and proposes life sentences, with felons serving a minimum of twenty years in prison without the possibility of parole, as alternatives to executions.[56] A sample of other single-issue groups using Web sites includes Murder Victims' Families for Reconciliation, a national organization of family members of murder victims who oppose capital punishment; Iowans Against the Death Penalty, which seeks to maintain Iowa as a state without capital punishment; Virginians for Alternatives to the Death Penalty, a statewide citizens' organization dedicated to educating the public about alternatives to the death penalty; and various state organizations working to abolish capital punishment, including Death Penalty Focus of California, Oklahoma Coalition to Abolish the Death Penalty, Texas Coalition to Abolish the Death Penalty, and the Washington Coalition to Abolish the Death Penalty.

Anti–capital punishment organizations point to racial bias as a compelling moral reason to oppose the ultimate sanction, as this 1991 statement by the Evangelical Lutheran Church in America explains:

> It is because of this Church's commitment to justice that we oppose the death penalty. . . . Despite attempts to provide legal safeguards, the death penalty has not been and cannot be made fair. The race of the victim plays a role in who is sentenced to death and who is sentenced to life imprisonment, as do the gender, race, mental capacity, age, and affluence of the accused. The system cannot be made perfect, for biases, prejudices, and chance affect whom we charge with a capital crime, what verdict we reach, and whether appeals will be successful.[57]

Multi-issue interest groups also get involved in single-issue politics and policy making by forming subsections of their organizations to focus on these issues. In the 1980s the ACLU had a Capital Punishment Project, whose director was active in a 1988 case involving a fifteen-year-old girl from Gary, Indiana, under a death sentence for stabbing an elderly woman. She became a cause célèbre for death penalty opponents, and even the pope asked for mercy in this instance. What constituted the legal challenge to the Indiana capital punishment statute was that Indiana, at that time, had the lowest age in the country, ten, for the death penalty. A bill was passed in the 1987 legislature to raise that age to sixteen.

The ACLU believes that capital punishment constitutes cruel and unusual punishment and thereby violates the Eighth Amendment to the U.S. Constitution. Execution, says the ACLU, "is a barbaric anachronism and should be abolished" in all its manifestations—electrocution, lethal injection, the gas chamber, hanging, and firing squad. The ACLU has an obvious civil libertarian perspective but also objects to the death penalty on moral grounds. Amnesty International, organized in London in 1961, is an independent worldwide movement that agitates for the release of all prisoners of conscience; fair and prompt trials for political prisoners; and an end to torture, "disappearances," and executions. Its position is that the death penalty is a denial of both the right to life and the right not to be subjected to cruel, inhuman, or degrading treatment or punishment.

Support for capital punishment comes from organizations that support a law-and-order approach to criminal justice and their local affiliates. When

Democratic governor Mario Cuomo fought the reinstatement of capital punishment in New York in 1989, law enforcement groups including the Patrolmen's Benevolent Association and the Metropolitan Police Conference led the counteroffensive in favor of the death penalty. And when New York governor George Pataki, a Republican, removed a prosecutor who was opposed to capital punishment, Pataki was supported by the Patrolmen's Benevolent Association. Organizations representing law enforcement officers, who are most in danger of being killed in the line of duty, especially support the death penalty for murders involving the police.

Congress

Congress plays a key role when crime control problems become national issues. Among the problems that reach the legislative agenda are gun control, organized crime, illicit drugs, hijacking, terrorism, and bank robbery. In 1970 the Justice Department pressed Congress to enact the Organized Crime Control Act, one provision of which "severely restricted the use of the Fifth Amendment by grand jury witnesses."[58] Congress also distributes crime control funds to state and local governments, a prominent example being the Omnibus Crime Control and Safe Streets Act of 1968. Most funds expended in the early years of that program were used by police departments to enhance their crime-fighting abilities, although the program supported a variety of rather liberal and innovative programs that emphasized experimentation in the areas of police–minority community relations and the "diversion of juveniles from the criminal justice system . . . and reforms aimed at more effective policing."[59] One issue on the national legislative agenda in 1974 was airline hijackings; Congress authorized the death penalty for hijackings that resulted in death.

In the 1980s the nation was concerned about drug-trafficking homicides, and again Congress considered the death penalty for certain drug-related murders. Senators who supported capital punishment tried to add the measure as an amendment to an appropriations bill for the Defense Department. Senator Alfonse D'Amato (R-NY), who sponsored the amendment, was not willing to withdraw it and allow the Pentagon budget to pass until he was assured by the Senate leadership that the death penalty provision would come before the Senate later for a separate vote. Opponents of the measure were threatening a filibuster to block any final vote on the budget if the amendment was not removed.[60] The death penalty debate continued into 1989, when the Senate Judiciary Committee sent legislation to the Senate authorizing the death penalty for more than twenty federal crimes, including assassination of the president, murder of a federal official or the official's family, bank robbery resulting in a death, espionage, murder of a foreign official, murder by a federal prisoner serving a life sentence, killing in the course of hostage taking, kidnapping in which death results, and murder for hire.[61] More problematic politically was an amendment that the committee added to this bill providing safeguards against racially biased applications of the death penalty. Sponsored by Senator Edward Kennedy (D-MA), its intent was to require "prosecutors to show by 'clear and convincing evidence' that racial disparities in sentencing are not the result of discrimination but reflect other non-racial factors." But Senator Strom Thurmond (R-SC), chief sponsor of the original legislation, was opposed to the amendment because "such a standard would keep prosecutors consumed with trying to develop race-based statistical evidence to prove that the race of the defendant or victim was incidental to the sentence sought."[62]

Implicit in these arguments is the law-and-order versus due process–civil libertarian debate. Kennedy argued that defendants in capital cases must be protected from the possibility that racial discrimination is a factor in court decisions, a civil libertarian argument, whereas Thurmond opposed those protections because they would hamper the ability of prosecutors to argue successfully for death sentences for persons convicted of capital crimes, a law-and-order argument. In its capital punishment debates, Congress focuses on many of the same issues that surface in Supreme Court deliberations, including imposition of capital punishment on persons under the age of eighteen and on persons who are mentally retarded. In the omnibus anticrime bill of 1994, capital punishment was prescribed for dozens of federal crimes, including treason, genocide, causing a death through a train wreck, lethal drive-by shootings, civil rights murders, and murders committed with a firearm during a federal drug felony. But to reassure the critics of capital punishment so the bill could pass both houses of Congress, these provisions were added to the final bill: "The law barred the federal government from imposing the penalty on persons under eighteen at the time of the offense and on those who are mentally retarded or lack the mental capacity to understand the death penalty and why it was imposed on that person." Another provision barred the execution of pregnant women.[63]

In 1996 Congress debated and eventually passed the Anti-Terrorism and Effective Death Penalty Act. Here the debate over capital punishment focused on a provision that would sharply restrict the ability of death-row inmates to appeal their sentences after they had exhausted their state-level appeals. Supporters wanted to limit prisoners to one habeas corpus appeal in order to reduce the long delays associated with executions, thereby increasing the number of executions that would take place by lessening the odds that death sentences would be overturned through multiple appeals. One observer noted that both supporters and opponents agreed that, if the measure withstood court challenges, it would "drastically accelerate executions by shaving years off appeals of most capital cases."[64] The Washington director of Human Rights Watch, an international human rights organization, was reported as saying that the "legislation not only ignores the international trend away from capital punishment, but also violates the spirit of international norms by proposing to make executions more common and errors in capital cases more likely."[65] When the bill finally passed the Senate in 1996, it was the fulfillment of efforts by congressional conservatives, beginning in Reagan's presidency, to rewrite habeas corpus rules, the only legal avenue open to state death row inmates to obtain a federal review of their cases.

When mistakes involving individuals convicted of capital crimes that they did not commit are uncovered, the debate over limiting the federal death penalty appeals process is renewed. This was the case in July 1996 when three Illinois men who had spent eighteen years on death row for a double murder that they did not commit were set free. Now that federal habeas corpus appeals by death row inmates are restricted to a six-month period after final state court appeals have been completed, others who are innocent yet are convicted will not have the time it takes to prove their innocence, assuming that they have the legal, investigative, and monetary resources to do so. In commenting on this case, Richard C. Dieter, director of the Death Penalty Information Center, reported that "the average length of time between conviction and execution is now about eight years," adding that "the restrictions probably meant that lengths of appeals would fall well below the average time it takes to discover new evidence of innocence."[66]

The latest development occurred in 2003 when the House of Representatives overwhelmingly passed the Innocence Protection Act, one provision in the much larger Advancing Justice Through DNA Technology Act (HR 3214/ S 1700). Partly motivated by the revelations in Illinois, Maryland, Arizona, and other states that convicted murderers were found innocent after subsequent DNA testing, the act would provide $25 million over five years to facilitate and improve DNA testing in federal, state, and local labs. The act would also ensure that convicted offenders could request DNA testing on evidence related to their case, help states provide competent and experienced lawyers at all stages of a death penalty case, and provide those charged with crimes and then proven innocent with some compensation for unjust incarceration. The lead sponsors in the House were both Republicans and Democrats, including the Republican chairs of both judiciary committees, Senator Orrin Hatch (R-UT) and Representative Jim Sensenbrenner (R-WI). The act has cleared the Senate Judiciary Committee by a vote of 12–7, but has yet to be passed by the entire Senate.

Presidency

Presidents occasionally have initiated crime policies and created programs that reflect their beliefs about the causes of criminal behavior and the appropriate crime prevention policies to be pursued. President John F. Kennedy promoted crime policies based on the assumption that lack of opportunity for youths in urban ghettos was the primary cause of much personal and property crime. But Kennedy's response to organized crime was much different, reflecting more fully the law-and-order school of thought that assumed that leaders of organized crime were not "victims" of environmental or socioeconomic factors. But it was during the Johnson administration that crime emerged as a highly visible political issue. Both Kennedy and urban riots of the late 1960s raised the political saliency of violence and crime, and President Johnson was well aware of public sentiment. Johnson's approach, similar to Kennedy's, involved a mixture of law-and-order policies and liberal social programs, notably labeled The Great Society, which included massive expenditures for welfare, education, and training intended to alleviate the causes of crime.

The sociogenic view of criminal behavior espoused by Lyndon Johnson took a backseat to the psychogenic/deterrence approach of Richard M. Nixon. President Nixon represented a complete repudiation of the sociogenic school of thought. Instead, he believed that drug addicts, thieves, and other lawbreakers were rational persons who chose to violate the rules of society and, as such, should be sternly dealt with by law enforcement agencies. Thus Nixon pushed for stringent punishments, saying: "The death penalty is not a sanction to be employed loosely or considered lightly, but neither is it to be ignored as a fitting penalty, in exceptional circumstances, for the purpose of preventing or deterring."[67] Gerald Ford, concerned about everyday street crime, advocated mandatory incarceration for anyone using a dangerous weapon when committing an offense, for people committing serious crimes such as hijacking, kidnapping, or trafficking in hard drugs, and for repeat offenders. But two other aspects of President Ford's crime philosophy were not indicative of a law-and-order approach, namely his preference for rehabilitation of some first-time offenders and his support for building humane prisons that minimized the violence prisoners experience from other prisoners and corrections officers.

With Jimmy Carter, a new emphasis in crime policy became evident. President Carter wanted persons of all economic classes to have "equal access" to justice. As he said in 1978, "Too often, the amount of justice that a person gets depends on the amount of money that he or she can pay. Access to justice must not depend on economic status, and it must not be thwarted by arbitrary procedural rules."[68] Seeking to create an image of U.S. justice as fully representative of the nation's diverse peoples, Carter stressed "special efforts to identify qualified minority and female candidates for judgeships."[69]

Ronald Reagan interpreted his 1980 election victory as direct evidence of a "conservative realignment" in American politics. In his first public speech on crime before the International Association of Chiefs of Police in 1981, President Reagan unveiled his ideological attack on the "social thinkers of the 1950s and 1960s who discussed crime only in the context of disadvantaged childhoods and poverty-stricken neighborhoods" and who "thought that massive government spending could wipe away our social ills." He concluded that speech with the call that only appropriate morals "can hold back the jungle and restrain the darker impulses of human nature."[70] With the exception of Nixon, Reagan's tough law-and-order agenda was unprecedented in recent decades. President Reagan appointed federal judges inclined to favor the prosecution in criminal cases. Moreover, because of the more extensive use of fixed sentences and tougher penalties coupled with more prosecutorial flexibility, during Reagan's tenure there were more persons incarcerated in federal prisons with longer sentences than in the previous administrations of presidents Ford and Carter. Near the end of his tenure, Reagan signed a bill that permitted the death penalty for murderers who had participated in at least two criminal operations involving drugs and for murderers who killed a police officer while committing a crime.[71]

President George H.W. Bush, who continued Reagan's strong law-and-order approach, demonstrated his commitment by supporting the death penalty. In a campaign speech to the Association for a Better New York, he called for the "swift" application of the death penalty to criminals convicted of drug-related murders and he challenged the Democrats running for president to do the same. When reporters questioned him about how executions could be speeded up without violating the due process rights of the convicted, he said, "We've got to find a way. Due process is fine, but we've got to find a way to speed it up."[72] President Bush maintained his tough anticrime stand by favoring mandatory death sentences for murders in drug-related cases and by urging that capital punishment be required (rather than just permitted) in drug cases involving the killing of a federal law enforcement officer.

In April 1995 the Alfred P. Murrah Federal Building in Oklahoma City was bombed and 168 men, women, and children were killed. In response to this tragedy, President Bill Clinton immediately urged Congress to pass counterterrorism legislation. Congress did act the following year and, by signing the Anti-Terrorism and Effective Death Penalty Act into law on April 25, 1996, Clinton authorized both new tools and penalties for federal law enforcement officials to use in fighting terrorism and a limit on habeas corpus appeals by death row inmates to a six-month period after their final state court appeals had been completed. The Clinton administration had not originally sought the time limit on appeals.[73]

Clinton actually implemented the death penalty when he was the governor of Arkansas in addition to his signing, as president, a crime bill in 1994 that made dozens of federal crimes subject to the death penalty. Yet capital punishment was an issue that former senator Bob Dole (R-KS) tried to use against Clinton in the 1996 presidential campaign. During a tour of California's death chamber, Dole voiced a strong law-and-order stand, saying that as president he would push for laws to speed up executions of condemned prisoners and appoint conservative judges who would be tough on criminals.[74] Dole also said that he had tried to speed up executions by proposing legislation in the Senate that limited the time period to one year during which death row inmates could file appeals. Although Dole accused Clinton of being soft on criminals because he on three occasions had vetoed limits on the right of appeal, nevertheless Clinton endorsed the death penalty several times during his presidency.

George W. Bush has been a staunch supporter of the death penalty, both as governor of Texas and as president. During his gubernatorial tenure, there were 152 executions, and very few death sentences were commuted. Bush also defended the Texas legal system as "fair and just" and said there was no need for a moratorium on executions. "As far as I'm concerned there has not been one innocent person executed since I've become governor."[75] Governor Bush vetoed legislation to provide funding for basic indigent defense, calling the bipartisan legislation "a threat to public safety." He similarly opposed bills to institute life without parole and to ban the execution of people with IQs under 65. As Bush once declared: "I'm going to uphold the law of the land and let the political consequences be what they may. If it costs me politically, it costs me politically. . . . I also keep in mind the victims, and the reason I support the death penalty is because it saves lives. That's why I support it, and the people of my state support it too."[76] As president, Bush has continued his strong support of the death penalty and even commented that Saddam Hussein, the Iraqi dictator seized by the U.S. military, should receive the "ultimate penalty" for his crimes against the people of Iraq.

Bureaucracy

As most death sentences are imposed by the states, there is virtually no substantive policy implementation by federal agencies. Presidents who voice strong support for the death penalty, like any policy issue, may try to symbolically engage the federal bureaucracy in order to focus public attention.

Both Reagan and Bush highlighted their support of the death penalty for drug-related murders to showcase the activities of the Drug Enforcement Administration (DEA). The attorney general and the solicitor general can be highly visible spokespersons for the death penalty. In the 1997 trial against the "Unabomber" (who for years had sent mail bombs to individuals across the country), Attorney General Janet Reno announced that the government would seek the death penalty in that case. Attorney General Richard Thornburgh in 1988 publicly supported Reagan's position on expanding the death penalty for federal crimes, including the assassination of senior government officials. Thornburgh said that he believed that the death penalty could serve as a deterrent to capital offenses, and he supported efforts to apply the punishment to cases in which prison guards and senior government officials were killed.[77]

Attorney General John Ashcroft in the second George W. Bush administration has probably been the most outspoken advocate of capital punishment. Ashcroft aggressively pursued the use of the death penalty in all relevant federal cases including in Puerto Rico, which has banned the death penalty since 1929. The Bush administration also sought the federal death penalty in states without capital punishment, a reversal of the Clinton administration's policy, which took into consideration local opposition to the death penalty. Attorney General Ashcroft went so far as to suggest that the "American Taliban" John Walker could have been subject to the death penalty for fighting against the United States.

In championing capital punishment, Ashcroft instructed and, where necessary, overruled federal prosecutors in order to pursue the death penalty. Federal law holds that, when federal and state governments both have jurisdiction to prosecute a crime, the federal government should become involved only in those cases in which a substantial federal interest is at stake. Under Attorney General Janet Reno in the Clinton administration, very few capital cases were prosecuted in states without the death penalty. But under Ashcroft, federal attorneys are instructed to consider the "appropriate punishment upon conviction," which means prosecuting defendants in those states without the death penalty. Ashcroft even personally contradicted a Justice Department report that suggested racial bias in the application of the death penalty, saying, "There is no evidence of racial bias in the administration of the federal death penalty."[78]

In a typical year there are approximately 20,000 murders in the United States with fewer than 300 of the convicted murderers receiving the death penalty. However, with no more than thirty murderers typically being executed in any recent year, most convicted murderers are more likely to die of old age than to receive a lethal injection or electrocution. Nonetheless, the use of the death penalty continues to generate much controversy regardless of the number of executions because it is the ultimate punishment with irrevocable results. We began this chapter by discussing the case of the Gary Ridgway—the "Green River Killer"—who was convicted of killing forty-eight women. Should Ridgway have received the death penalty as just punishment for his crime, or is his sentence of forty-eight consecutive life sentences just because putting him to death would constitute legalized homicide? As we have discussed in this chapter, the answer to this question depends on one's notion of morality.

Summary of Propositions

1a (single-issue groups): The evidence is mixed. Many important groups are professional groups and multi-issue organizations, although there are many single-issue groups that generate public awareness.

1b (absolutist politics): Supported. The very nature of the death penalty—life or death—validates this proposition. Proponents see it as the ultimate penalty for horrific crimes, while opponents believe it is immoral, regardless of the crime, for the state to kill anyone.

2a (judicial activism): The evidence is mixed. Since the 1980s the Supreme Court has restricted postconviction reviews and relieved the federal courts of the necessity to ensure that fairness prevailed in the growing number of state court cases involving the death penalty. In certain tailored situations, however, the courts have asserted the primacy of individual rights.

2b (incorporation): Not supported. Although federal courts regularly are asked to review state laws on capital punishment and have held that sanctioning the death penalty for certain crimes or certain defendants violates the Eighth Amendment, the Supreme Court refused to nullify capital punishment as violating the cruel and unusual punishment clause.

3a (presidential symbolism): It is supported insofar as presidential advocacy of capital punishment is largely rhetorical, although President George W. Bush seems to be more aggressive in his advocacy of the death penalty than other presidents since executions commenced in 1977.

3b (partisan presidents): There is support for this proposition, with a caveat regarding Clinton since he, as governor and president, endorsed and implemented capital punishment.

4a (Congress and states): Not supported, because there is much common ground between Congress, the federal courts, and the majority of states in upholding the constitutionality of the death penalty.

4b (Congress and elections): Supported, by the fact that most voters support capital punishment and Congress increasingly adds more federal crimes that warrant the death penalty.

5a (public opinion and ideology): Supported, because the majority of the public for several decades has expressed conservative views supporting capital punishment.

5b (law and society): Supported, insofar as allegations that racial bias in the criminal justice system targets African-American defendants for the death penalty, but spares whites who commit the same crimes may partly explain why there is more opposition to capital punishment by the NAACP and among blacks who are polled on this question.

6a (federal agencies): Supported, because rarely does the federal government execute somebody for violating a federal crime.

6b (federal implementation): Not supported, because the implementation of capital punishment mandated by a federal court does not involve administrative discretion, though there is flexibility at the prosecutorial stage. The Clinton administration deferred to the sensitivities of states without capital punishment, for example, by not seeking the death penalty for federal capital cases in those jurisdictions, whereas Attorney General Ashcroft pursued the death penalty regardless of state policy.

7a (federalism): Supported, because capital punishment historically rests under the jurisdiction of state government, with the notable exception of the Supreme Court's imposition of a moratorium on executions between 1972 and 1976, during which the states had to redraft their death statutes to conform with judicial guidelines.

7b (compliance): Not supported, because the implementation of federal capital punishment laws does not depend upon state authorities or private decision makers.

For Further Insight Into the Capital Punishment Debate

Bedau, Hugo Adam, ed. *The Death Penalty in America: Current Controversies.* New York: Oxford University Press, 1996. Good overview of the death penalty controversies.

Galliher, John, Larry Koch, David Keys, and Teresa Guess. *America without the Death Penalty: States Leading the Way.* Boston: Northeastern University Press, 2002. History of capital punishment in the United States and the shift by some states away from its use.

Megivern, James. *The Death Penalty: An Historical and Theological Survey.* Mahwah, NJ: Paulist Press, 1997. Good summary of religious issues and the death penalty.

Palmer, Louis J. *The Death Penalty: An American Citizen's Guide to Understanding Federal and State Laws.* London: McFarland, 1998. Excellent overview of the laws and regulations pertaining to the death penalty.

Sarat, Austin. *When the State Kills.* Princeton, NJ: Princeton University Press, 2001. General scholarly assessment of the death penalty and its application.

www.clarkprosecutor.org/html/links/dplinks.htm. This Web site for the Clark County

www.clarkprosecutor.org/html/links/dplinks.htm. This Web site for the Clark County Prosecuting Attorney has more than one hundred links to other relevant Web sites.

www.deathpenaltyinfo.org. Web site for the Death Penalty Information Center, a non-profit organization that provides analysis and information on this issue.

www.law.cornell.edu/topics/death_penalty.html. Web site for the Cornell School of Law Death Penalty Center, which provides extensive coverage of the legal issues.

www.ojp.usdoj.gov/bjs. The Bureau of Justice Statistics, U.S. Department of Justice, is the best source for official death penalty statistics, including the annual report *Correctional Populations in the United States.*

5

Gay Rights

Lifestyle or Immorality?

Margaret E. Ellis

Gay rights, because they involve highly personal notions of sexual intimacy and morality, have become a highly controversial social regulatory policy for both the "moral" conservative and the liberal "accommodationist." In 1986 the Supreme Court upheld the constitutionality of laws criminalizing homosexual sodomy, only to strike down antisodomy laws in a Texas case seven years later. In the short time span between *Bowers v. Hardwick* (1986) and *Lawrence v. Texas* (2003), the United States experienced a remarkable metamorphosis in social attitudes toward homosexuality and the civil rights of gays and lesbians. Public opinion has not proven an insurmountable impediment, for example, in the adoption of state laws that provide protection for gay rights in employment practices and personal privacy.

In April 1993, 300,000 supporters of the gay and lesbian movement converged on Washington, D.C., to protest against oppression based on sexual identity. This demonstration signaled the progress the gay rights movement had made since its beginning with the 1969 Stonewall riots in New York City. In April 2000 the Millennium March on Washington, D.C., took place, but this time with a much different cohort of supporters. In the seven intervening years, the number of organizations and sponsors at both the national and state level had grown tremendously. The issue of gay rights no longer languishes at the margins of the political agenda but is now a major focus of elected officials and their constituencies.

For the participants, these marches marked a call for further legal protections as well as a celebration for the few victories in hand. For many who observed the gatherings, however, the marches represented a collection of misguided individuals who were more deserving of condemnation than legal protection. Opponents of gay rights portray homosexuals as immoral sinners,[1] claim that societal disapproval of homosexuality is justified for the protection of both the traditional family unit and future generations, blame homosexuals for the spread of sexually transmitted diseases, especially AIDS, and assert that homosexuals are disproportionately likely to be pedophiles. This dichotomy of views illustrates the chasm that must be bridged in order to understand the difficulties in dealing with this social issue. Gay rights are not simply a constitutional question. The issue involves the moral structure of society and strains the outer limits of tolerance for those who feel that sexual orientation does not warrant equal protection of the law.

Advocates of gay and lesbian civil rights argue that the only "immorality" in this issue is to define constitutional rights as "special rights" because of one's religious or moral bias against homosexuality.[2] Such a definition deviates from the legal tradition of equal protection and shifts the issue from openness and tolerance to mandating serious legal consequences for such behavior. In a democratic society, if the law of the land reflects the consensus of the majority, then who will determine the morality of that consensus? Many Americans now perceive gays and lesbians as a minority group that deserves legal protection from discrimination. While there are traditional religious arguments that homosexuality is wrong and therefore can be condemned, those arguments are directed at conduct, not at the legality of a certain group enjoying the benefits of life, liberty, and the pursuit of happiness.[3]

Presidency

Although domestic policies and even foreign policies are developed through cooperation between the executive and legislative branches, the political problem often lies in the president's ability to formulate a viable policy that has acceptance among the general public. According to Paul Light, at the start of a term the president often is faced with a large number of campaign promises and is forced to prioritize that policy agenda to a manageable size. By the end of the term, on the other hand, the policy stream is reduced to a trickle and the president's focus turns to reelection.[4] This presidential policy stream provides a partial explanation of the presidential role in gay rights policy making. Policy making is normally considered to be rather pragmatic in that policy should be formulated with an eye toward whatever works, rather than following one ideological or philosophical criterion. One conventional definition within government of what will work is "that which is already working," because an ongoing policy already enjoys public support. Thus, because policy tends to change slowly and incrementally, presidents do not attempt to initiate radical changes in existing policy.

The first time the issue of gay civil rights surfaced in a presidential election was 1980. That campaign, however, did not target votes of gay constituents but rather sought to discredit candidates who openly supported gay rights. The Democratic contenders in the primaries largely supported the homosexual agenda, but the race for the GOP nomination became a contest to see which candidate could be the most staunchly antigay. Reagan positioned himself most advantageously by alluding to the Bible, declaring that "in the eyes of the Lord, homosexuality is an abomination," and left it to George H.W. Bush and John Connally (a former Texas governor and Democrat who became a Republican) to bicker over which legal rights gays should or should not be allowed to exercise. Reagan interjected that the objection to gay rights was not that American citizens should be deprived of their legal rights but that this "alternative lifestyle" was not one society could condone.

The underlying purpose of this campaign debate was not to resolve any issues but to create a significant voting cue for the electorate when choosing between President Carter and his Republican opponent. The conservative wing of the Republican Party converged on the issue of gay rights, focused on the Democratic platform's endorsement of gay rights, and depicted Carter as the candidate of homosexuals. Emphasizing that the next president would have the opportunity to make several Supreme Court appointments translated into the need to protect the country from an overly liberal judiciary that would advance the cause of the gay community. This strategy by the New Right and the Moral Majority did not have much impact on how America viewed the rights of other minority groups, however, because support for women's rights remained strong even as opposition to the gay rights agenda increased.

In 1988 gay rights again influenced a presidential campaign, when Democratic candidate Michael Dukakis, then governor of Massachusetts, refused to pledge himself to signing an executive order banning discrimination on the basis of sexual orientation in federal jobs, though he presented a more moderate position toward gay rights. Republican George Bush deftly took a seemingly centrist position when he answered a questionnaire from the National Gay and Lesbian Task Force with the statement "I believe all Americans have fundamental rights guaranteed in our Constitution."[5] This position, relaxed by comparison with the Reagan agenda, eased concerns in the gay community that the election of yet another Republican president would lead to even more discrimination. The inability of Michael Dukakis to meet this political challenge, along with his other missteps, meant that the votes of many white gay males helped to ensure Bush's victory.

The issue of gays in the military captured the national spotlight during the 1992 presidential campaign when candidate Bill Clinton announced his intention, if elected, to overturn the military's existing ban on gays. Gay rights activists at the 1992 Democratic convention came forward with tremendous support for Clinton, with the potential to be a major constituency since homosexuals numbered more than a hundred delegates. Gay rights groups also donated more than $3 million to the Clinton campaign, ranking them along with the Jewish community, the entertainment industry, and environmentalists as the party's biggest contributors.

Shortly after his election, rumors circulated that President Clinton would remain true to his word and would sign an executive order overturning a long-standing military policy. This decision was apparently made completely without any consultation with military professionals and, therefore, sparked a backlash. A number of highly respected policy experts—military, civilian, Republican, and Democratic—strongly advised against this move, and veterans' groups, including the American Legion and the Veterans of Foreign Wars, criticized the plan. President Clinton eventually agreed to consult with military leaders on how best to make this change, making it very clear, however, that the change would take place. The only negotiable point was the method by which the change would be effected.

Military policy on homosexuality has had a complex history despite the fact that, before the armed forces of the United States were formally organized, gays were bearing arms for the nation. Friedrich von Steuben, a known homosexual, was appointed by General George Washington as the first inspector general of the army. Steuben's contribution to the training and discipline of the troops of the Continental army was credited as indispensable to the success of the Revolution.[6] During the Civil War, both Union and Confederate armies employed homosexual soldiers in battle notwithstanding the existence of regulations prohibiting homosexual acts by soldiers. Excluding homosexuals from the military began during World War I, and during World War II homosexuality was classified as mental illness. Psychiatrists helped formulate regulations barring anybody with homosexual tendencies from serving in the military and setting forth treatment requirements for those persons identified as having the "disease" after joining the armed forces. Dishonorable discharges resulted if psychiatric treatment failed.[7]

This policy remained until 1982, when the Department of Defense instituted a new policy that voided all clauses in the military regulations that would allow the retention of anyone discerned to be homosexual, on the grounds that such individuals would "damage the image of the military in the eyes of the American people, our allies, and our potential adversaries and make military service less attractive."[8] This policy was incorporated into the Uniform Code of Military Justice and remained until 1993, when President Clinton partially lifted the ban.

Clinton's desire to totally lift the ban was quickly characterized as a test of the new president's political power. The polarization of the debate pushed the issue to the top of Clinton's political agenda, forcing Clinton to deal with one of the most sensitive, value-laden issues of the day. Without congressional support and a clear mandate from the electorate, President Clinton backed away from taking full responsibility for this policy reversal, and he decided to send the proposal to the Department of Defense for review and recommendation. Some observers suggested that Clinton's actions had been a symbolic gesture, aimed at gaining the support of a crucial voting bloc, when in reality Clinton learned that it was not politically prudent to make such a controversial decision unilaterally even though that decision was within the scope of presidential authority.

In January 1993, 72 percent of those surveyed believed that homosexuals could effectively serve in the armed forces, but 50 percent did not support Clinton's proposal to lift the ban.[9] By May of 1993, 60 percent did not support the president's position,[10] and opposition within the armed forces increased to 74 percent, including 81 percent who believed violent acts against homosexuals would occur.[11] The 1994 compromise between President Clinton and his military and political opponents was labeled the "don't ask, don't tell" policy. The first version was actually called "don't ask, don't tell, and don't pursue," and it meant that military officials would agree not to actively identify lesbians and gay men in the armed forces. Senator Samuel Nunn (D-GA), who chaired the Armed Services Committee, objected and the final wording omitted the third clause, which was intended to order recruiters not to ask recruits if they were gay, and left this issue to the discretion of the secretary of defense.

In a 1996 study of the "don't ask, don't tell" policy, the Service Members Legal Defense Network (SMLDN) reported that the military had discharged 722 service members for homosexuality in fiscal 1995, an increase of 21 percent over 1994.[12] The Department of Defense reported the discharge of 850 service members for homosexuality in 1996, 997 members in 1997, and 1,145 in 1998.[13] While President Clinton envisioned the policy as creating a "zone of privacy" for lesbian and gay soldiers, the policy has not lived up to its original billing. In February 2000 the Pentagon issued a press release announcing that the rate of discharge from the military for homosexuality was 73 percent higher than the rate in 1993. In response to this increased level of persecution and reports of increased harassment, the Pentagon instituted new training programs to prevent antigay harassment and improper investigations.[14]

Nor did the new policy end litigation by gay and lesbian members of the armed forces. In *Able v. United States,* 88 Fed 1280 (2nd Cir. 1998), a federal district held that the policy violated the plaintiffs' right to equal protection, but this decision was reversed by the Second Circuit Court of Appeals. At the end of 2003 three high-ranking officers—Retired Brigadier General Keith Kerr, Retired Rear Admiral Alan Steinman, and Retired Brigadier General Virgil Richard—revealed that they were gay and called for a repeal of the policy. The three retired officers called "don't ask, don't tell" a failure that, in addition to wasting resources, was creating a hostile and sometimes violent workplace. In 1999, when President Clinton was asked about the success of the law, he commented that, since Congress had enacted the policy into law, it would now be up to the next president to try to get Congress to change the law.[15]

But the next president, George W. Bush, had a more pressing gay rights issue to address during his administration. Beginning with the passage of the Defense of Marriage Act (DOMA) in 1996, which President Clinton signed into law, a politicized conflict surfaced between gay Republicans and their party. Shortly after his inauguration, members of the Log Cabin Republicans, a political advocacy group of gay men and lesbians, attempted to meet with President Bush. Although the group was given a policy briefing in the Old Executive Office Building, President Bush did not meet with the group. Christian social conservative groups, who had also demanded, and got, a meeting with the president, warned him that his reelection could be in jeopardy if he courted what they call the "homosexual lobby." Bush has stated his opposition to giving gays legal coverage that would grant their domestic partners health and tax benefits or to rolling back the "don't ask, don't tell" policy. The executive director of the Log Cabin Republicans, Patrick Guerriero, estimated that a million gay people voted for Bush in 2000.[16]

In an effort to moderate his image on gay rights, President Bush has supported legislation to allow crime prosecutions to weigh a victim's sexual orientation, an issue long supported by the gay and lesbian community. In response to the 2003 decision of the Massachusetts Supreme Court allowing same-sex marriages (not just same-sex unions), however, President Bush publicly declared his support for a constitutional amendment to ban same-sex marriage. Under enormous pressure in an election year from his conservative supporters to address an issue of critical importance to many of his Christian backers, the president called the union of a man and a woman "the most fundamental institution of civilization" that cannot be separated from its "cultural, religious, and natural roots" without weakening society.[17] His declaration immediately ignited a furious debate between conservatives, who applauded it, and gays, who denounced it.

Congress

Following *Bowers v. Hardwick,* 478 U.S. 186 (1986), which upheld state antisodomy laws, Congress began to pursue an increasingly antigay agenda. Senator Jesse Helms (R-NC), conservative and stridently antigay, introduced a number of different legislative initiatives to counter what he (and many others) perceived to be inappropriate legal and political gains by gays. Helms asserted that government has the right not to fund the advancement of a "homosexual lifestyle," giving as justification his belief that government has a duty to protect the public from the seduction and conversion of heterosexuals to a homosexual lifestyle. The opposition did not view gay rights legislation in terms of civil rights but as the imposition of an immoral lifestyle. According to Barry Adam, this backlash was fueled by the belief that laws protecting gays from discrimination would lead to child molestation, gay recruiting, threats to the traditional family, and an overall national gay conspiracy to destroy the moral fiber of this country.[18]

The emotionalism of this argument was fueled by the panic generated by the uncontrolled spread of the HIV virus. The failure of Congress to provide funding for AIDS research during the early 1980s, though later perceived to be a partial cause for the spread of this disease, reflected the widespread viewpoint that the sexual conduct of homosexuals was primarily responsible. Donald Haider-Markel's research on gay rights policy and AIDS policy finds a strong relationship between increased opposition to restrictive AIDS legislation and increased support for gay rights.[19] As the seriousness of the AIDS epidemic and nature of the disease was effectively communicated to the general public, antipathy for gay rights lessened. Both these factors provided the political impetus for Congress to act decisively on gay rights legislation.

During the 1990s the spread of the HIV virus and AIDS became a priority issue for most policy makers. In 1985 the Centers for Disease Control (CDC) began funding programs aimed at changing sexual behavior, including initiatives undertaken by numerous gay organizations across the nation. These organizations provided education materials and other services, including graphic and explicit descriptions of safe sex practices. Private funds were used for producing the most provocative materials[20] and limits were placed on federal funding for materials that might "be judged by a reasonable person to be offensive to most educated adults."[21]

In 1987 Senator Helms introduced an amendment to an appropriations bill to prohibit the flow of any federal funds through the CDC to either private groups or state and local governments that would be used "to provide AIDS education, information, or prevention materials and activities that promote or encourage, directly or indirectly, homosexual activities."[22] Helms's objection was not simply the provision of these educational materials to the general public but rather the alleged promotion of a homosexual lifestyle. Representative William Dannemeyer (R-CA), a staunch opponent of gay rights, warned that it would be beneficial to study how extensively "the movement of homosexuality in America" has changed "the cultural values of our society so that we will accept and equate homosexuality on a par with heterosexual life."[23] Senator Helms observed that "every AIDS case can be traced back to a homosexual act" and, therefore, funding of safe-sex materials would contributed to the spread of AIDS because of the contagiousness of homosexuality.[24] Senator Helms also mentioned that the distribution of the material was ineffective because "the people who are spreading the disease do not pay attention to it anyhow." The literature was also criticized as being pornographic.

Subsequently, the CDC created new funding guidelines aimed at eliminating any material that could be considered obscene and also established a peer review panel of ordinary citizens to approval all materials before they were distributed. These guidelines were ultimately challenged in the courts and found to be unconstitutional. The United States District Court of the Southern District of New York held that the CDC obscenity standard provided no real guidance to AIDS educators and, as such, was outside the statutory authority of the CDC. The vagueness and ambiguity of the guidelines were found to have a chilling effect on the expression of sexual identity in public discourse, resulting in a form of self-censorship by AIDS educators.[25] Freedom of speech affords more reliable support for protecting lesbian and gay rights than other constitutional doctrines.

In the debate over funding safe-sex educational materials, the congressional decision focused on the morality of the homosexual "lifestyle" rather than on the need to uphold constitutional doctrine. The challenge for legislators would be to maintain objectivity in their decision making and to look beyond the current debate, but this perspective is not within the job description of elected representatives. The theory of morality policy making suggests that congressional voting on lesbian and gay issues is driven by partisanship, ideology, religious affiliation, and constituency preferences.[26] The Defense of Marriage Act of 1996 nicely illustrates the morality politics framework.

After the Hawaii state court ruling that favored same-sex marriage in *Baehr v. Lewin,* the overwhelming public outcry caused Congress to act quickly and decisively.[27] The Defense of Marriage Act (DOMA) of 1996 had two purposes: (1) it prevented states from being forced by the full faith and credit clause of the Constitution to recognize same-sex marriages validly celebrated in other states; and (2) it defined marriage as the union between one man and one woman. In May, 1996 Senate majority party leader Robert Dole (R-KS), on the eve of securing the GOP presidential nomination, introduced the Defense of Marriage Act as similar legislation was being introduced into the House of Representatives. Critics questioned the constitutionality of the legislation with respect to the Article IV clause of the Constitution that reads: "Full Faith and Credit shall be given in each State to the public Acts, Records, and judicial Proceedings of every other State. And the Congress may by general Laws prescribe the Manner in which Such Acts, Records, and Proceedings shall be proved, and the Effect thereof." The Supreme Court has ruled that this clause *does* require a state to recognize and enforce valid judgments entered by the courts of another state but has not interpreted the clause in order to limit a state that chooses to impose its own laws over the laws of another state. In light of this critical question, the Supreme Court ruling in May 1996 in *Romer v. Evans* raised serious doubts about the constitutionality of DOMA's definition of marriage, which was intended to negate any possibility of federal benefits for same-sex couples.

The House Judiciary Committee attempted to defuse the constitutional questions by asserting that the federal government had "an interest in maintaining and protecting the institution of heterosexual marriage because it has a deep and abiding interest in encouraging responsible procreation and children."[28] But Congressman Barney Frank (D-MA), an avowed homosexual, repeatedly scoffed at the bill, saying: "This is not the defense of marriage, but the defense of the Republican ticket." In response, Representative Charles Canady (R-FL), who stressed that the federal government should not give an implicit sanction to gay marriage, countered. "What is at issue here is whether we choose to give moral equivalency to same-sex marriage." Congressman Sonny Bono (R-CA), who offered Congressman Frank an unusual personal apology for not opposing the bill, told Frank. "I simply can't handle this yet. I wish I was ready, but I can't tell my son it's okay." To that, Frank replied that he and other gays were seeking tolerance and fair treatment, not approval: "If it bothers people, turn your heads."[29] The bill passed both chambers of Congress with perfunctory hearings and little, if any, consideration of the constitutional issues. In this election year, President Clinton immediately signed the bill, thus depriving the GOP of a powerful wedge issue in the 1996 campaign. In response, moreover, thirty-seven states from 1995 through 2004 passed legislation prohibiting the recognition of same-sex marriage by their courts.[30]

However, in its June 26, 2003, ruling in *Lawrence v. Texas,* the Supreme Court struck down a Texas law that made homosexual sex a crime.[31] Most legal scholars anticipated that the Court, if it struck down the law, would do so on very narrow grounds. But the high court went much further by overturning *Bowers v. Hardwick* (1986). By holding that a prohibition of homosexual relations is a violation of equal protection, the Supreme Court somewhat eroded the argument that same-sex marriage could not be a real marriage because it could not be legally consummated. The language of the opinion also suggests that the justices have accommodated a much broader view of the historical and anthropological background of homosexuality as well as the legal positions of other Western nations. Most importantly, *Lawrence* reflects a new recognition and respect for the human dignity of gays and lesbians.[32]

Judiciary

The constitutionality of a "suspect classification" based upon sexual discrimination is a delicate issue. The question at hand is whether the government can draw legal distinctions between citizens based on their sexual orientation without violating the equal protection clause. The legal arguments tend to revolve around the perception that gay rights differs from other civil rights because gay rights are identified by sexual conduct rather than a state of being. This dichotomy between *behavior* and *identity* drives the controversy about the legitimacy of gay men and lesbians' seeking civil rights protection. Opponents of gay rights term antidiscrimination laws for gays as "special rights" while supporters counter that the protection of civil rights for gays is consistent with the fundamental aspects of full, genuine citizenship.[33]

Much of the conflict between homosexual activists and their foes springs from disagreement over the nature of homosexuality. Gays and lesbians usually allege that their sexual leaning is either an inborn trait or an immutable and healthy psychological condition developed in early childhood. Opponents of gay rights contend that homosexual behavior is acquired or learned from others and, therefore, can be discarded or changed by the individual. This debate has significant political implications because, if sexual orientation is truly inborn and immutable, the argument for broad civil rights protections is valid. If so, then gays and lesbians might be recognized by the courts as a "suspect class," a discrete and insular minority displaying immutable characteristics and lacking political power. This classification would require that any government regulation of gay rights would have to meet the "strict scrutiny" standard of judicial review and be narrowly tailored to address a "compelling" government interest. The application of the strict scrutiny imposes a higher burden of proof on the government and, in all likelihood, would result in much more extensive civil rights protections. On the other hand, if sexual orientation is viewed as sexual preference, the suspect classification would not be forthcoming, nor would strict scrutiny for anti-gay rights actions be required as would be the case when a fundamental right, such as free speech or the right to privacy, is infringed.

Because this question of sexual orientation versus sexual preference remains unanswered, opponents of gay rights continue to argue that homosexuals are asking for "special rights." The argument surrounding special rights is that gay rights represent the efforts of homosexuals to carve out an entirely new area of civil rights law by basing protections for minorities on behavior rather than on immutable characteristics. This line of thinking holds that, since homosexuals already have all the civil rights everyone else has, basing their claim for protection against discrimination based on sexual orientation is unreasonable. The core of this argument is that private sexual activity between consenting adults is not the basis for legal distinctions since everyone is protected by the same rules of fairness and protection from discrimination. Supporters of gay rights quickly point out that, in fact, antigay laws *do* draw a distinction based on the private sexual activity between consenting adults, thereby identifying certain people whom the law treats differently.

The volume of litigation involving gay rights issues appears to be increasing, partly a result of the more routine and more public involvement of gays in economic, social, and political activities but also from the increased salience of the gay rights issue. From 1986 through its 2003 session, the Supreme Court addressed the issue of gay rights more than a dozen times in diverse areas of law.[34] In 1986 the high court first addressed sodomy laws in its ruling in *Bowers,* an issue the justices revisited in the 2003 *Lawrence* case. Following a relatively long period when the Supreme Court did not grant certiorari to any major gay rights case, in 1996 the Court ruled in *Romer v. Evans* that the Colorado state constitution (Amendment 2) violated the equal protection clause by setting gays and lesbians aside as a differentiated group. In contrast, the Court ruled in fourteen major gay rights cases between 2000 and 2003. In 2000 the Court considered the use of student fees at public universities in *Board of Regents of the University of Wisconsin System v. Southworth,* ruling that public universities can use mandatory student fees to support campus groups even though some students may disagree with some groups' views. The case in question involved self-identified Christian conservative students at the University of Wisconsin who objected to a number of groups, one among them being the Lesbian, Gay and Bisexual Campus Center. Also in 2000 the Supreme Court ruled in *Boy Scouts of*

America v. Dale that the Boy Scouts of America can exclude homosexuals from serving in leadership roles. This decision overturned a New Jersey Supreme Court ruling that held the Boy Scouts as subject to state antibias laws. The majority opinion concluded that forcing the scouts to accept a homosexual leader placed an unconstitutional burden on the organization's "expressive purpose."[35]

Rulings in 2001 and 2002 on sex offender information requirements, employer discrimination, the operation of a sex-related business, and California's three-strikes law all had implications for gay rights. Because, in many states, an eighteen-year-old male who has consenting sex with a seventeen-year-old male can be considered a sexually violent predator, identification requirements and mandatory sentencing requirements can affect gays. And because it is a felony in some states for two adults of the same sex to have consensual sex, the fact that twenty-six states and the federal government now have some version of three-strikes laws means that multiple arrests for engaging in sex with a same-sex partner could result in life imprisonment.[36]

By far the most important decision by the U.S. Supreme Court in recent decades is *Lawrence v. Texas*. Legal professionals and scholars alike called the decision "historic and transformative." Suzanne Goldberg, a professor at Rutgers Law School who represented the plaintiffs in the Texas courts, said that the decision would affect "every kind of case" involving gay people, including employment, child custody, and visitation and adoption.[37] The decision was met with much contempt by social conservatives who equated the *Lawrence* decision with the Court's earlier ruling in *Roe v. Wade*, arguing that none of the rights enunciated by the justices in those cases could be found in either the text of the Constitution or the history of jurisprudence. Phyllis Schlafly, president of the Eagle Forum, a conservative group based in St. Louis, remarked that if the Court could overturn a decision like *Bowers,* which was made seventeen years ago, perhaps there was still hope to overturn *Roe.*[38] Gary Bauer, former contender for the GOP presidential nomination and the president of American Values, said, "Once again, an activist Supreme Court has substituted its judgment over the decisions of the citizens of Texas, who, through their elected representatives, had made a moral and legal judgment about behavior."[39]

The argument that the *Lawrence* decision is an indication of a shift in the Court's position on social regulatory policy fails to take into account the exclusiveness of this decision. Texas was one of just four states to apply a criminal felony sodomy law to same-sex partners (the others were Oklahoma, Kansas, and Missouri). Nine other states had criminal sodomy laws on their books, that in theory if not in practice, applied to opposite-sex couples as well as same-sex partners.[40] Few states criminalized only homosexual sex between consenting adults when *Lawrence* was decided whereas, at the time *Bowers* was decided, a majority of the states applied their criminal sodomy laws in this manner.

In *Bowers v. Hardwick,* 478 U.S. 186 (1986), the Supreme Court upheld a Georgia law that made acts of sodomy performed by anyone in any place a crime. The 5–4 decision was one of the most controversial and widely publicized Supreme Court decisions of 1986. The Georgia law had been challenged by Michael Hardwick, a homosexual who had been arrested for acts of sodomy performed in private places, but the high court ruled that there was no fundamental right to engage in homosexual sodomy. This decision was a considerable blow to the gay rights movement, because it meant that the "right to privacy" doctrine would not protect homosexual activities in one's home. Surveys conducted during the 1980s and 1990s showed that about 75 percent of respondents believed that sexual relations between two adults of the same sex were wrong. Since Hardwick had not raised a First Amendment objection to the sodomy laws, the Supreme Court ruled solely on his privacy concerns and, because the Court could not identify the involvement of a fundamental right, it used a "rational basis" standard of judicial scrutiny to uphold the state antisodomy law. The *Bowers* decision was decided by one vote, and much speculation followed about the degree to which the justices applied constitutional doctrine or were influenced by public opinion. The dissenters in *Bowers* admonished the majority for its "almost obsessive focus on homosexual activity" and pointed out that the ruling went against prior decisions upholding the right to privacy.

Ten years after *Bowers,* the Supreme Court ruled in *Romer v. Evans* (1996) that Amendment 2, which was added to the Colorado state constitution, violated the equal protection clause of the U.S. Constitution because it abridged the right of gays and lesbians to participate equally in the political process. Amendment 2, ratified by Colorado voters in a 1992 referendum, precluded all legislative, executive, or judicial action designed to protect the status of individuals based on their homosexual, lesbian, or bisexual orientation or conduct. The Court's 6–3 decision held that Colorado may not "deem a class of persons a stranger to its own laws." Much has been made of the historical significance of this decision, with *Romer* being equated with the landmark 1954 racial desegregation ruling in *Brown v. Board of Education. Romer* was viewed as the first step in that direction for gays and lesbians. For the first time, the Supreme Court ruled in favor of gay and lesbian civil rights by taking a strong moral stance against discrimination. While precedent and doctrine were evoked, the persuasiveness of the argument in *Romer* rested on its moral foundation. Matt Coles of the American Civil Liberties Union (ACLU) said the ruling was the "first time the Supreme Court has said that government cannot justify discrimination simply out of hostility and fear."[41] Though not recognizing gays and lesbians as a suspect class, the Court did find that discrimination based on sexual orientation nullifies specific legal protections for this targeted class in all transactions in housing, sale of real estate, insurance, health and welfare services, private education, and employment. Justice Antonin Scalia filed a forceful dissent, accusing the majority of taking sides in a "cultural war" through "an act not out of judicial judgment but of political will." Justices William Rehnquist and Clarence Thomas also dissented, accusing the majority of "inventing a novel and extravagant constitutional doctrine to take the victory away from traditional forces." Rehnquist later said, "The Colorado Amendment was an eminently reasonable means of preventing the piecemeal deterioration of the sexual morality favored by a majority of Coloradans."[42]

In the 2003 *Lawrence* decision, the Supreme Court held (5–4) that a Texas statute making it a crime for two persons of the same sex to engage in certain intimate sexual conduct was a violation of the due process clause of the Fourteenth Amendment. The state courts, relying on *Bowers v. Hardwick,* had ruled that the statute was not unconstitutional under the due process clause. The opinion in *Lawrence* reflected the shift in public opinion and, again, led to speculation that the Supreme Court was merely responding to changing social attitudes. Writing for the Court, Justice William Kennedy began by addressing the initial substantive statement in *Bowers,* namely whether the Constitution confers a fundamental right upon homosexuals to engage in sodomy, as a "failure of the Court to appreciate the extent of the liberty at stake."[43] His opinion then articulates the liberties defined in the Constitution that allow homosexual persons the right to choose to have relationships in the confines of their own homes and in their own private lives, also citing the abortion decision in *Planned Parenthood of Southeastern Pennsylvania v. Casey* as yet another example of "the emerging awareness that liberty gives substantial protection to adult persons in deciding how to conduct their private matters pertaining to sex."[44]

Federalism

Our system of federalism allows policy makers to choose those issues for which the federal government will accept primary responsibility and to leave more controversial, politically sensitive issues for the states to handle. When an advocacy coalition encounters opposition to gay rights at the federal level, that coalition is likely to move the issue to the state level.[45]

Discrimination in housing, employment, and public accommodations gravely concerns the gay community. When the 1974 attempt failed to amend the 1964 Civil Rights Act to include gays and lesbians in the federal ban on discrimination, the effort to add sexual orientation to antidiscrimination laws moved to the state and local levels. Elaine Sharp points out that, because rights-based federal laws receive minimal attention by the federal government, state and local governments often must implement these policies on their own. Sharp uses the term "culture wars" to describe how implementation of the right to abortion, gay rights, and other highly moralistic issues is forced to the level of local government. State governments are thus relieved of policy innovation while maintaining some discretion over the implementation of the policy by city governments.[46]

Research on antidiscrimination policies for lesbians and gays suggests that states are most likely to adopt these policies when gay interest groups have significant resources, the salience of the issue is low, partisanship is avoided, conservative religious forces can be neutralized, the policy change can be framed as incremental in nature, and the gay community has the support of political elites.[47] The change from twelve years of rule by the Reagan and Bush administrations to the friendlier Democratic administration of Bill Clinton, along with gays' and lesbians' increased political participation at the state and local level and the influx of organized interest group support, created a much more amenable environment for heightened protection of gay rights.

The first gay rights ordinances were adopted in the early 1970s, primarily in university communities such as Berkeley and Palo Alto, California; Boulder, Colorado; Ann Arbor and East Lansing, Michigan; and Austin, Texas. Of the twenty-eight jurisdictions that passed such laws or policies before 1977, eighteen could be classified as college communities. Several cities with sizable and organized gay and lesbian populations, including Detroit, Minneapolis, San Francisco, Seattle, and Washington, D.C., as well as Atlanta, Chicago, Los Angeles, New York, and Philadelphia, adopted gay rights ordinances before 1975. By 1999 forty states had statutes, usually dealing with public employment and housing, that prohibited discrimination on the basis of sexual orientation. Though estimates differ, approximately 150 city and county governments have now adopted sexual orientation nondiscrimination ordinances, although the nature and scope of those ordinances vary widely.[48]

The issue of same-sex marriage has surfaced with intensity since the Hawaii Supreme Court ruling in *Baehr v. Lewin* (1993), the first to declare that state refusal to recognize same-sex marriages would be found unconstitutional absent a compelling state interest to justify the restriction.[49] Soon after *Baehr,* the state legislature responded with legislation defining heterosexual marriage between a man and woman and, the following year, created a Commission on Sexual Orientation and the Law to advise the state of Hawaii on how to treat same-sex couples as a matter of policy.[50] What eventually emerged from these efforts was a Reciprocal Beneficiary Law, under which Hawaiian adults living in partnerships that could not be eligible for marriage (whether same-sex or opposite-sex) could become "reciprocal beneficiaries" entitled to recognition for certain purposes specified in the statute, including employee benefits eligibility for partners of public employees of the state.[51]

In response to the *Baehr* ruling, the religious right organized to lobby states to prohibit the recognition of same-sex marriages. By late 1998, thirty states had adopted policies banning the recognition of same-sex marriage.[52] Then, in December 1999, the Vermont Supreme Court held in *Baker v. State of Vermont* that same-sex couples are constitutionally entitled to all of the protections and benefits provided through law to opposite-sex married couples. The Vermont high court did not consider the issue of the denial of a marriage license for same-sex couples and, rather than order the issuance of marriage licenses to same-sex couples, held that the legislature must remedy the constitutional violation brought about by the denial of this right. The Vermont legislature responded by passing a civil union statute, creating an institution parallel to marriage for same-sex partners.[53] The Vermont civil union law made available to same-sex couples a legal status akin to marriage, and within the next year seven more states and the District of Columbia adopted some form of same-sex union while even more states adopted a partnership registry system. In November 2003 the Massachusetts Supreme Court went even further by legalizing same-sex marriage in *Goodridge v. Department of Public Health,* arguing that any policy short of marriage would be invalid. Despite numerous attempts to block the implementation of this policy, Massachusetts began issuing valid marriage licenses to gay and lesbian couples on May 17, 2004, thereby becoming the first state in the United States to legally recognize same-sex marriage. However, the Massachusetts legislature responded by taking the preliminary step necessary for submitting a constitutional amendment to the electorate in 2006. If adopted, it would sanction same-sex unions but not same-sex marriages in Massachusetts.

Major cities in California, New York, and Oregon began issuing licenses despite provisions in their constitutions that would not allow this action, and thousands of gay and lesbian couples rushed to states where they could get the marriage licenses. Courts in these states have issued injunctions to stop the issuance of these licenses, once again centering the resolution of this moral conflict in the judiciary. Over the past decade, state court decisions have reflected the gradual shift in societal acceptance of homosexuality, and given the time to build support and appropriate legal strategies, gays and lesbians may make great strides with this approach. Presumably, discrepancies between the state laws will lead to federal litigation, but most potential litigants are currently waiting for the outcome of the high court decisions in those states where the issuance of marriage license is being challenged.

However this contentious issue is resolved, the outcome would have a significant impact not only on states but on the interpretation of a wide variety of federal laws. Federal laws where benefits, rights, and privileges are contingent upon marital status include Social Security, housing subsidies, food stamps, veterans' benefits, taxation, civil service and military benefits, employment benefits, immigration, naturalization, and alien laws; trade, commerce, and intellectual property policies; financial disclosure and conflict of interest concerns; crimes and family violence incidents; loans, guarantees, and payments; and federal natural resources law. Although states have retained the sovereign authority to regulate marriage, this authority can be subjected to federal regulation. While state authority to regulate marriage is subject to some constitutional limitations (for example, miscegenation laws were found to be an unconstitutional violation of the equal protection clause), for opponents of same-sex marriage the most expeditious approach to dealing with this issue would be congressional action.

A related question is the ability of gay and lesbian couples to adopt children, which is also under state jurisdiction. In 1997, in response to a lawsuit filed by more than 200 gay couples, New Jersey became the first state to permit adoptions by homosexuals and unmarried couples under state law. While gays and lesbians were able to adopt children individually prior to this policy change, the threat of federal litigation for violation of equal protection rights of gay and lesbian couples persuaded New Jersey to permit this type of adoption. Twenty-two states now allow gays and lesbians to adopt children through state-run or private adoption agencies.

Conservative groups argue that placing children with homosexuals is morally or ethically wrong and could lead to the children either "becoming gay" or being pressured to become gay. The Family Research Council (FRC) maintains that placing babies in gay or lesbian homes deprives the child of a mother's or father's love and that children have the best chance to thrive in "married, mother-and-father-based families." While there may be a growing acceptance of gay or lesbian couples, the issue of adoption by these couples still provokes a decidedly moralistic response. In late 1999, for example, the Oklahoma lower house passed a bill that would have barred joint adoption by any couple—heterosexual or homosexual—living together in any manner "not solemnized as marriage" by state law. (Same-sex marriage remains banned by Oklahoma law.) The bill's sponsor, Republican Representative Tim Pope, commented, "They say you can't legislate morality. Why not? We legislate morality every day of the week!"[54]

Bureaucracy

The agencies that come to mind in respect to issues of homosexuality are the National Institutes of Health (NIH) and the Centers for Disease Control and Prevention (CDC). The obvious reason is their direct role in dealing with the HIV/AIDS epidemic. Most key health and scientific research agencies fall under the umbrella of the U.S. Public Health Service, which is directed by the assistant secretary for health of the Department of Health and Human Services. NIH, CDC, and the Food and Drug Administration are among the agencies that constitute the Public Health Service.

NIH consists of various separate institutes that oversee laboratory research into health matters. Two of the largest institutes at NIH are those involved in AIDS research—the National Cancer Institute and the National Institute of Allergy and Infectious Diseases. There is abundant literature on the struggle to adequately fund these research efforts, showing how both politics and hysteria played a role in delaying any funding to confront that disease. The federal government viewed the struggle as a budget problem; public health officials saw it as a political problem; gay leaders blamed the delay on lack of access and credibility; and the media regarded it as a homosexual problem that did not interest anyone else. Until it was discovered that HIV/AIDS could be communicated through means other than homosexual behavior, it was considered a "gay disease" and, as such, became a morality politics issue.

Morality policies issues are highly salient, with little need for people to acquire any information (technical or otherwise) to participate in the debate. The saga of the HIV/AIDS epidemic is a classic example of how the lack of information can drive public policy in an inappropriate manner and how, once new information is disseminated, policy innovation can undergo a tremendous transformation. Disease can mobilize several types of groups to political activity: those who have the disease, those who have friends or loved ones with the disease, and those who have little personal stake but feel impelled to protect themselves and/or society from the disease. The politics of AIDS involves all three groups, resulting in each group adopting a political position best suited to its own interests and politics.

As early as 1920, congress was conducting investigations at naval training bases to determine the extent to which homosexuals were contributing to "immoral conditions" on the base. In the 1950s members of Congress expanded the debate over homosexuality by linking homosexuality to Communism, calling homosexuals a threat to national security. This specter of a security threat was raised in the context of possible Communist infiltration of the government, as alleged by the 1953 McCarthy hearings. Witnesses testifying at the hearings suggested that homosexuals could be blackmailed by Communist spies and that the enemy's knowledge of such immoral behavior could be used as an espionage tool.

The HIV/AIDS epidemic stimulated profound changes in lesbian/gay politics in the 1980s. The various responses, or lack of response, to the epidemic on the part of government, the insurance and medical-scientific industries, the mass media, and religious leaders clearly brought the gay and lesbian community together to form a massive grassroots movement to galvanize attention on the issue. Through the concerted efforts of the Public Health Service, NIH, and CDC, funding for research to combat this disease was finally procured; since that time, Congress has approved the expenditure of billions of dollars for educational programs, research, and medical care. Between 1987 and 1996, moreover, state legislatures enacted over 200 bills addressing HIV/AIDS-related issues, such as testing, blood bank screening, confidentiality, housing, insurance, prisons, informed consent, counseling, and medication programs.

Such was not the case with the military. By the early 1990s the debate over homosexuals in the military took a different turn. The military remained firmly entrenched in its conviction that homosexuals not only presented a threat to national security and adversely affected the troop morale but also presented a medical risk to other military personnel. Following Department of Defense Directive 1332.14, the military openly and intentionally excluded gays and lesbians from the armed forces in order to "maintain the public acceptability of military service and to prevent breaches of security." The rationale for the ban against homosexuals was based on "military necessity" and the military's singular mission, as stated by the secretary of defense on March 26, 1992, to defend American from enemies foreign and domestic: anything or anyone who interferes with or inhibits the military's ability to accomplish this task threatens America's national security.

Among the most obvious dangers homosexuals allegedly pose for the military is the threat of AIDS. The argument is that, once relieved of the need to restrain their sexual behavior or hide their homosexual tendencies, homosexual and bisexual service members would be more likely to contract HIV and to spread the virus through peacetime training injuries or through the blood supply during wartime. With an increase in AIDS cases among homosexual members, the military could expect a dramatic increase in personnel costs related to medical cases and personnel turnover. And there would be reason to anticipate that the military's generous medical benefits would provide an incentive for increasing numbers of homosexuals to enter the military. The crux of this argument is that, given all these liabilities, homosexuals present a large and unnecessary medical risk to the armed forces. In sum, there is no military necessity to place American service personnel at risk by lifting the ban against homosexuals serving in the armed forces. In February 1996 Congress enacted legislation to require the mandatory discharge of members of the armed forces who tested positive for the virus that causes AIDS. The measure, included in a $265 billion military authorization bill, required the Defense Department to begin ousting HIV-infected personnel regardless of their ability to perform their jobs.

Interest Groups

Although most pressure groups represent interests of direct, material benefit to their members, members of gay rights organizations are also concerned with the principle or morality of the proposed policy. The oldest and best-known gay organization focusing on AIDS is the Gay Men's Health Crisis (GMHC). Founded in 1981 in New York City, GMHC mainly provides AIDS education, counseling, and social services to assist the sick "in much the same way that a family, community, or groups of friends would."[55] The AIDS Coalition to Unleash Power (ACT UP), established partially in reaction to GMHC's lack of political activity, has operated primarily as an "agitator" organization to ring attention and focus on gay rights issues.[56] Lambda Legal Defense and Education Fund is a national organization committed to achieving full recognition of the civil rights of gays and lesbians, and those with HIV/AIDS through "impact litigation" (lawsuits meant to set precedent), education, and public policy work; Lambda remains among the most active and influential of these groups.[57] Currently, the Human Rights Campaign Foundation is the primary sponsor of several nationwide programs designed to increase activism and to promote the advancement of gays, lesbians, and bisexuals on campuses, in the workplace, and in private affairs, primarily focusing on issues affecting the health needs and civil rights of lesbians and gays. State and local groups such as Oregon Right to Pride, the Dallas Gay and Lesbian Alliance, the Massachusetts Gay and Lesbian Political Caucus, and the Southeast Alaska Gay Alliance are also active in large numbers. Since the Stonewall riots of 1969 in New York City, supporters of gay rights have functioned under the interest group model of politics.

Experts identify two main sources of opposition to gay rights: religious conservatives and certain segments of the business community. Gays are perceived as a threat to the social values and cultural dominance of people committed to a particular vision of society. They frequently refer to homosexuality as a violation of Judeo-Christian tradition, leaving the impression that all such religious communities perceive homosexuality to be sinful. The Christian Coalition, the Eagle Forum, and Concerned Women for America are among the most active religiously based groups that regard homosexual behavior as fundamentally wrong and sinful. The Roman Catholic Church differentiates between orientation, which is not considered sinful, and behavior, which is not accepted. Unlike Protestant fundamentalists, however, Roman Catholics do not attempt to "convert" homosexuals to heterosexuality but rather seek to help them adopt a lifestyle the church finds appropriate.

The Christian right is the major force behind the efforts to enact antigay referenda, notably Colorado's Amendment 2 in 1992, which was orchestrated by Colorado for Family Values (CFV). Other such efforts were not successful. CFV's counterpart in Oregon, Oregon Citizens' Alliance, twice failed to gain passage of similar antigay initiatives in 1992 (Measure 9) and in 1994 (Measure 13). In 1995 the Idaho Citizens' Alliance narrowly lost its statewide referendum campaign (the same year that Maine's electorate also rejected a similar antigay measure). Although the center of opposition to gay rights is located in traditionalist religious communities, sole reliance on moralistic and value-laden arguments is not appealing to the general public. Thus, opponents have learned to state their objections not in terms of religious beliefs but rather in terms of "cultural" or "social" traditions. Claiming to be open-minded and tolerant of societal differences, opponents emphasize that they do not want to encourage discrimination but instead want to build a live-and-let-live atmosphere, meaning that although gays can do what they please, the government ought not to give them legal endorsement.

The morality politics model of policy making involves issues that tend to engage religious forces, partisanship, high saliency, and resistance to compromise solutions. The interest group model of policy making, on the other hand, claims that interest groups fare best when they limit the scope of the conflict and discreetly lobby policy makers for public policy. In the interest group model, policy making is determined by interest group resources, supportive elites, incremental adjustments of past policies (like adding sexual orientation to existing antidiscrimination laws), and sometimes the existence of an educated population. While interest group politics has been important to the gay rights movement in previous decades, the morality politics model more aptly describes the long-term prospects for this issue.

Public Opinion

Over the past decades, the ongoing political debates about gay rights have focused on employment nondiscrimination, then gays in the military, and now same-sex marriage. Issues concerning gays and lesbians have received increased coverage in the national media and, as a result, people who had never given much thought to the subject are now gaining new information with which to evaluate old prejudices. Public opinion can change in response to events and new information. Judging by opinion surveys, however, ordinary citizens do not have a high regard for gays and lesbians. To summarize a vast array of past polling material, gays have been perceived as people who choose to pursue an unhealthy and immoral lifestyle and whose code of behavior makes them unfit to occupy some important positions in society. Homosexual conduct is still regarded as "always wrong" by two-thirds to three-fourths of the adult population, and the prospect of contact with gays inspires discomfort among many heterosexuals. Believing that gays are likely to "recruit" or molest children, the public is decidedly hostile to the notion of putting gays in positions of direct contact with children, either as teachers or adoptive parents.

The saliency of same-sex marriage as a public policy issue is reflected in numerous public opinion surveys. Four in ten voters say they would not vote for a candidate who disagrees with them on gay marriage, even if they agree with the candidate on most other issues. By comparison, 34 percent say they would not support a candidate who disagrees with them on abortion, and 32 percent expressed that opinion about a candidate's stance on gun control. Gay marriage may be a personal issue for many people but is a make-or-break issue for true opponents. Supporters of gay marriage generally say that a candidate's stance would not affect their vote but, among gay marriage opponents, the issue has a disproportionate impact on conservative Republicans, evangelical Christians, and voters age sixty-five and older.[58] Despite the broad opposition to gay marriage, the public remains divided over a constitutional amendment to ban the practice. An ABC News/*Washington Post* poll conducted in 2004 showed that 46 percent of respondents support a constitutional amendment while 45 percent believe that it should be up to each state to make its own laws regarding homosexual marriage.[59]

Nonetheless, opinion polls over the past twenty years yield two important shifts in public attitudes towards gays and lesbians. First, only a minority of Americans hold very negative views of gays and lesbians; second, public attitudes have rapidly changed in recent years. Disapproval of homosexual activity reached its peak around 1988 and has been steadily declining since that time. Though it is uncertain what caused this shift, a partial explanation may be the sympathetic depiction of gays and lesbians in the popular media, particularly television. A second explanation may be that personal contact with openly gay individuals has increased in recent years. Regardless of the causes, greater acceptance is rising more among women than men, particularly as women age. The older women become, the more liberal they become, but men do not. That women are much warmer toward gays and lesbians than men is a common finding in the literature.[60]

In the 1970s, the early supporters of gay rights were drawn heavily from three population groups—universities, communities with large gay populations, and communities with many government employees—and the people most likely to support gay rights ordinances were either affiliated with universities or university-oriented. By the 1990s university students accounted for less than half of those who support protection for gays. The political environment surrounding gay and lesbian issues is quite different in the 1990s than during the 1970s. Numerous reasons are given for this change: an attitude of increased tolerance by Americans for all kinds of people, a pronounced shift in the public attitudes against governmental discrimination at any level, and the increased willingness of homosexuals to openly and actively pursue civil rights. Also, gay candidates have gained political power. During the 1998 general election, six openly gay and lesbian candidates ran for election to the U.S. House of Representatives, and three won—incumbents Barney Frank (D-MA), Jim Kolbe (R-AZ), and Tommy Baldwin (D-WI). There were many more successful candidates at the state and local level that year, and this trend has continued into the twenty-first century. There are now more than 200 openly lesbian and gay public officials in the United States.

Changes take place in public opinion incrementally. The adoption of antidiscrimination ordinances for gays and lesbians developed over the course of two decades. Though society still does not give full recognition to homosexuality, the current trend toward giving all citizens equal protection under the law finds the public willing to accept fewer restrictions on gays and lesbians.

Summary of Propositions

1a (single-issue groups): Unsupported, because the gay and lesbian organizations as well as the Christian right are multi-interest groups.

1b (absolutist politics): Supported, insofar as gays demand legal and social equality while the opponents characterize homosexuality as immoral behavior.

2a (judicial activism): Supported, by such decisions as *Romer* and *Lawrence*.

2b (incorporation): Supported, by the Supreme Court reversal of *Bowers* that held state antisodomy laws to violate the due process clause.

3a (presidential symbolism): Supported, because presidential agenda setting rarely goes beyond speech making.

3b (partisan presidents): Supported, for Republicans and arguably supported with respect to President Clinton, though Clinton signed the Defense of Marriage Act of 1996.

4a (Congress and states): Supported, insofar as most states and Congress defended the institution of heterosexual marriage.

4b (Congress and elections): Supported, with respect to the issue of same-sex marriage and arguably regarding gays in the military.

5a (opinion and ideology): Unsupported, by recent surveys showing greater acceptance of gay rights by the American people.

5b (law and society): Supported, in the sense that the gay rights movement has a history of mounting legal and social challenges to laws seen as unjust and unfair to homosexuals.

6a (marginal agencies): Supported, insofar as the key federal agencies involved with the gay community deal with the HIV/AIDS epidemic.

6b (federal implementation): Supported, as evidenced by the battle within the Clinton administration over allowing gays in the military.

7a (federalism): Supported, because heterosexual marriage is defined by state law, but unsupported with respect to extending gays and lesbians coverage under antidiscrimination legislation.

7b (compliance): Supported, because achieving legal and social equality for gays and lesbians would require a concerted effort by states, localities, and the private sector.

For Further Insight Into the Gay Rights Debate

Duberman, Martin. *Stonewall.* New York: Dutton, 1993. Uses personal accounts of six gays and lesbians to chronicle the 1969 police raid on the Stonewall, a Greenwich Village gay bar, which inaugurated the modern gay rights movement.

Marcus, Eric. *Making Gay History: The Half Century Fight for Lesbian and Gay Equal Rights.* Pymble, Australia: Perennial, 2002. The stories of more than sixty people are the means for documenting the struggle for gay rights over five decades.

Shilts, Randy. *The Mayor of Castro Street: The Life and Times of Harvey Milk.* New York: St. Martin's, 1988. Biography of a grassroots organizer from Castro Street, a gay neighborhood, who was elected the first openly gay city supervisor in San Francisco but later assassinated.

The Boys in the Band (stage play and film). Written by Mark Crowley and directed by William Friedkin. When it opened off-Broadway in 1968, it was the first mainstream stage play to break the social taboo of homosexuality and portray gays on their own terms.

The Incredibly True Adventures of Two Girls in Love (film). A lesbian romantic comedy directed by Maria Maggenti about two high school girls who are drawn to each other.

Love! Valour! Compassion! (film). What began in 1994 as an off-Broadway stage production that won a Tony Award for best play by Terrence McNally, is now a film directed by Joe Manello. Its eight characters are gays who face real-world problems in coping with their sexual and platonic relationships.

www.LambdaLegal.org. Web site for the Lambda Legal Defense and Education Fund, the national organization dedicated to equal rights for gays and lesbians.

6

God or Country

Debating Religion in Public Life

Ted G. Jelen

One of the salient features of American politics in the post–World War II era is the frequency with which religious beliefs and values have been voiced in the making of public policy. Religiously motivated activists have played key roles in political struggles over civil rights, foreign policy, welfare, abortion, feminism, and gay rights, to name but a few issues. Not surprisingly, the political expression of religious belief has provoked opposition and countermobilization. Religious activists have not only been criticized for the substantive policy positions they espouse but also because the propriety of religious involvement in the political process itself has been questioned. Some adversaries raise objections to religiously motivated political activity, arguing that politics and religion should be divided by, in the words of Thomas Jefferson, "a wall of separation."[1] This chapter illuminates the issue of church-state relations and accounts for the diverse positions that can be taken on the relationship between the sacred and the secular.

The Religion Clauses

The source of the persistent conflict in the United States over church-state relations is the fact that the relationship between the sacred and the secular is a matter of constitutional principle. Religious freedom is considered so fundamental as to reflect the basic social contract, and its constitutional context involves the following clauses in the First Amendment: "Congress shall make no law respecting an establishment of religion, or prohibiting the free exercise thereof." Termed the "establishment clause" and the "free exercise clause," respectively, they have provided the legal setting within which church-state relations are contested in American politics. This issue has become a problem for our political system because there is little agreement on what the sparse language of the religion clauses mean. The tension over church-state relations results because the establishment clause appears to offer freedom *from* religion while the free exercise clause promises freedom *of* religion.[2]

Establishment Clause

To oversimplify somewhat, there are two general positions with respect to the establishment clause that might be termed accommodationism and separationism.[3] An accommodationist might argue that the proper relationship between church and state is "benevolent neutrality," wherein the establishment clause is interpreted to mean that government is simply prohibited from extending preferential treatment to any particular religion.[4] However, this "nonpreferentialism" stance does not proscribe government support to religion in general.[5] The state is not required to be neutral between religion and irreligion. Accommodationism is based on two important assumptions. First, accommodationists believe that religion has beneficial consequences for the social order. Religion provides a nonarbitrary basis for moral human behavior and thus limits the scope of political conflict.[6] Second, religion is regarded by accommodationists as a source of social cohesion. Differences between religious denominations are confined to distinctions over *doctrine* and do not typically result in different prescriptions or proscriptions about human behavior.[7] In the United States, a "Judeo-Christian tradition" is thought to provide a moral basis for political life, or what Peter Berger has termed a "sacred canopy" beneath which political affairs can be conducted.[8] Religion is thought to perform a "priestly" function of legitimating political authority.[9] This sentiment was voiced by Alexis de Tocqueville in the 1830s, and his words are quoted with approval by many religious conservatives who assert the consensual nature of American religion when applied to political affairs:

> The sects that exist in the United States are innumerable. They all differ in respect to the worship which is due to the Creator, but they all agree in respect to the duties which are due from man to man. . . . Moreover, all the sects of the United States are comprised within *the great unity of Christianity, and Christian morality is everywhere the same.* . . . Christianity,

therefore, reigns without obstacle, by universal consent; the consequence is . . . that every principle of the moral world is fixed and determinate, although the political world is abandoned to the debates and experiments of men.[10]

By contrast, separationists have argued that the diversity of American religions makes religion a dangerous stranger to democratic discourse. Religious belief makes absolute truth claims, which cannot be compromised by believers.[11] James Madison in *The Federalist* No. 10 mentions religion as a fertile source of "faction," which he regards as an important source of political instability.[12] Many analysts, pointing to the sectarian violence experienced in other nations, have contrasted those situations with the religious harmony experienced in the United States.[13] Therefore, separationists see the establishment clause as promoting the depoliticization (or domestication) of religious belief by confining religion to a "private sphere" of activity.[14] Separationists generally view the establishment clause quite broadly, arguing that it prohibits government assistance to religion in *any* form.[15] As Justice Hugo Black stated in his opinion in *Everson v. Board of Education,* 330 U.S. 1 (1947): "The 'establishment of religion' clause of the First Amendment means at least this: Neither a state nor the Federal government can set up a church. Neither can pass laws which aid one religion, *aid all religions,* (emphasis added) or prefer one religion over another." In sum, separationists would prohibit the most general assistance to religion, even if a large majority favored such assistance.

It is not surprising that many accommodationists regard separationism as hostile to religion. A recent collection of essays written from an accommodationist perspective is titled *The Assault on Religion.*[16] However, many separationists are quite religious and regard a strict boundary between the sacred and the secular as beneficial to both spheres.[17] Therefore, separationists believe that the political role of religion is enhanced by strict independence from government assistance. In a religiously pluralistic society, religion is often thought to perform the prophetic role of social critic by reminding the political actors about standards outside the secular realm of politics.[18] This critical role might be compromised if religious bodies depended directly or indirectly on government support.[19]

Free Exercise Clause

There are also two perspectives with respect to the free exercise clause. A. James Reichley offers a distinction between the communalist and libertarian understandings of religious free exercise.[20] Adherents of both positions regard religious *beliefs* as inviolate, but communalists and libertarians differ on the extent to which religiously motivated *conduct* should be protected from government regulation.

Essentially, the communalist view of the free exercise clause involves two assumptions. First, the protection of religious free exercise means that religiously motivated groups can attempt to enact their policy preferences into law. Religious motivations are legitimate warrants or justifications for public policy positions.[21] Second, religious *practices* can be regulated to the extent that they violate the moral or religious sensibilities of popular majorities. From the communalist viewpoint, actions that are otherwise illegal deserve no special protection if they are religiously motivated, because the free exercise clause simply means that government may not single out religious practices for special regulation. The communitarian view of free exercise is quite narrow and substantially qualifies the idea that free exercise is an inalienable right.[22] However, this reading of the free exercise clause is quite consistent with the majoritarian, consensual assumptions that underlie an accommodationist reading of the establishment clause. If one purpose of religion is to promote an ethical consensus on fundamental rules of conduct, it follows that religious groups outside this consensus will pose problems for democratic politics.

A libertarian view of free exercise, by contrast, would believe, with certain exceptions, that religious practices are exempt from government regulation. Unless government can show that a particular religious practice has immediate and harmful consequences (e.g., human sacrifice), a libertarian perspective on the free exercise clause would allow religiously motivated exemptions from otherwise valid laws. Underlying the libertarian view of religious free exercise is the assumption that, under most circumstances, the requirements of citizenship can be trumped by religiously derived obligations. Religion is thought to produce a "higher" obligation that governments are bound to respect.[23]

Frequently, issues are encountered that involve questions of both religious establishment *and* free exercise. Such issues typically arise because modern government provides services that were not contemplated by the Framers of the Constitution. In our era of activist government, one question frequently raised is whether a government service to religious groups constitutes unconstitutional "establishment" or whether withholding those services entails a restriction on the free exercise of religion. In 2002 the U.S. Supreme Court ruled against a college student in the state of Washington who was denied a taxpayer-funded scholarship because he elected to major in theology. State officials denied him the scholarship, arguing that subsidizing his desire to become a minister was an unconstitutional violation of the establishment clause. Others (including the Bush administration) argued that denial of the scholarship represents an infringement on his free exercise rights by making the study of religion more costly than other majors.[24]

Other free exercise claims ask government to liberate religiously motivated citizens from certain obligations of citizenship. During certain periods of American history, the federal government conscripted young men for military service but granted exemptions or allowed substitute service for those people whose religious convictions forbade engaging in warfare. The existence of a legal classification for "conscientious objectors" has typically been justified via reference to the free exercise clause since it is unjust (and unconstitutional) for government to require citizens to violate their religious beliefs. However, it has also been argued that legal provision for conscientious objectors may violate the establishment clause.[25] If religious denominations vary to the degree that they condemn warfare (as they clearly do) and if exemption from the risk of military service has value (as it clearly does), the government may well be discriminating in favor of "peace churches" (Mennonites, Quakers) by allowing their adherents to avoid conscription. Access to the status of conscientious objector might be regarded as a governmentally created inducement to join particular churches, which would violate even a very narrow reading of the establishment clause.[26]

The general point is that there are very real tensions between the establishment and free exercise clauses. If government is active, whether to promote education or raise armies, simple proscriptions against interference or discrimination will be inadequate to guide public authorities. But note that this view of the tensions between the two religion clauses is more characteristic of separationists than accommodationists. Accommodationists are likely to argue that the free exercise and establishment clauses are consistent and mutually supportive,[27] but that interpretation is contingent on a particular (narrow) reading of the establishment clause and typically involves granting one clause (usually, the free exercise clause) priority over the other.[28]

A Typology of Church-State Positions

Because there are varying combinations of perspectives on the religion clauses, it is possible to construct a typology of possible church-state positions (Table 6.1). Each cell represents the trade-off between positions on religious establishment and free exercise. Accommodationists might take either the libertarian or communalist position on the free exercise clause. Those who are also communalists (the upper left-hand quadrant) might be termed Christian preferentialists because they would likely view the establishment clause quite broadly (permitting certain neutral types of government assistance to religion)

Table 6.1

A Typology of Church-State Relations

		Establishment clause	
		Accommodationist	Separationist
Free exercise clause	Communalist	Christian preferentialist	Religious minimalist
	Libertarian	Religious nonpreferentialist	Religious free-marketeer

Source: Ted G. Jelen and Clyde Wilcox, *Public Attitudes Toward Church and State* (Armonk, NY: M.E. Sharpe, 1995), p. 25.

and also would be willing to restrict the free exercise prerogatives of minority religious sects falling outside a presumed cultural consensus. They might regard the United States as being a "Christian nation" or adhering to a "Judeo-Christian tradition." On the other hand, libertarian accommodationists (lower left-hand quadrant) might be termed "religious nonpreferentialists" because they might favor neutral government affirmation of religious values and tolerate the free exercise claims of nonconventional religious groups.

Separationists with a libertarian perspective on the free exercise clause (lower right-hand quadrant) might be termed religious free-marketeers because they support the free exercise claims of all religious groups but oppose government support for or affirmation of any religion. Free-marketeers might favor confining religion to a private sphere of activity, but permitting maximum religious freedom within that sphere. Finally, separationists who are communalists (upper right-hand quadrant) might be considered religious minimalists because they want to minimize the role of religion in public life. They may regard government restrictions on the activities of unconventional or unpopular religious sects as desirable but also may seek to minimize government support for any religious groups, majority or minority. A minimalist position entails the view that religion deserves no special protection and that government should not support religious expression.[29]

Public Opinion

It is unlikely that arcane legal considerations about religious establishment or free exercise penetrate the consciousness of ordinary citizens. Nevertheless, the mass public does appear to have well-formed attitudes about church-state relations,[30] although such attitudes are not necessarily consistent in any logical or ideological sense. This is not surprising, since American attitudes about the relationship between God and Caesar are subject to two conflicting forces. First, Americans are a highly religious people.[31] Relative to citizens of other industrialized nations, the extent of religious belief, affiliation, and practice is unusually high, which means that periodically some citizens are strongly tempted to translate their religious principles into public policy. Second, and conversely, the principle of the constitutional separation of church and state (a phrase that appears nowhere in the U.S. Constitution) is a powerful symbol in American political discourse. While there is little agreement about the precise meaning of church-state separation, the principle itself is generally accepted in American politics.

Public attitudes toward church-state relations can be summarized easily. At the abstract, symbolic level, there exists ample support for the separationist view of the establishment clause and the libertarian view of the free exercise clause, though such support is by no means unanimous. Recent scholarship finds that nearly two-thirds of Americans endorse a "high wall of separation" between church and state, although only about half reject any kind of government assistance to religion.[32] On free exercise, a survey of residents in the District of Columbia area showed near unanimity that "people have the right to practice their religion as they see fit, even if their practices seem strange to most Americans," although support for religious free exercise drops dramatically if the question of lawbreaking is raised. Only 21 percent disagreed when asked if "it is important for people to obey the law, even if it means limiting their religious freedom."[33]

When concrete applications of the religious clauses are raised, public attitudes become more complex. With respect to religious establishment, Americans make distinctions among public displays of religious symbols (such as Christmas decorations on public property), financial support for religious institutions, and religious socialization in public schools. Free exercise attitudes are similarly structured, with respondents distinguishing between religious groups they consider dangerous (e.g., cults, Satanists) and groups considered strange but harmless (e.g., students who seek to wear religious apparel in public schools). Thus, attitudes about concrete applications of establishment issues are organized around an activity-based heuristic whereas free exercise attitudes are structured in terms of group orientations.[34]

Furthermore, there exist systematic differences in church-state attitudes at varying levels of abstraction. Many people appear to be abstract separationists but concrete accommodationists, meaning that they endorse the general principle of church-state separation but express support for prayer in public schools, tuition tax vouchers, and publicly funded nativity scenes. Many Americans seem to be abstract libertarians but concrete communalists with respect to religious free exercise, because they endorse the principle of religious free exercise in the abstract while backing restrictions on a variety of religious practices, such as the ritual use of hallucinogenic drugs by Native Americans, religious solicitation at airports, and released time from work for religious holidays celebrated by minorities, such as Jews.

There is nothing unusual about a disparity between public support for a general principle and public resistance when applying that principle in concrete situations.[35] In this case, the disparity results from a lack of familiarity with the range of possible applications of the First Amendment. Genuine religious diversity is not experienced by most Americans. Focus group data reveal, for example, that some advocates of school prayer change their minds when faced with the prospect that a classroom might include polytheists (e.g., Hindus). In this situation, school prayer advocates concede the difficulty of composing a true nondenominational prayer to accommodate those students but are not willing to rotate prayers to satisfy minority religious traditions. As one focus group participant explained, "I don't want my children praying to Buddha."[36]

In summary, while the symbols of religious freedom and church-state separation receive high levels of support from mass publics, many Americans are quite accommodationist (on establishment questions) and communalist (on free exercise questions). In addition, the Christian Right is a formidable political force at the level of the mass electorate, with approximately one American in six identifying as a "supporter" of the Christian Right.[37] There is a strong pro-Republican voting trend among evangelical Christians who today are among the most reliable components of the GOP electoral base.[38]

Interest Groups

A bewildering array of interest groups makes demands relevant to the relationship between church and state.[39] Some groups are ad hoc, formed in response to the increased salience of particular issues,[40] while single-issue groups (such as Operation Rescue) combine a narrow focus with greater longevity. Still others have more general issue orientations (e.g., Pax Christi, the Christian Coalition).[41] A few groups, such as the American Civil Liberties Union, People for the American Way, and Americans United for Separation of Church and State, are focused on perceived violations of the establishment clause and advocate separationist positions. They tend to confine their activites to legal work and public education,[42] frequently filing amicus briefs in court cases and monitoring legislation and court decisions.

These groups operate at a comparative disadvantage due to the disparity between abstract public support for separationism, but concrete public support for governmental policies that accommodate religion. Even direct mail appeals, presumably sent to group members or sympathizers, often contain detailed explanations of why apparently innocuous policies are subversive of church-state separation. A recent issue of *Church and State* (the publication of Americans United for Separation of Church and State), for example, contained an article detailing why a proposed religious freedom amendment to the Constitution would actually be subversive of religious freedom.[43] Given the tremendous legitimacy enjoyed by organized religion in the United States, separationist groups have the more difficult case to make.

On the other hand, accommodationist groups like the Moral Majority and the Christian Coalition have been able to compete in a wider range of political arenas. While some accommodationist groups, such as the American Center for Law and Justice, focus on litigation to counteract the activities of separationist groups, the Christian Coalition has lobbied legislatures at all levels of government and participated in election campaigns.[44] The actual effectiveness of religious interest groups is the subject of some dispute. Matthew Moen argues that, while the Christian Right has fallen short of its earlier goal of transforming American politics, Christian Right groups have penetrated state and local party organizations and have achieved some notable legislative successes.[45] The Christian Coalition, having shifted its focus from national politics to the state and local level, has been quite effective in influencing city councils and school boards.

The political maturation of the Christian Right has been accompanied by a shift in interest group rhetoric. Early pronouncements of the New Christian Right tended to emphasize the language of religious establishment, as when Jerry Falwell, in his 1980 book *Listen, America!,* argued that the United States is a Christian nation and that God would hold the nation collectively responsible for the moral corruption that, in his view, characterized American culture.[46] Falwell also argued that political elites had established a belief system, termed "secular humanism," that was the practical equivalent of religious establishment.

By contrast, more contemporary representatives of the Christian Right have cast their public appeals in the language of religious free exercise. Both Ralph Reed (until recently the executive director of the Christian Coalition)[47] and Stephen Carter[48] attempt to show how certain government policies inhibit the free exercise of religious belief and practice in the United States. Many policies, seemingly fair and reasonable at first glance, might violate a libertarian understanding of the free exercise clause. For example, it has been alleged that legislation prohibiting discrimination against gays may violate the free exercise clause by forcing Christians into social and business interaction with persons with whom they are religiously forbidden to associate.[49]

Also, proponents of school prayer now emphasize its "voluntary" nature and argue against allowing school authorities to persecute the expression of religious beliefs.

Accommodationist groups have come to eschew specific religious doctrines in favor of arguments that emphasize secular and individualist values such as fairness, freedom, or choice. Advocates of "creation science" (who argue that the account of creation in Genesis is literally true) now avoid public assertions of the authoritative truth of the biblical account and, instead, advocate "equal time" provisions that would require the teaching of creationism as an alternative to evolution. The different theories of life's beginnings would be placed side by side, with students encouraged to make up their own minds. Such appeals to "fairness" or "equality" may be more effective than an insistence on the veracity of a particular reading of the scriptures.[50]

Thus, organized groups that seek an accommodationist understanding of the establishment clause have shifted their public arguments to reflect a libertarian understanding of the free exercise clause. Obviously, the new emphasis on free exercise is more compatible with Lockean individualism, which arguably dominates the American political culture. By focusing on the rights of the believer rather than on the authority or truth of religious doctrine, religious groups may have neutralized the prospects for separationist countermobilization. Most groups that address church-state relations are organized around issues implicating the establishment clause, though free exercise issues may surface without much connection to establishment issues. In such cases, interest groups sometimes form ad hoc coalitions that are not institutionalized or stable over time. In response to the *Smith* (1990) decision (see below), a diverse coalition of Orthodox Jews, mainline Protestants, Southern Baptists, and the American Civil Liberties Union formed in support of the Religious Freedom Restoration Act.[51] But "pure" questions of free exercise generally are posed by unpopular religious minorities that lack the resources for sustained political mobilization.[52]

Federalism

Thomas P. "Tip" O'Neill (D-MA), former Speaker of the House of Representatives, is said to have observed that "all politics is local." There is a good deal of truth in that assertion with respect to church-state relations. A large majority of the conflicts between politics and religion are raised by the actions of state or local governments. This local focus should not be surprising because citizens have more direct contact with local governmental bodies than with remote federal agencies in Washington. "Retail" religious politics often involves questions of aesthetics, zoning, local taxation, and expecially public education. A very high percentage of church-state questions deal with the education of schoolchildren, because education is very decentralized and, for most Americans, public schools represent their most sustained contact with government at any level.

Localized concerns attain the status of constitutional issues largely because of the "incorporation" doctrine (see Introduction).[53] The religion clauses were first applied to subnational governments in *Cantwell v. Connecticut* 310 U.S. 296 (1940).[54] While the scope of the doctrine of incorporation remains controversial, there is now general agreement that *both* religion clauses of the First Amendment properly apply to the actions of subnational governments.[55] Constitutional issues at the state and local levels frequently arise from the particular contours of public opinion—many Americans are abstract separationists but concrete accommodationists. When localities deal with such issues as Sabbath observances, holiday displays with religious themes, or school curricula, they are operating at an applied level where many Americans are unaware that constitutional principles are highly relevant. The mass public wants the presumed benefits of religious accommodation without considering (or taking seriously) the possible constitutional conflicts. For example, parents who are concerned about juvenile delinquency may advocate organized public prayer in school or the posting of the Ten Commandments as reminders of a shared moral and ethical code that is much more important, to them, than a clause in the First Amendment. On church-state issues, accommodationist public opinion is likely to be formidable at the subnational level. Not only are accommodationist beliefs rather popular[56] but research shows that churches are important agents for political socialization.[57] The socializing effects of religious observance, moreover, are strongest among the evangelical, pietistic congregations that are most favorably disposed to the teaching of creationism and school prayer.[58] Citizens with separationist views do not typically have comparable opportunities for social interaction and, in addition, may regard themselves as politically isolated on such issues.[59]

A number of recent controversies correspond to this pattern. In 1999, the Kansas State School Board passed, and then rescinded, revised curricular standards that would have limited the teaching of evolution in Kansas public schools.[60] In Alabama, Roy Moore, chief justice of the state supreme court, was removed from office for his refusal to remove a large (two-and-half-ton) monument to the Ten Commandments from the rotunda of the Alabama State Judicial Building, after being ordered to do so by the U.S. Court of Appeals for the Eleventh Circuit.[61] The decision to remove Justice Moore was unpopular in Alabama, and Moore has been mentioned as a possible candidate for statewide office. The record of compliance with court decisions banning prayer in public schools has been spotty in some regions of the country, because local school districts have often defied unpopular court decisions.[62] Several states recently have authorized the use of tax credits or tuition vouchers for the parents of children who attend private schools. While characterized as an educational reform measure, this policy does have establishment clause implications since most educational institutions that would benefit from these programs are religious. In sum, accommodationist policies have been enacted by many subnational governments in response to generally supportive public attitudes.[63]

The electoral incentives for local politicians to enact popular measures that involve establishment issues may be strong, whereas those governing elites may risk weak or no political sanctions for supporting legislation that is patently unconstitutional.[64] More typically, issues involving the free exercise clause pertain to the religious rights of small, unpopular, and politically impotent minorities, so it might require a great deal of political courage (or an electoral death wish) for a state legislator or local official to support the rights of Native Americans to ingest peyote or to advocate publicly the right of some Muslim immigrants to engage in female genital mutilation.[65] Therefore, in terms of the typology developed above, state and local policy making in most areas of the United States is likely to take on a Christian preferentialist tone.

Judiciary

Respecting the establishment clause, the Supreme Court usually takes a separationist position, arguably since its rulings in *Everson v. Board of Education* and *Engel v. Vitale,* 370 U.S. 421 (1962).[66] *Everson* incorporated the establishment clause and *Engel* was the first decision banning organized school prayer. At this writing, the operative (and controversial) precedent is *Lemon v. Kurtzman,* 403 U.S. 602 (1971), in which Chief Justice Warren Burger outlined a three-pronged test to determine whether the establishment clause has been violated by an act of government. The *Lemon* test would require that a policy be invalidated if that policy (1) has a religious purpose, (2) has a religious effect of either advancing or inhibiting religion, or (3) requires an "excessive entanglement" between government and religion.[67] A government policy is unconstitutional if *any* of these conditions is violated.

Following the logic of *Lemon,* the high court has struck down laws that require public schools to devote "equal time" to the teaching of creationism and evolution (*Edward v. Aguillard,* 482 U.S. 578 [1987]) as well as several legal maneuvers designed to restore prayer in public schools.[68] The Court, for example, disallowed an Alabama statute mandating a "moment of silence" in public schools (*Wallace v. Jaffree,* 472 U.S. 38 [1985]) and also at a high school graduation ceremony (*Lee v. Weisman,* 112 S.Ct. 2649 [1992]).[69] It also held that any government assistance to religious schools must be narrowly defined, with a clear secular purpose. It is constitutional for a state to provide mathematics textbooks to parochial schools, because the state has a legitimate secular purpose in promoting mathematics instruction, but state assistance to instructors of parochial schools would be unconstitutional (*Abington Township School District v. Schempp,* 374 U.S. 203 [1963]; *Allegheny County v. ACLU,* 492 U.S. 573 [1989]).

In recent years, the Court seems to have relaxed its strict separationist interpretation of *Lemon* by permitting state funding for a sign-language interpreter for a deaf student enrolled in a parochial school (*Zobrest v. Catalina Foothills School District,* 113 S.Ct. 2462 [1993]) and by requiring public schools to allow religious groups the use of school facilities after hours if such opportunities are extended to nonreligious groups (*Lamb's Chapel v. Center Moriches Union Free School District,* 113 S.Ct. 2142 [1993]).[70] However, there seems to be no general shift by the Court toward a more accommodationist reading of the Constitution, nor any serious attempt to overrule or seriously modify *Lemon.*[71]

One ruling at the end of its 1996–1997 term does suggest that the Supreme Court may be moving in an accommodationist direction on certain issues involving the establishment clause. On June 23, 1997, in the case of *Agostini v. Felton,* no. 96–552 (1997), the justices overturned on a 5–4 vote a 1985 ruling (*Aguilar v. Felton*) that had prohibited the use of publicly funded instructors for special or remedial education in parochial schools. While some observers suggested that *Agostini* signaled a change in the Court's jurisprudence on establishment issues, it should be noted that *Agostini* does not threaten the framework enunciated in *Lemon.* Indeed, Justice O'Connor's majority opinion made a clear argument that *Aguilar* was being overturned because the majority believed that the *Lemon* test had been misapplied in the 1985 case. The somewhat ambivalent approach toward religious establishment is well illustrated in the case of *Zelman v. Simmons-Harris* (536 U.S. 639 [2002]). Voting 5–4, the high court upheld the constitutionality of providing tuition vouchers for the parents of children who attend private schools. Although an accommodationist result, the Court used the *Lemon* framework in the majority and concurring opinions. The fact that most educational institutions that would benefit from vouchers are religious schools did not violate the "effects" prong of the *Lemon* test because the pattern was the result of "uncoerced, individual choices" on the part of parents. At this time, the potential scope of the Court's apparent accommodationist shift remains unclear.[72]

Until recently, the Supreme Court had adopted a libertarian stance toward issues involving the free exercise clause.[73] Although the free exercise of religion has never been an absolute right,[74] the Court has been quite willing to protect the prerogatives of unconventional religious groups. Thomas Robbins suggests that the Supreme Court historically has applied a three-prong test for evaluating the constitutionality of free exercise claims. The three criteria in question were derived from *Sherbert v. Verner,* 374 U.S. 398 (1963), and *Wisconsin v. Yoder,* 406 U.S. 205 (1972). Under the Sherbert-Yoder test,[75] government must show that "it has a compelling interest which justifies the . . . right to [restrain] free exercise of religion."[76] Such regulations are subjected to "strict scrutiny" by the courts, which requires the government to justify the abridgement of religious free exercise by showing that a particular regulation is *essential.* This is quite a formidable hurdle for public policy since government bears a substantial burden of proof. If the centrality of a government regulation of religious practice has been established, the burden of proof under Sherbert-Yoder shifts to the persons or groups who claim that their religious free exercise has been violated. The religious practice must be so "central" to the religion that the government regulation involves a "substantial infringement" on that religious practice. The courts take into consideration whether the compelling governmental regulation that restricts religious free exercise is the "least restrictive alternative" available by which the state can achieve its secular goals. A policy might well be deemed unconstitutional if government objectives can be achieved by less intrusive means.[77]

Under Chief Justice William Rehnquist, the Supreme Court's traditional deference to free exercise claims appears to be changing. In *Employment Division v. Smith,* 110 S.Ct. 1595 (1990), the Court ruled that Native Americans who used the hallucinogenic drug peyote during a religious ritual were not entitled to legal protection under the free exercise clause. The majority opinion by Justice Antonin Scalia argued that activities otherwise prohibited by a state criminal code do not enjoy special protection for religious reasons unless such an exception was made explicit by the legislature.[78] Because of *Smith,* the criteria appears to have shifted away from the "compelling [state] interest" standard of Sherbert-Yoder toward a more communalist understanding of the free exercise clause.[79] Consistent with the consensual nature of an accommodationist reading of the establishment clause, the *Smith* decision may signal that the high court will accord legislative acts (and, perhaps by extension, popular majorities) increasing deference. Those implications of *Smith* caught the attention of the U.S. Congress, which enacted the Religious Freedom Restoration Act of 1993 to reverse the *Smith* decision. But the Supreme Court had the last word, also at the end of its 1996–1997 term. Its 6–3 decision in *City of Boerne v. Flores* (1997) ruled that the congressional action to void the ruling in *Smith* was not a legitimate application of Congress's enforcement powers under the Fourteenth Amendment. As Justice Kennedy stated in his majority opinion, it is the prerogative of the courts and not Congress to determine the meaning of a constitutional right. In her dissent, Justice O'Connor endorsed Kennedy's view of the separation of powers but argued that the high court should have used *Boerne* as the vehicle to overturn the 1990 *Smith* decision, where she had dissented, and restore the Sherbert-Yoder standard to free exercise jurisprudence.[80] In terms of my typology (Table 6.1), the Supreme Court has moved from being a religious free-marketeer toward religious minimalism.

Congress

Congress has not been proactive in enacting legislation with respect to church-state relations but, for the most part, has reacted (usually ineffectually) to controversial decisions of the Supreme Court. Members of Congress frequently have sought to represent accommodationist public opinion. However, due perhaps to the religious diversity of Congress and the two-thirds majorities required to pass constitutional amendments, most congressional efforts to counteract separationist rulings have not been successful.

The tendency for Congress to take accommodationist positions has been exacerbated by recent trends in public opinion and legislative redistricting. In an electorate that is increasingly independent, partisan majorities in state legislatures are likely to create very safe districts for incumbents rather than create as many competitive districts as possible. This minimax redistricting strategy reduces the number of competitive districts in the House of Representatives.[81] To the extent that evangelical Christians are *realigning* in the direction of the Republican Party while much of the rest of the electorate is *dealigning,* it follows that many safe Republican districts will likely contain many evangelicals in the GOP coalition. Thus, to the extent that Congress represents constituent opinion, issues of religious importance may be salient to an increasingly large (and strategically located) evangelical electorate.[82]

Much congressional attention to church-state relations has been devoted to that hardy perennial issue, school prayer. School prayer is an "easy" issue because most Americans favor some form of school prayer; members of Congress have frequently sought to pass amendments to bills, House and Senate resolutions, and constitutional amendments which would permit the practice.[83] Since the *Engel* decision in 1962, nearly a hundred such measures have been introduced in the Senate and several hundred have been introduced in the House.[84] Most of the constitutional amendments in question have used the language of free exercise, emphasizing the voluntary or noncoercive aspects of school prayer. A proposed amendment by Senators Strom Thurmond (R-SC), Orrin G. Hatch (R-UT), Lawton Chiles (D-FL), James Abdnor (R-SD), Don Nickles (R-OK), and Jesse A. Helms (R-NC) is typical of the genre: "Nothing in this Constitution shall be construed to prohibit individual or group prayer in public schools or other public institutions. No person shall be required by the United States or any state to participate in prayer. Neither the United States nor any state shall compose the words of any prayer to be said in public schools."[85]

Such measures typically receive majorities in the House and Senate but fall short of the two-thirds required to pass a constitutional amendment. Members of Congress also have tried to remove school prayer from the Supreme Court's appellate jurisdiction, without success. Congressional reaction to federal court rulings extends to other policies as well. Early in 1997 House Republicans introduced a "sense of Congress" resolution that backed a judge who had refused (contrary to earlier precedent and a court order) to remove a display of the Ten Commandments from his courtroom.[86] This resolution was nonbinding, lacking the force of law, but represented the accommodationist stand in public opinion. In 1993 Congress passed the Religious Freedom Restoration Act (RFRA) to reverse the Supreme Court ruling in *Smith* and to reinstate the compelling state interest standard in cases involving religious free exercise. In an unexpected legal twist, as noted before, RFRA was subjected to a court challenge (*City of Boerne v. Flores,* 1997) that allowed the Supreme Court to declare that act of Congress to be unconstitutional.[87] Finally, Representative Ernest J. Istook Jr. (R-OK) proposed a constitutional amendment that, to a large extent, would enact an accommodationist interpretation of the establishment clause. It read: "To secure the people's right to acknowledge God according to the dictates of conscience; the people's right to pray and to recognize their religious beliefs, heritage, or traditions on public property, including schools, shall not be infringed. The government shall not require any person to join in prayer or other religious activity, initiate or designate school prayers, discriminate against religion, or deny a benefit to religion."[88]

Given the frequency with which local governments attempt to accommodate religious belief in public institutions and the general popularity of an accommodationist reading of the establishment clause (plus the highly positive symbol of religious free exercise), it is not clear why congressional attempts to amend the Constitution have not been successful. Congressional impotence may result from a reluctance by a sizable minority of members to revise the Constitution (itself regarded in a civil religion sense as a "sacred" document)[89] and from the religious diversity represented in the Congress.[90] Since mainstream Protestant denominations as well as Catholics, Jews, and non-Christians have been indifferent or hostile to the Christian preferentialist tendencies of some localities, the representatives from those mainline denominations may be sufficient in numbers to prevent the formation of the two-thirds majority needed to amend the Constitution.[91]

Presidency

Issues involving religious establishment and free exercise have not been high priorities for American presidents until quite recently.[92] With the exceptions of Ronald Reagan and George W. Bush, few presidents since *Engel* have made strong pronouncements or policy initiatives with respect to religion. Since 1964 (the first presidential election after *Engel*), GOP platforms have routinely offered support for school prayer while Democratic platforms have generally ignored the issue.[93] This difference no doubt reflects deep religious differences in the activist base of the two parties.[94] Once elected, however, presidents of both parties have done little more than voice symbolic support for religion, making few public appeals for specific policies. President George H.W. Bush invoked religious values as underlying his vision of "a thousand points of light" and President Clinton publicly praised Stephen Carter's pro-free exercise work, *The Culture of Disbelief*. President Kennedy, when commenting upon the *Engel* decision, used the occasion to urge people to pray privately.[95] Modern presidents do not place high priority on issues involving church-state separation. Their conventional strategy has been to make proreligious statements while avoiding controversies associated with particular church-state issues.

It is ironic that explicit support for religious separationism has come from presidents whose religious identities are distinctive. John Kennedy, whose Catholicism was something of an electoral liability, supported the *Engel* decision, albeit with a notable lack of enthusiasm.[96] Jimmy Carter, whose credentials as a born-again Christian constituted a moderately important issue in the presidential campaign of 1976, took a separationist position on school prayer (which he modified after becoming president).[97] These examples suggest that presidents identified with a *specific* denomination outside the mainline protestant tradition have been particularly wary of endorsing religious accommodationism for fear of alienating potential supporters from outside their faith.[98]

One exception to the passive presidential role in church-state relations was Ronald Reagan. Reagan, who was elected with the support of several leaders of the Christian Right, invoked religious imagery frequently to express his opposition to abortion and school prayer. Reagan often cited his understanding of the Found or praised the desirability of religion. Once he declared, "If we could get government out of the classroom, maybe we could get God back in."[99] Reagan did propose a school prayer amendment in 1982 but, once again, Congress did not pass it.[100] Several analysts have suggested that even Reagan, who was perhaps the most publicly pro-religion president in modern times, gave only passive and rhetorical support to religious accommodation or free exercise.

It is not obvious why there has been so little presidential activity with respect to church-state relations. Perhaps presidents want to husband their limited political capital and avoid such controversial issues as school prayer or tuition tax credits. It also might be the case that demographic groups largely opposed to religious accommodation (members of minority religions) are concentrated in large, urban areas rich in electoral votes, making support for school prayer partially costly for presidential candidates. The logic of presidential selection may encourage presidential passivity in church-state relations.[101]

The George W. Bush administration witnessed a more aggressive approach to church-state relations than has typically been the case. The president proposed (and Congress passed) a number of measures in support of "faith-based initiatives." These initiatives would allow religious organizations that provide social services to compete for government support so long as the provision of social services was separated from the religious mission of those organizations. Public support for such measures is high but diminishes when Americans are faced with the possibility that unpopular religious groups (e.g., Nation of Islam, Buddhists, Church of Scientology) may receive public assistance.[102] Despite a host of constitutional and practical problems,[103] the Bush administration has pursued the promotion of Faith-Based Organizations (FBOs) quite aggressively. This reversal by the Bush administration may be a strategic adaption to an altered electoral landscape, in which the mobilization of GOP core voters has a higher priority than attracting more moderate swing voters.

Bureaucracy

Issues relating to religious establishment or free exercise have received little attention from the federal bureaucracy. One prominent exception involves the Reagan administration. Reagan's solicitor general, Rex Lee, submitted amicus briefs in numerous court cases supporting religious accommodationism in issues involving the constitutionality of state legislative chaplains, publicly sponsored nativity scenes, school prayer, and aid to parochial schools.[104] Cabinet officials from the Departments of Justice and Education testified before Congress in favor of the school prayer amendment submitted by the Reagan administration.[105] Since religious organizations usually are exempt from federal taxes, the Internal Revenue Service (IRS) is rarely involved in church-state issues. In one case affecting Bob Jones University, however, the IRS revoked its religious tax exemption because the university had a policy of official racial discrimination.[106] The university argued (unsuccessfully) that the free exercise clause provided an exemption from federally mandated rules proscribing discrimination. In addition, there are strict limitations on the political activity of tax-exempt organizations, and several religious organizations (including the United States Catholic Conference) have limited their participation in politics as a result of this policy.[107] Nonetheless, in relatively few cases has a tax exemption actually been revoked for this reason.

The second Bush administration again represents an exception to this general pattern. Government agencies like AmeriCorps, the Senior Corps, and the Peace Corps have been subsumed under the Corporation for National and Community Service, which is also charged with administering federally sponsored faith-based organizations.[108] Some empirical research shows that, in certain settings, the religious character of FBOs is ubiquitous, suggesting that the constitutional issues of religious establishment may not be resolved very easily.[109] Wuthnow and his associates have reported that FBOs are not considered more effective than government agencies by the recipients of social services.[110] Although the involvement of federal agencies in church-state relations has traditionally been quite limited, it is unclear whether the second Bush administration represents a new chapter in this relationship or simply a temporary interruption in the previous pattern of noninvolvement.

In summary, the conflict over the proper relationship between church and state will likely be an enduring feature of American politics. The task of "rendering unto Caesar that which is Caesar's, and to God that which is God's" is not easily accomplished. Two features of religious politics suggest that the general issue will resist stable resolution.

First, church-state relations in the United States largely involve interactions between subnational governments and the federal courts. The distribution of religious beliefs and practices in some localities may approximate the consensus that Alexis de Tocqueville envisioned a century and a half ago. In those states and communities, an accommodationist reading of the establishment clause seems reasonable due to the lack of any genuine religious and ethical diversity. Where local religious hegemony exists, religiously marginalized citizens typically have recourse only to the courts since they would fare poorly in elections. Thus, church-state relations is one issue area in which the classic dilemma between majority rule and minority rights is played out.

A second feature of religious politics is the inherent tension between the two religion clauses. Unless one takes a hard accommodationist position on the establishment clause, many public policies exemplify *both* religious establishment and free exercise because modern government at all levels provides services unbeknownst to the Framers of the First Amendment. Given governmental activism, the constant question is whether granting tax exemptions to religious organizations or using grant funds to pay for school lunches or transportation for religious groups to public facilities constitutes unconstitutional religious establishment. Or, conversely, is the withholding of such benefits from religious groups a denial of their free exercise? And if those benefits are granted to religious organizations, would governmental requirements, such as accreditation for private schools or bans on political activity, also interfere with the free exercise of religion? *Lemon v. Kurtzman* suggests that individual claims and particular government policies will be evaluated by the Supreme Court on a case-by-case basis.

One possible solution to these dilemmas is to adopt an accommodationist position on the establishment clause and apply the establishment clause only to discrimination in favor of *particular* denominations or traditions. From this perspective, neutral, nondiscriminatory assistance to religion would pose no constitutional issue. However, I would suggest that religious accommodation on a national scale may not be politically possible. Accommodationism assumes, as did de Tocqueville, a religious or ethical consensus, which does not currently exist in the United States, if indeed it ever did.[111] Many Americans profess either very casual or nonexistent religious convictions, and the increasing number of non-European immigrants suggests that Christianity no longer "rules by universal consent." Also the presumed ethical consensus of which de Tocqueville wrote does not appear to be viable today since issues like abortion, gay rights, and women's rights are increasingly debated *within* Christian denominations.[112] Finally, any attempt to implement a thoroughly accommodationist perspective on the establishment clause would raise the question of what is or is not a bona fide religion.[113]

It is thus difficult to imagine how issues of religious freedom and church-state separation can ever be resolved in our current constitutional format. We are, as Justice William O. Douglas argued, "a religious people," with a natural desire to see our most sacred beliefs and values enacted into public policy. We are also a people who value personal and spiritual autonomy, and freedom from government interference. These different national characteristics can be expected to provide a dynamic for conflict over church-state relations for the foreseeable future.

Summary of Propositions

1a (single-issue groups): Unsupported, to the degree that most organizations involved in church-state issues are general interest groups, for example, the Christian Coalition and the American Civil Liberties Union.

1b (absolutist politics): Supported, certainly by those adversaries who support the Christian preferentialist versus the religious free-marketeer views of the two religion clauses.

2a (judicial activism): Supported, because federal courts very often take positions unpopular with accommodationist majorities.

2a (incorporation): Supported, because the Supreme Court has incorporated the establishment clause and the free exercise clause to the fifty states. However, there is some evidence that federal courts are becoming more deferential to states and localities and, by extension, to popular majorities that favor accommodationist policies.

3a (presidential symbolism): Supported, for most presidents in the post–World War II era. President George W. Bush may be a prominent exception, although the results of faith-based initiatives remain uncertain at this writing.

3b (partisan presidents): Supported, since Democrats are often on the defensive given that there are very few separationist constituencies in the United States.

4a (Congress and states): Supported. In such policies as school prayer, Congress has voiced opposition to the decisions of federal courts.

4b (Congress and elections): Supported with respect to several church-state issues.

5a (opinion and ideology): Supported, because polls reflect accommodationist rather than separation views in public opinion and there is little evidence of an intense, separationist minority in the mass public.

5b (law and society): Supported, especially when public policy targets school prayer, religious observances at graduations and sporting events, and the teaching of evolution.

6a (marginal agencies): Supported, as this generalization is historically true, but again President Bush's faith-based initiatives would grant greater discretion to federal agencies to distribute resources to religiously based service organizations.

6b (federal implementation): Supported because, for most of the postwar era, any discretion by federal agencies in the church-state area was limited by legal precedents set by federal courts.

7a (federalism): Supported, because a great deal of policy making in the church-state area deals with public education, historically a matter of state concern. However, today most church-state policies involve constitutional issues and, because the doctrine of incorporation has never been challenged with respect to the religion clauses, there are few church-state issues in which state jurisdiction would not be contested.

7b (compliance): Supported, especially when church-state issues affect public education. In such school-related matters as prayer and the teaching of evolution, outright defiance of court decisions is not uncommon.

For Further Insight Into the Debate Over God and Country

Carter, Stephen L. *The Culture of Disbelief: How American Law and Politics Trivialize Religious Devotion*. New York: Basic Books, 1993. This Yale law professor defends religious activism in the public sphere and argues that the trivialization of religion has eroded our First Amendment protections. Political activism should be grounded in religious belief.

Hunter, James Davison. *Culture Wars*. New York: Basic Books, 1991. This influential book by a sociologist of religion argues that many moral conflicts divide people with "orthodoxy" religious values against people with "progressive" views about religion in society.

Hunter, James Davison. *Before the Shooting Begins*. New York: Free Press, 1994. Argues that the "culture wars" based on religious values pose dangers for democratic politics, because political rhetoric is the primary weapon in this ideological battle to impose a new cultural consensus on American society.

Inherit the Wind. (1960). First dramatized on Broadway and later filmed by director Stanley Kramer starring Spencer Tracy, it portrays the 1925 Scopes "Monkey Trial" in Tennessee when Clarence Darrow (for the defense) and William Jennings Bryan (for the prosecution) clashed over a science teacher who was accused of violating state law by teaching evolution.

Levy, Leonard. *The Establishment Clause: Religion and the First Amendment*. Chapel Hill: University of North Carolina Press, 1994. Argues that the history of the Establishment Clause indicates that the Framers were opposed to more than the establishment of one state religion insofar as they would oppose government support for any church or all religions.

Reed, Ralph. *Politically Incorrect: The Emerging Faith Factor in American Politics*. Dallas: World Publishing, 1994. Then executive director of the Christian Coalition, Ralph Reed argues that pluralism in America should include political participation by all denominations including evangelical Christians.

www.aclj.org. Web site for American Center for Law and Justice.

www.aclu.org. Web site for American Civil Liberties Union.

www.au.org. Web site for Americans United for the Separation of Church and State.

www.cc.org. Web site for the Christian Coalition.

http://eagleforum.org. Web site for Eagle Forum, an ideologically conservative group.

http://family.org. Web site for Focus on the Family.

www.pfaw.org. Web site for People for the American Way, an ideologically liberal group.

Gun Control

Constitutional Mandate or Myth?

Robert J. Spitzer

> A well regulated Militia, being necessary to the security of
> a free state, the right of the people to keep and bear Arms,
> shall not be infringed.
> —*Second Amendment, U.S. Constitution*

> The NRA, the foremost guardian of the traditional right to "keep
> and bear arms," believes that every law-abiding citizen is entitled to
> the ownership and legal use of firearms, and that every reputable
> gun owner should be an NRA member.
> —*Motto, The American Rifleman*

> A powerful lobby dins into the ears of our citizenry that . . . gun
> purchases are constitutional rights protected by the Second Amend-
> ment. . . . There is under our decisions no reason why stiff state laws
> governing the purchase and possession of pistols may not be enacted.
> There is no reason why pistols may not be barred from anyone with
> a police record. There is no reason why a State may not require a
> purchaser of a pistol to pass a psychiatric test. There is no reason
> why all pistols should not be barred to everyone except the police.
> —*Associate Justice William O. Douglas*
> *Adams v. Williams (1972)*

The issue of gun control has proven to be one of the most highly charged and enduringly controversial in American politics, yet surprisingly little writing has incorporated a dispassionate examination of gun control policies and politics. The purposes of this chapter are to inquire whether the state has the authority to regulate guns under the Second Amendment and, if so, how to explain the existing pattern of weak national gun control laws.

Mistrust of standing armies was a pervasive sentiment during the revolutionary period in America and was related directly to the bearing of arms by citizens. Samuel Adams wrote in 1776, for example, that a "standing army, however necessary it be at some times, is always dangerous to the liberties of the people."[1] Samuel Seabury characterized the standing army as "the MONSTER,"[2] and George Washington observed that "mercenary armies . . . have at one time or another subverted the liberties of almost all the Countries they have been raised to defend."[3] A reliance on the citizen-soldier became synonymous with the revolutionary spirit. In the Declaration of Independence, Thomas Jefferson complained that King George III "has kept among us, in Times of Peace, Standing Armies, without the consent of our Legislatures. He has affected to render the Military independent of and superior to the Civil Power." The Declaration of Independence also complained that the British were "quartering large Bodies of Armed Troops among us" and "protecting them, by a mock Trial, from Punishment for any Murders which they should commit on the Inhabitants of these States." The British only compounded these grievances by hiring Hessian mercenaries to fight against colonial troops during the Revolution. The colonists relied on state-based militias to fight the war, rather than risk vesting a national government with a national army that might later pose a threat to the people's liberties. Even by 1788 the Army of the Confederation consisted of only 697 men and officers.[4]

Despite these concerns, the Framers recognized that a standing army was a necessity. Article I, Section 8, of the Constitution grants Congress the power "to raise and support armies" (although the fear of standing armies caused the Framers to limit appropriations for the military to two years), to "provide for calling forth the militia," and to "provide for organizing, arming, and disciplining, the militia."[5] The modern militia is no longer an eighteenth-century citizen army but is now the National Guard since passage of the Militia Act of 1903 and the National Defense Act of 1916.

Fears of a standing army also influenced the writing of the Bill of Rights. The congressional committee reviewing proposed amendments reported out this text for what eventually became the Second Amendment: "A well regulated militia, composed of the body of the people, being the best security of a free state, the right of the people to keep and bear arms shall not be infringed; but no person religiously scrupulous shall be compelled to bear arms."[6] The primary change in the final text was the omission of the last phrase; Elbridge Gerry and others felt that the religious exemption could result in numerous citizens exempting themselves from military service, which might necessitate the baneful standing army.[7]

The Framers sought in the Second Amendment assurance that states could maintain their militias against a mischievous or unreliable federal army and against the encroachments of other states. Absent from these debates was any discussion or justification of an individual "right" to bear arms aside or apart from citizen service in a militia. The concept of individualism had relevance only insofar as individuals during the early years of the country's history had to supply their own arms while serving in the militia. For example, Congress created uniform state militias through the Uniform Militia Act of 1792, which allowed the calling up of "every free, able-bodied, white male citizen of the respective States [between the ages of eighteen and forty-five] in the militia. Each man was to provide his own weapons, two flints, 24 rounds of ammunition for a musket or 20 rounds for a rifle."[8] This kind of armed force was mobilized by President Washington in 1794, for example, to suppress the Whiskey Rebellion. The debate today about whether the Second Amendment refers to an "individual" or "collective" right to bear arms is directly relevant to the gun control issue. The individual interpretation is championed by the National Rifle Association (NRA), but the weight of scholarly opinion argues against the NRA position,[9] although some scholars agree that the Second Amendment secures an individual right to bear arms.[10]

Interest Groups

Pro-Gun Groups

National Rifle Association

The NRA was formed in 1871 by Colonel William C. Church, editor of the *Army and Navy Journal,* and by George W. Wingate, an officer in the New York National Guard. The NRA's beginnings paralleled a rising interest in rifle shooting competitions, which resulted partly from the Union army's relatively poor marksmanship skills during the Civil War. The organization languished until 1900, when Albert Jones, an officer in the New Jersey National Guard, with the aid of New York governor Theodore Roosevelt, revived interest in forming a group to support marksmanship. The then-forgotten NRA became the vehicle for implementing Jones's plan, and in 1905 the NRA became the primary channel for the sale of government surplus weapons and ammunition to rifle clubs under Public Law 149. In 1921 C.B. Lister, a promotions manager, assumed leadership of the NRA, and due to his efforts, the NRA became affiliated with two thousand local sportsmen's clubs; its membership grew tenfold by 1934. The NRA swiftly became the largest and best-organized association of firearms users in the nation.

The NRA is now headquartered in Virginia, where prolific information is kept on the NRA's 4 million members and on legislators. In a few hours, correspondence can be rapidly routed to Congress by mobilizing this huge membership. In 1994 the NRA generated revenues of $148 million.[11] Fifty percent of the NRA's revenues come from membership fees and another 15 percent from advertising, mainly by gun manufacturers, in its monthly magazines: *The American Rifleman, The American Hunter,* and *America's First Freedom.*[12] The NRA fosters member devotion by emphasizing the gun as a cultural phenomenon, not simply as a political issue. Beyond this, the NRA has benefited from a kind of quasi-governmental status; federal law for decades stipulated that surplus military arms could be sold only to civilians who belonged to the NRA. This led to an ironic occurrence in 1967 when 400 members of the Detroit Police Department had to join the NRA in order to obtain surplus army carbines for riot control.[13] A court order ended this special privilege in 1979, the result of a legal challenge by the National Coalition to Ban Handguns (NCBH). The federal government continues to subsidize NRA activities by allowing the organization to hold annual shooting matches at federal military installations at no expense to the NRA and by allowing it the special favor of building target ranges on federal lands.[14]

Institute for Legislative Action (ILA)

In 1975, this special branch of the NRA coordinates legislative efforts. One of ILA's primary responsibilities is to apply political pressure on federal and state elected officials and to provide the NRA membership with current information and alerts on impending firearms legislation and court rulings. The ILA has become the primary power center within the NRA and its potency has been widely noted. For example, the *Washington Post* observed that "few lobbies have so mastered the marble halls and concrete canyons of Washington."[15] The ILA now consumes over a quarter of the NRA budget, expending considerable resources in communications with NRA members. In virtually every year since the end of the 1970s, the NRA has spent more money on emotionally charged internal communications than any similar group.[16]

In one very controversial instance, the NRA suffered severe criticism from a fund-raising letter sent out shortly before the bombing of the Murrah federal office building in Oklahoma City on April 19, 1995. In the six-page letter, signed by NRA executive vice president Wayne LaPierre, federal government agents were compared to Nazis, in that they were said to wear "Nazi bucket helmets and black storm trooper uniforms" and to "harass, intimidate, *even murder* law-abiding citizens." Many expressed outrage at the letter, and former president George H.W. Bush publicly resigned his life membership in the organization, calling the NRA letter a "vicious slander on good people."[17] The adverse publicity stemming from the NRA's perceived extremism contributed to the decline in its membership. After reaching a high point of about 3.5 million members in the early 1990s, NRA membership dipped to about 2.8 million by 1997. In an effort to rehabilitate the NRA's reputation, give it a more palatable public face, and beat back an internal power challenge from an even more extremist faction, actor Charlton Heston was elected president in 1998, a position to which he was annually reelected (the organization's two-term limit was waived) until his retirement in 2003, owing to the onset of Alzheimer's disease. Under Heston's tenure, membership grew to 4 million, and the organization exercised unrivaled sway within the George W. Bush administration and among Republican congressional leaders.

NRA PAC

The Institute for Legislative Action also manages the NRA's political action committee (PAC), which is called the Political Victory Fund. Formed in 1976, the NRA PAC has funneled millions of dollars to gun control foes. Throughout the 1980s and 1990s, the NRA has consistently been one of the top-spending political organizations in the country. In 1988, for example, it funneled $1.5 million to George H.W. Bush's presidential campaign; four years later, however, it withheld support from Bush because of his support for restrictions on imports of assault weapons. It also sat out the 1996 presidential contest because President Bill Clinton was a supporter of tough gun laws while his opponent, Bob Dole, backed away from his antigun control positions of prior years. In the 1994 elections, the NRA PAC spent $5.3 million on direct campaign contributions, making it the biggest-spending PAC in that year's election. In 1995 and 1996 it raised and spent over $6.6 million. In the 1999–2000 cycle, the NRA PAC raised more than $20 million for federal and state elections. Like most PACs, the Political Victory Fund gives most of its money to incumbents. It also favors Republicans over Democrats. From 1978 to 1996, the NRA gave about 84 percent of its money to Republicans. This ratio shifted even more dramatically in the 2000 elections, when it gave 94 percent of its money to Republicans.

The PAC also devotes considerable resources to independent expenditures (money spent independent of the campaign of the candidate for whom the money is used). In 1994 it spent $1.5 million on independent expenditures, accounting for more than a fourth of all the independent money spent by PACs that year. Increasingly, these independent expenditures have been used to attack opponents in Congress and elsewhere through "stealth" tactics, that is, ads that attack opponents on other issues to conceal the fact that the gun issue is the primary motivation.[18]

But the NRA does not confine its activities to the legislative branch. Through its Firearms Civil Rights Legal Defense Fund, founded in 1978, the NRA helps to finance legal battles in the courts. This organization, a tax-exempt fund supported by individual and corporate donations, is under the guidance of the Institute for Legislative Action. From 1993 to 1996, the organization provided money to seventy-eight cases. In 1996, for example, the organization gave about $20,000 to aid in the legal defense of Bernhard Goetz, a man who shot four reputed attackers on a New York City subway in the 1980s.[19]

Other Pro-Gun Groups

Single-issue pro-gun groups have sprung up mainly because they believe that the NRA is not strident enough in its opposition to gun control legislation. One such group is the Citizens Committee for the Right to Keep and Bear Arms, headquartered in Washington, D.C. It was founded in 1971 because of the belief that the NRA was not maintaining a tough enough stand on the gun issue. It includes a research arm, the Second Amendment Foundation, that publishes gun-related literature.[20] The Gun Owners of America (GOA) was founded in 1974 by H.L. Richardson, a California state senator and former director of the NRA. The organization is today headed by Larry Pratt, and it claims about 150,000 members.

Pro-Gun Arguments

The symbolic importance of the Constitution is evident in much NRA literature, with one recurring theme being that the Second Amendment provides absolute protection for any individual's right to own guns. The NRA also opposes essentially every gun control measure, including waiting periods for gun ownership, which the NRA had supported until the 1970s. An analysis of NRA rhetoric by Raymond S. Rodgers identifies five logical and rhetorical fallacies. The first is the failure to define terms—for example, the options that are included under the term *gun control*. The second is the use of the "big lie"—that the Second Amendment guarantees an inalienable right to bear arms. The third, the "slippery slope" fallacy, argued that any gun regulation invariably will lead to a total ban on guns and even to authoritarianism.[21] The fourth was the use of "bully tactics" such as name calling, as when gun control advocates are called "gun-grabbers." The fifth is improper appeals to authority, such as using endorsements by celebrities rather than relying on evidence or reasoning.

Gun Control Groups

Brady Campaign to Prevent Gun Violence

The ideological antithesis of the NRA is the Brady Campaign to Prevent Gun Violence, known before 2001 as Handgun Control, Inc. (HCI). Based in Washington, D.C., the Brady Campaign is the largest of the gun control groups. The Brady Campaign, chaired by Sarah Brady, is affiliated with the Brady Center to Prevent Gun Violence (before 2001, the Center to Prevent Handgun Violence), a nonprofit educational and legal-action organization founded in 1983. Brady also chairs this group. Although formed in 1974 by business-man Pete Shields, the organization had few resources or capabilities until the early 1980s, when the murder of ex-Beatle John Lennon spurred interest and fund-raising. By 1981, membership surpassed 100,000.

HCI contributed money to congressional campaigns for the first time in 1980, when it gave $75,000. That year, by comparison, the NRA contributed $1.5 million to campaigns. By the 1991–1992 election cycle, HCI had spent $280,000. In the 2000 election cycle, it spent over ten times as much on campaigns as it had in 1996, amounting to over $4 million, though still a fraction of NRA spending. The Brady Campaign has sought to copy the NRA's tactical and organizational methods, particularly by building grassroots sup-port among members willing to write letters, make phone calls, vote, and contribute money. By 1990, membership reached 250,000 and by 1998 topped 400,000; the organization maintained a mailing list of over a million names. Today, its annual budget tops $7 million.[22]

HCI's original agenda was to restrict, but not ban, the ownership of pistols and revolvers (particularly cheap handguns called Saturday night specials). Its focus shifted in the 1980s when Sarah Brady became its chief public advocate (she has headed the organization since 1989). Brady achieved pub-lic visibility when her husband, James Brady (press secretary to President Ronald Reagan), was seriously injured in the 1981 assassination attempt upon the president. Four years later, Brady joined the HCI board in reaction to efforts by gun control opponents in Congress to gut much of the 1968 Gun Control Act (see below). In the late 1980s she and her husband became the chief advocates for enactment of a waiting period for purchase of a handgun, legislation that became known as the Brady bill and was enacted in 1993. In 2001, the Brady Campaign subsumed the Million Mom March organization, a grassroots movement that briefly captured national attention when it staged one of the largest rallies ever held in the nation's capital on Mother's Day in 2000. It was organized to support stronger gun laws in the aftermath of the 1999 shooting at Columbine High School in Colorado.

Other Gun Control Groups

Another gun control group, the National Coalition to Ban Handguns (NCBH), was founded in 1974 with a grant from the United Methodist church. The NCBH is composed of a group of national religious, educational, and social organizations. The NCBH was renamed the Coalition to Stop Gun Violence (CSGV) in 1990. The CSGV tends to be more militant and aggressive in its lobbying efforts than the Brady Campaign, but it has been overshadowed by the larger and more visible Brady group. More recently, a pro-gun control research group based in Washington, D.C., the Violence Policy Center, headed by Josh Sugarmann, has engaged in high-visibility research to promote gun control policy. Proponents of stricter regulations, unlike the NRA, have rallied the support of other organizations not exclusively concerned about the gun issue. The U.S. Conference of Mayors in 1972 adopted a strongly worded resolution that "urges national legislation against the manufacture, importation, sale and private possession of handguns" and that "urges its members to extend every effort to educate the American public to the dangerous and appalling realities resulting from the private possession of handguns." The NAACP also has endorsed stricter gun laws. In 2003 the NAACP sponsored a lawsuit against several gun manufacturers, arguing that irresponsible marketing practices by gun manufacturers caused unique harm to its constituency. Its arguments met with some public sympathy, but not in the courts. The American Bar Association, the American Medical Association, and other professional organizations have lined up strongly in favor of stricter gun laws.

Gun Control Advocacy Literature

The gun control literature emphasizes crime statistics, the "collective" meaning of the Second Amendment, and supplies anecdotes to buttress its arguments for more gun regulations. In recent years, the Brady Coalition has adopted a tone reminiscent of NRA literature, for example when it began a 1993 appeal to members with the bold lettering "WE MUST GET THESE KILLING MACHINES OFF OUR STREETS!"

Each year about 30,000 people die as a result of the suicidal, homicidal, and accidental use of guns. The number of firearms in private ownership has dramatically increased, from 60 million in 1968 to 150 million guns in circulation in 1982, to 240 million by 2003. The increase in the total number of guns belies the fact that fewer American homes have guns. In the 1960s, about half of all homes had one or more guns; by 2001, that proportion had fallen to about a third of all homes (the average number of guns per gun-owning household has increased).[23] Of the total, two-thirds are long guns (rifles and shotguns) and a third are handguns. Compared to the population as a whole, gun owners are likely to be male, white, less educated, older, people with higher incomes, Republicans, Protestants, and manual workers. Two subgroups show the greatest degree of gun ownership—residents of the South and persons living in towns under 2,500 population or in rural areas. Fewest guns are owned by easterners and by people living in cities of 1 million or above.

Antigun literature emphasizes that handguns pose a special danger, because they are the weapons used in about 80 percent of gun-related crimes. Historian Richard Hofstadter observes that the United States is the only modern Western nation that clings to the "gun culture."[24] From 1993 to 1995, America had a firearm death rate of 13.7 per 100,000 people, with the nearest competitor nations being France at 6.3, Norway at 4.3, Canada at 3.9, Australia at 2.9, Israel at 2.8, and England at 0.4.[25] The advocates of stricter gun control legislation claim that other nations' much lower death rates from guns are a consequence of stronger laws and lower rates of gun possession.

Public Opinion

As early as 1938, pollsters began measuring public opinion on gun control. The Gallup Poll in that year found that 79 percent of the respondents favored "gun control."[26] Since 1959 Gallup has asked, "Would you favor or oppose a law which would require a person to obtain a police permit before he or she could buy a gun?" The affirmative response rate to that question has fluctuated between 68 and 78 percent.[27] Gallup also asked whether laws governing the sale of guns should be more or less strict (Table 7.1). Those responses reveal a consistently high level of support. Women are more likely to favor stricter laws than men, as are young adults (age 18 to 29), the college-educated, and people living in the East and in urban areas. In addition, the National Opinion Research Center surveyed the public on whether police permits should be required for gun ownership (Table 7.2). These responses show much public support for that requirement, despite vehement opposition from gun groups. A variation of this question was used by researchers Howard Schuman and Stanley Presser to measure intensity of feelings on both sides of the gun controversy.[28] They found that supporters of the permit law were more intense than the opponents, but when respondents were asked whether they ever wrote letters or contributed money to support their gun views, the opponents were much more likely to have done so than the supporters. One

Table 7.1

Gallup Polls on Gun Control (in percent)

Question: "In general do you feel that the laws covering the sale of firearms should be made more strict, less strict, or kept as they are?"

	More strict	Less strict	Kept as is
1975	69	3	24
1980	59	6	29
1981	65	3	30
1983	59	4	31
1986	60	8	30
1990	78	2	17
1991	68	5	25
1993	70	4	24
1995	63	13	23
1996	61	9	26
1999	65	5	28
2000	61	7	30

Source: Leslie McAneny, "Americans Tell Congress: Pass Brady Bill, Other Tough Gun Laws," *Gallup Poll Monthly,* March 1993, p. 2. Updates from Gallup.

Table 7.2

National Opinion Research Center Surveys on Permits for Gun Ownership (in percent)

Question: "Would you favor or oppose a law which would require a person to obtain a police permit before he or she could buy a gun?"

	1972	1977	1985	1996	2002
Favor	70	72	72	81	80
Oppose	27	26	27	18	19

Sources: National Opinion Research Center, *General Social Surveys* (July 1982), p. 87; *Public Perspective* (February–March, 1997), p. 27. Update by National Opinion Research Center.

reason for this differential, they suggest, was the superior organizational effectiveness of antigun control forces.

Other gun measures find wide support as well. According to Gallup, 81 percent of Americans supported universal handgun registration in 1993. A 1988 survey found 84 percent favoring laws requiring anyone carrying a gun outside the home to be licensed to do so. Throughout the 1990s, over 90 percent of Americans supported a waiting period for purchase of a handgun, and 66 percent favored banning semiautomatic assault weapons in

1993 (the measure was enacted the following year).[29] Despite the wealth of public opinion findings favoring gun control, the opposition can point to survey results indicating support for the use of guns in hypothetical situations of danger or criminal assault. For example, a Gallup poll found overwhelming support (72 percent) for using a gun against a likely assailant.[30]

Federalism

Much of the emotional commitment that feeds the gun culture stems from a long tradition linking guns to the nation's frontier development. Slogans such as "the guns that won the West" and "arm[s] that opened the West and tamed the wild land" underestimate the central role played by homesteaders, ranchers, business owners, and the general movement of larger settlements across America's western lands.[31] Even after the frontier disappeared, mythic attachments to the gun remained, as reflected in the argument that a boy should be allowed to own a gun because a .22 caliber rifle was a "character builder."[32]

It is difficult to overemphasize the grassroots nature of the gun culture. Obvious regional differences exist, for example, between Morton Grove, Illinois, where handgun ownership in the home was banned, and Kenesaw County, Georgia, where local leaders passed an admittedly frivolous law making it a crime *not* to own a gun. Forty-four states make some mention of a right to bear arms in their constitutions; those that do not are California, Iowa, Maryland, Minnesota, New Jersey, and New York. Except for California, none of these states is located in the South or West, where the gun culture is strongest. One study devised a measure of the strictness of state handgun laws using seven possible types of regulation. Most states fell in the middle of the distribution, having neither very strict nor very weak gun laws. Generally, states with strict handgun control laws tended to have large populations, were eastern, and committed more resources to criminal justice.[33]

Presidency

The first president to associate himself aggressively with organized gun interests was soldier-hunter-sportsman Theodore Roosevelt. While governor of New York, Roosevelt took an active hand in encouraging marksmanship. As president, Roosevelt helped revive the National Rifle Association and was himself a member. He also encouraged the establishment of firing ranges in public schools. During the term of President Calvin Coolidge, Congress dealt with several modest but controversial gun control measures, yet Coolidge offered no leadership on the issue. Franklin D. Roosevelt was the first president to actively promote gun-restricting legislation as part of a larger federal assault on crime and gangsterism. The modest gun control legislation that was enacted into law in 1934 and 1938 was the result of this effort. For most subsequent presidents, the gun issue was primarily one more symbolic ribbon to be acquired. Notably, Presidents Dwight Eisenhower, John Kennedy, Richard Nixon, Ronald Reagan, and George H.W. Bush were all life members of the NRA. Ironically, it was the Kennedy assassination that prompted renewed interest in stronger gun regulations. President Lyndon B. Johnson stood behind the gun control efforts of the 1960s, but he was not especially successful as compared to his enormous impact on major social welfare legislation.[34]

President Reagan took a consistent and prominent stand against gun control. Even after the assassination attempt on his life in 1981, Reagan said in an interview that "if anything, I'm a little disturbed that focusing on gun control as an answer to the crime problem today could very well be diverting us from really paying attention to what needs to be done if we're to solve the crime problem." He also said that existing gun control laws had proven ineffective in regulating guns.[35] After leaving the presidency, however, Reagan reversed himself, endorsing the Brady bill, which passed in 1993, and the assault weapons ban that passed in 1994. George H.W. Bush similarly opposed gun control efforts during his presidency, and he was endorsed by the NRA in 1988. Four years later, however, the NRA repudiated Bush when he endorsed a ban on the import of assault weapons. After his presidency, as noted before, Bush turned in his life NRA membership because the NRA stridently criticized agents of the Bureau of Alcohol, Tobacco, and Firearms.

President Bill Clinton strongly supported new gun controls, notably the Brady bill and the assault weapons ban. His role was clearly important to their passage, yet the country's increasingly strong support for gun control coupled with increasing criticism of the NRA were greater factors in gaining those enactments. President George W. Bush has been, by far, the contemporary president most friendly to the cause of gun rights groups. With the exception of his announcement that he would sign the extension of the assault weapons ban (set to lapse in 2004) if it reached his desk, Bush has aligned himself with the NRA on virtually every other gun measure, including cancellation of a federal gun buy-back program, the barring of law enforcement attempts to gain access to federal gun records, support for a bill to provide the gun industry with immunity from product liability lawsuits, successful opposition in the United Nations to a proposal to restrict the international small arms trade, and a reinterpretation of the Second Amendment (advanced by Attorney General John Ashcroft) that for the first time asserted that it protected an individual "right to bear arms" right to own guns aside from citizen service in militias.[36]

The national political parties have consistently disagreed on gun control.

The Republicans have articulated a long-standing support for gun owner-ship, and the Democrats exhibit a similar consistency in favor of stronger gun regulations. The issue first appeared in party platforms in 1968, and both political parties have treated the issue in their platforms under the category of crime and criminal justice.[37] The 1968 Republican Party platform urged "control [of] indiscriminate availability of firearms" but also "safeguarding the right of responsible citizens to collect, own and use firearms . . . retaining primary responsibility at the state level." The 1972 Republican platform again endorsed citizen rights to "collect, own and use firearms," but also included "self-defense" as a purpose and emphasized efforts "to prevent criminal access to all weapons," especially cheap handguns, while relying mainly on state enforcement. The 1976 GOP platform was terser; it simply stated, "We support the right of citizens to keep and bear arms." The Republican Party also stated its opposition to federal registration of firearms and advocated harsher sentences for crimes committed with guns. The 1976 document conformed fully to NRA policy.

In 1980 the Republican platform wording was the same as in 1976, with an added phrase urging removal of "those provisions of the Control Act of 1968 that do not significantly impact on crime but serve rather to restrain the law-abiding citizen in his legitimate use of firearms." The 1984 platform dropped any reference to the Gun Control Act or to gun registration and said instead that citizens ought not to be blamed for "exercising their constitutional rights" (which presumably meant an "individual" right to bear arms). The 1988 platform supported "the constitutional right to keep and bear arms" and called for "stiff, mandatory penalties" for those who used guns in crime. This wording was kept in 1992 (despite the NRA's refusal to endorse Bush), along with additional wording tying gun ownership to national defense and criticizing efforts at "blaming firearm manufacturers for street crime." The 1996 platform mentioned the Second Amendment, emphasizing firearms training, and a plan to conduct instant background checks for gun purchases. It also endorsed mandatory penalties for crimes involving guns. The 2000 platform paralleled that of 1996, invoking the Second Amendment, the importance of self-defense, and promising vigorous enforcement of existing gun laws. It also stated express opposition to gun licensing and registration.

The 1968 Democratic Party platform urged "the passage and enforcement of effective federal, state and local gun control legislation." A specific proposal appeared for the first time in 1972 when, after calling for "laws to control the improper use of hand guns," the Democratic Party asked for a ban on Saturday night specials. The 1976 platform again called for strengthening existing handgun controls as well as banning Saturday night specials. But the platform also urged tougher sentencing for crimes committed with guns and, in a partial reversal, affirmed "the right of sportsmen to possess guns for purely hunting and target-shooting purposes." The 1980 platform advocated the same position and reaffirmed that the Democratic Party supported the rights of sportsmen to possess guns for sporting purposes. This softening of the Democratic Party's stand on gun control probably reflected the caution of its presidential candidate, Jimmy Carter. The 1984 Democratic Party platform, reflecting the liberal views of nominee Walter Mondale, made a modest turn to the left by dropping any reference to the sporting use of guns. The platform again called for tough restraints on snub-nosed handguns. The 1988 platform backpedaled on earlier tough language. Its only specific gun regulation proposal was a call for enforcement of the ban on "cop killer" bullets enacted in 1986. It also made a vague reference to the procuring of weapons by professionals who carry them as an impediment to the jobs performed by police, teachers, and parents.

The 1992 Democratic platform was stronger and more specific. After asserting that it was "time to shut down the weapons bazaars," it endorsed a waiting period for handgun purchases and a ban on "the most deadly assault weapons." It also called for swift punishment of those who commit gun crimes, shutting down the black market, and stiff penalties for those who sell guns to children. In a bow to hunters (of whom Clinton is one), the platform also said, "We do not support efforts to restrict weapons used for legitimate hunting and sporting purposes." The 1996 platform applauded the enactment of the Brady law and the assault weapons ban, and the protection of legitimate hunting and sporting uses of guns. The 2000 platform extolled candidate Al Gore's record of standing up to the gun lobby, citing past successes of the Clinton-Gore administration, including the Brady law and the assault weapons ban, reductions in juvenile gun crimes, and also promises of a continued tough approach to crime and especially gun crime. The platform also called for mandatory gun locks, a photo license ID system, full background checks, and more federal gun prosecutors and prosecutions.

Congress

Seven major federal gun control laws have been enacted in the past century. The first was the National Firearms Act of 1934, which came as a response to gang violence and the attempted assassination of President Roosevelt the year before. The act's main purpose was to end possession of machine guns, sawed-off shotguns, silencers, and other gangster weapons. Congress went a step further in 1938 by passing the Federal Firearms Act, which regulated the interstate shipment of firearms and ammunition by establishing federal licensing of manufacturers, importers, and dealers of guns and ammunition.

The act also prohibited the shipment of firearms to people under indictment, fugitives, and some convicted felons. Two laws were passed in 1968. One was incorporated in Title IV of the Omnibus Crime Control and Safe Streets Act, which banned the transportation of pistols and revolvers across state lines and forbade the purchase of handguns in stores in a state where the buyer did not reside. The Omnibus Crime Control and Safe Streets Act was passed the day after the assassination of Robert Kennedy and two months after the murder of Martin Luther King Jr.

Gun Control Act of 1968

The key provisions of the Omnibus Act were incorporated into the Gun Control Act of 1968, the second enactment of that year. This statute provides an ideal case study to highlight the political processes affecting a direct effort to regulate firearms. The main arena of conflict was Congress, where numerous efforts were made on the floor to amend this legislation. Lobbying by interest groups was heavy, but the president's influence over the final bill was minimal.[38] The enactment of PL 90–618 was spurred by recent assassinations and a wave of public sentiment favoring tougher gun laws. President Johnson had been outspoken in his support for stronger gun laws since taking office in 1963, but congressional action was not forthcoming. On June 6, 1968, President Johnson urged Congress "in the name of sanity . . . in the name of safety and in the name of an aroused nation to give America the gun-control law it needs."[39]

The Johnson proposal was introduced into the House on June 10, 1968, as HR 17735 by Judiciary Committee chair Emanuel Celler (D-NY), a gun control advocate, and by Senator Thomas Dodd (D-CT), also a champion of gun control, who chaired the Judiciary's Subcommittee on Juvenile Delinquency. The House Judiciary Committee initially voted 16–16 on the bill, thus keeping it in the committee. After an agreement to reconsider the legislation, however, it was finally reported out on June 21 with the addition of qualifying amendments. The House Rules Committee approved a rule for the bill on July 9, after holding the legislation for nearly three weeks. Rules Committee chair William Colmer (D-MS), a gun control opponent, released the bill only after extracting a promise from Celler that he would oppose any efforts to add registration and licensing provisions to the bill on the floor of the House.

The House of Representatives passed HR 17735 on July 24 after four days of vigorous floor consideration characterized by numerous attempts to amend the bill. Forty-five attempts were made to amend this legislation on the floor of the House, including four roll call votes plus one more on final passage. In the more liberal Senate, the gun control bill met with greater support, and more debate centered on whether to strengthen the law or not. Subcommittee hearings began on June 26, and testimony was received from a wide variety of persons including NRA president Harold W. Glassen, who said that the legislation was part of an effort to "foist upon an unsuspecting and aroused public a law that would, through its operation, sound the death knell for the shooting sport and eventually disarm the American public."[40]

The Senate subcommittee approved the measure unanimously and forwarded it to the full committee, where the bill encountered stiff opposition. The bill was delayed and weakened by gun control opponents, including Judiciary Committee chair James Eastland (D-MS). Efforts to push the bill through were hampered by the absence at various times of gun control supporters, including Senator Edward Kennedy (D-MA), who was still mourning the loss of his brother. Finally, the bill was sent by committee to the Senate floor, where it was debated for five days. The opening salvo came from Senator Dodd, who accused the NRA of "blackmail, intimidation and unscrupulous propaganda."[41] Seventeen formal motions were made to amend this bill in the Senate. After the bill's passage on September 18, a conference committee ironed out differences with the House, and President Johnson signed the bill on October 22.

As enacted, PL 90–618 restricted interstate shipment of firearms and ammunition and prohibited the sale of guns to minors, drug addicts, mental incompetents, and convicted felons. The act strengthened licensing and record-keeping requirements for gun dealers and collectors, extended the tax provisions of the National Firearms Act of 1934 to include destructive devices not originally covered, and banned the importation of foreign-made surplus firearms. But the law did not ban the importation of handgun parts, which effectively allowed for the circumvention of the import ban. One year later, however, a key provision of the act, requiring sellers of shotgun and rifle ammunition to register purchasers, was repealed in an amendment tacked onto a tax bill. This rider was authored by Senator Wallace F. Bennett (R-UT) along with forty-six Senate cosponsors.[42]

Firearms Owners Protection Act of 1986

Repeated efforts were made to weaken the 1968 gun law. Success came in 1986 with enactment of the Firearms Owners Protection Act, also known as the McClure-Volkmer Bill (S 49, HR 4332, PL 99–308). This act amended the 1968 Gun Control Act by allowing for the legal interstate sale of rifles and shotguns as long as the sale is legal in the states of the buyer and seller. The act also eliminated record-keeping requirements for ammunition dealers, made it easier for individuals selling guns to do so without a license unless they did so "regularly," allowed gun dealers to do business at gun shows, and prohibited the Bureau of Alcohol, Tobacco, and Firearms (ATF) from issuing regulations requiring centralized records of gun dealers. In addition, the act limited to one per year the number of unannounced inspections of gun dealers by the ATF and prohibited the establishment of any system of comprehensive firearms registration. Finally, the act barred future possession or transfer of machine guns and retained existing restrictions (except for transport) on handguns. The passage of this legislation spanned two years and was the culmination of a protracted lobbying effort by the NRA, joined by the Gun Owners of America and the Citizens Committee for the Right to Keep and Bear Arms.

Consideration of S 49 began first in the Senate, where attempts to weaken the 1968 gun law had been approved by the Judiciary Committee in 1982 and 1984. Floor consideration was not obtained, however, until 1985, the first time the full Senate had considered any gun legislation since 1972. Once on the floor, the bill was subjected to a barrage of amendments designed to strengthen gun controls; none of these amendments, however, was accepted. The chief Senate sponsors, James A. McClure (R-ID) and Orrin Hatch (R-UT), argued that the proposed restrictions would have no effect on crime fighting but instead represented unjustified limitations on sportsmen, hunters, and dealers. The one significant restriction imposed by the Senate was a ban on the importation of parts for Saturday night specials. The final vote on S. 49 was 79–15, with the strongest support coming from westerners. The relatively speedy passage of this bill was attributed to the pressure from the NRA and its allies and sympathetic Judiciary Committee chairman (Strom Thurmond, R-SC) and majority leader (Robert Dole, R-KS) in the Republican-controlled Senate.[43]

The gun control forces were caught unaware by the speedy Senate action. This set the stage for a full-scale fight in the House of Representatives in 1986. Although the gun lobby achieved an important victory, in the process it alienated some longtime allies—law enforcement organizations. Police dissatisfaction with NRA positions had been growing for some time, and even during Senate consideration of S. 49, Handgun Control had enlisted the support of five national police organizations. In 1986 national law enforcement groups lined up almost unanimously with gun control proponents. Such organizations as the National Sheriffs' Association, the International Association of Chiefs of Police, the National Organization of Black Law Enforcement Executives, the National Troopers Association, the Police Executive Research Forum, the Police Foundation, and the Fraternal Order of Police became increasingly alarmed about the criminal and safety consequences of weak gun regulations. Law enforcement officials were particularly alienated by the NRA stand against controlling armor-piercing bullets and favoring the legal possession of submachine guns and automatic weapons.[44]

Deliberations on the McClure-Volkmer Bill in the Democratic-controlled House posed a far greater problem for the gun lobby. Judiciary Committee chair Peter Rodino (D-NJ), a staunch proponent of gun control, had announced that the bill came "DOA—dead on arrival." Many proponents of gun control felt reassured, despite the Senate action, because they had confidence that Rodino would not allow a gun decontrol bill out of his committee. Rodino's comments infuriated the gun lobby, however, and a discharge petition was begun, spearheaded by House bill sponsor Harold L. Volkmer (D-MO). If signed by a majority of the House membership, a discharge petition would force the bill from the committee to the House floor. The opponents of gun control argued that this bill was necessary to eliminate burdensome and unnecessary restrictions on gun dealers and legitimate owners. The ATF countered that, in fact, most of its prosecutions under the gun law involved individuals with prior criminal or felony records.[45] Despite its well-known support for the NRA, the Reagan administration played a minimal role in these proceedings. Officially, the administration supported S. 49, but the Justice Department offered no testimony at committee hearings. Further, internal ATF memos released to the press revealed doubts about some of the decontrol provisions. Public comments by Attorney General Edwin Meese were similarly equivocal.[46]

Notwithstanding the firm opposition of Congressmen Peter Rodino and William J. Hughes (D-NJ, chair of the Subcommittee on Crime), the full Judiciary Committee held a markup session on the bill and reported it to the floor on a unanimous vote. This remarkable turn of events occurred in March as the result of the discharge petition, the first successful petition since 1983. By reporting to the floor first (March 11) before completion and filing of the discharge petition (March 13), gun control forces hoped to salvage some parliamentary flexibility that would allow prior consideration of legislation retaining more gun restrictions. This maneuver failed, however, because Representative Volkmer was able to offer his version of the bill as a substitute for that of the Judiciary Committee.

On April 9 Congressman Hughes offered a package of law enforcement amendments, including a ban on interstate sale and transport of handguns and stricter record-keeping regulations. The package was rejected by a wide margin (176–248). During the vote, police officers stood in full uniform at "parade rest" at the entrance to the House floor. After several other votes on motions to strengthen certain gun control provisions (none was successful), the House adjourned and then reconvened the next day. This time, on the third try, the House approved (233–184) a ban on interstate handgun sales after proponents stressed the difference between sale and transport. A final amendment to bar all future possession and sale of machine guns by private citizens also passed. The bill was approved by a lopsided 292–130 vote on April 10.

Analysis of the voting behavior on the key package of amendments offered by Congressman Hughes revealed that antigun control voters were most numerous in the South and border states (83 percent against), followed by the West and Rocky Mountain region (59 percent against), the Midwest (50 percent against), and then the East (38 percent against). Regions with heavily rural populations and high rates of gun ownership (and presumably heavy NRA influence) provided the strongest support for the progun lobby, but the NRA did well even in some large states such as Pennsylvania and Texas. In terms of partisanship, House Republicans heavily favored the NRA, with only 40 voting for the Hughes package versus 138 against. The Democrats were less cohesive on this question; they split almost evenly, with 138 for the amendments and 110 against.

NRA applied dual pressure from below (grassroots) and above (lobbying) on the Congress, devoting $1.6 million to its efforts compared to the paltry $15,000 spent by police organizations.[47] The relative inexperience of police lobbyists also hurt their cause. As one congressman observed, "The police misunderstood the force of lobbying. Lobbying is not standing in long lines at the door. Lobbying is good information early; it is a presence when minds are being made up."[48] The House-passed bill, HR 4332, differed from the Senate version in a few specifics. They were resolved by the unusual action of enacting a separate bill (S. 2414). Its purpose was to clarify certain sections and to appease police officers, who finally succeeded in persuading Senator Thurmond to take up their appeal. The added provision made clear that guns transported across state lines must be unloaded and locked in an area of the motor vehicle other than the passenger compartment. The clarifying bill also provided for easier government traces of guns and restored certain record-keeping provisions. In this form, the bill was signed by President Reagan on May 19, 1986.

This legislative case study parallels the experience of the 1968 Gun Control Act in important ways. First, President Reagan's impact was minimal, despite his clear opinions on this subject. Second, the level of political intensity was high, especially in the House. The successful and rare application of a discharge petition coupled with the unusual clarifying bill at final passage illustrates how both conflict and political instability caused these disruptions in legislative routine. The large number of floor amendments revealed the inability of the proponents and opponents of decontrol to resolve their differences within the committees of either house. Third, interest group activity again was abundant and of critical importance to the final outcome.

The Brady Bill

From 1987 to 1993, gun control proponents placed their primary emphasis on enacting a national waiting period for handgun purchases in order to, first, allow authorities to conduct a background check on the prospective purchaser in order to void handgun purchases by felons, the mentally incompetent, and others who should not have handguns and, second, provide a cooling-off period for those who seek to buy and perhaps use a handgun in a fit of temper or rage. The so-called Brady bill (named after James Brady, the former White House press secretary) was first introduced in early 1987 in the Senate by Howard Metzenbaum (D-OH) and in the House by Representative Edward F. Feighan (D-OH). It quickly became the top priority of HCI and Sarah Brady, James Brady's wife and HCI leader. The NRA opposed the measure, although as late as the mid-1970s the NRA had supported such a waiting period.[49]

The Brady bill struggle first emerged on the floor of Congress in a House vote in 1988 (the bill was defeated). In 1991 and 1992 both the House and the Senate passed different versions of the bill, but the revised version of the bill stalled in the Senate. The effort climaxed in 1993, when supporters promoted a bill requiring a waiting period of five business days. House Judiciary Committee approval was won on November 4, despite the objections of committee chair and gun control opponent Jack Brooks (D-TX), who also boosted the bill's chances by consenting with reluctance to separate the measure (HR 1025) from a new crime bill. Six days later, the full House approved the Brady bill after fending off several amendments (sponsored by Republicans and Representative Brooks) designed to weaken the bill. One such amendment, to phase out the waiting period after five years, was adopted. The final vote to pass the bill, HR 1025, was 238–189.[50]

Following the lead of the House, the Senate separated the Brady bill (S 414) from the larger crime package. The bill faced a Republican filibuster almost immediately, but this move was forestalled by an agreement between the political party leaders to allow floor consideration of a substitute version that included two NRA-backed provisions. The first called for all state waiting periods to be superseded by the federal five-day waiting period (twenty-four states had waiting periods of varying lengths in 1993; twenty-three also had background checks).[51] This was objectionable to Brady supporters because many states had waiting periods longer than five days, and the move was seen as a violation of states' rights. This amendment was stricken from the bill by a Senate floor vote. The second measure called for ending the five-day waiting period after five years. It survived a vote to kill it. The Senate then faced another filibuster, which looked as though it would be fatal to the bill. Brady supporters and congressional allies all conceded that the bill was dead for the year. The postmortems proved to be premature, however, as the Republicans, sensing a rising tide of impatience that would allow them to win no further concessions from Democratic leaders, decided to end their opposition on November 20. The bill was passed that day by a 63–36 vote.[52]

The bill then went to a contentious House-Senate conference on November 22. The House passed the conference version early in the morning of the twenty-third. Senate GOP leader Robert Dole (R-KS), however, balked at the compromise, calling it unacceptable. Senate Democratic leader George Mitchell (D-ME) threatened to reconvene the Senate after the Thanksgiving break in order to obtain final action. The two finally reached an accommodation, and the bill was approved in the Senate by voice vote on November 24, with a promise to consider several modifications in early 1994. President Clinton signed the bill into law on November 30.[53] The Brady law codified a five-business-day waiting period for handgun purchases. It also authorized $200 million per year to help states upgrade their computerization of criminal records; increased federal firearms license fees from $30 to $200 for the first three years, and $90 for renewals; made it a federal crime to steal firearms from licensed dealers; barred package labeling for guns being shipped, to deter theft; required state and local police to be told of multiple handgun sales; and mandated that police make a "reasonable effort" to check the backgrounds of gun buyers.

In policy terms, the impact of the Brady law was modest, but measurable. First, the law does not actually require local police to conduct background checks, and there are wide variations in state record-keeping practices. Second, state experiences with waiting periods showed that about 1 to 2 percent of prospective gun buyers were denied sales as the result of background checks, a figure that may be more significant than it appears because roughly a quarter of state prison inmates reported purchasing their guns legally.[54] The ATF reported that it conducted about 90,000 Brady background checks each week, using the National Criminal Information Computer system. About 16 percent of those checks came up with criminal records, and 6 percent identified convicted felons.[55] From 1994 through the end of 2000, the Brady law blocked about 600,000 gun purchases to felons, illegal aliens, and others.[56]

The political consequences of enacting the Brady bill far outstripped its policy consequences. A crucial realignment in favor of the Brady bill occurred in the House between 1988 and 1991, when about thirty-five House members switched their votes to support the bill, citing repugnance at the NRA's continued strong-arm tactics. The 1991 House vote thus helped to deflate the NRA's image of invulnerability. According to Representative Charles E. Schumer (D-NY), a Brady bill supporter, "People realized that there's life after voting against the NRA."[57] The partisan pattern observed in other gun control votes emerged here as well. More Democrats than Republicans supported the Brady bill but both parties were split. In the House, 184 Democrats supported Brady, with 69 opposed; the Republican split was 54 in favor and 119 opposed.[58] Northern Democrats provided the greatest support for Brady (82 percent); southern Democrats provided the lowest Democratic support (55 percent). As with previous gun control votes, most opposition came from southern, western, and rural representatives, regardless of party, and strongest support came from urban representatives.[59] The election of Bill Clinton put an incumbent in the White House who was sympathetic to the aims of gun control proponents. Still, the bill's near-passage in 1992 clearly suggested that the time for its enactment had come, and Clinton's primary focus during his 1992 campaign and first year in office was on domestic policy issues, not gun control. Indeed, many in the Clinton administration were caught by surprise when President Clinton began to aggressively promote gun control in late 1993.[60]

Assault Weapons Ban

In the forefront of gun control efforts in the 1980s and 1990s were moves to regulate or ban various styles of semiautomatic assault weapons. A semiautomatic weapon is one that fires a round with each pull of the trigger. Some wooden-stocked hunting rifles are semiautomatic. Assault-style semiautomatic weapons have large clips holding twenty to thirty bullets, are compact in design, have barrels under twenty inches in length, take intermediate-sized cartridges, include extensive use of stampings and plastics, weigh six to ten pounds, and were designed for military use. They often have pistol grips, grenade launchers, and bayonet fittings. These traits underscore assault weapons' military combat function.[61]

The key event spurring supporters of a ban on such weapons was a schoolyard massacre in Stockton, California, in January 1989, when five children were killed and twenty-nine others were wounded in a shooting spree by a man using a Chinese AK-47 assault rifle. Within weeks, thirty states and many localities were considering bans on these weapons.[62] Two years later, the worst such massacre in American history occurred in Killeen, Texas, when George J. Hennard killed twenty-two people and himself, and wounded twenty-three others, in a cafeteria.

Responding to advice from his staff and First Lady Barbara Bush, George H.W. Bush reversed his opposition to regulation of assault weapons within the space of a month, issuing in March 1989 an executive order to temporarily ban the importation of certain assault rifles. The temporary ban was subsequently expanded to include a larger number of weapons, then made permanent, thus earning Bush the ire of the NRA. President Bill Clinton expanded the scope of the import ban in 1993, also by executive order, to include assault-style handguns, like the Uzi.

In November 1993 the Senate passed a ban on the manufacture of nineteen types of assault weapons but also included a provision allowing gun dealers to sell guns that had already been produced. The measure also exempted 650 types of hunting weapons.[63] That same month, the Senate passed a bill making it a federal crime to sell handguns to minors. In the spring of 1994 the House took up the assault weapons ban. From the start, however, ban supporters were not optimistic that the House would approve the measure. In April President Clinton strongly endorsed the ban, enlisting the help of several cabinet secretaries, most notably treasury secretary and gun owner Lloyd Bentsen. Ban supporters received unexpected help from Representative Henry Hyde (R-IL), a staunch conservative who in past years had opposed gun measures. Thanks partly to Hyde's backing, the measure cleared the Judiciary Committee on April 28 despite the opposition of committee chair Jack Brooks (D-TX).[64]

As the House floor vote approached, bill supporters feared defeat because they were probably fifteen votes shy and the Democratic leadership was split. House Speaker Tom Foley (D-WA) opposed the measure, while Majority Leader Richard Gephardt (D-MO) favored it. Yet, in a stunning finale, the assault weapons ban managed to pass by a two-vote margin, 216–214, on May 5. The drama was heightened when Representative Andrew Jacobs Jr. (D-IN), at the urging of several colleagues, switched his vote from nay to yea in the final seconds of the roll call vote. On the final roll call, 177 Democrats were joined by 38 Republicans plus one independent in favor, with 137 Republicans and 77 Democrats opposed. Although more Democrats than Republicans supported the measure, party was not the deciding factor because the main opposition came from southern and western representatives.[65]

Because the assault weapons ban was included in a larger crime bill that had passed the House and Senate in different versions, a conference committee was called to iron out those differences. Bill supporters initially predicted that the conference committee would complete its work by the end of May, but it did not report a bill back to the House and Senate until the end of July. In August opponents actually defeated the bill on the House floor in a procedural vote. Despite this setback, supporters regrouped, won passage, and after a similarly tumultuous Senate debate, HR 3355 was signed by President Clinton on September 13.[66]

The assault weapons ban outlawed the sale and possession of nineteen specified types as well as dozens of other copycat weapons that possessed characteristics similar to those designated weapons. It specifically exempted over 650 sporting rifles and limited gun clips to those that could hold no more than ten bullets. Existing assault-style rifles were exempted from the ban, and Congress was given the power to review the inclusion of any additional weapons under the terms of the measure. With the ban scheduled to sunset in 2004, both sides geared up for a bruising battle over the law's renewal. In a blow to those who oppose its renewal, President George W. Bush promised to sign the bill if it got to his desk, although he did not work actively for its renewal. Despite the measure's popularity, the bill lapsed in September 2004.[67]

Bureaucracy

The Bureau of Alcohol, Tobacco, and Firearms (ATF) was established in 1972 within the Treasury Department when legal authority related to alcohol, tobacco, and firearms was transferred from the Internal Revenue Service. The bureau was organized according to two sections: regulatory enforcement and criminal enforcement. Matters dealing with gun regulations, including licensing, gun tracing, illegal firearms transport and possession, and explosives were handled by the Section on Criminal Enforcement. In 2003 the ATF was reorganized as the Bureau of Alcohol, Tobacco, Firearms, and Explosives as part of the Homeland Security Act of 2002. Most ATF employees (about 4,600 people) who specialize in firearms and explosives investigations were transferred to the Justice Department, and the remaining 500 ATF employees who specialize in alcohol and tobacco taxes and trade stayed under the Treasury Department.[68]

A spokesperson for the ATF reported that during 1980 the bureau conducted only 103 investigations of firearms dealers and that 10 dealer licenses out of the 180,000 nationwide were revoked.[69] In 1985 ATF fielded only 400 inspectors to monitor more than 200,000 gun merchants.[70] In 1994 about 250 agents were responsible for overseeing 280,000 dealers.[71] Much ATF reluctance to enforce gun laws more aggressively stems from continued NRA harassment, but the ATF also suffered a serious loss of prestige over its handling of a raid on the heavily fortified and armed compound of the Branch Davidian cult near Waco, Texas, in February 1993. Four ATF agents were killed and twenty were wounded in an initial assault on the compound, leading to a two-month standoff until ATF and FBI agents stormed the fortress, killing nearly all of those inside. The new ATF director, John Magaw, worked to improve agency morale and effectiveness during the Clinton administration.[72]

Clinton administration support for gun control meant an expanded mission for the ATF. In 1994, for example, ATF extended the prohibition on armor-piercing bullets to certain bullets that formerly could not be fired from handguns. Rapid-fire, "street sweeper" shotguns (developed for military and riot control purposes in South Africa) were subjected to strict ATF regulation on the directive of Treasury Secretary Lloyd Bentsen. Owners of the 18,000 such weapons in circulation were required to submit to registration, fingerprinting, and photographing. Dealers in such weapons were also subjected to new fees and regulations.[73] Under President George W. Bush, critics differed on the impact of the 2003 organizational changes on ATF gun regulation enforcement. Some argued that Attorney General Ashcroft, a gun rights supporter, would further weaken ATF enforcement activities, while others argued that, by elevating the agency's status, the reorganization could have the opposite effect.

Judiciary

Gun control does not immediately conjure up an image of judicial activism because the Second Amendment has not been centrally involved in fundamental rights adjudication. This amendment is accorded little significance by most legal experts. Irving Brant argues that the Second Amendment "comes to life chiefly on the parade floats of rifle associations and in the propaganda of mail-order houses selling pistols to teenage gangsters."[74] J.W. Peltason writes that the Second Amendment "was designed to prevent Congress from disarming the state militias, not to prevent it from regulating private ownership of firearms."[75] In state courts, various rulings generally have upheld the power of states to regulate firearms and have associated the right to bear arms with service in a militia.[76]

Five Supreme Court cases serve as precedent for interpreting the Second Amendment. The first is *U.S. v. Cruikshank,* 92 U.S. 553 (1876). Cruikshank was charged with thirty-two counts of depriving blacks of their constitutional rights, including two counts alleging that he had deprived blacks of firearms possession. The Court ruled that the right "of bearing arms for a lawful purpose is not a right granted by the Constitution, nor is it in any manner dependent upon that instrument for its existence." Speaking for the Court, Chief Justice Morrison Waite said that "the Second Amendment declares that it shall not be infringed; but this, as has been seen, means no more than that it shall not be infringed by Congress." At this juncture, the Supreme

Court established two principles that it (and lower federal courts) consistently have upheld. First, the Second Amendment does not bar the regulation of firearms; second, the Second Amendment is not "incorporated" or applied to the states through the due process and equal protection clauses of the Fourteenth Amendment.

Ten years later, the Supreme Court ruled in *Presser v. Illinois,* 116 U.S. 252 (1886), that an Illinois law that barred paramilitary organizations from drilling or parading in cities or towns without a license from the governor was constitutional. Herman Presser challenged the law after he was arrested for marching his fringe group through Chicago streets. In upholding the Illinois statute, the Supreme Court reaffirmed that the Second Amendment did not apply to the states. Speaking for the court, Justice William B. Woods discussed the relationship between the citizen, the militia, and the government:

> It is undoubtedly true that all citizens capable of bearing arms constitute the revered reserved military force or reserve militia of the United States as well as the States; and, in view of this prerogative of the General Government, as well as of its general powers, the States cannot, even laying the constitutional provisions in question out of view, prohibit the people from keeping and bearing arms, so as to deprive the United States of their rightful resource for maintaining the public security, and disable the people from performing their duty to the General Government. But, as already stated, we think it clear that sections [of the Illinois law] under consideration do not have this effect.

In 1894 the Supreme Court ruled in *Miller v. Texas,* 153 U.S. 535 (1894), that a Texas law prohibiting the carrying of dangerous weapons did not violate the Second Amendment. Here again the Court said that the right to bear arms did not apply to the states. This reasoning was reaffirmed three years later in the case of *Robertson v. Baldwin,* 165 U.S. 275 (1897).[77] The final case in this sequence is *U.S. v. Miller,* 307 U.S. 174 (1939). *Miller* was founded on a challenge to the National Firearms Act of 1934, which regulated the interstate transport of certain weapons. Jack Miller and Frank Layton, both of whom were convicted of transporting an unregistered twelve-gauge sawed-off shotgun (having a barrel less than eighteen inches long) across state lines under the 1934 act, challenged its constitutionality by claiming that the law violated the Second Amendment and also represented an improper use of the commerce power. Turning aside those arguments, the high court ruled that the federal taxing power could be used to regulate firearms and that firearms registration was legal. Beyond this, the Supreme Court was unequivocal in

saying that the Second Amendment must be interpreted by its "obvious purpose" of ensuring the effectiveness of the militia. Speaking for the Court,
Justice James C. McReynolds wrote:

> In the absence of any evidence tending to show that possession or use of a
> "shotgun having a barrel of less than eighteen inches in length" at this time
> has some reasonable relationship to the preservation or efficiency of a well
> regulated militia, we cannot say that the Second Amendment guarantees
> the right to keep and bear such an instrument. Certainly, it is not within
> judicial notice that this weapon is any part of the ordinary equipment or
> that its use could contribute to the common defense.

Supreme Court rulings aside, over forty lower federal court rulings from
the 1940s to the present have confirmed the militia-based meaning of the
Second Amendment. In 2001, however, the Fifth Circuit Court of Appeals
embraced the individualist view for the first time in *U.S. v. Emerson,* 270
F.3d 203 (5th Cir. 2001). The anomalous decision gave hope to those seeking
to ratify a new interpretation of the Second Amendment, thus encouraging
more gun rights supporters to seek favorable court rulings. It also increased
pressure on the Supreme Court to revisit the Second Amendment.[78]

Summary of Propositions

1a (single-issue groups): Supported, because the NRA is the foremost opponent of gun control laws and because, in addition, single-issue groups operate on both sides of this issue.

1b (absolutist politics): Supported, by the uncompromising opposition of
the NRA and, even more so, of other single-issue progun lobbies that believe
the NRA is not strident enough.

2a (judicial activism): Supported, by the large body of case law on gun
control issues even though the Supreme Court has handed down few rulings
over two centuries.

2b (incorporation): Unsupported, because the Supreme Court has not interpreted the Second Amendment as guaranteeing an "individual" right to
bear arms.

3a (presidential symbolism): Supported, though Clinton may be an exception to this generalization.

3b (partisan presidents): Supported, because the major gun laws were enacted under Democrats Johnson and Clinton, whereas Republicans—with
few exceptions—are reluctant to offend the NRA.

4a (Congress and states): Unsupported, because the Supreme Court has signaled to Congress and the state legislatures that gun control laws are constitutionally permissible.

4b (Congress and elections): Unsupported, because Congress would enact stronger gun laws if legislators were constrained by popular electoral pressures rather than NRA lobbying.

5a (opinion and ideology): Unsupported, because public opinion supports the liberal position favoring stronger gun laws.

5b (law and society): Supported, insofar as any gun control enforcement is resisted by the NRA and its like-minded constituents.

6a (federal agencies): Supported, to the degree that the ATF has jurisdiction over cigarette and alcohol tax enforcement and bombings as well as gun control and recently was given the added responsibility of investigating explosives, beyond the limitations of inadequate ATF resources to monitor gun sales.

6b (federal implementation): Supported, because clearly pressure from the NRA, its allies in Congress, and some presidents means that the ATF will not aggressively enforce gun control policy.

7a (federalism): Supported, because states had gun laws prior to the first federal gun control statute.

7b (compliance): Supported, in the sense that the ATF relies on state and local law enforcement authorities as partners in gun control enforcement and, given its inadequate resources coupled with congressional prohibitions on ATF monitoring of gun dealers, the implementation of gun control policy seemingly relies heavily on voluntary compliance by gun dealers.

For Further Insight Into the Gun Control Debate

Carter, Gregg, ed. *Encyclopedia of Guns in American Society.* 2 vols. Santa Barbara, CA: ABC-CLIO, 2002. A interdisciplinary compilation of every major aspect of the gun control issue.

Cornell, Saul, ed. *Whose Right to Bear Arms Did the Second Amendment Protect?* Boston: Bedford/St. Martin's, 2000. Essays that analyze the historical basis of the Second Amendment and the arms-bearing tradition.

DeConde, Alexander. *Gun Violence in America.* Boston: Northeastern University Press, 2001. A sweeping examination of gun practices and politics from colonial times to the present.

Kennett, Lee, and James LaVerne Anderson. *The Gun in America.* Westport, CT: Greenwood, 1975. Historical treatment of the role of guns and gun control in American development.

Spitzer, Robert J. *The Politics of Gun Control,* 3rd ed. Washington, DC: CQ Press, 2004. A political, policy, and legal analysis of all elements of the gun control issue.

Spitzer, Robert J. *The Right to Bear Arms.* Santa Barbara, CA: ABC-CLIO, 2001. Examination of the right to bear arms in history and law.

Vizzard, William J. *Shots in the Dark: The Policy, Politics, and Symbolism of Gun Control.* Lanham, MD: Rowman and Littlefield, 2000. A look at the gun issue, including the role of the Bureau of Alcohol, Tobacco, and Firearms.

www.bradycenter.org. Web site for Brady Campaign to Prevent Gun Violence.

www.atf.gov. Web site for the Bureau of Alcohol, Tobacco, Firearms and Explosives.

www.gunowners.org. Web site for Gun Owners of America.

www.nra.org. Web site for the National Rifle Association.

www.vpc.org. Web site for Violence Policy Center, advocates for gun control.

Guns and Mothers. This documentary by Sugar Pictures, first aired on PBS on May 14, 2003, examines the gun control issue from the perspectives of two women on opposing sides.

Bowling for Columbine. This 2002 documentary by Michael Moore is a highly critical examination of the American gun culture.

8

Hate Crimes

Protected Prejudice or Punishable Motive?

Scott Yenor and Jon Schaff

The existence of illiberal attitudes poses a challenge to a liberal society. Liberal societies are designed to protect human freedoms, including free thought, free speech, and political association. The legal system guarantees these rights by treating individuals equally without regard to their thoughts, speech, or political associations. Punishment and incarceration demonstrate our commitment to equal justice and reaffirm society's commitment to protecting itself. They are a quintessential expression of our commonality, unity, and solidarity. At the same time, liberal society's commitment to limited government seems to preclude government from actively shaping the manner in which freedom is exercised. Because liberal tolerance seems to protect intolerant beliefs, as a consequence various racial, religious, ethnic, and homosexual groups have mobilized around the goal of eradicating through persuasion what they perceive as hatred, bigotry, and intolerance that is beyond liberal government's coercive powers.

Collective denunciations of bigotry and pleas for tolerance presume the existence of a community, a concept somewhat in conflict with liberalism's emphasis on individual rights. The apparently liberal desire to eradicate illiberal prejudice leads to the formation of group identity and therewith identity politics. Smith and Tatalovich define identity politics as "campaigns by 'victim' groups—women, racial and ethnic minorities, homosexuals and indigenous peoples—to elevate their social status by gaining political recognition and legal rights as members of groups, not as autonomous individuals."[1]

Interest groups that form around such goals find themselves pleading for government to use its coercive power to fight illiberal bigotry. Hate crime laws, which offer enhanced criminal penalties for criminal conduct motivated by "hatred" or disfavored prejudice, surfaced in the mid-1980s when self-proclaimed marginalized groups appropriated the language of "identity politics" and "victim's rights." Coupled with liberalism's commitment to tolerance and humanity, the pluralism of modern societies allows the airing of grievances by such marginalized groups, giving rise to hate crimes laws.

Judiciary

Judicial doctrine on hate crimes derives from judicial doctrine on hate speech. Laws against hate speech aim to deter and punish the expression of offensive, insulting, and threatening thoughts. Hate crime laws aim to deter and punish conduct related to insulting, threatening, and prejudiced motives. Hate crimes laws force courts to differentiate expressive speech from proscribable conduct and to distinguish the punishment of thoughts from the punishment of motives. Supreme Court jurisprudence on hate speech is more ambiguous than its doctrine on hate crimes legislation. With some qualifications, laws curbing hate speech are constitutionally impermissible although states have wide-ranging authority to enact hate crimes legislation.

Hate speech or "fighting words" are unconstitutional according to a World War II–era case (*Chaplinsky v. New Hampshire*). In this case, the defendant was convicted of insulting a city marshal, whom he called "a God-damned racketeer" and a "damned fascist." The Supreme Court upheld Chaplinsky's conviction on the grounds that words "which by their very utterance inflict injury or tend to incite an immediate breach of the peace" are not protected by the Constitution.[2] The Court subsequently has allowed the "inflict injury" portion of *Chaplinsky* to wither on the legal vine while narrowing the "immediate breach" portion. Neither laws against group libel, local ordinances meant to keep hate groups from marching, nor campus speech codes—all arguably instances of hate speech—have found support in the federal courts. It is notable that the Supreme Court has never sustained a conviction under the "fighting words" doctrine since *Chaplinsky. Chaplinsky* now appears to be just a shadow of an exception.

The Supreme Court seems more willing to draw limits around what it calls expressive conduct. The most famous instance of protecting expressive conduct appears in *Texas v. Johnson* (1989), wherein the high court held that "flag-burning was 'conduct' sufficiently imbued with elements of 'communication' to implicate the First Amendment."[3] Supreme Court jurisprudence on hate crime laws began with *R.A.V. v. St. Paul* (1992). R.A.V. and friends burned a wooden cross on a black family's lawn in violation of a St. Paul, Minnesota, ordinance proscribing symbolic conduct that would arouse "anger, alarm, or resentment in others on the basis of race, color, religion, or gender."[4] The majority opinion worried that the ordinance singled out only ideas that "communicate messages of racial, gender or religious intolerance" because such "selectivity . . . creates the possibility that the city is seeking to handicap the expression of particular ideas." Writing for the majority, Justice Antonio Scalia asserted that St. Paul "has sufficient means at its disposal to prevent such behavior without adding the First Amendment to the fire."[5]

The Court plumbed the meaning of "sufficient means" ten years later in *Virginia v. Black.* Unlike the St. Paul ordinance, *Virginia* did not single out specific cultural groups but focused on threatening, intimidating conduct. This approach satisfied the Court, but the specific provision that cross-burning be considered *"prima facie* evidence of an intent to intimidate" runs afoul of the First Amendment because it "ignores all of the contextual factors that are necessary to decide whether a particular cross burning is intended to intimidate." Sometimes, the Court reasoned, cross-burning is "core political speech," as when one burns a cross as a symbol of political affiliation or to signify pride in one's heritage. Cross-burning with the intent of intimidation is "constitutionally proscribable," as when a Klansman burns a cross on a black family's lawn with the hope of scaring them out of the neighborhood. Circumstances determine the message, and only laws that pay attention to circumstances can pass constitutional muster. *Black* leaves the door open for localities to limit intimidating hate speech, but only narrowly tailored, nuanced laws can pass through that door. Laws that in effect proscribe much "core political speech" under the guise of limiting intimidation are not permissible.[6]

This issue leads to the related question of hate crime statutes that impose enhanced penalties for violators who target victims because of their race, creed, gender, or sexual orientation. The constitutionality of these enhancement provisions depends on the distinction between conduct and speech, since hate crimes laws force the judiciary to evaluate what is being targeted for enhanced punishments. There is general consensus that state legislatures wanted to single out prejudiced *motives* for extra punishment. At issue is whether the intent of the law is to punish offensive motives, thoughts, or expressions under the guise of punishing criminal conduct. In *Wisconsin v. Mitchell,* a unanimous Supreme Court upheld penalty enhancements provisions because they were aimed at punishing conduct not protected by the First Amendment.[7] The high court held that penalty enhancement provisions must not be content neutral because they target conduct (where certain motives are disfavored) instead of expression (where neutrality is required). The Supreme Court also noted that defendants cannot be punished for "abstract beliefs," thus limiting the kind of evidence used to prove that someone was motivated by a disapproved prejudice.[8] Concrete beliefs that illustrate a clear connection between a disfavored prejudice and the criminal act are punishable. Bigotry unrelated to a committed crime is not sufficient to justify enhanced penalties. Penalty enhancement provisions are akin to "aggravating circumstances" when juries or judges decide punishments. Evidence of racial animus can be an aggravating factor, for instance, when courts decide whether to put a convicted murderer to death.[9] While it places some limits on state action, *Mitchell* provides a largely open field for political branches to enact penalty enhancement statutes for crimes implicating a disfavored motivation. State courts generally have followed the federal judiciary in permitting penalty enhancement provisions under state constitutions. In sum, judicial hurdles to hate crime laws are quite low across the federal and state judicial systems.

Interest Groups

Minority groups have framed the hate crimes issue with uncommon skill. The Anti-Defamation League (ADL) has advocated hate crimes legislation and the centralized collection of hate crime statistics since the late 1970s. Before those efforts could achieve results, however, it was necessary to convince the attentive public and sympathetic legislators that a need existed for such laws. That goal could only be accomplished if the ADL made allies of like-minded minority advocates, such as the National Association for the Advancement of Colored People (NAACP), the National Gay and Lesbian Task Force, and the Southern Poverty Law Center. Led by the ADL, its allied groups collected data by mining local newspapers, through victim self-reporting, and with the aid of community activist reports. With the help of sympathetic sociologists and criminologists, they convinced the national media—and Congress—that an "epidemic" of hate crimes was sweeping the nation.[10] Advocacy groups that lobbied for the Hate Crimes Statistics Act (HCSA) emphasized how the collection of hate crime statistics would assist states in making policy decisions on the nature of punishments for hate crimes, raise public consciousness about the alleged epidemic of hate crimes, and send the message that the national government sided with the victims of such crimes.[11]

Congress

This campaign succeeded in convincing Congress to pass legislation requiring the collection of national hate crime statistics.[12] The bill was first proposed in 1985, when the Subcommittee on Criminal Justice of the House Judiciary Committee conducted sympathetic hearings. Ethnic and religious groups testified about the need for data collection, specifically emphasizing the need to "send a message" to violent bigots around the country that the federal government will not tolerate attacks on minorities. The House of Representatives approved its version of HCSA in 1985 but Congress adjourned before the Senate could act. Eventually the bill would embrace a broader political coalition as it moved toward enactment.

A revised bill, which included crimes motivated by anti-homosexual prejudice under the definition of hate crimes, was introduced in the next Congress. Although the bill involved only the collection of statistics, the inclusion of sexual orientation as the equivalent of racial or ethnic identity was an important step in furthering the gay rights agenda. The only controversy that erupted over HCSA resulted from including sexual orientation as a hate crime category. Senator Jesse Helms (R-NC) and five conservative Republicans on the House Judiciary Committee perceived the hidden agenda of the leading homosexual advocacy groups (People for the American Way and the ADL) that including antihomosexual violence in the HCSA was the first step toward recognizing substantive rights for homosexuals.[13]

Nonetheless, the political calculations underlying HCSA made the bill difficult for Congress to resist. HCSA allowed members of Congress, especially liberals, to shore up their symbolic opposition to disfavored prejudices and crimes without facing the kind of legitimate opposition they confronted when defending affirmative action. Also, the legislation involved little or no cost to the federal government. Hate crime legislation is moral policy making without the moral conflict, for the most part. Legislators could oppose violent prejudices and sound a clarion call for law and order.[14] The HCSA passed the House (368–47) and Senate (92–4) and was signed by President George H.W. Bush in 1990. The HCSA was amended to include crimes motivated by bias against people with disabilities under the Violent Crime and Law Enforcement Act of 1994. In a later development, the Church Arson Prevention Act of 1996 removed the "sunset" provision from HCSA.

Advocacy groups saw the HCSA as one prong of a national strategy. The HCSA depends on the voluntary compliance of state and local agencies that collect criminal justice statistics to allocate resources for the investigation of hate crimes and the tabulation of hate crime data. Armed with statistics that they anticipated would show an alarming trend toward more hate crimes, advocates would try to convince states to pass laws enhancing punishments for crimes motivated by racial, ethnic, gender, religious, and homosexual prejudice. Without the Supreme Court ruling in *Mitchell v. Wisconsin* allowing states the discretion to maneuver legislatively, the strategy of moving the hate crime policy agenda from data collection to penalty enhancement would have stalled.

Bills federalizing hate crimes and providing for enhanced penalties have been introduced regularly since the mid-1990s. First proposed in 1994, the Violent Crime Control and Law Enforcement Act would have provided enhanced sentences not to exceed three years when local agencies determine that a criminal offense is a hate crime. But only hate crimes committed while the victim was exercising a federally protected activity would have been subjected to enhanced punishment. This proposal languished, so advocacy groups changed strategies and sought to increase the federal role in investigating and prosecuting hate crimes.

Originally proposed in 1998, the Hate Crimes Prevention Act (HCPA) aimed at removing impediments to federal jurisdiction over hate crimes by expanding federal jurisdiction to all hate crimes if state authorities decline to prosecute, if the state requests that the Justice Department assume jurisdiction, or if the state has no hate crime statute. This bill proposed dual jurisdiction over hate crimes, with the local governments having, in effect, the first chance to investigate and prosecute hate crimes. The federal legislation would have set minimal standards, or a benchmark, below which no local or state government could fall, an approach that would allow the federal government to oversee hate crime investigations and prosecutions at the subnational level in order to assure equal enforcement across all jurisdictions. The bill also ensured that hate crimes would apply to all groups for which hate crime statistics are being collected.

HCPA passed the House and Senate in the 106th Congress but died in conference committee. Its Senate proponents added this legislation as a rider to more important legislation. In 2000, for instance, it passed the Senate by a vote of 57–42 as an amendment to the defense authorization bill, and in 2003 Senator Edward Kennedy (D-MA) stalled foreign aid legislation with a threat to add the bill as an amendment, causing Majority Leader Bill Frist (R-TN) to pull the foreign aid bill from the floor.[15] A majority of Republicans view this legislation as political demagoguery but are reluctant to articulate a principled opposition that singling out hate crimes for special condemnation undermines social cohesion as embodied in the criminal code. One alternative offered by Senator Orrin Hatch (R-UT), chairman of the Judiciary Committee, was a bill that makes certain hate crimes punishable with the death penalty. Hatch's maneuver would place many pro-hate crime but anti-death penalty liberal Democrats in a conflicted position.

The logic for renaming HCPA the Local Law Enforcement Enhancement Act (LLEEA) of 2001 was explained by then Majority Leader Tom Daschle (D-SD) in a colloquy with Senator Kennedy, the bill's chief sponsor. Daschle asked, "How can anyone be opposed to a bill with the title Local Law Enforcement Enhancement Act?"[16] The old bill was given a new wrapper to showcase its least controversial feature, implying that the legislation is concerned about enhanced local law enforcement rather than expanding federal jurisdiction or punishing hate crimes. The bill currently has fifty cosponsors in the Senate, including forty-two Democrats and seven Republicans. The GOP cosponsors include the moderates or liberals within the party: Senators Olympia Snowe (R-ME), Susan Collins (R-ME), Arlen Specter (R-PA), Lincoln Chafee (R-RI), and Gordon Smith (R-OR). The 206 cosponsors in the House of Representatives include 192 Democrats, 1 Independent, but only 23 Republicans. Again the majority of Republican cosponsors come from the Northeast, whereas most Democrats who chose *not* to cosponsor this legislation reside in the South or border states.

Presidency

Presidential leadership on the issue of hate crimes has been episodic. President George H.W. Bush signaled support for the HCSA in 1989 at a fund-raiser for a Senate candidate in Rhode Island, saying, "I was proud to endorse the hate crimes bill to identify and fight bigotry."[17] Bush expressed his support throughout the year and on April 23, 1990, signed the Hate Crimes Statistics Act into law. Calling HCSA "a significant step to help guarantee civil rights for every American," Bush added, "One of the greatest obligations of this administration and the Department of Justice is the guarantee of civil rights to all Americans." Moreover, President Bush declared, "hate breeds violence, threatening the security of our entire society. We must rid our communities of the poison we call prejudice, bias, and discrimination." The law Bush signed required the attorney general to collect data on "crimes motivated by religion, race, ethnicity, or sexual orientation," but Bush also directed the Department of Justice to establish a toll-free number to allow victims to report hate crimes. Bush vowed, "I will use this noble office, this bully pulpit, if you will, to speak out against hate and discrimination everywhere it exists."[18]

Bill Clinton was far more active on the subject of hate crimes than either Bush or President George W. Bush. As part of the 1994 Crime Act, Clinton signed the Hate Crimes Sentencing Enhancement Act, which provided for lengthier sentences for people convicted of a hate crime. When he was precluded from running for further offices, Clinton tried to bring hate crimes into the public consciousness. A year before the infamous hate crimes against James Byrd, a black man dragged to his death in Texas, and Matthew Shephard, a homosexual beaten to death in Wyoming, Clinton denounced hate crimes in his June 7, 1996, radio address. Echoing the earlier arguments made by his predecessor at the passing of the HCSA, Clinton maintained that "[h]ate crimes leave deep scars not only on the victims, but on our larger community." Labeling hate crimes "acts of violence against America itself," Clinton called on America "to mount an all-out assault on hate crimes."[19] President Clinton's speech and his actions to this point were, for the most part, symbolic and educational, as he hoped to shape public opinion.

Building on those admonitions, Clinton hosted a White House Conference on Hate Crimes later in 1997. Addressing the conference, he discussed what role the federal government could play in curbing hate crimes. Clinton asserted that Congress should make "current law tougher to include all hate crimes that cause physical harm . . . [and] prohibit crimes committed because of a victim's sexual orientation, gender or disability." "All Americans," said Clinton, "deserve protection from hate." He then announced that fifty FBI agents would be diverted from other duties to hate crimes enforcement. President Clinton continued speaking out against disfavored prejudice, at one point arguing that "the number one security threat" to the nation was "the persistence of old, even primitive, hatreds."[20]

Given his public stance, it is not surprising that President Clinton claimed to be a passionate supporter of the aforementioned Hate Crimes Prevention Act (HCPA). On June 24, 1998, Clinton sent a letter to the party leadership of the House and Senate urging them to pass the HCPA. According to Clinton, the bill would eliminate the "needless jurisdictional requirements" that prevent federal law enforcement from prosecuting local hate crimes. Clinton continued, "There is nothing more important to the future of this country than our standing together against intolerance, prejudice, and violent bigotry."[21] It would seem that hate crime legislation was an important priority for President Clinton since he vetoed the FY 2000 appropriations bill for the Commerce, State, and Justice departments because it did not include HCPA. In his veto message of October 26, 1999 Clinton chastised Congress for not including HCPA in the appropriations bill, stating that the United States must "maintain a system that vigorously protects and rigorously respects the civil rights of individuals" and that failure to pass hate crimes legislation imperiled this laudable goal.[22] However, Clinton later capitulated and signed a modified spending plan without the HCPA.

In September 2000, in an apparent effort to highlight the differences between Democratic presidential candidate Al Gore and Republican candidate George W. Bush, Clinton spoke at the White House and urged Congress to pass federal hate crimes legislation. Surrounding himself with those involved in well-publicized hate crimes, including the Laramie, Wyoming, police officer who investigated the Matthew Shephard case, the president argued that this legislation would "enhance the government's ability to prosecute violent crimes motivated by race, color, religion or national origin, and would authorize federal prosecution of crimes motivated by sexual orientation, gender, or disability." Clinton urged Congress to appropriate federal money to state and local governments to "help with investigation and prosecutions to ensure that perpetrators of hate crimes are brought to justice." President Clinton, known by some supporters as The Man from Hope, stated, "It is for me a sad and painful irony that at the beginning of a new century I have done so much to fill with opportunity for the American people and to bring full hope to the world, with all the modern gadgets we enjoy, we are still bedeviled by mankind's oldest failure—fear of the other."[23]

Legislative inaction on hate crime continues in the post–Clinton era, and its importance as a symbolic rallying cry for Democrats will continue to make it a staple of national elections. This issue did surface during the 2000 presidential race when Vice President Gore made his support for national hate crimes legislation central in his efforts to rally minority voters, especially black voters, to his cause. In speaking before the NAACP, Gore touted his support for hate crimes legislation as well as his support for affirmative action and activist judges, and his opposition to school vouchers. Hate crimes also were mentioned in two of the presidential debates between Gore and Bush. In the October 11, 2000, debate, during a discussion of racial profiling, Gore brought up the vicious killing of James Byrd, cleverly pointing out that this murder had occurred in Bush's home state of Texas. Gore stated, "And as for singling people out because of race, you know, James Byrd was singled out because of race, in Texas, and other Americans have been singled out because of their race or ethnicity." Gore laid out an argument against hate crimes that echoed the argument originally made by George W. Bush's father: "And that's why I think that we can embody our values by passing a hate crimes law. I think these crimes are different. I think they're different because they're based on prejudice and hatred. They're intended to stigmatize and dehumanize a whole group of people." Asked by the debate moderator if he had a different view of the matter, George W. Bush stated, "No, I don't, really, on hate crimes laws. No, we've got one in Texas. And guess what? The three men who murdered James Byrd, guess what's going to happen to them? They're going to be put to death." In the October 17, 2000, debate, Gore reiterated his support for a federal hate crimes statute, again bringing up the death of James Byrd, but Bush had no more to say on the matter.[24]

The current Bush administration has not made hate crimes legislation a priority. The Bush White House barely mentioned the LLEEA during its first term, though the bill enjoyed substantial support in both houses of Congress. Although Bush did not actively fight its enactment, he has done nothing to promote it. President Bush's relative inaction on this matter is not surprising, given the lack of support among Republicans for such legislation and its lack of issue saliency with the general public.

Public Opinion

With the news-making murders of James Byrd and Matthew Shephard in 1998, the issue of hate crimes legislation reached the broad American public in a dramatic fashion. Subsequent public opinion polls have indicated broad, though not necessarily deep, and ambivalent support for hate crimes legislation. Activists and advocacy groups seized on the Byrd and Shephard murders to begin a nationwide public relations campaign for more extensive state hate crime laws and a federal hate crime statute. The Human Rights Campaign, a leading gay rights interest group, conducted an exit poll during the November 1998 congressional election. Fifty-six percent of all respondents indicated support for federal hate crimes legislation (HCPA), while 23 percent were opposed. But 21 percent had no opinion on the issue.[25]

The Gallup public opinion firm conducted a more comprehensive poll in 1999.[26] Individuals were asked to respond to the following question: "Some states have special laws that provide harsher penalties for crimes motivated by hate of certain groups than the same penalties for the same crimes if they are not motivated by this kind of hate. Would you favor or oppose this type of hate crime law in your state?" Seventy percent of respondents indicated support for hate crimes legislation, while 25 percent were opposed. Gallup tried to determine if Americans thought that hate crimes were a problem in the United States but found that only 13 percent of respondents said they knew somebody who was capable of committing a hate crime. Eighty-six percent said they knew no such person. Also, only 13 percent of the respondents feared being the victim of a hate crime, with 86 percent indicating they did not fear this. Given the scenario that their state already had hate crimes legislation, then over 80 percent of respondents gave support to covering such groups as racial minorities, women, and religious and ethnic minorities under those hate crimes statutes.[27] Slightly fewer would support "sexual orientation" (75 percent being supportive), which compares favorably to a Gallup poll in 2000 that found 71 percent supporting protection of gays and lesbians against hate crimes laws and 81 percent supporting hate crimes to protect racial minorities.[28] Based on these results, it seems that Americans do not object to hate crimes legislation though they do not seem to regard hate crimes as a problem of great urgency.

Other polls confirm this conclusion. In 1999 Gallup asked about one particular hate crime, the murder of six people at a Jewish community center in the Los Angeles area by Bufford Farrow, a member of the Aryan Nations.[29]

While 96 percent of those polled supported either capital punishment or life imprisonment with no parole (55 percent and 41 percent, respectively) for Farrow, only 34 percent believed that he should receive harsher punishment because he was motivated by racist and anti-Semitic beliefs. Sixty-four percent said he should receive the same punishment "as anyone convicted of the same crimes would receive, without regard for his motive." This indicates that, while Americans may support the general notion of hate crimes legislation, they are still uncertain about the law treating offenders differently based upon beliefs and motivations. When Americans are asked to evaluate the trade-off between two core values—tolerance for minorities and opposition to prejudice, on the one hand, versus equal treatment for equal crimes—public opinion seems to be ambivalent.

A minor gender gap appears with hate crimes. While both sexes give wide approval to hate crimes legislation, 88 percent of women support hate crimes measures, whereas male support is lower at 78 percent.[30] Similarly, there is bipartisan support for hate crimes laws, though with fewer Republicans (75 percent) supportive than Democrats (90 percent).[31]

Although there may be broad public support for hate crimes legislation, the issue does not have much saliency with the voting public. One poll in late 2003 asked registered voters about the most important issues in the 2004 presidential election, but neither hate crimes nor any civil rights issue was mentioned by more than 1 percent of respondents.[32] The lack of political saliency may partly explain why the federal government and certain states lack comprehensive hate crimes legislation despite overwhelming public approval.

Bureaucracy

Because the federal government has not preempted the investigative and prosecutorial powers of the states over hate crimes, hate crime legislation has only marginally increased the administrative scope of the federal bureaucracy. Under the HCSA, the attorney general must establish "guidelines for the collection of such data including the necessary evidence and criteria that must be present for the finding of manifest prejudice."[33] The attorney general has delegated this responsibility to the FBI Uniform Crime Reporting (UCR) Program. With the help of local law enforcement and advocacy groups like the ADL and NAACP, the UCR Program wrote a guide for hate crime data collection in 1991 and revised the guidelines in 1999. This guide lays out the criteria local law enforcement should use in classifying incidents as hate crimes. The FBI established uniform hate crime standards, emphasizing that the offender's crime must be motivated, in part at least, by a disfavored bias against the victim's race, religion, disability, sexual orientation, or ethnicity.

But the bulk of the law enforcement duty of collecting data falls on state and local police agencies, which can submit quarterly and annual reports on the number, types, and locations of hate crimes in their jurisdictions. However, compliance with the HCSA is *voluntary*, though nearly all states and a majority of localities provide hate crime information to UCR. According to the best evidence, fewer than 36 percent of all police departments in the largest 250 American cities have special officers or task forces charged with investigating and tracking hate crimes.[34] Smaller cities devote fewer resources to the investigation of hate crimes and are less likely to report hate crime statistics to the FBI (see Table 8.1).[35]

The Justice Department also created a training guide to instruct local police officers on how to identify, investigate, and report hate crimes. Local law enforcement agencies are charged with the duty of investigating the crimes and of finding "sufficient, objective facts" to conclude that a disfavored motivation provoked the crime.[36] The UCR Program recommends that police departments adopt a two-tiered decision-making process. First, the responding police officers should ask "whether there is any indication that the offender was motivated by bias." If this permissive criterion is met, the second stage requires that hate crime specialists "carefully sift through the facts using more stringent criteria" in order to make a final determination.[37]

The UCR seeks to guide police training with a series of indicators that are believed to accompany bias-motivated crimes—for example, if racial epithets are uttered during the offense, if the offender and victim are of different races, if the victim is a minority "overwhelmingly outnumbered" by the majority of residents in the neighborhood where the victim lives, and if other people in the area *believe* that the crime was motivated by a disfavored bias.[38] Consistent with the Supreme Court ruling in *Mitchell,* the UCR cautions law enforcement personnel that all these indicators must be evaluated in context. To use the agency's example, during the commission of a crime an offender might express "a well-known and recognized epithet used against blacks" to refer to the victim. If the offender is black and the victim is black, such an epithet is not an indication of a hate crime. If the offender is white and the victim is black, such an epithet is an indication of a hate crime.[39] A too rigid application of these indicators would mean that nearly any crime could be a hate crime, while a properly contextualized application of the indicators winnows down the number of possible hate crimes.

UCR reporting has shown a clear trend: Hate crimes are *not* sweeping the country. In no year since reporting began has the percentage of reported crimes motivated by a disfavored bias reached the level of .001 percent of

Table 8.1

Jurisdictions Reporting Hate Crimes, 1995–2001

	1995	1996	1997	1998	1999	2000	2001
States reporting	45	49	48	46	48	48	49
Police departments reporting	9,500	11,354	11,211	10,730	12,122	11,690	11,987
Percent of U.S. population covered by reporting jurisdictions	75	84	83	80	85	84	85

Source: See multiple issues of Federal Bureau of Investigation, *Hate Crime Statistics* (Washington, DC: U.S. Government Printing Office, 1995–2002), page 2 (for agencies reporting) and Table 11 on page 20 (for number of states reporting).

Table 8.2

Hate Crimes as Compared to Total Criminal Offenses

	1995	1996	1997	1998	1999	2000	2001
Total criminal offenses[a]	13,863	13,474	13,175	12,476	11,643	11,606	11,877
Hate crimes	9,895	10,706	9,861	9,235	9,301	9,430	11,451
Hate crimes as percent of total offenses	0.00071	0.00079	0.00075	0.00074	0.00080	0.00081	0.00096

Source: See multiple issues of Federal Bureau of Investigation, *Crime in the United States* (Washington, DC: U.S. Government Printing Office, 1996–2002), page 5; see multiple issues of Federal Bureau of Investigation, *Hate Crime Statistics* (Washington, DC: U.S. Government Printing Office, 1995–2002), Table 1, page 9.
[a]In thousands.

the total number of crimes (Table 8.2). The worries of critics who fear potential abuses of hate crime statutes and the possibility that every crime may be labeled a hate crime have not materialized. On the other hand, advocates of hate crime legislation have rationalized the low numbers as resulting from bureaucratic failures and underreporting by local law enforcement agencies.

Given these statistics, it seems apparent that hate crime laws were not initiated "as a direct response to the level of hate crime."[40] The bureaucratic implementation of hate crime statistics collection, in fact, depends mostly on the attitudes of local police, the pressures by advocacy groups, and support from politicians. A statistical model by Donald Haider-Markel indicates that the strength of interest groups, especially gay and lesbian groups, has the most positive effect on spurring local law enforcement to collect hate crime statistics.[41] Therefore, since there has been no evidence of increased violence in the United States against these marginalized groups, hate crimes legislation is symbolic politics whereby those groups attempt to gain legitimacy in the eyes of the law and, more importantly, in the eyes of society.

Federalism

Because the collection of hate crime statistics by local agencies is voluntary, the implementation of hate crime statistics laws depends on the attitudes of police and prosecutors. States approach hate crimes differently from one another. Though some states cover a wide variety of suspect groups, a small handful of states provide practically no enhanced penalties for them. Over time, patterns of policy diffusion and innovation emerged as some types of legislation became more prevalent.

By 1989 forty-two states had enacted victim rights laws, helping to create "a victim ideology and corresponding victim industry."[42] Along with victim rights legislation, many states passed laws defining "discriminatory violence."[43] By 1990 twenty-eight states had laws that could be described as "hate crimes" laws, mainly located in the East (ten states), Midwest (seven), and the West (eight).[44] But only three southern states—Florida, Oklahoma, and Tennessee—had passed any kind of hate crimes legislation. The 1990s saw passage of laws creating and/or enhancing penalties for hate crimes. Forty-nine states plus Washington, D.C., have some hate crimes legislation, with Wyoming the lone exception. Forty-seven states cover some kind of "bias motivation" or "intimidation" (Table 8.3).

One area with wide variation among the states involves the groups deserving of protection through legislation. In the late 1980s most states covered the categories of race, religion, color (as distinct from race), and national origin. Since then, a second set of categories—most prominently

Table 8.3

Anti-Defamation League State Hate Crime Statutory Provisions

	Bias motivated violence and intimidation— criminal penalty	Civil action	Race, religion,[a] ethnicity	Sexual orientation	Gender	Disability	Other[b]	Institutional vandalism	Data collection[c]	Training for law enforcement personnel[d]
AL	✓		✓		✓	✓		✓	✓	✓
AK	✓		✓	✓	✓	✓			✓	✓
AZ	✓		✓			✓				
AR		✓						✓		
CA	✓	✓	✓	✓	✓	✓	✓	✓	✓	
CO	✓	✓	✓	✓				✓	✓	
CT	✓	✓	✓	✓	✓	✓	✓	✓	✓	
DC	✓	✓	✓	✓		✓	✓	✓		
DE	✓		✓	✓		✓		✓		
FL	✓	✓	✓	✓			✓	✓	✓	
GA	✓[e]							✓		
HI	✓	✓	✓					✓		
ID	✓	✓	✓		✓	✓		✓	✓	✓
IL	✓		✓	✓		✓	✓	✓		✓
IN							✓			
IA	✓	✓	✓	✓	✓	✓	✓	✓	✓	✓
KS	✓	✓		✓		✓			✓	✓
KY	✓		✓	✓	✓	✓		✓	✓	✓✓
LA	✓		✓	✓		✓		✓	✓	
ME	✓	✓	✓	✓	✓	✓	✓	✓	✓	✓
MD	✓	✓	✓	✓		✓		✓	✓	✓
MA	✓	✓	✓	✓	✓	✓		✓	✓	
MI	✓		✓	✓	✓	✓	✓	✓	✓	
MN	✓		✓	✓	✓			✓	✓	
MS	✓		✓	✓	✓	✓		✓	✓	
MO	✓		✓	✓	✓	✓		✓	✓	

MT
NE
NV
NH
NJ
NM
NY
NC
ND
OH
OK
OR
PA
RI
SC
SD
TN
TX
UT
VT
VA
WA
WV
WI
WY

Source: ©2003 Anti-Defamation League.

aThe following states also have statutes criminalizing interference with religious worship: AR, CA, DC, FL, ID, MD, MA, MI, MN, MS, MO, NV, NM, NY, NC, OK, RI, SC, TN, VA, WV.

b"Other" includes political affiliation (CA, DC, IA, LA, WV) and age (CA, DC, FL, IA, HI, KS, LA, ME, MN, NE, NM, NY, VT).

cStates with data collection statutes which include sexual orientation are AZ, CA, CT, DC, FL, IL, IA, MD, MI, MN, NV, OR, TX, and WA: those which include gender are AZ, DC, IL, IA, MI, MN, TX, and WA.

dSome other states have administrative regulations mandating such training.

eThe Georgia statute enhances criminal penalties for crimes in which the defendant "intentionally selected" the victim or property "because of bias or prejudice."

fThe Utah statute ties penalties for hate crimes to violations of the victim's constitutional or civil rights.

ancestry, gender, sexual orientation, and disability—have become more common in state law.[45] Forty-five states now have added penalties for those committing a crime motivated by racial, religious, and ethnic prejudices (see Table 8.3). Less common are laws covering sexual orientation (thirty states), persons with disabilities (twenty-nine), and gender (twenty-six). The Anti-Defamation League recommends that ten societal attributes be covered; currently, fourteen states have laws covering at least eight of those ten criteria, whereas four states have laws covering fewer than two.[46] States employ different methods to identify and punish hate crimes, though penalty enhancements and generic "ethnic intimidation" laws are most common. These methods are the least controversial means of punishing disfavored prejudices, because penalty enhancement statutes and ethnic intimidation statutes operate within existing state criminal codes and do not require the creation of separate criminal codes for bias-motivated crimes.

States also differ in defining the "motivation" needed to categorize a crime as one of "hate." The most common and broadest standard, according to Jennes and Grattet, is the "because of" standard. For example, the Virginia statute reads: "intentionally selects the person against whom the offense is committed *because of* his [etc.]"[47] In identifying hate crimes, many statutes also seek evidence of prejudice on the part of the offender, a showing of "maliciousness" in intent, or the demonstration of an "intent to terrify, intimidate, threaten, harass, annoy, or offend."[48] The latter three clauses require a higher evidentiary threshold than the relatively loose "because of" standard. The "because of" standard has no descriptors that require interpreting the precise nature of the perpetrator's motives. One can imagine, for example, that an attack against an Asian-American occurs "because of" a particular person's race, yet the perpetrator might *not* have a definable prejudice against Asians as a group. In some states, this example would be defined as a hate crime; in others, it might not be.

New York State provides a prototypical definition of a hate crime. The Hate Crimes Act of 2000 begins with a legislative finding that "criminal acts involving violence, intimidation and destruction of property based upon bias and prejudice" have increased in New York State. The statute reads: "The intolerable truth is that in these crimes, commonly and justly referred to as 'hate crimes,' victims are intentionally selected, in whole or in part, because of their race, color, national origin, ancestry, gender, religion, religious practice, age, disability, or sexual orientation."

> A person commits a hate crime if the perpetrator intentionally selects the person against whom the offense is committed or intended to be committed in whole or in substantial part because of a belief or perception regarding

the race, color, national origin, ancestry, gender, religion, religious practice, age, disability or sexual orientation of a person, regardless of whether the belief or perception is correct. (NY CLS Penal § 485.05)

The Alabama hate crimes law, in contrast to New York law, enhances penalties against persons "who [have] been found guilty of a crime, the commission of which was shown beyond a reasonable doubt to have been motivated by the victim's actual or perceived race, color, religion, national origin, ethnicity, or physical or mental disability" (Code of Alabama § 13A-5-13). Categories such as gender and sexual orientation are not covered in Alabama.

The penalty depends on whether the perpetrator is convicted of a misdemeanor or a felony and on the class of felonies. In New York, for example, a hate crime conviction is a "violent felony offense." While there are many caveats in the New York State penal code, generally Section 485.12 holds true:

When a person is convicted of a hate crime pursuant to this article and the specified offense is a misdemeanor or a class C, D or E felony, the hate crime shall be deemed to be one category higher than the specified offense the defendant committed, or one category higher than the offense level applicable to the defendant's conviction for an attempt or conspiracy to commit a specified offense, whichever is applicable. (NY CLS Penal § 485.12)

Alabama, again for comparison, has different hate crime penalties depending on the type of crime to which the "hate" is attached. Misdemeanors as hate crimes are sentenced as Class A misdemeanors with a minimum of three months' imprisonment. Felonies with a hate crime mandate a minimum of five years for Class C, ten years for Class B, and fifteen years for Class A (Code of Alabama § 13A-5-13).

In terms of implementing hate crime statistics, twenty-five states mandate data collection. Michigan, for example, commands:

The chief of police of each city or village, the chief of police of each township having a police department, and the sheriff of each county within this state shall report to the department of state police, in a manner prescribed by the department, information related to crimes motivated by prejudice or bias based upon race, ethnic origin, religion, gender, or sexual orientation. (MCL § 28.257a)

Twelve states require training for law enforcement personnel to help them in identifying when a crime might be bias-motivated. The Minnesota statute on this subject reads:

The board (of peace officer standards and training) must prepare a training course to assist peace officers in identifying and responding to crimes motivated by the victim's race, religion, national origin, sex, age, disability, or characteristics identified as sexual orientation. The course must include material to help officers distinguish bias crimes from other crimes, to help officers in understanding and assisting victims of these crimes, and to ensure that bias crimes will be accurately reported. (Minn. State. § 626.8451)

The Kentucky law states that the Department of Criminal Justice Training "shall include in each basic law enforcement training course a unit of training relating to identifying, responding to, investigation of, and reporting of bias-related crime cases." There must also be a biennial in-service training on "bias-related" crime (KRS § 15.331).

To conclude, the following generalizations seem warranted. First, almost every state has some kind of hate crimes legislation that punishes crimes motivated by race, ethnicity, and religion. Second, several states cover such categories as sexual orientation, gender, and disability. Third, states that prosecute hate crimes typically have chosen the most plastic criteria for what motivation constitutes "hate."

Summary of Propositions

1a (single-issue groups): Unsupported, because minorities have not utilized single-issue groups to pursue the hate crimes policy agenda.

1b (absolutist politics): Supported, insofar as the tolerance of liberal society for diversity has been insufficient to recognizing that certain marginalized groups deserved added protection from prejudice.

2a (judicial activism): Unsupported, insofar as the Supreme Court, while upholding the constitutionality of hate crimes legislation, has not been the primary political actor for achieving policy change.

2b (incorporation): Unsupported, because no provision in the Bill of Rights has not applied to all fifty states.

3a (presidential symbolism): Supported. Both George H.W. Bush and Bill Clinton endorsed laws on hate crimes, but the legislation originated in Congress.

3b (partisan presidents): Supported, only to the degree that Clinton, a Democrat, exhibited commitment to hate crimes policy whereas this issue was not on the policy agenda of George W. Bush.

4a (Congress and states): Unsupported, because Congress has not followed the example of the states in enacting federal hate crimes legislation, whereas the Supreme Court has signaled that state hate crimes legislation was permissible.

4b (Congress and elections): Supported, insofar as electoral constraints seemingly permit Congress (like the majority of states) to enact hate crimes legislation, although Congress has responded by enacting a law to collect hate crime statistics but not to enhance punishments at the federal level.

5a (opinion and ideology): Unsupported, because liberals more than conservatives support hate crime legislation and polls indicate that public opinion is supportive.

5b (law and society): Supported. Hate crimes legislation is not highly salient for the general public, whereas, on the other hand, its impact on curbing prejudiced attacks on minorities by bigots remains an open question.

6a (federal agencies): Supported, because federal agencies currently play a minor role in the statistics-gathering function and would have only backup responsibilities even if pending bills become law.

6b (federal implementation): Supported, to the degree that any pressures on the FBI from Congress, the presidency, and advocacy groups would favor enforcement of hate crimes legislation.

7a (federalism): Supported, because crime control historically is under state jurisdiction, and, with respect to hate crime penalty enhancements, most states have acted before Congress even considered such legislation.

7b (compliance): Supported, because the FBI relies on voluntary compliance by state and local law enforcement agencies to collect hate crime statistics; compliance with hate crimes legislation depends on the voluntary cooperation of state officials.

For Further Insight Into the Hate Crimes Debate

A Campus of Difference. This program, a component of the Anti-Defamation League's A World of Difference Institute, provides development and delivery of diversity and antibias training and resources on college and university campuses throughout the United States.

From Swastika to Jim Crow. This film tells the little-known story of two different cultures that share elements of a common burden of oppression. Directed by Joel Sucher and Steven Fischler.

Hate Comes Home. This virtual-experience interactive CD-ROM allows users to become the lead characters in a plot immersed in everyday occurrences of bias and hate-motivated behavior in which they can save lives if they choose correctly. www.adl.org/education/hate_comes_home2.asp.

The Laramie Project. This movie explores the aftermath of the murder of twenty-one-year-old Matthew Shepard in Laramie, Wyoming.

Life Is Beautiful. This Italian movie depicts the Holocaust as it affected Italian Jews.

Schindler's List. This Steven Spielberg movie depicts the Holocaust and one coura-
geous man who saved scores of Jews.

Shoah. This 1985 movie, named for the Hebrew word meaning "chaos" or "annihila-
tion," is a nine-and-one-half-hour documentary containing interviews with Holocaust survivors.

www.tolerance.org/teach/. Web site for Teaching Tolerance, maintained by the Southern Poverty Law Center, and designed as a clearinghouse for lesson plans on how
to teach racial tolerance in a K-12 curriculum.

9

Pornography

Freedom of Expression or Sexual Degradation?

Byron W. Daynes

Ever since the eighteenth century, government has tried to cope with the problems associated with obscenity and pornography. The first judicial ruling on this issue came in 1815, when a Pennsylvania court held it illegal to exhibit any picture of nude bodies for profit. This was followed in 1821 by Vermont's enactment of the first state antiobscenity law. But the politicalization of obscenity had to await Supreme Court decisions of the 1960s and the outcry that followed a 1970 report of the President's Commission on Obscenity and Pornography.

Efforts to halt the spread of pornography have not always been effective, for many reasons. Most importantly, the enforcement of antipornography laws frequently collides with constitutional guarantees of free expression, but another problem is the sheer size, complexity, and profitability of the pornographic market, which includes hard-core videos, live sex acts, adult cable programming, hotel movies, peep shows, sexual devices, pay-per-view movies on both satellite and cable, sex magazines, and Internet sites.[1] On the Internet, which Mark Alexander describes as "spaceless and anonymous, there is no way to be sure who accesses material once it is placed into cyberspace."[2] The most troubling characteristic that makes pornography difficult to control is suggested by Richard C. Morais, who observes, "Even as pornography becomes more appallingly graphic, it is becoming more mainstream. Phone companies, cable companies, hotel chains and now investment bankers are all part of the act. It may be the ultimate case of defining smut-down."[3] Pornography is so mainstream, in fact, there was even a 2003 singing group in the United States called "The New Pornographers."[4] How does one limit a market so variegated and so widespread that potentially controls so many resources, with profit estimates for 2003 ranging between $2.6 and $14 billion?[5]

A third problem involving obscenity and pornography is that there has never been a clear definition of what *obscenity* means, nor has there been consensus on the guidelines used by the Supreme Court,[6] despite the agreement of a majority of justices in *Miller v. California* (1973)[7] that an obscene work is that which the average person, applying community standards, would find when taken as a whole would appeal to prurient interest; and is depicted or described in a patently offensive way, lacking serious literary, artistic, political, or scientific value.

While obscenity as a concept may sound somewhat convoluted to the reader, *pornography* is even more obscure. We need only recall Justice Potter Stewart's now infamous concurrence in the 1964 *Jacobellis v. Ohio* case, in which, after puzzling over whether the film he was viewing was hard-core pornography and thus obscene, he finally stated in exasperation, "I shall not today attempt further to define the kinds of material I understand to be embraced within that shorthand description [of hard-core pornography], and perhaps I could never succeed in intelligently doing so. But *I know it when I see it,* and the motion picture involved in this case is not that" (emphasis added).[8]

Stewart's exasperation reflects what James S. Tyre said about pornography, namely, that unlike obscenity, pornography is a "layperson's term, with no particular legal significance."[9] Until pornography becomes "hard-core" or obscene, it will be considered constitutionally protected expression—with one major exception, namely, child pornography. "Child porn"[10] allows the government to use any power it wishes to punish violators of children whether any of the standards of *Miller* are referred to or not. While the First Amendment protects adult access to information, double standards do prevail in order to protect a child's welfare. Child pornography, unlike other types of pornography, does unify citizen disgust because virtually everyone—with the possible exception of pedophiles—dislikes it. Everyone is concerned as to how widespread it has become, caused, in part, by the ease of Internet access and digital photography that, in the wrong hands, have combined to create "homemade" child pornography.[11] Even the adult entertainment industry is concerned, so much that those who established 3,000 adult sites on the Internet organized Adult Sites Against Child Pornography (ASACP) to help eliminate child pornography.[12]

Judiciary

The judicial dilemma in dealing with obscenity and pornography is well captured by constitutional law scholar Louis Fisher, who expresses his own concerns with this area of the law:

> I approach obscenity and pornography with heavy heart and wry amusement. Readers are unlikely to comprehend judicial declamations about prurient interest, lascivious matter, lewdness, lust, socially redeeming values and contemporary community standards. Students are baffled to encounter plaintiffs called "12 200-ft Reels of Super 8 mm. Film." Still this is an important area of First Amendment law, and there is some instruction in the court's willingness to adjudicate and offer guidance for an overwhelmingly thankless task.[13]

The Warren Court (1953–1969), dedicated to free expression, saw obscenity as a barrier to protected expression and, therefore, wanted to minimize its impact. Yet, after many years of adjudicating this issue, the Warren Court finally admitted it could not satisfactorily define what obscenity was, instead deciding to define what obscenity *was not,* and what protected expression should be. The problem with that strategy is that the Court's efforts became so all-inclusive and unmanageable that the term *obscene* all but disappeared. In *Roth v. United States* (1957) the Court decided that a work could be considered obscene if the average person thought that the dominant theme of the material taken as a whole "appealed to prurient interests."[14] These standards were significantly broadened in subsequent cases. In *Manual Enterprises v. Day* (1962),[15] for instance, Justice John Harlan said that for a work to be obscene it should have "prurient interest" as well as being "patently offensive"; also, it should fail all the *Roth* tests individually and be "utterly without redeeming social value." This "social value" test was viewed by civil libertarians as the most important criterion since it all but eliminated any possibility that a work might be considered obscene, since virtually every work, it could be argued, has at least a modicum of social value and importance.

In at least two respects, the Burger Court (1969–1986) approach was identical to that of the Warren Court. The Burger Court also insisted on viewing the movies and reading the books before making a judgment, and the Burger Court was just as reluctant to define obscenity. The most important case it decided was *Miller v. California,* as noted earlier. The *Miller* standards replaced the open-ended "utterly without redeeming social value" test, specifying particular actions that could be considered obscene, such as patently offensive representations or descriptions of ultimate sexual acts, normal or perverted, actual or simulated; and patently offensive representations or descriptions of masturbation, excretory functions, and lewd exhibitions of the genitals.[16] In doing this, however, the Court sent mixed messages to the states about the importance of "local community standards" as a controlling factor, because once the Court outlined its "universal" list of obscene acts, the discretion of juries, legislatures, and judges in determining obscenity based on community standards was limited.

Child·pornography posed a major challenge to the Burger Court obscenity criteria, because child pornography did not conveniently fit the *Miller* standards. Following the lead of Congress and state legislatures, the Supreme Court agreed that stricter standards should govern when children were the objects of obscenity. Whether the material was obscene or not, therefore, was less important than whether children were being victimized through sexual exploitation. Child pornography was not to be judged "as a whole" but could be banned based on "isolated passages." Thus, the Burger Court began judging child pornography by the very standard that the Warren Court had discarded.

The focus of the Rehnquist Court (1986–present) has been child pornography and pornography in the mass media, and especially challenging were its cases on indecency in cyberspace.[17] In 1996 Congress passed the Communications Decency Act (CDA)[18] to prohibit the knowing transmission of indecent messages to minors over the Internet.[19] In June 1997 *Reno v. American Civil Liberties Union* held that the section of the CDA that shielded minors from these messages on the Internet proved to be an "unacceptably heavy burden on protected speech." Legislative vagueness also was deemed by the Court majority as having a "chilling effect on free speech."[20]

Twenty-first-century Court cases have also focused on the potential conflicts between pornography and free expression. In the *City of Erie et al. v. PAP's A.M., tdba "Kandyland"* 529 U.S. 277 (2000),[21] the Supreme Court upheld the constitutionality of an Erie, Pennsylvania, city ordinance that restricted "nude live entertainment" within the city limits, stating that nude dancing had a negative impact on the public health, safety, and welfare of the community by facilitating an "atmosphere conducive to violence, sexual harassment, public intoxication [and] prostitution." Justice Sandra Day O'Connor observed that she did not feel that such a ban prevented the dancers from expressing themselves.[22] That same year, the Playboy Entertainment Group challenged the Telecommunications Act of 1996, designed to shield children from those cable channels principally devoted to sexually oriented programming. In *United States v. Playboy Entertainment Group* (2000) Justice Anthony Kennedy, writing for the majority, agreed that the law violated the rights of adults who wanted to view lawful sexually oriented programming.[23] It was clear to him that children could be protected in other ways less restrictive than the ban. The next year, *Ashcroft v. American Civil*

Liberties Union (2002) evaluated whether commercial speech could be harmful to minors. This 8–1 ruling held that "local community standards" could be applied to protect children from potential harm.[24]

Two other cases in 2002 dealt with differing aspects of pornography. *Ashcroft v. Free Speech Coalition* (2002) determined that those provisions of the Child Pornography Protection Act (CPPA) of 1996 that broadened child pornography to include "virtual images" and digital likenesses of persons engaged in sexual activity went too far.[25] *City of Los Angeles v. Alameda Books* (2002) focused on a Los Angeles ordinance that prevented concentrations of adult entertainment establishments built closer than 1,000 feet from each other or built nearer than 500 feet to a religious institution, a school, or a public park. Justice O'Connor, for the majority, supported the city ban but never questioned whether conclusions drawn about increasing crime rates based upon a 1977 study were still valid.[26] The first 2003 obscenity decision, *United States et al. v. American Library Association, Inc., et al.* (2003), upheld the Children's Internet Protection Act (CIPA), which required public libraries receiving federal funds to use Internet filters to protect children from exposure to pornography.[27]

From these cases, one might reasonably conclude that the courts have made the most exhaustive examination of pornography of any of our governmental institutions. Yet this case law has not been very satisfying to the justices. No member of the Supreme Court has been more dissatisfied than Justice William Brennan, who spent nearly two decades wrestling with how obscenity should be defined. In a 1973 dissent in the case of *Paris Adult Theatre I v. Slaton* (1973), Brennan indicated that obscenity could not be defined "with sufficient specificity and clarity to provide fair notice to persons who create and distribute sexually oriented materials." Therefore, he was willing to forgo any restrictions imposed by state and federal governments on sexually oriented materials except to protect juveniles and unconsenting adults.[28]

Congress

The Supreme Court and the Congress often have been at cross-purposes in dealing with pornography and obscenity. Congress first attempted to restrict obscenity in the nineteenth century, with the enactment of the Tariff Act of 1842, which prohibited obscene prints and visual depictions, and since the 1950s Congress has legislated in such critical areas as the distribution of obscenity through the U.S. mails, limitations on obscene expressions, and the protection of children (Table 9.1). Few members of Congress could hope to win election or reelection by campaigning in support of expanding access to free expression, since the risk of being seen as "soft on pornography" would

Table 9.1

Number of Measures on Obscenity Introduced in Congress, 1956–2003

	1956–1960	1961–1965	1966–1970	1971–1975	1976–1980
Mail/postal services	7	3	6		
Protection from obscenity	1				
State control over obscenity	1				
Transportation of obscenity	1		2		
Study of obscenity	3	2	4		
Sale of obscenity		1			
Obscenity and subversion	1				
Criminal code and obscenity					3
DC bill on obscenity		1	1		
Obscene communications			1		
Children and obscenity			2	1	9
Advertising of obscenity			4		
Definition of obscenity			2	1	2
Victims of obscenity					
Importation of obscenity					
Education					
Arts and obscenity					
Internet					
Enforcement of laws					
Total by year	14	7	22	2	14

Source: Congressional Record, Congressional Quarterly Weekly Reports for each yearly period; Thomas: Legislative Information on the Internet, http://thomas.loc.gov/.

be too great. Moreover, in legislating against obscenity, Congress has not necessarily been guided by judicial definitions on what is obscene but has developed its own working assumptions.[29]

However, Congress did share one perspective with the courts when lawmakers began to confront child pornography. Its assumptions regarding obscenity and pornography were as useless to Congress as past judicial guidelines had been to the Supreme Court. Nonetheless, the House of Representatives on April 20, 1994, made crystal clear where it stood by voting a "sense of Congress" amendment to the Equal Justice Act of 1994. It declared that the House recognized child pornography as "a serious national problem" and Congress has a "compelling interest in the protection of children from abuse." Passage was overwhelming, with 425 yea votes to 3 nays.[30]

The congressional response to child pornography has taken various forms.

1981–1985	1986–1990	1991–1995	1996–1997	1998–2000	2001–2003[1]	Total
	1	1		1		19
						1
		2				3
		1				4
						9
		2				3
						1
2						5
						2
1	9	2	1			14
5	17	7	3	2		46
	1					5
						5
2	5	3				10
1	1					2
	1					1
	1	1				2
		4		1	1	6
		1			1	2
11	36	24	4	4	2	140

[1]Includes only the first eight months of 2003.

In 1985 Congress focused on Internet pornography and passed the Computer Pornography and Child Exploitation Act of 1985. In 1986 children as victims were the object of concern when Congress passed the Child Abuse Victims' Rights Act. In 1987 and 1988 Congress approved two bills with the same title—the Child Protection and Obscenity Enforcement Acts—which became public law. By 1988 there were approximately thirty-two federal laws that dealt with child pornography.[31]

Perhaps most controversial among the recent spate of antipornography bills was the 1996 Communications Decency Act (CDA). The CDA, in amending § 223(a) and (d) of Title 47 of the U.S. Code, made illegal the transmission of obscene or "indecent" and "patently offensive" material to a minor by means of a telecommunications device, or over the Internet.[32] This covered any "comment, request, suggestion, proposal, image, or other communication that, in context, depict[ed] or describ[ed], in terms patently offensive as measured by contemporary community standards, sexual or excretory activities or organs."[33] The final vote on the Conference report in both the House and the Senate showed overwhelming support on the part of Republicans for the act. Overall, there were 414 votes in support of the measure and 16 against, with 4 persons not voting. Breaking this down by party it meant that all of the Republicans (236) were in support of the bill, and they were joined by 178 Democrats; 15 Democrats voted in oppositions to the bill.[34] In the Senate the vote showed a similar pattern. The total vote showed ninety-one senators supporting the measure and five in opposition, with three senators not voting. Of the ninety-one in support of the measure fifty-one of them were Republicans and forty were Democrats. Voting against the measure were four Democrats and one Republican, with two Democrats and one Republican not voting. [35] Thus the CDA became officially a part of the Telecommunications Act of 1996, and almost at the same time the American Civil Liberties Union (ACLU) brought a suit into Federal Court in the Eastern District of Pennsylvania to enjoin the act. After taking into account the unique qualities of the Internet, the District Court enjoined its enforcement of the Communications Decency Act. The Department of Justice then filed an appeal that went directly to the Supreme Court for final judgment.[36]

When challenged, the Supreme Court ruled in *Reno v. American Civil Liberties Union* (1997) that the section of the CDA that shielded minors from "indecent" and "patently offensive" materials on the Internet was an "unacceptably heavy burden on protected speech."[37]

Other so-called "C-laws" passed by Congress during the 1990s are known by their acronyms: CDA, COPA, CIPA, CPPA, and two COPPAS.[38] On July 23, 1998, the Senate passed a second Communications Decency Act, known as CDA II, making it a crime for Web sites to distribute "harmful" material to children and requiring most libraries and schools to filter federally funded Internet access as well as banning Internet gambling. The House has yet to pass it.[39] Congress's interest in child welfare and victimization continued with the passage of the Child Online Protections Act (COPA) in 2000, prohibiting Web site operators from allowing children to observe pornography on the World Wide Web even if that material was legal and protected for adults.[40]

In 2002 Congress passed this concurrent resolution: "That it is the sense of Congress that the Federal obscenity laws should be vigorously enforced throughout the United States."[41] Congress insisted on procedures to protect children despite the Supreme Court having declared many of those same protections unconstitutional. For example, the Child Obscenity and Pornography Prevention Act of 2002 (COPPA) reinstated the idea of treating so-called "morphed" images, which made it appear that "prepubescent" children were illicitly engaged in sex, as if they were real children, but, as before, the Supreme Court declared this law unconstitutional.[42]

Another line of attack was Public Law 107–317, or the Dot Kids Implementation and Efficiency Act of 2002, which created a child-friendly, second-level Internet domain for children called "kids.us." It was intended to be a network, monitored by the National Telecommunications and Information Administration, that would include all content appropriate for children under age thirteen.[43] The 2003 version of the Child Obscenity and Pornography Prevention Act (COPPA) was designed to protect children from "online marketers" by making it illegal to keep data on children under thirteen years of age when their parents were not involved.[44] The House of Representatives even tried to ban from the Internet photographs of children under seventeen years of age who are fully clothed but strike suggestive poses, incorporating this provision in the Child Modeling Exploitation Prevention Act (CMEPA) for 2003.

Legislation that focused on pandering and solicitation is the Child Obscenity and Pornography Prevention Act of 2003, designed to prevent "trafficking in child pornography and obscenity,"[45] while another measure introduced in 2003—the Protecting Children Against Crime Act of 2003 (S. 810) —is intended to eliminate "the statute of limitations for child abduction and sex crimes, providing for registration of child pornographers as sex offenders."[46] Another bill introduced in the Senate during the 108th Congress, which would protect children and adults who use the Internet, was S. 800, entitled Truth in Domain Names Act of 2003. The intent of this bill was to offer a safeguard against deception on the Internet so the public can avoid mistakenly linking onto a pornography site due to a misleading domain name. It carried a penalty of a four-year prison sentence as well as a fine.[47] Finally, there was the awkwardly named Prosecutorial Remedies and Other Tools to End the Exploitation of Children Today Act of 2003, intended to both fund the Amber Alert system for rescuing kidnapped children and prevent the transmission of digitally created images that are made to appear as if children are having sex. Although the Supreme Court had spoken to this issue before, Congress nonetheless followed the sentiment of President George W. Bush who stated, when signing the bill, "Obscene images of children, no matter how they are made, incite abuse, raise the dangers to children and will not be tolerated in America."[48]

Presidency

During the 1950s and 1960s, presidents generally did not devote much attention to the issue of pornography beyond their desire to safeguard the postal system, and only a few contemporary presidents elevated pornography as a priority on their social agenda. One political constraint on presidential leadership, as Floyd Abrams suggests, has to do with First Amendment issues:

> First Amendment claims tend to be made by unpopular people or institutions who wish to say unpopular things. . . . To lend meaningful support to First Amendment protections, a President must be prepared to put aside popular political positions and defend the rights of those who say things of which the public thoroughly disapproves. They include a cadre of sometimes disagreeable candidates [such as] Nazis and pornographers. . . . To protect such people and institutions to the fullest requires a good dose of political courage.[49]

Democrats John F. Kennedy and Lyndon B. Johnson gave support to existing laws protecting free expression. At a 1962 news conference, Kennedy, when asked about a Supreme Court decision that prevented the postmaster general from restricting pornographic matter in the mails, responded that existing laws already governed such distribution and that the post office's main responsibility was not to make judgments regarding the nature of pornography but, rather, to carry out the law. Lyndon Johnson's major response to the pornography problem was his appointment in 1968 of an eighteen-member Presidential Commission on Obscenity and Pornography to study the effects of obscenity and make recommendations.

In contrast, Republicans Richard Nixon and Ronald Reagan made obscenity and pornography campaign issues and spoke out forcefully against their spread. Much of Nixon's concern grew from his desire to blame congressional Democrats for inaction on his legislative agenda, including his measures against pornography and obscenity. Nixon also appealed for public opposition to pornography, maintaining that "when indecent books no longer find a market, when pornographic films can no longer draw an audience, when obscene plays open to empty houses, then the tide will turn. Government can maintain the dikes against obscenity, but only people can turn the tide."[50] This issue was galvanized by the 1970 report of the Presidential Commission on Obscenity and Pornography, which was soundly rejected by the Senate and repudiated by President Nixon.[51] Nixon and the Senate were particularly concerned about its conclusion that there was no convincing evidence that exposure to explicit sexual materials played any meaningful role in causing criminal behavior and delinquency among either adults or young people, nor did such exposure have any adverse effects on public attitudes toward sex and sexual conduct.[52]

Since 1984 Republican presidents could rely on GOP party platforms to support their antipornography campaigns,[53] but Democrats have not enjoyed such party support. The 1984 GOP platform stated that "the Republican Party has deep concern about gratuitous sex and violence in the entertainment media, both of which contribute to the problem of crime against children and women. To the victims of such crimes who need protection we gladly offer it."[54] President Reagan gave full support to this plank by focusing considerable attention on the problem. He felt, despite what the 1967 presidential commission had concluded, that there was a link "between child molesting and pornography" and between "pornography and sexual violence."[55] Because of his dissatisfaction with the 1967 commission, Reagan asked Attorney General Edwin Meese to establish a new presidential commission to investigate the effects of obscenity on society. In May 1985 Meese named a new, eleven-member commission. Unlike the previous commission, which was largely staffed with social scientists, criminologists, and attorneys, the Meese Commission was staffed with law enforcement personnel. Not surprisingly, its final report was very different from the 1967 recommendations. It argued that "substantial exposure to sexually violent materials . . . [bore] a causal relationship to antisocial acts of sexual violence and, for some subgroups, possibly to unlawful acts of sexual violence."[56]

George H.W. Bush chose to focus his efforts on child pornography, which seemed a safe and noncontroversial aspect of the problem, and specifically the issue of unsolicited mailings to children.[57] However, President Bush also became embroiled in a controversy over the National Endowment for the Arts (NEA) when it funded works of art that Bush considered to be "filth." He encouraged John Frohnmayer, NEA chair, to avoid funding the "excessive cases."[58]

President Clinton similarly tried to limit his involvement with this issue to the evils of child pornography, but his efforts were not free of controversy: Clinton became the first president to be challenged by congressional critics with being "soft" on child pornography.[59] Twenty-two senators and eighty-two representatives bitterly complained to Attorney General Janet Reno that the Clinton administration had retreated from its prosecution of Stephen A. Knox, a graduate student who had possessed three videotapes featuring young girls fully clothed though in provocative poses. Knox did not believe his videos were "sexually explicit" or pornographic because previously those designations had been reserved for the "lascivious exhibition of the genitals or pubic area." President Clinton agreed with Knox's assessment and instructed the Justice Department to convey his opinion to the Supreme Court, but eventually the high court ignored Clinton's position and let Knox's conviction stand.[60]

Partly due to this criticism, Clinton adopted a stronger stand on pornography in his second term, integrating it with his focus on family values. Concerned about the potential dangers of the Internet, Clinton issued an executive order to establish a working group of parents, teachers, librarians, and industry leaders to recommend what might be done to protect children from Internet pornography.[61] Clinton was particularly interested in E-chip technology that would allow parents, through electronic filtering, to have greater control over what images their children saw on the Internet. He also encouraged the Internet community to develop safety labels similar to those seen on food products[62] and, moreover, supported United Nations efforts to protect children by signing, on July 5, 2000, two U.N. Optional Protocols. One was the Convention on the Rights of the Child on Involvement of Children in Armed Conflict; the other one was the Sale of Children, Child Prostitution and Child Pornography.[63] The Senate passed these two protocols and they were entered into force in 2002.[64] Clinton pointed out that these two protocols, along with the Convention on the Worst Forms of Child Labor, which he signed in 1999, should offer strong protections for the world's children.[65]

During his 2000 presidential campaign, George W. Bush promised to "vigorously enforc[e] federal anti-pornography laws,"[66] and his appointment of John Ashcroft as attorney general signaled the seriousness of that commitment.[67] But the terrorist attacks on September 11, 2001, the wars in Afghanistan and Iraq, and the jobless economic recovery forced Bush to downgrade the pornography issue on his list of priorities. Yet in October 2002 he found time to convene a White House Conference on Missing, Exploited, and Runaway Children, at which sexual exploitation of children on the Internet by "cyberpredators" was one of the topics he discussed.[68] That same month, Bush addressed federal, state, and law enforcement officers to share his concerns about sexual exploitation and pornography, again specifically mentioning sexual predators of children who operated through the Internet.[69] After the conferences, Bush urged the Senate to provide additional funding and new legislation to stop online predators who "stalk children," asking for increased funding from $6.5 million to $12.5 million for the Internet Crimes Against Children Task Force.[70]

Bureaucracy

The key agencies involved with pornography have been the Federal Communications Commission (FCC), the Federal Bureau of Investigation (FBI), the U.S. Postal Service, and the U.S. Customs Service. The Department of Justice (DOJ) under George W. Bush also deserves mention, given the leadership style of Attorney General John Ashcroft.

Department of Justice

John Ashcroft firmly lead the DOJ to focus its effort on child pornography, probably more so than any attorney general in recent history. On June 6, 2002, in an address to the Federal Prosecutors' Symposium on Obscenity at the National Advocacy Center in Columbia, South Carolina, Ashcroft indicated that his department was "committed unequivocally to the task of prosecuting obscenity."[71] He said that the Child Exploitation and Obscenity Section (CEOS) had received an additional $1 million to hire five information technology specialists and two prosecutors, staffers devoted "full-time to making prosecutions against child pornography and obscenity offenders using the Internet. This initiative will allow CEOS to wage an aggressive battle to protect children and families from individuals who use computers to abuse, exploit and assault them." Ashcroft also said that the Department of Justice would revise the U.S. attorneys' manual to allow the DOJ to preempt local U.S. attorneys in the prosecution of child pornography and obscenity cases. Thus, with the policy change, "CEOS can pursue cases after simply notifying the U.S. Attorney of the need to do so."[72] One task force within DOJ is the Internet Crimes Against Children Task Force. Although it had its beginning under the Clinton administration in 1998, having trained some 1,900 investigators and 1,500 prosecutors through 2002, President Bush hoped to double the funding level for this program.[73]

The Justice Department, along with the U.S. Postal Service, completed in 2001 a two-year child pornography sting operation that involved 37 states and resulted in 150 searches and ultimately some 100 arrests. Some customers resided outside the United States, making this an international operation, although a primary source for the child pornography ring was a Fort Worth company called Landslide Productions. A business that grossed $1 million a month,[74] the company was all but dismantled following the federal sting investigation.

Federal Communications Commission (FCC)

Although the Federal Communications Act (1948) prohibits the FCC from censoring questionable material on the airwaves, the U.S. Code (18 USC § 1464) authorizes the FCC to look for any "obscene, indecent, or profane language by means of radio communication."[75] The FCC has used the *Miller v. California* precedent and judicial instructions from *FCC v. Pacifica Foundation* to prohibit offensive descriptions of "sexual or excretory activities or organs."[76] However it was not until March 2001 that the FCC finally adopted its "Indecency Guidelines" to assist broadcasters in making such judgments. The important criteria to be applied to broadcasting are "(1) the explicitness or graphic nature of the description or depiction of sexual or excretory organs or activities; (2) whether the material dwells on or repeats at length description of sexual or excretory organs or activities; (3) whether the material appears to pander or is used to titillate or whether the material appears to have been presented for its shock value."[77] The FCC has focused most of its attention on removing indecency from broadcasts that occupy the hours of 6 A.M. to 10 P.M.[78]

Federal Bureau of Investigation (FBI)

Prior to 1955, the FBI could only arrest individuals who transported obscene materials on common carriers, but that year Congress passed new legislation making any interstate transportation of pornography illegal, whether by common carrier or private automobile. The potential for FBI enforcement of pornography laws today was illustrated in 1996 when an organized pornography ring was broken up. A federal grand jury charged sixteen persons who participated in a pedophilia club by sharing original pictures on-line and recounting their sexual experiences with others on the Internet.[79] The FBI also conducts computer stings, one occurring in December 1996 when facilities in some twenty cities were searched to determine which computer networks and Internet services were soliciting children for illicit sex. This operation involved fifty-one of fifty-six FBI field offices along with local and state police from Virginia, Maryland, Florida, and the District of Columbia. Over the three-year period of this operation, eighty arrests were made and sixty-six felony convictions were handed down.[80] Among other FBI activities are its "Parent's Guide to Internet Safety"[81] and the "Innocent Images National Initiative" (IINI), which investigates and identifies sexual predators who use the Internet. The IINI caseload increased from 113 cases in 1996 to 2,370 in 2002 and the FBI expects many more cases in the future, anticipating that President Bush will increase the number of undercover investigators.[82]

U.S. Customs Service

Although U.S. Customs has no legal authority to make judgments about what is or is not obscene, the nature of its work gives it leverage to determine what books, magazines, devices, and films enter the country. Most foreign films are given a review before being allowed to enter the United States, and U.S. Customs also spot-checks suspicious packages and in cooperation with the U.S. Postal Service withholds first-class mail. Customs does have the legal authority to prohibit the mailing of sexually oriented advertisements, to prohibit any "office of the United States" from aiding in the importation of obscene or "treasonous" books or articles,[83] and to prohibit the actual "importation or transportation into the United States" of any obscene material.[84]

Beginning in 1983, the U.S. Customs Service redirected its effort against child pornography and, since 2000, has conducted pornography investigations through "Operation Hamlet." Its objective, to disrupt an international ring of child molesters, was achieved when twenty-five persons were arrested, including fourteen Americans.[85] Its more recent activities were summarized by Acting U.S. Customs Commissioner Charles Winwood in 2001, at a press conference, following a successful joint operation with the Moscow city police that shut down a Russian Web site. As the commissioner stated, "The message today should be unmistakable to anybody in that [child pornography] supply chain. The United States Customs Service is engaged with other law enforcement agencies here and abroad in a worldwide assault on the producers, distributors and purchasers of child pornography."[86]

Customs usually cooperates with other domestic and foreign investigative units. U.S. Customs agents in 2001, for example, operated in Denmark with the Cyber-Smuggling Center of the Danish National Police to stop child pornography. In this country, Customs worked with the Cassia County sheriff in 2002 to arrest a suspect from Burley, Idaho, who operated a photography business for producing child pornography.[87] Since 1992, according to Commissioner Winwood, U.S. Customs arrested "more than 1,000 people for offenses related to child pornography, with 320 arrests in 2000 alone."[88] In 1998 one of its largest operations against child porn was conducted when 32 federal search and seizure warrants were enforced by Customs officials in 22 states as part of a worldwide investigation that sought evidence against 100 persons in fourteen countries.[89]

U.S. Postal Service

The role of the U.S. Postal Service in combating pornography has caused more concern among civil libertarians than the work of any other agency, because Congress has armed postal investigators with sufficient statutory authority to detain and restrain mail as well as broad powers over fraud and false advertising when the mails are used to deliver the products ordered by consumers.[90] The U.S. Postal Service has resorted to seizure, exclusion, branding certain publications as unmailable, blocking the mail sent to certain persons through the use of mail covers, and revoking mailing privileges. Sometimes postal inspectors have operated independently, as they did in 1996 when they closed a $500,000-a-year child pornography ring headed by three Americans who were operating from Acapulco, Mexico. This investigation turned out to be the largest child pornography distribution ring U.S. law enforcement had seen up to that time. Thousands of videos and still photographs involving some 300 Mexican boys as young as seven years old were seized, with the consequence that some 56 individuals were arrested throughout the United States for having received the material by mail order.[91]

At other times, the U.S. Postal Service has worked in conjunction with other agencies through task forces. The successful "Operation Avalanche"— a two-year cooperative effort between the U.S. Postal Service and 30 federally funded Internet Crimes Against Children task forces—led to the disassembling of the "largest commercial child photography enterprise ever uncovered" and to charges against more than 120 people.[92]

Interest Groups

Amicus curiae (friend of the court) briefs filed with the Supreme Court and congressional testimony are primary instruments by which interest groups try to influence public policy on pornography. Data on the types of interest groups that acted as amici in major Supreme Court obscenity cases from 1957 to 2003 (Table 9.2) show that, since 1985, there has been much more lobbying of the courts by groups seeking to *expand* public access as compared to those groups favoring restriction. One likely reason for this pattern is the willingness of the Supreme Court to take on more cases involving controversial social issues than they have taken on before. There were also more court petitions than testimonies by interest groups before Congress (Table 9.3). This difference held for every type of interest group except governmental agencies and business/labor organizations, who testified before congressional committees more frequently than they filed amicus briefs. Undoubtedly there is a policy bias with respect to judicial versus congressional decision making that encourages open-access groups to petition the courts whereas anti-access groups appeal to Congress. Yet it is surprising that such an overwhelming number of interests are attracted to the Supreme Court as compared to Congress. This applies to single-issue and multi-issue groups, law-related interest groups as well as authors and press organizations.

The American Civil Liberties Union (ACLU) was one of the most active groups supporting information access, whereas Citizens for Decency Through Law and Morality in Media were the most active in trying to restrict public access. Publishers Marketing Association and Freedom to Read were just as tenacious in opposing censorship, as generally civil libertarians, authors, presses, libraries, museums, and artists favor freer access to information except where minors and nonconsenting adults are involved.

Single-issue groups like the antiobscenity Citizens for Decency Through Law have been especially strident in their advocacy, more so than other groups, and numerous single-issue groups that have petitioned Congress over the years have been affiliates of the Citizens for Decency Through Law. Two other such groups are Eradication of Smut and Morality in Media, the latter

Table 9.2

Amicus Curiae Briefs to the Supreme Court on Obscenity Cases[a]

Interest groups filing briefs	To restrict access			To expand access		
	1957–1984[b]	1985–1997[c]	1998–2003[d]	1957–1984	1985–1997	1998–2003
Parent/child	2	24	15			
Single-issue	2	83	6		17	9
Law-related		73	6		59	8
Religious	1	45	2	2	31	
Museums/libraries			3	2	35	
Multi-issue		86		2	1	4
Arts				9	44	23
Author/press				5	47	12
Government			15	23		42
Education						6
Labor/business			2			1
Women's groups			2			3
Media						7
Total	5	311	51	43	234	115

[a]Through October 2002 term (ended June 2003).
[b]Included in this period are forty-two obscenity cases.
[c]Included in this period are twenty-one obscenity cases.
[d]Included in this period are six obscenity cases.

Table 9.3

Interest Group Testimony to Congress on Obscenity[a]

Interest group	To restrict access to obscenity 1957–1984[b]	1985–1998[c]	To expand access to obscenity 1999–2003[d]	1957–1984	1985–1998	1999–2003	Total number of statements
	Number of statements						
Government	8	30	3	4			45
Parent/child	1	4	6				11
Single-issue	14	14					28
Law-related	1	2	1	4			8
Religious	38	8	1	2			49
Health-related	11			1			12
Education	3	1		1		1	6
Multi-issue	10	4	1	2	6		23
Arts	3			2			5
Authors/press	7			13	9		29
Fraternal/ethnic	3						3
Labor/business	4			1	2		7
Women's groups	4						4
Museums/libraries			1	1	2		4
Computer/Internet			9		8		17
Media		1			1		2
Victims/potential victims		1	5				6
Total	107	65	27	31	28	1	259

[a]Includes first eight months of 2003.
[b]Included in this period are thirty-seven congressional hearings.
[c]Included in this period are sixteen congressional hearings.
[d]Included in this period are five congressional hearings.

of which filed five amicus briefs before the Supreme Court in 2000. Curiously, feminist groups have not been highly visible among those groups critical of pornography. Most active before the Supreme Court in recent years has been Feminists for Free Expression, which filing three amicus briefs in the six cases that the Court heard since 2000, whereas Concerned Women for America supported restrictions of expression, with two amicus briefs filed during the same period.

How effective are antipornography groups at the grass roots? One study of censorship campaigns in eighteen communities determined that failed to suppress pornography because the booksellers successfully appealed to the courts and to local officials. That study concluded that, because antipornography groups were unable to rally public opinion, "those who attempted to censor basically had to do so alone" and had to settle for limited, short-term, or symbolic successes.[93] However, increased awareness of child pornography, the expansion of Internet access, and the use of federal funds for the arts all have encouraged greater activity on the part of antipornography interest groups. Such groups as the American Family Association, Pat Robertson's *700 Club,* and the Christian Action Network actively have opposed funding for the National Endowment for the Arts, whereas the American Arts Alliance, the American Council for the Arts, and the Arts Coalition for Freedom of Expression have been equally active in supporting government funding.[94] The Religious Alliance Against Pornography served as a sympathetic audience for George H.W. Bush, who addressed the members in October 1991 about the horrors of pornography, encouraging them to continue to stand firmly against it.[95]

Shortly after George W. Bush appointed John Ashcroft as attorney general, the National Coalition for the Protection of Children & Families and the Religious Alliance Against Pornography, petitioned both Bush and Ashcroft to be firm in prosecuting illegal pornography. Believing that they enjoyed access to this new administration, these conservative and family oriented groups stated that they were "speaking out against 'white-collar pornographers' that pander pornographic materials not protected by the First Amendment," were requesting that "enforcement of federal obscenity laws be among the highest priorities for the United States Department of Justice," and were distributing their petition through General Motors and other companies.[96]

Another example of single-issue activism was the outreach efforts of the National Coalition for the Protection of Children & Families during Pornography Awareness Week (October 27–November 3). In 2002 this group encouraged concerned individuals to: (1) clean up the local video store; (2) encourage zoning to prevent the location of sexually oriented businesses near schools, churches, or residential areas; (3) protect children by overseeing the public libraries to make sure that Internet filters were installed; (4) distribute educational materials discussing the harmful effects of pornography; (5) raise the issue in their local churches; (6) encourage members of Congress to counteract obscenity; (7) sign a "fight corporate porn" petition and encourage Attorney General Ashcroft to "prosecute illegal obscenity"; (8) use filtering software in the home; (9) talk to children in the home about the limits beyond which they should not go on the Internet; and (10) talk to the children about pornography and about the prevalence of sex in the community in its music, movies, and television.[97]

Federalism

Although recognized as a universal problem affecting nearly all cities and states, some cities and counties have enacted unusual ordinances in their attempts to control pornography, though many of these laws raise serious constitutional questions. In 1983 an ordinance introduced to the Minneapolis City Council defined pornography as "the sexually explicit subordination of women; graphically depicted, whether in pictures or words" and categorized it as one type of discrimination based on gender.[98] By this definition, individuals could bring lawsuits based on the city's civil rights ordinance. The antipornography ordinance was adopted by the Minneapolis City Council but vetoed by Mayor Donald Fraser on the grounds that it was ambiguous and vague. Despite its failure in Minneapolis, this proposal influenced other communities across America, including Indianapolis, where a similar antipornography ordinance was adopted by the Indianapolis City and County Council in May 1984. The Indianapolis definition of pornography paralleled the Minneapolis ordinance, defining pornography as "the graphic sexually explicit subordination of women, whether in pictures or in words" and then adding many of the specific clauses in the *Model Anti-pornography Civil Rights Ordinance*.[99] The Seventh Circuit Court of Appeals rejected the Indianapolis pornography ordinance for several reasons. To begin with, the ordinance did not use any of the accepted standards that the Supreme Court had developed over time for determining when material is obscene, including "prurient interest," "offensiveness," or "local community standards." A second and, perhaps, more important concern was the way women were depicted in the work. If women were referred to in the approved fashion stressing equality, the activity involved would be approved regardless of how sexually explicit it was; on the other hand, the Court indicated that if women were referred to in a disapproving way depicting them as subversive or as enjoying humiliation, the activity would be unlawful regardless of the "literary, artistic or political qualities of the work taken as a whole." The decision was appealed to the Supreme Court the next year, but was later denied a rehearing.[100]

There has been much frustration among state and local officials who try to monitor pornographic materials. Although Albany, New York, was successful in 1985 in passing a law against the display of "offensive sexual material" in public areas,[101] the next year Maine voters turned back an attempt to make it a crime to sell or promote pornographic materials. The Christian Civil League of Maine was the principal interest group behind the referendum attempt, but opponents managed to convince voters that the issue was really censorship.[102] While the Supreme Court allowed Ohio (in *Osborne v. Ohio,* 1990) to ban the private possession of pornography, that very same year the high court refused to allow Dallas, Texas, to license "adult" businesses (in *FW/PBS v. Dallas,* 1990).[103] In 1994, 80,000 Colorado citizens signed a petition to amend the Colorado constitution to remove what they considered a too permissive free-speech clause. Supporters of the amendment argued that this clause made the Colorado document even more liberal than the U.S. Constitution in its interpretation of what obscenity is,[104] but the referendum was defeated.

One policy on which state, local, and federal authorities can agree is their collective opposition to child pornography. All but a few states have enacted strong prohibitions against child pornography. The fines and penalties are strong, severe in many cases, with states generally mandating felony penalties for violating child antipornography laws, and many states restrict child pornography whether or not the material has been deemed obscene.[105] Even had the Supreme Court supported community standards for obscenity cases, it is doubtful that there would be sufficient consensus among local decision makers on what community standards should prevail. In a study of Detroit, for example, Douglas H. Wallace found that there was no uniform standard or criterion among the respondents. Instead, Wallace found a gap between "sexual liberals" and "sexual conservatives" that prevented any possible agreement on a single contemporary community standard.[106] Even in an Idaho town of 43,000, where one might expect more homogeneous views, a 1978 study found that "pornography was dichotomized differently by different individuals."[107]

The Internet poses additional difficulties for states. In 1996 the Georgia legislature went so far as to outlaw pictures of marijuana on the Internet, and the previous year the Georgia legislature attempted to bar the transmission of "fighting words" or vulgar expressions that might influence minors on the Internet. What Georgia legislators did not consider in their zeal to protect children from Internet transmissions is that whatever restricts access to children also frequently limits the freedoms of adults. Utah thought it had a novel solution to this dilemma when the governor in 2000 selected Paula Houston to be Utah's first "Porn Czar" to advise communities on legal and illegal policies in combating the communities' problems with pornography.[108] The Utah experiment lasted only two years however, the victim of budget cuts.[109]

Public Opinion

Is pornography a salient issue for most citizens? There is enough opinion research to draw some conclusions about how public opinion assesses the pornography problem. To begin, it is clear that pornography is all-pervasive in almost all communities. A 1977 Gallup poll found that X-rated movies, adult bookstores, and even massage parlors existed in communities of all sizes, from cities with more than 1 million people to towns with populations of 2,500. Only in rural areas were movie theaters not showing X-rated films.[110] Today, with the Internet bringing all types of information directly into the home, 80 percent of those polled in a 2001 Princeton survey indicated that they were "very concerned" and another 12 percent were "somewhat concerned" about the problem of pornography.[111]

Despite the 1967 presidential commission, which suggested that there was no evidence linking pornography to social deviancy, most citizens believe such a relationship exists. The link for some people, as explained by one researcher, is that "pornography is the theory, and rape the practice."[112] Regarding that connection, the National Opinion Research Center asked national samples during 1988, 1991, 1993, and 1994 whether sexual materials caused people to commit rape. A majority said yes in the first three surveys, falling slightly to 48 percent in 1994.[113] Even if the link between pornography and crime is not as firm in the public mind today, people still make the connection between pornography and a decline in moral values in society. A 1999 Peter Hart poll found that 62 percent of respondents felt that pornography on the Internet was a major cause of the decline in moral values in the United States.[114]

While 92 percent of people in 1986 agreed with Supreme Court Justice Potter Stewart that they could determine for themselves what pornography was, there was little agreement about what exactly should be considered pornographic and what should be done about the problem.[115] Most commonly branded as pornographic, in one 1986 poll, were depictions of sexual intercourse in magazines (84 percent), X-rated movies (77 percent), and depictions of homosexual sex acts (86 percent).[116] Seventy-six percent of those who responded to an International Communications Research poll in July of 2000 felt that, while government was making an effort to control pornography, government was not exerting enough control over the negative aspects of child pornography.[117] Surveys have consistently shown that a majority of the public wants more protective standards for children under eighteen years of age, designed to prevent their exposure to pornography.[118] Since 1988 more than 50 percent told pollsters they would support bans on questionable material for minors, and one-third of Americans would impose that ban on people of all ages.[119]

Summary of Propositions

1a (single-issue groups): Supported, only when single-issue groups opposed pornography; but was not supported in the anticensorship lobby composed of multi-interest groups.

1b (absolutist politics): Supported, by single-issue groups. Opponents of absolutist politics, made up largely of multi-interest groups, saw laws restricting adult access to pornography as violating First Amendment guarantees.

2a (judicial activism): Supported, because the importance of the First Amendment to the courts guarantees that the issues of pornography will always reach the courts for a final resolution.

2b (incorporation): Unsupported, in a purely legal sense, because obscenity is not a "protected freedom," although the Supreme Court often invalidates state and local antipornography laws on the basis of protecting freedom of the press and of expression, stating that such expression is not pornographic.

3a (presidential symbolism): Unsupported, because some presidents have gone beyond rhetorical leadership to appoint study commissions or convene conferences.

3b (partisan presidents): Supported, because Republicans more often than Democrats have politicized this issue and have included this issue in their presidential campaigns.

4a (Congress and states): Supported, because congressional as well as state antipornography laws have been invalidated by federal courts on the basis of First Amendment guarantees.

4b (Congress and elections): Supported, because legislators at the state and federal levels view antipornography campaigns, especially regarding child pornography, as popular with the electorate.

5a (opinion and ideology): Supported, because public opinion sees a link between access to pornography and antisocial acts, with significant majorities opposing child pornography.

5b (law and society): Supported, insofar as law enforcement and antipornography campaigns have acted to limit the growth of the massive and diversified pornography industry.

6a (federal agencies): Supported, in the sense that the federal agencies involved with antipornography enforcement were not established solely to enforce antipornography laws; moreover, the priority given antipornography enforcement by the Department of Justice can vary widely from administration to administration.

6b (federal implementation): Supported, with respect to adult pornography, inasmuch as the judiciary and "regulated" interest groups have been less supportive of censorship of adult pornography than presidents, members of Congress, and moralistic interest groups. Federal implementation has not been supported with regard to child pornography.

7a (federalism): Supported, insofar as the states have a long history of attempting to suppress obscenity and pornography.

7b (compliance): Supported, in the sense that most successful antipornography "sting" operations by the federal government have involved cooperation with state and local law enforcement authorities and, at times, agencies in foreign countries.

For Further Insight Into the Pornography Debate

Frontline, "American Porn" PBS, 2002, @ www.pbs.org/wgbh/pages/frontline/shows/porn/etc/synopsis.htm. There are two versions of this documentary, which gives an insider's look at the most successful pornography business and its profits. *Frontline* decided to make a second version of "American Porn" in which some explicit images and language were electronically masked. Both versions have been offered to television stations. Both versions mask frontal nudity but in the specially edited version additional material is "black boxed" or bleeped. However, the film's sequences in both versions are exactly the same and the narration also is the same.

Nightline, "Dirty Business: Growing Pornography Business," ABC, March 16, 2002. This *Nightline* program examines the business of pornography in detail. Ted Koppel and associates examine the pornography market and the businesses that feed the market through interviews with those involved. The program shows how the market has moved from the porn shops and adult movie houses to the privacy of the Internet. Item #N020315.

Patently Offensive: Porn Under Siege, 1992. (Distributed by Filmmakers Library, 124 East 40th St., New York, NY 10016). This video shows interviews with Ralph Ginzburg, Al Goldstein, Barry Lynn, P.E. Dietz, Frederick Schauer, and Andrea Dworkin, as well as people in the Women Against Pornography movement, the National Organization for Women, and the National Christian Association. The people interviewed comment on the economic, legal, social, and moral implications of pornography and look at such concerns as censorship, artistic freedom, family values, and individual rights.

Pornography: First Amendment Right or State-Sanctioned Violence Against Women? Films for the Humanities & Sciences, (#H1H10983-A).

Ratings, Morals, and Sex on TV, 1998. (Distributed by Showtime Video, 1813 Westchester Ave., Bronx, NY 10472). This documentary looks at how airwaves are controlled. Interviewed are television producers, critics, journalists, and others, including Tim Doyle, Stuart Elliott, Ted Harbert, Marta Kauffman, David Milch, Robert Peters, and Frank Rich.

The Sexual Exploitation of Children: Taking a Stand (Films for the Humanities & Sciences). Filmed in the Dominican Republic, Sweden, the Netherlands, Germany, Thailand, Sri Lanka, and Britain, this documentary discusses how children are victimized through prostitution, pedophilia, and pornography and also examines the efforts of several international organizations, including Interpol, ECPAT International, and Swedish Save the Children, involved in this problem. There is a special focus on Internet porn and sex tourism. The film contains some explicit material (#HLN31407).

"Sexual Harassment and Pornography." *20th Century with Mike Wallace*, National Television System Committee (ASIN: #0767012348).

The Story of X: 100 Years of Adult Film and Its Stars, 1998. (Distributed by Playboy, P.O. Box 809, Itasca, IL 60143–0809). This video interviews producers, historians, and critics, including David Friedman, Andrea Dworkin, Russ Meyer, and Donald Wildmon, who discuss the role of women, concerns of free speech, and challenges to taste and candor. The film also uses clips from historically important films.

Notes

Foreword

1. Theodore J. Lowi, "The Welfare State, The New Regulation and the Rule of Law," in Allan Schnaiberg et al., *Distributional Conflicts in Environmental Resource Policy* (London, England: Gower Publishing Co., Ltd., 1986), p. 113. My thanks to Schnaiberg for suggesting, albeit for different purposes, the first antinomy between error and sin.

2. New York State Consolidated Laws Domestic Relations, Sec. 11.

3. *Loving v. Virginia*, 388 U.S. 1 (1967). What an ironic title.

4. Paul Starr, "Judicial Overreach," *The American Prospect*, March 2004, p. 18. (Emphasis added.)

5. Theodore J. Lowi, *The End of the Republican Era* (University of Oklahoma Press, 1995, 1996).

Introduction

1. Theodore J. Lowi, "American Business, Public Policy, Case Studies, and Political Theory," *World Politics* 16 (July 1964), pp. 677–715.

2. Theodore J. Lowi, "Four Systems of Policy, Politics and Choice," *Public Administration Review* 32 (July–August 1972), pp. 298–310.

3. T. Alexander Smith, *The Comparative Policy Process* (Santa Barbara, CA: Clio Press, 1975), p. 90.

4. T. Alexander Smith and Raymond Tatalovich, *Cultures at War: Moral Conflicts in Western Democracies* (Peterborough, Ontario: Broadview Press, 2003).

5. Max Weber, *Economy and Society* (New York: Bedminster, 1968), pp. 302–307, 901–940. See also Gerard A. Brandmeyer and R. Serge Denisoff, "Status Politics: An Appraisal of the Application of a Concept," *Pacific Sociological Review* 12 (1969), pp. 5–11.

6. Joseph R. Gusfield, *Symbolic Crusade: Status Politics and the American Temperance Movement* (Urbana: University of Illinois Press, 1963); Louis A. Zurcher Jr., R. George Kirkpatrick, Robert G. Cushing, and Charles K. Bowman, "The Anti-Pornography Campaign: A Symbolic Crusade," *Social Problems* 19 (Fall 1971); J. Wilbur Scott, "The Equal Rights Amendment as Status Politics," *Social Forces* 64 (December 1985), pp. 499–506; John Higham, "Another Look at Nativism," *Catholic*

Historical Review 44 (July 1958); Raymond Tatalovich, *Nativism Reborn? The Official English Movement and the American States* (Lexington: University of Kentucky Press, 1995); Ann L. Page and Donald A. Clelland, "The Kanawha County Textbook Controversy: A Study of the Politics of Life Style Concern," *Social Forces* 57 (September 1978); Matthew C. Moen, "School Prayer and the Politics of Life-Style Concern," *Social Science Quarterly* 65 (December 1984).

7. Seymour Martin Lipset, *Political Man: The Social Bases of Politics* (Garden City, NY: Anchor Books, 1963), p. 92.

8. This formulation is a slight modification of James Anderson's conceptualization of the administrative decision making process. See James E. Anderson, *Public Policymaking*, 4th ed. (Boston: Houghton Mifflin, 2000), p. 221.

9. Kenneth J. Meier, *The Politics of Sin: Drugs, Alcohol, and Public Policy* (Armonk, NY: M.E. Sharpe, 1994), p. xiv.

Chapter 1

1. Neal Devins, *Shaping Constitutional Values: Elected Government, the Supreme Court, and the Abortion Debate* (Baltimore: Johns Hopkins University Press, 1996), p. 145. For Justice Ginsburg's remarks, see Laurie Shrage, *Abortion and Social Responsibility: Depolarizing the Debate* (London: Oxford University Press, 2003), p. 131. For McCorvey's reactions to Roe after more than thirty years, see Liza Porteus, "'Roe' Seeks to Overturn Historic Abortion Ruling," Fox News Channel, www.foxnews.com/printer_friendly_story/0,3566,89663,00.html.

2. James C. Mohr, *Abortion in America: The Origins and Evolution of National Policy*, (New York: Oxford University Press, 1978).

3. Marie Costa, *Abortion: A Reference Handbook* (Santa Barbara, CA: ABC-CLIO, 1996), p. 6.

4. Nanette J. Davis, *From Crime to Choice: The Transformation of Abortion in America* (Westport, CT: Greenwood Press, 1985), p. 211.

5. Ibid.

6. Karen O'Connor, *No Neutral Ground? Abortion Politics in an Age of Absolutes* (Boulder, CO: Westview Press, 1996), p. 21.

7. Linda Gordon, *Woman Body, Woman Right: Birth Control in America* (New York: Penguin, 1990), pp. 50–51.

8. Laurence H. Tribe, *Abortion: The Clash of Absolutes* (New York: W.W. Norton, 1990), p. 34.

9. Carroll Smith-Rosenberg, *Disorderly Conduct: Visions of Gender in Victorian America* (New York: Alfred A. Knopf, 1985), p. 222.

10. Davis, *From Crime to Choice*, p. 213.

11. Ibid., pp. 212–213.

12. Raymond Tatalovich, "Abortion: Prochoice Versus Prolife," in *Social Regulatory Policy: Moral Controversies in American Politics*, ed. Raymond Tatalovich and Byron W. Daynes. (Boulder, CO: Westview Press, 1988), p. 178.

13. See the following sources for estimates of illegal abortions obtained from 1900 through 1950: Marie E. Kopp, *Birth Control in Practice: Analysis of Ten Thousand Case Histories of the Birth Control Clinical Research Bureau* (New York: Arno Press, 1972), pp. 121–127, 207; F.I. Taussig, *Abortion, Spontaneous and Induced* (St. Louis: C.V. Mosby, 1936), pp. 387–388; Raymond Pearl, *The Natural History*

of the Population (London: Oxford University Press, 1939), pp. 202–203; and Daniel Callahan, *Abortion: Law, Choice and Morality* (New York: Macmillan, 1970).

14. Costa, *Abortion: A Reference Handbook,* p. 12.

15. Leslie J. Reagan, *When Abortion Was a Crime: Women, Medicine, and Law in the United States, 1867–1973* (Berkeley: University of California Press, 1997), pp. 219–220.

16. Costa, *Abortion: A Reference Handbook,* p. 11.

17. Reagan, *When Abortion Was a Crime,* p. 224. For the pre-*Roe* abortion politics in New York and Pennsylvania, see Rosemary Nosiff, *Before Roe: Abortion Policy in the States,* (Philadelphia: Temple University Press, 2001).

18. O'Connor, *No Neutral Ground?* p. 29.

19. Barbara Hinkson Craig and David M. O'Brien, *Abortion and American Politics* (Chatham, NJ: Chatham House, 1993), p. 434.

20. See Raymond Tatalovich and Byron W. Daynes, *The Politics of Abortion: A Study of Community Conflict in Public Policy Making* (New York: Praeger, 1981), p. 27, and Tatalovich, "Abortion: Prochoice Versus Prolife," pp. 180–181.

21. David J. Garrow, *Liberty and Sexuality: The Right to Privacy and the Making of* Roe v. Wade (New York: Macmillan, 1994), pp. 591–594.

22. Mary C. Segers and Timothy A. Byrnes, "Introduction: Abortion Politics in American States," in *Abortion Politics in American States,* ed. Mary C. Segers and Timothy A. Byrnes, (Armonk, NY: M.E. Sharpe, 1995), p. 5.

23. The nineteen cases decided from 1973 to 1989 were *Roe v. Wade, District Attorney of Dallas County,* 410 U.S. 113 (1973); *Doe v. Bolton,* 410 U.S. 179 (1973); *Bigelow v. Virginia,* 421 U.S. 809 (1975); *Connecticut v. Menillo,* 423 U.S. 9 (1975); *Bellotti v. Baird (I),* 428 U.S. 132 (1976); *Planned Parenthood of Central Missouri v. Danforth,* 428 U.S. 52 (1976); *Maher v. Roe,* 432 U.S. 464 (1977); *Beal v. Doe,* 432 U.S. 438 (1977); *Poelker v. Doe,* 432 U.S. 519 (1977); *Colautti v. Franklin,* 439 U.S. 379 (1979); *Bellotti v. Baird (II),* 443 U.S. 622 (1979); *Harris v. McRae,* 448 U.S. 297 (1980); *Williams v. Zbaraz,* 448 U.S. 358 (1981); *H.L. v. Matheson,* 450 U.S. 398 (1981); *City of Akron v. Akron Center for Reproductive Health,* 462 U.S. 416 (1983); *Planned Parenthood Association of Kansas City, Mo. v. Ashcroft,* 462 U.S. 476 (1983); *Simopoulos v. Virginia,* 462 U.S. 506 (1983); *Thornburgh v. American College of Obstetricians and Gynecologists,* 476 U.S. 747 (1986), and *Webster v. Reproductive Health Services,* 492 U.S. 490.

24. Tatalovich, "Abortion: Prochoice Versus Prolife," p. 183.

25. U.S. Supreme Court Decisions Concerning Reproductive Rights: 1965–2003. www.naral.org/facts/scotus_decisions_choice.cfm.

26. Segers and Byrnes, "Introduction: Abortion Politics in American States," p. 7.

27. Irene Davall, "Which Way After Webster? Throughout the U.S., Six-Hour Drives Are Not Uncommon for Women Needing Abortions," *On the Issues* 17 (Winter 1990), p. 8.

28. American Civil Liberties Union, "Parental Involvement Laws," 2001, www.aclu.org/library/parent.html. See also American Civil Liberties Union, "Parental Rights Legislation," 1996, www. aclu.org/library/parentrt.html, and Allison Beth Hubbard, "The Erosion of Minors' Abortion Rights: An Analysis of *Hodgson v. Minnesota* and *Ohio v. Akron Center for Reproductive Health,*" *UCLA Women's Law Journal* 1 (Spring 1991), pp. 227–244. http//cnn.com/US/8703/31/ scotus.wrap/index.html.

29. David A. Gardey, "Federal Power to the Rescue: The Use of Section 1985(3) Against Anti-Abortion Protestors," *Notre Dame Law Review* 67 (1992), pp. 707–743.

30. Lissa Shults Campbell, "Critical Analysis of *Bray v. Alexandria Women Health Clinic* and the Use of 42 U.S.C. Section 1985(3) to Protect a Woman's Right to an Abortion," *University of Kansas Law Review* 41 (Spring 1993), pp. 569–589.

31. Amy L. Mauk, "RICO Abortion Protesters Subject to Civil RICO Actions *National Organization for Women, Inc. v. Scheidler*, No. 92 780, 1994 U.S. LEXIS 1143 (Jan. 24, 1994), *Suffolk University Law Review* 28 (Spring 1994), pp. 288–297.

32. Jennifer J. Seibring, "If It's Not Too Much to Ask, Could You Please Shut Up? *Madsen v. Women Health Ctr., Inc.*, 114 S. Ct. 2516 (1994)," *Southern Illinois University Law Journal* 20 (Fall 1995), pp. 205–222.

33. Linda Greenhouse, "High Court Backs Limits on Protest at Abortion Clinic," *New York Times,* July 1, 1994.

34. Tatalovich, "Abortion: Prochoice Versus Prolife," pp. 185–186.

35. Devins, *Shaping Constitutional Values,* p. 92. See also Rachael K. Pirner and Laurie B. Williams, "*Roe* to *Casey*: A Survey of Abortion Law," *Washburn Law Journal* 32 (Winter 1993), pp. 166–189. For information on Justice Blackmun's papers, see Religious Coalition for Reproductive Choice, "Blackmun Papers Reveal That Roe Almost Overturned," March 15, 2004, www.rcrc.org/news/current/blackmun_papers.htm.

36. Deborah R. McFarlane and Kenneth J. Meier, *The Politics of Fertility Control: Family Planning and Abortion Policies in the American States* (New York: Chatham House Publishers of Seven Bridges Press, 2001), p. 70.

37. N.E.H. Hull and Peter Charles Hoffer, *Roe v. Wade: The Abortion Rights Controversy in American History* (Lawrence: University of Kansas Press, 2001), pp. 266–267.

38. Feminist Majority, "Roe v. Wade Day—Protecting Abortion Access," n.d., www.feminist.org/rights/roevwade/supremecourt.org.

39. Craig and O'Brien, *Abortion and American Politics,* p. 249.

40. Kenneth Jost, "Abortion Debates: Will More Restrictions Be Enacted," *Congressional Quarterly Researcher* 13 (March 21, 2003), p. 254.

41. Barbara Norrander and Clyde Wilcox, *Understanding Public Opinion* (Washington, DC: Congressional Quarterly, 2002), p. 130.

42. Jost, "Abortion Debates," p. 254.

43. Abortion: Bills and Proposals, n.d., www.publicagenda.org/issues/major_proposals_detail.cfm?issue_type=abortion&list=2.

44. John Kenneth White, "E Pluribus Duo: Red State vs. Blue State America: An Analysis of the O'Leary Report/Zogby International Values Poll," 2003, pp. 3 and 31–33. The Red States (voted for George Bush) are Alabama, Alaska, Arizona, Arkansas, Colorado, Florida, Georgia, Idaho, Indiana, Kansas, Kentucky, Louisiana, Mississippi, Missouri, Montana, Nebraska, Nevada, New Hampshire, North Carolina, North Dakota, Ohio, Oklahoma, South Carolina, South Dakota, Tennessee, Texas, Utah, Virginia, West Virginia, and Wyoming. The Blue States (supported Al Gore) were California, Connecticut, Delaware, Hawaii, Illinois, Iowa, Maine, Maryland, Massachusetts, Michigan, Minnesota, New Jersey, New Mexico, New York, Oregon, Pennsylvania, Rhode Island, Vermont, Washington, and Wisconsin. The District of Columbia is included with the Blue States.

45. See Linda J. Beckman and S. Marie Harvey, eds., *The New Civil War: The Psychology, Culture, and Politics of Abortion* (Washington, DC: American Psychological Association, 1998).

46. Suzanne Staggenborg, *The Pro-Choice Movement: Organization and Activism in the Abortion Conflict* (New York: Oxford University Press, 1991), p. 3.

47. Feminist Majority Foundation, "Reproductive Rights," www.feminist.org/rights; National Organization for Women, "Reproductive Rights Steadily Eroded in the States," now.org/issues/abortion//031704states.html.

48. Costa, *Abortion: A Reference Handbook,* pp. 190, 203, and 212–213.

49. National Abortion Rights Action League, "About Us," n.d., www.naral.org/about/index.cfm.

50. Staggenborg, *The Pro-Choice Movement,* p. 145.

51. Barbara M. Yarnold, *Abortion Politics in the Federal Courts: Right Versus Right* (Westport, CT: Praeger, 1995), pp. 116, 223.

52. Raymond Tatalovich and Byron W. Daynes, "The Lowi Paradigm, Moral Conflict, and Coalition-Building: Pro-Choice Versus Pro-Life," *Women and Politics* 13 (1993), pp. 39–56.

53. O'Connor, *No Neutral Ground? Abortion Politics in the Age of Absolutes,* pp. 84–85, 146–147. See the Christian Coalition's mission at www.cc.org/mission.php and its proclaimed victories at www.cc.org/victories.php.

54. Costa, *Abortion: A Reference Handbook,* pp. 192–193.

55. Keith Cassidy, "The Right to Life Movement: Sources, Development, and Strategies, *Journal of Policy History* 7 (1995), pp. 128–159; see www.operation saveamerica.org of Operation Save America's activities.

56. Charles S. Clark, "Abortion Clinic Protests: Is Violence Changing the Abortion Debate? *Congressional Quarterly Researcher* 5 (April 7, 1995), pp. 297–320; Jill Petty, "Enemies of Choice," *Ms.* (May/June 1995), pp. 44–47; National Abortion Rights Action League, "Justifiable Homicide and the Anti-Choice Movement," *NARAL Factsheets,* 1996, www.naral.org/facts/homicide.cfm.

57. National Right to Life, "Diary of An Unborn Baby," n.d., www.nrlc.org/abortion/facts/fetusdevelopment.html.

58. Gary Leber, "We Must Rescue Them," in *The Ethics of Abortion: Pro-Life vs. Pro-Choice,* ed. Robert M. Baird and Stuart E. Rosenbaum, rev. ed. (Buffalo, NY: Prometheus Books, 1993), p. 139.

59. Mark A. Graber, *Rethinking Abortion: Equal Choice, the Constitution, and Reproductive Rights* (Princeton, NJ: Princeton University Press, 1996), p. 24; Leber, "We Must Rescue Them," p. 139.

60. *The Gallup Poll Monthly,* July 1996 (no. 370), p. 38.

61. Kristin Luker, *Abortion and the Politics of Motherhood* (Berkeley: University of California Press, 1984), p. 145.

62. Luker, *Abortion and the Politics of Motherhood,* p. 146.

63. Craig and O'Brien, *Abortion and American Politics,* p. 46.

64. Ibid., pp. 158–159.

65. Tatalovich, "Abortion: Prochoice Versus Prolife," p. 198.

66. Craig and O'Brien, *Abortion and American Politics,* pp. 169–170; Tatalovich, "Abortion: Prochoice Versus Prolife," p. 200.

67. O'Connor, *No Neutral Ground?* pp. 116–119.

68. Raymond Tatalovich, *The Politics of Abortion in the United States and Canada: A Comparative Study* (Armonk, NY: M.E. Sharpe, 1997), pp. 157–158.

69. William Saletan, *Bearing Right: How Conservatives Won the Abortion War* (Berkeley: University of California Press, 2003), pp. 250–251.

70. Lawrence Lader, *A Private Matter: RU-486 and the Abortion Crisis* (Amherst, NY: Prometheus Books, 1995), pp. 115–117; Karen Freeman, "Planned Parenthood to Test 2 Abortion Drugs," *New York Times,* September 12, 1996; Tamar Lewin,

"Abortion Group to Advise Doctors on Drug Used to End Pregnancy," *New York Times,* March 30, 1996.

71. Frank Bruni and Marc Lacey, "Bush Acts to Deny Money Overseas Tied to Abortion," *New York Times,* January 23, 2001.

72. Laura Mansnerus, "Abortion Rights Group Files Suit Over Bush Family Planning Rule," *New York Times,* June 7, 2001; Planned Parenthood, "President Bush Sued by Center for Reproductive Law and Policy," Press Releases, www.planned parenthood.org/research/news.

73. Robert Pear, "Thompson Says He Will Order a New Review of Abortion Drug," *New York Times,* January 20, 2001.

74. Lars Noah, "A Miscarriage in the Drug Approval Process? Mifepristone Embroils the FDA in Abortion Politics," *Wake Forest Law Review* 36 (2001), p. 591.

75. Planned Parenthood Federation, "Another Dubious Appointment," Press Releases, www.plannedparenthood.org/research /news.

76. Katherine Q. Seelye, "Bush Gives His Backing for Limited Research on Existing Stem Cells," *New York Times,* August 10, 2001; National Committee for a Human Life Amendment, Key Votes on Abortion: 107th Congress 2001. www.nchla/com/votes/2001overall.pdf.

77. National Organization for Women, "The Bush Administration's Reproductive Rights Record," www.now.org/issues/abortion/roe30/record.html?/printable.

78. Minnesota Citizens Concerned for Life, "Pro-Life Record of President George W. Bush," www.mccl-inc.org/PresBush66.pdf.

79. O'Connor, *No Neutral Ground?* p. 67.

80. Tatalovich, *The Politics of Abortion in the United States and Canada,* p. 98.

81. Craig and OBrien, *Abortion and American Politics,* pp. 112–113.

82. Raymond Tatalovich and David Schier, "The Persistence of Ideological Voting on Abortion Legislation in the House of Representatives, 1973–1988," *American Politics Quarterly* 21 (1993), pp. 125–139.

83. Mark J. Wattier and Raymond Tatalovich, "Senate Voting on Abortion Legislation Over Two Decades: Testing a Reconstructed Partisanship Variable," *American Review of Politics* 16 (1995), pp. 167–183.

84. Raymond Tatalovich and David Schier, "The Persistence of Ideological Cleavage in Voting on Abortion Legislation in the House of Representatives, 1973–1988," in *Understanding the New Politics of Abortion,* ed. Malcolm L. Goggin (Newbury Park, CA: Sage, 1993), pp. 118–119.

85. Robert Pear, "Abortion Clinic Protests Drop Under New Law," *New York Times,* September 24, 1996, p. A13; American Civil Liberties Union, "The ACLU's Role in Stopping Clinic Violence," 1996, www.aclu.org/library/clinicvi.html.

86. Jerry Gray, "White House Says Clinton Plans to Veto Bill Banning Late-Term Abortions," *New York Times,* October 27, 1995.

87. Center for Reproductive Law and Policy. 2001. *The Bush Global Gag Rule: A Violation of International Human Rights and the U.S. Constitution.* New York: Center for Reproductive Law and Policy.

88. Katherine Q. Seelye, "Three Bills Offered to Settle Debate on Late-Term Abortions," *New York Times,* 1997, www.nytimes.com/yr/mo/day/news/washpol/senate-abortion.html; newsroom/ntn/politics/051697/politics8_4470.html.

89. CNN/AllPolitics, "Will an AMA Endorsement Sway Any Votes?" www.cnn.com/allpolitics/1997/05/20/abortion.ama/index.html; CNN/AllPolitics, "AMA Recommends Alternatives To So-Called 'Partial Birth' Abortions," www.cnn.com/allpolitics/

1997/05/14/ama.abortion/index.html; CNN/AllPolitics, "Senate Votes to Bank Late-Term Abortions: Bill Likely to be Vetoed by Clinton," www.cnn.com/allpolitics/storis/1999/10/21/abortion.senate/index.html.

90. National Organization for Women, "105th Congress: Rolling Back Women's Rights," October 1998, www.now.org/issues/election/analysis1998/key.html.

91. National Right to Life Committee Scorecard, "U.S. Congress 1999 Roll Call Votes on Abortion and Other Right-to-Life Issues," January 2000, www.nrlc.org/federal/scorecardexplaination.

92. Susan A. Cohen, "Congress in 2000: Actions to Date on Major Reproductive Health Issues," *The Guttmacher Report* 3 (December 2000), www.guttmacher.org/pubs/journals/gr030611.html.

93. Robin Toner, "Critics Seek to Overturn Abortion Rule," *New York Times,* February 16, 2001, National Committee for a Human Life Amendment, Key Votes on Abortion: 107th Congress 2001, www.nchla.com/votes/midyear-total08.01.02.pdf.

94. NARAL Pro-Choice America, Congressional Record on Choice: 107th Congress, 2nd Session, 2002 (February 11, 2003).

95. Robert B. Bluey, "Lawsuits Challenge Partial-Birth Abortion Ban," *Cybercast News Service,* October 31, 2003, www.cnsnews/culture/archive/200310/cul2003103/ at www.cnsnews.com/mainsearch/search.html.

96. Glen A. Halva-Neubauer, "The States After *Roe:* No 'Paper Tigers,' " in *Understanding the New Politics of Abortion,* ed. Malcolm L. Goggin (Newbury Park, CA: Sage, 1993), pp. 186–189.

97. Ibid., p. 179.

98. "Issue Brief: Minors' Access to Abortion Services," www.naral.org/issues/youngwomen/young_fs.cfm. American Civil Liberties Union, "Reproductive Rights: Low-Income Women," www.aclu.org/reproductiverights/reproductiverightslist.cg=fm?c=146.

99. Linda Feldmann, "Abortion Foes Push Restrictions in Legislatures Across the Country," *Christian Science Monitor,* January 22, 1997.

100. Katherine Q. Seelye, "States Move to Ban Controversial Abortion Procedure," *New York Times,* May 5, 1997, www.nytimes.com/yr/mo/day/news/national/abort-states.html. NARAL, "NARAL Pro-Choice America Issue Brief: Bans on Abortion Procedures," www.naral.org/facts/im_bans.cfm.

101. Alan Guttmacher Institute, "Monthly State Update: Major Developments in 2004," (as of August 1, 2004) www.guttmacher.org/statecenter/updates/index.html pba.

102. National Abortion Rights Action League, Pro-Choice America, *Who Decides: A State-by-State Review of Abortion and Reproductive Rights* (NARAL, 2003), pp. xx–xii.

103. Alan Guttmacher Institute, State Policies in Brief: "'Choose Life' License Plates," February 1, 2004; ibid., "Mandatory Counseling and Waiting Periods for Abortion," February 1, 2004; ibid., "Parental Involvement in Minors' Abortions," February 1, 2004; ibid., "Restricting Insurance Coverage of Abortion," February 1, 2004; ibid., "Refusing to Provide Health Services," February 1, 2004. www.agi-usd.org/.

104. Malcolm L. Goggin and Christopher Wlezian, "Abortion Opinion and Policy in the American States," in *Understanding the New Politics of Abortion,* ed. Malcolm L. Goggin (Newbury Park, CA: Sage, 1993), p. 201; Jean Reith Schroedel, *Is the Fetus a Person? A Comparison of Policies Across the Fifty States* (Ithaca: Cornell University Press, 2000), pp. 99, 160.

105. Ruth Ann Strickland and Marcia Lynn Whicker, "Political and Socio-Economic

Indicators of State Restrictiveness Toward Abortion," *Policy Studies Journal* 20 (1992), pp. 598–617; Maureen Rand Oakley, "Abortion Restrictions and Abortion Rates: Has State Abortion Policy Been Successful?" *Politics and Policy* 31 (September 2003), pp. 472–487.

Chapter 2

1. U.S. Commission on Civil Rights, *Affirmative Action in the 1980s: Dismantling the Process of Discrimination* (Washington, DC: U.S. Commission on Civil Rights, 1981), pp. 3–5.

2. See Morris Abram, "Affirmative Action: Fair Shakers and Social Engineers," *Harvard Law Review* 99 (1986), pp. 1312–1326.

3. Quoted in Carl Cohen, "The DeFunis Case, Race, and the Constitution," *The Nation,* February 8, 1975, pp. 135–145.

4. Ellis Close, *Color-Blind: Seeing Beyond Race in a Race-Obsessed World* (New York: HarperCollins, 1997).

5. The states were Alaska, California, Colorado, Connecticut, Delaware, Hawaii, Idaho, Illinois, Indiana, Iowa, Kansas, Massachusetts, Michigan, Missouri, New Jersey, New Mexico, New York, Ohio, Oregon, Pennsylvania, Rhode Island, Vermont, Washington, and Wisconsin. Bureau of National Affairs, *State Fair Employment Laws and Their Administration* (Washington, DC: BNA, 1964), p. ii.

6. "University's Leaders Are Torn by Affirmative-Action Ban," *New York Times,* January 28, 1996, B. Drummond Ayres Jr., "California Regents Postpone a Ban on Affirmative Action," *New York Times,* February 16, 1996.

7. Kathryn Wexler, "The Fight Over Affirmative Action," *Washington Post National Weekly Edition,* March 11–17, 1996.

8. B. Drummond Ayres Jr., "Foes of Affirmative Action Complete California Drive," *New York Times,* February 22, 1996.

9. B. Drummond Ayres Jr., "Foes of Affirmative Action Are Gaining in Ballot Effort," *New York Times,* February 6, 1996.

10. Paul M. Barrett and G. Pascal Zachary, "Affirmative Action Foes Advance in California," *Wall Street Journal,* February 21, 1996.

11. Wexler, "The Fight Over Affirmative Action."

12. William Claiborne, "The Dulling of a Cutting-Edge Issue," *Washington Post National Weekly Edition,* June 17–23, 1996.

13. Sam Howe Verhovek, "Vote in California Is Motivating Foes of Anti-bias Plans," *New York Times,* November 10, 1996.

14. Glenn C. Loury, "When Color Should Count," *New York Times,* July 28, 2002, www.nytimes.com/2002/07/28/opinion/28LOUR.html.

15. www.infoplease.com/spot/affirmativetimeline1.html.

16. Congressional Quarterly, *Congress and the Nation* (Washington, DC: Congressional Quarterly, 1964), 1:1634.

17. Ibid., 1:1629.

18. Ibid., 1:1610.

19. Ibid., 1:1635.

20. See, generally, Charles and Barbara Whalen, *The Longest Debate: A Legislative History of the 1964 Civil Rights Act* (New York: New American Library, 1985), especially chapter 3.

21. Congressional Quarterly, *Congress and the Nation,* 1:93a, 96a, and 1637.

22. See Gary Bryner, "Congress, Courts, and Agencies: Equal Employment and the Limits of Policy Implementation," *Political Science Quarterly* 96 (1981), pp. 411–430.

23. Congressional Quarterly, *Congress and the Nation,* 2:174.

24. Ibid., 2:503.

25. Quoted in *Washington v. Davis,* 426 U.S. 229 (1976).

26. Congressional Quarterly, *Congress and the Nation,* 3:250–251.

27. Sheilah A. Goodman, "Trying to Undo the Damage: The Civil Rights Act of 1990," *Harvard Law Review* 14 (1991), pp. 185–189.

28. Other civil rights cases effectively overturned by Congress include *Alyeska Pipeline Serv. Co. v. Wilderness Soc'y,* 421 U.S. 240 (1975); *General Elec. Co. v. Gilbert,* 429 U.S. 125 (1976), overturned by Pregnancy Discrimination Act, 92 Stat. 2076 (1978); *United Air Lines, Inc. v. McMann,* 434 U.S. 192 (1977), overturned in the Age Discrimination in Employment Act Amendments of 1978, 92 Stat. 189 (1978); *City of Mobile v. Bolden,* 466 U.S. 55 (1980); *Grove City College v. Bell,* 465 U.S. 555 (1984), overturned in the Civil Rights Restoration Act of 1987, 102 Stat. 28; *Smith v. Robinson,* 468 U.S. 992 (1984), overturned in the Handicapped Children's Protection Act of 1986, 100 Stat. 796; *Atascadero State Hosp. v. Scanlon,* 473 U.S. 234 (1985); and *United States Dep't of Transp. v. Paralyzed Veterans of America,* 477 U.S. 597 (1986).

29. 104th Congress, S. 1085.

30. Deval L. Patrick, assistant attorney general for civil rights, testimony provided in a hearing of the Committee on Labor and Human Resources, *Affirmative Action, Preferences, and the Equal Employment Opportunity Act of 1995,* 104th Congress (April 30, 1995), pp. 30–33; Steven A. Holmes, "Veto Threat on Bill to Ban Hiring Rules," *New York Times,* December 8, 1995.

31. Steven A. Holmes, "White House to Suspend a Program for Minorities," *New York Times,* March 8, 1996.

32. Rep. Charles Canady, testimony provided in a hearing of the Committee on Labor and Human Resources, *Affirmative Action, Preferences, and the Equal Employment Opportunity Act of 1995,* p. 9.

33. Barrett and Zachary, "Affirmative Action Foes Advance in California."

34. *Congressional Record* 110 (1964), p. 8921.

35. *Hopwood v. Texas,* 78 F.3d 932, *cert. denied,* 116 S.Ct. 2591 (1996).

36. U.S. Senate, Committee on Labor and Human Resources, *Committee Analysis of Executive Order 12246,* 97th Cong. (Washington, DC: U.S. Government Printing Office, 1982).

37. E.O. 9664, 3 C.F.R. 1943; E.O. 10210, 3 C.F.R. 1949; and E.O. 10308, 3 C.F.R. 1949.

38. E.O. 10479, 3 C.F.R. 1953; E.O. 10577, 3 C.F.R. 1954.

39. 3 C.F.R. 1963.

40. E.O. 11375, 32 *Fed. Reg.* 14303.

41. Dom Donafede, "Blacks Await Performance of Promise," *National Journal,* November 30, 1974, p. 1810.

42. See James W. Singer, "A Shake-up May Be in Store for Job Discrimination Efforts," *National Journal,* May 4, 1977, pp. 746–747; Bryner, "Congress, Courts, and Agencies," p. 417.

43. Eric Press and Ann McDaniel, "A Right Turn on Race?" *Newsweek,* June 25, 1984, pp. 29–31.

44. Nicholas Lemann, "Clinton, the Great Communicator," *New York Times,* January 20, 1997.

45. Barrett and Zachary, "Affirmative Action Foes Advance in California."

46. Paul M. Barrett, "Foes of Affirmative Action Target SBA's 8(a) Program," *Wall Street Journal,* March 18, 1996.

47. Holmes, "White House to Suspend a Program for Minorities."

48. Paul M. Barrett, "Affirmative Action for U.S. Contracts Is Limited in Rules Using 'Benchmarks,'" *Wall Street Journal,* May 23, 1996.

49. Paul M. Barrett, "White House Memo on Federal Hiring Shows Defense of Affirmative Action," *Wall Street Journal,* March 4, 1996.

50. David Von Drehle, "Court Mirrors Public Opinion," *Washington Post,* June 23, 2003.

51. U.S. Senate, Committee on Labor and Human Resources, *Committee Analysis of Executive Order 12246,* p. 12.

52. 33 *Fed. Reg.* 7804.

53. 41 C.F.R., sec. 60–2.10, 1970.

54. Ibid.

55. *Contractors Association of Eastern Pennsylvania v. Secretary of Labor,* 442 F. 2d 159, 3rd cir. (1971), *cert. denied,* 404 U.S. 854.

56. *New York Times,* December 21, 1969, p. 39.

57. Congressional Quarterly, *Congress and the Nation,* 3:498.

58. U.S. Commission on Civil Rights, *Affirmative Action in the 1980s,* p. 2.

59. Congressional Quarterly, *Congress and the Nation,* 2:374.

60. Allan R. Meyerson, "As Federal Bias Cases Drop, Workers Take Up the Fight," *New York Times,* January 12, 1997.

61. Barbara Rosewicz, "EEOC Flexes New Muscles in Mitsubishi Case, But It Lacks the Bulk to Push Business Around," *Wall Street Journal,* April 29, 1996.

62. Kirsten Downey Grimsley, "The Rodney Dangerfield of Agencies," *Washington Post National Weekly Edition,* February 19–25, 1996.

63. The balance of the cases were closed for other reasons, such as the charging party withdrawing the charge or successful conciliation. See www.eeoc.gov/stats/race.html.

64. Shirley J. Wilcher, deputy assistant secretary for federal contract compliance, U.S. Department of Labor, testimony provided in a hearing of the Committee on Labor and Human Resources, *Affirmative Action and the Office of Federal Contract Compliance* (June 5, 1995), pp. 11–18.

65. Barrett, "Foes of Affirmative Action Target SBA's 8(a) Program."

66. See Rochelle L. Stanfield, "The Black-Jewish Coalition—Shaken but Still Alive After Young Incident," *National Journal,* November 3, 1979, pp. 1849–1852.

67. Congressional Quarterly Researcher, *Issues for Debate in American Public Policy,* 4th ed. (Washington, DC: CQ Press, 2004), pp. 81–98.

68. Tom W. Smith and Paul B. Sheatsley, "American Attitudes Toward Race Relations," *Public Opinion* (October–November 1984), p. 15.

69. Andrew Hacker, "Goodbye to Affirmative Action?" *New York Review of Books,* July 11, 1996, p. 25.

70. Rochelle L. Stanfield, "The Wedge Issue," *National Journal,* April 1, 1995, p. 791.

71. Louis Jacobson, "A Speak-No-Evil Veil Lifted," *National Journal,* April 1, 1995, p. 836.

72. Seymour Martin Lipset and William Schneider, "The Bakke Case: How Would It Be Decided at the Bar of Public Opinion?" *Public Opinion* 1 (March–April 1978), pp. 41–42.

73. www.understandingprejudice.org/readroom/articles/affirm.htm. The balance of respondents answered "don't know" or refused to answer.

74. Von Drehle, "Court Mirrors Public Opinion."

75. Anthony Neely, "Government Role in Rooting Out, Remedying Discrimination Is Shifting," *National Journal,* September 22, 1984, p. 15.

76. Douglas Huron, "It's Fashionable to Denigrate Hiring Quotas—but It's Wrong," *Washington Post National Weekly Edition,* August 27, 1984.

77. John David Skrentny, *The Ironies of Affirmative Action: Politics, Culture, and Justice in America* (Chicago: University of Chicago Press, 1996).

78. "The Jack Kemp Reverse," *New York Times,* August 15, 1996; Katharine Q. Seelye, "Dole Declares Strong Opposition To Preferences for Sex and Race," *New York Times,* March 25, 1996.

Chapter 3

1. Peter Singer, *Animal Liberation: A New Ethics for Our Treatment of Animals* (New York: Avon Books, 1975), p. ix.

2. Gary L. Francione, *Rain Without Thunder: The Ideology of the Animal Rights Movement* (Philadelphia: Temple University Press, 1996), pp. 12–13.

3. James M. Jasper and Dorothy Nelkin, *Animal Rights Crusade* (New York: Free Press, 1992), p. 7.

4. Ibid.

5. Ibid., p. 1.

6. T. Alexander Smith and Raymond Tatalovich, *Cultures at War: Moral Conflicts in Western Democracies* (Orchard Park, NY: Broadview Press, 2003), p. 83.

7. Jasper and Nelkin, *Animal Rights Crusade*, p. 27.

8. Ibid., pp. 26–28.

9. Ibid., p. 29.

10. Ibid., p. 168.

11. Susan Finsen and Lawrence Finsen, "Animal Rights Movement," in *Encyclopedia of Animal Rights and Welfare* (Westport, CT: Greenwood Press, 1998), p. 52.

12. Adam Parker, "Animal Rights Group Is Taking Its Message to the Ballet," *Christian Science Monitor,* December 22, 2003.

13. Jasper and Nelkin, *Animal Rights Crusade,* pp. 31, 37.

14. Ibid., pp. 56–61.

15. Ibid., p. 3.

16. Ibid., pp. 21–22.

17. Ibid., p. 5.

18. Theodore Lowi, "Foreword," in *Moral Controversies in American Politics: Cases in Social Regulatory Policy,* ed. Raymond Tatalovich and Byron W. Daynes (Armonk, NY: M.E. Sharpe, 1998).

19. Jasper and Nelkin, *Animal Rights Crusade,* pp. 3–4.

20. Finsen and Finsen, "Animal Rights Movement," p. 52.

21. Jasper and Nelkin, *Animal Rights Crusade,* p. 3.

22. Ibid., p. 4.

23. Finsen and Finsen, "Animal Rights Movement," p. 52.

24. Ibid., p. 52.

25. Jasper and Nelkin, *Animal Rights Crusade,* p. 3.

26. Ibid., p. 3.

27. Ibid., p. 55.

28. Ibid., pp. 131–133.

29. Ibid., pp. 129–134.

30. Ibid., p. 153.

31. Ibid., p. 9.

32. Ibid., p. 2.

33. Parker, "Animal Rights Group Is Taking Its Message to the Ballet."

34. Jasper and Nelkin, *Animal Rights Crusade,* p. 127.

35. Kris Novak, "Animal Rights Attacks Spark FBI Terror Investigation," *Nature Medicine* 9, no. 10 (October 2003), p. 1230.

36. Margaret Jasper, *Animal Rights Law* (Dobbs Ferry, NY: Oceana Publications, 2002), p. 7.

37. Ibid., pp. 8–9.

38. Ibid., pp. 17–18.

39. Jasper and Nelkin, *Animal Rights Crusade,* p. 82.

40. Ibid., pp. 83–84.

41. Patrick Jonsson, "'Right to Hunt' vs. Animal Rights: What's Fair Game?" *Christian Science Monitor,* April 3, 2002.

42. Debra West, "One Person's Hunt, Another's Slaughter," *New York Times,* May 11, 1999.

43. Jim Robbins, "Montana Ban on Private Hunting Means an Excess of Elk," *New York Times,* November 25, 2000.

44. West, "One Person's Hunt, Another's Slaughter."

45. Jasper and Nelkin, *Animal Rights Crusade,* pp. 84–85.

46. Ibid., p. 140.

47. Jasper, *Animal Rights Law,* p. 16.

48. Ibid., pp. 28–29.

49. Jasper and Nelkin, *Animal Rights Crusade,* p. 157.

50. Smith and Tatalovich, *Cultures at War,* pp. 175–176.

51. M. Dane Waters, "2002 Initiatives and Referenda," *Spectrum: The Journal of State Government* (Winter 2003), pp. 20–21.

52. Douglas Jehl, "Officials Loath to Act as Water Meant for Endangered Fish Flows to Dry Western Farms," *New York Times,* July 9, 2001.

53. Jasper and Nelkin, *Animal Rights Crusade,* p. 140.

54. Jasper, *Animal Rights Law,* p. 15.

55. Jasper and Nelkin, *Animal Rights Crusade,* p. 140.

56. Jasper, *Animal Rights Law,* pp. 15–16.

57. Ibid., pp. 17–19.

58. Joseph Mendelson III, "Should Animals Have Standing? A Review of Standing Under the Animal Welfare Act," *Boston College Environmental Affairs Law Review* 24, no. 4 (Summer 1997), p. 795.

59. Tim Friend, "Violence Escalates Over Animal Research," *USA Today,* December 8, 1999.

60. Jasper, *Animal Rights Law,* p. 17.

61. Jasper and Nelkin, *Animal Rights Crusade,* pp. 61–62.

62. Jasper, *Animal Rights Law,* p. 19.

63. Jasper and Nelkin, *Animal Rights Crusade,* pp. 70–71.

64. Ibid., p. 73.

65. Jasper, *Animal Rights Law,* pp. 31–32.

66. Jasper and Nelkin, *Animal Rights Crusade,* p. 81.

67. Jasper, *Animal Rights Law,* pp. 11–13.

68. Jasper and Nelkin, *Animal Rights Crusade,* p. 85.

69. Jasper, *Animal Rights Law,* p. 22.

70. Peter Carruthers, *The Animals Issue: Moral Theory in Practice* (New York: Cambridge University Press, 1992), p. xii.

71. Jasper and Nelkin, *Animal Rights Crusade,* p. 22.

72. Jeremy Waldron, "The Right to Private Property," cited in Gary L. Francione, *Animals as Property* (Detroit: Michigan State University, Detroit College of Law, 1996).

73. Gary L. Francione, *Animals as Property* (Detroit: Michigan State University, Detroit College of Law, 1996), p. 2.

74. Ibid., p. 4.

75. William Glaberson, "Legal Pioneers Seek to Raise Lowly Status of Animals," *New York Times,* August 18, 1999.

76. Patricia Leigh Brown, "The Warp and Woof of Identity Politics for Pets," *New York Times,* March 18, 2001.

77. Glaberson, "Legal Pioneers Seek to Raise Lowly Status of Animals."

78. Jasper and Nelkin, *Animal Rights Crusade,* p. 126.

79. Ibid., p. 126.

80. Mendelson, "Should Animals Have Standing?"

81. Ibid.

82. Jasper, *Animal Rights Law,* pp. 39–40.

83. Ibid., p. 20.

84. Mendelson, "Should Animals Have Standing?"

85. Virginia S. Albrecht and James N. Christman, "Overview, The Endangered Species Act," *FindLaw,* (1999), http://profs.lp.findlaw.com/endanger.

86. Ibid.

87. Douglas Jehl, "White House to Delay a Decision on Breaching Dams in Northwest," *New York Times,* July 20, 2000.

88. Douglas Jehl, "Cries of 'Save the Suckerfish' Rile Farmers' Political Allies," *New York Times,* June 20, 2001.

89. Erica Werner, "Endangered Species Act Targeted," *Washington Post,* January 13, 2004.

90. Douglas Jehl, "Rare Arizona Owl (All 7 Inches of It) Is in Habitat Furor," *New York Times,* March 17, 2003.

91. Glaberson, "Legal Pioneers Seek to Raise Lowly Status of Animals."

92. David Malakoff, "Groups Sue to Tighten Oversight of Rodents," *Science,* February 5, 1999, p. 767.

93. David Malakoff, "Activists Win Big on Rodent, Bird Rules," *Science,* July 21, 2000, p. 377.

94. David Malakoff, "Senate Says No to New Rodent Rules," *Science,* February 25, 2002, p. 1440, and "Congress Clears Way for Rodent Rules," *Science,* November 23, 2001, p. 1637.

95. Mendelson, "Should Animals Have Standing?"

96. Jasper, *Animal Rights Law,* p. 32.

97. Ibid., p. 21.

98. Harold Herzog, "Sociology of the Animal Rights Movement," in *Encyclopedia of Animal Rights and Welfare* (Westport, CT: Greenwood Press, 1998), p. 53.

99. Associated Press national telephone poll of 1,004 adults, taken November 10–14, 1995; ICR Survey Research Group of Media, PA. Margin of sampling error of plus or minus three percentage points.

100. Jasper and Nelkin, *Animal Rights Crusade,* p. 137.

101. American Medical Association, *AMA Surveys of Physician and Public Opinion on Health Care Issues: 1989* (Chicago, IL: American Medical Association, April 1989); Foundation for Biomedical Research, *Members of the American Public Comment on the Use of Animals in Medical Research and Testing* (Washington, DC: Foundation for Biomedical Research, 1985); I. Groller, "Do Animals Have Rights?" *Parents,* May 1990, p. 33; L. Pifer, K. Shimizu, and R. Pifer, "Public Attitudes Toward Animal Research: Some International Comparisons," *Society and Animals* 2 (1994), pp. 95–113.

102. Roper Center for Public Opinion (Question ID: USNORC.480246.R08), *POLL Database* (Storrs, CT: Roper Center for Public Opinion, 1988).

103. Roper Center for Public Opinion (Question ID: USNORC.480246.R10 and USNORC.480246.R22), *POLL Database* (Storrs, CT: Roper Center for Public Opinion, 1988).

104. Groller, "Do Animals Have Rights?"

105. Foundation for Biomedical Research, *Members of the American Public Comment;* Pifer, Shimizu and Pifer, "Public Attitudes Toward Animal Research"; S. Plous, "Attitudes Toward the Use of Animals in Psychological Research and Education: Results from a National Survey of Psychologists," *American Psychologist* 51 (1996), pp. 1167–1180; S. Plous, "Attitudes Toward the Use of Animals in Psychological Research and Education: Results from a National Survey of Psychology Majors," *Psychological Science* 7 (1996), pp. 352–358.

106. Plous, "Attitudes Toward the Use of Animals in Psychologists" and "Attitudes Toward the Use of Animals in Psychology Majors."

107. Cate Barnett Alexander, "Animal Research Poll Was Misleading," *Chronicle of Philanthropy,* January 10, 2002.

108. Associated Press poll, 1995.

109. Jeanne Williams, *Animal Rights and Welfare* (New York: H.W. Wilson, 1991), p. 8.

110. Herzog, "Sociology of the Animal Rights Movement."

111. Jasper and Nelkins, *Animal Rights Crusade,* p. 171.

112. Parker, "Animal Rights Group Is Taking Its Message to the Ballet."

113. Barbara Whitaker, "Killing and Maiming of Imperiled Pelicans Stun Officials," *New York Times,* January 23, 2003, and "Rare Charges Filed in Wounding of Sea Lion," *New York Times,* April 4, 2003.

114. *New York Times*, "Is a Bird Hunt Pest Control or Murder of Crows?" February 2, 2003.

115. John M. Broder, "In West Hollywood, A Cat's Right to Scratch May Become a Matter of Law," *New York Times,* January 25, 2003.

116. Thomas Lueck, "Giuliani Criticizes Limits on Spraying for Mosquitoes," *New York Times,* July 22, 2000.

Chapter 4

1. "Green River Killer Avoids Death in Plea Deal," *CNN*, November 6, 2003, http://cHnn.com.

2. Allan Bormel, "Green River Killer," *The Reality Check*, July 1, 2004, www.therealitycheck.org/guestcolumnist/abormel11213.htm.

3. "Green River Killer Plea Saves County $16 Million," *Talk Left*, November 9, 2003, www.talkleft.com/.

4. For example, see Ramsey Clark, *Crime in America* (New York: Simon and Schuster, 1970).

5. See Edward C. Banfield, *The Unheavenly City Revisited* (Boston: Little, Brown, 1974).

6. Saleem A. Shah and Loren H. Roth, "Biological and Psychophysiological Factors in Criminality," in *Handbook of Criminology,* ed. Daniel Glaser (Chicago: Rand McNally, 1974), pp. 101–173.

7. Raymond Paternoster, *Capital Punishment in America* (New York: Lexington Books, 1991), p. 4.

8. Ibid., p. 10.

9. Ibid., pp. 11, 14.

10. Ibid., p. 21.

11. See "Executions" and "Prisoners on Death Row," Bureau of Justice Statistics, U.S. Department of Justice, 2003, www.ojp.usdoj.gov/.

12. Mark Costanzo and Lawrence T. White, "An Overview of the Death Penalty and Capital Trials: History, Current Status, Legal Procedures, and Cost," *Journal of Social Issues* 50 (1994), p. 8.

13. "Capital Punishment: Is There Any Habeas Left in This Corpus?" *Loyola University Chicago Law Journal* 27 (1996), pp. 523–614.

14. Bryan Stevenson, "The Hanging Judges of the Rehnquist Court, *The Nation*, October 14, 1996, p.12.

15. Ibid.

16. "Prisoners on Death Row by Race," Bureau of Justice Statistics, U.S. Department of Justice, 2003, www.ojp.usdoj.gov/.

17. Ibid.

18. United States General Accounting Office, Report to Senate and House Committees on the Judiciary, *Death Penalty Sentencing: Research Indicates Pattern of Racial Disparities* (Washington, DC: General Accounting Office, 1990), p. 5.

19. Eric Baumer, Steven Messner, and Richard Rosenfeld, "Explaining Spatial Variation in Support for Capital Punishment: A Multilevel Analysis," *American Journal of Sociology* 108 (2003), p. 850.

20. As reported in a Gallup poll, March 2001, www.gallup.com/poll/.

21. "Support for Death Penalty Still Very Strong in Spite of Widespread Belief That Some Innocent People Are Convicted of Murder," *Harris Poll #41*, August 17, 2001, www.harrisinteractive.com/.

22. As reported in a Gallup poll, February 2000, www.gallup.com/poll/.

23. As reported in a Pew Research Center for the People and the Press poll, July 2003, http://people-press.org/.

24. "Green River Killer Plea Saves County $16 Million."

25. Costanzo and White, "Overview of the Death Penalty and Capital Trials," p. 12.

26. Linda Greenhouse, "Death Sentences Against Retarded and Young Upheld," *New York Times,* June 27, 1989.

27. Stephen Wermiel, "Death Penalty Edicts Compound Confusion Say Critics of the Court," *Wall Street Journal,* May 10, 1984.

28. Ibid.

29. Interview with former Supreme Court Justice Lewis F. Powell in E.R. Shipp, "Ex-Justice Powell Says Lawmakers Should Reconsider Capital Punishment," *New York Times,* August 8, 1988.

30. Stephen Labaton, "Bars on Death Row: By Curbing Appeals, Terrorism Bill Shifts Powers to State Court Judges," *New York Times*, April 19, 1996.

31. Linda Greenhouse, "Right to Lawyer Curbed for Death Row Inmates," *New York Times,* June 24, 1989.

32. Linda Greenhouse, "Supreme Court, 9–0, Upholds Death Penalty in the Military," *New York Times,* June 4, 1996.

33. Ibid.

34. Robert Reinhold, "Outgoing Governor in New Mexico Bars the Execution of 5," *New York Times,* November 27, 1986.

35. Ibid.

36. Mario M. Cuomo, "New York State Shouldn't Kill People," *New York Times,* June 17, 1989.

37. Rachel L. Swarns, "In Clash on Death Penalty Case, Pataki Removes Bronx Prosecutor," *New York Times,* March 22, 1996, p. A16.

38. David Von Drehle, *Among the Lowest of the Dead: The Culture of Death Row* (New York: Times Books, Random House, 1995), p. 279.

39. Ibid.

40. Ibid., pp. 282–283.

41. Ibid., p. 283.

42. Human Rights Watch, *Modern Capital of Human Rights? Abuses in the State of Georgia* (New York: Human Rights Watch, 1996), p. 53.

43. Ibid., p. 57.

44. Patrick Arden, "The Redemption of Gov. Ryan," *Salon.Com,* January 16, 2003, www.salon.com/.

45. Mireya Navarro, "After Fire at Execution, Florida Lawmakers Defend Use of Electric Chair," *New York Times,* March 27, 1997.

46. Ibid.

47. Michael Engel, *State and Local Politics* (New York: St. Martin's Press, 1985), p. 154.

48. Francis T. Cullen, Timothy S. Bynum, Kim Montgomery Garrett, and Jack R. Greene, "Legislator Ideology and Criminal Justice Policy: Implications from Illinois," in *The Politics of Crime and Criminal Justice,* ed. Erika S. Fairchild and Vincent J. Webb, (Beverly Hills, CA: Sage, 1985), p. 69.

49. For additional information on this issue, see David H. Getches, Charles F. Wilkinson, and Robert A. Williams Jr., *Federal Indian Law: Cases and Materials,* 3rd ed. (Washington, DC: Congressional Quarterly Press, 1995).

50. *United States Code,* Title 18—Crimes and Criminal Procedure, Section 3598, p. 608.

51. This tripartite division of labor is taken from Stuart Scheingold, *The Politics of Law and Order* (New York: Longman, 1984), pp. 228–229.

52. Ibid., p. 180.

53. "ABA House of Delegates Approves Call for Halt in U.S. Executions Until Death Penalty Fairness Assured—Press Release," February 3, 1997, www.abanet. org/media/feb97/death.html.

54. Ibid.

55. "National Coalition to Abolish the Death Penalty," in *Congregation of the Condemned: Voices Against the Death Penalty*, ed. Shirley Dicks (Buffalo, NY: Prometheus Books, 1991), p. 221.

56. "Southern Coalition on Jails and Prisons," in *Congregation of the Condemned: Voices Against the Death Penalty*, ed. Shirley Dicks (Buffalo, NY: Prometheus Books, 1991), p. 238.

57. Evangelical Lutheran Church in America, "A Social Statement on the Death Penalty," December 28, 1995, www.elca.org/dcs/death.html.

58. Joseph F. Sheley, *America's "Crime Problem": An Introduction to Criminology* (Belmont, CA: Wadsworth, 1985), p. 33.

59. Scheingold, *Politics of Law and Order,* p. 85.

60. "Death Penalty Amendment Stalls Vote on Pentagon Bill," *New York Times,* May 19, 1988.

61. Joan Biskupic, "Law/Judiciary: Death-Penalty Expansion Bill Is Moved to Senate Floor," *Congressional Quarterly: Social Policy* (October 21, 1989), p. 2805.

62. Ibid.

63. "Death Penalty Debate: Action in Congress," *Congressional Quarterly Researcher* 5, no. 9 (March 10, 1995), p. 206.

64. Stephen Labaton, "Bill on Terrorism Gains Momentum in the Congress," *New York Times,* April 16, 1996.

65. Ibid.

65. Stephen Labaton, "Stopping Amendments from Democrats, Senate Easily Passes a Counterterrorism Bill," *New York Times,* April 18, 1996.

66. Don Terry, "After 18 Years in Prison, 3 Are Cleared of Murders: Official Apologizes for 'a Terrible Injustice,'" *New York Times,* July 3, 1996.

67. Richard M. Nixon, *Public Papers of the President of the United States* (Washington, DC: U.S. Government Printing Office, 1968), p. 781.

68. Jimmy Carter, *Public Papers of the President of the United States* (Washington, DC: U.S. Government Printing Office, 1978), p. 839.

69. Ibid.

70. Bertram Gross, "Reagan's Criminal 'Anti-crime' Fix," in *What Reagan Is Doing to Us,* ed. Alan Gartner, Colin Geer, and Frank Riessman, (New York: Harper and Row, 1982), pp. 87–88.

71. Julie Johnson, "Reagan Signs Bill to Curb Drug Use," *New York Times,* November 19, 1988.

72. Gerald M. Boyd, "Execution Backed in Drug Slayings: Bush Urges Swift Penalties, Citing Murder of Officer," *New York Times,* April 14, 1988.

73. Alison Mitchell, "President Signs Bill on Terrorism and Death Penalty Appeals," *New York Times,* April 25, 1996.

74. Katharine Q. Seelye, "Dole Tours Death Chamber in San Quentin and Calls for Speedier Executions," *New York Times,* March 24, 1996.

75. Associated Press, "134 Texas Executions Are Fair and Just," *New York Times,* June 21, 2000.

76. Ian McCaleb, "Uphold Law on Death Penalty; and Think of Victims," *CNN.Com,* June 22, 2000, www.cnn.com.

77. Philip Shenon, "Wider Death Rule for U.S. Crimes Backed by the Attorney General," *New York Times,* October 19, 1988.

78. "Ashcroft: No Death Penalty Race Bias," *CBSNEWS.Com,* June 6, 2001, www.cbsnews.com.

Chapter 5

1. Michael Nava and Robert Dawidoff, *Created Equal: Why Gay Rights Matter to America* (New York: St. Martin's Press, 1984), p. 139.

2. For more discussion on this point, see John M. Finnis, "Law, Morality, and Sexual Orientation," *Notre Dame Law Review* (1994), pp. 11–40; Richard F. Duncan, "Who Wants to Stop the Church: Homosexual Rights Legislation, Public Policy, and Religious Freedom," *Notre Dame Law Review* 69 (1994), pp. 393–445; Samuel A. Marcosson, "The 'Special Rights' Canard in the Debate Over Lesbian and Gay Civil Rights," *Notre Dame Journal of Law, Ethics & Public Policy* 9 (1995), pp. 137–183.

3. Dennis Altamn, *The Homosexualization of America, The Americanization of the Homosexual* (Boston: Beacon Press, 1983).

4. Paul Light, "The Presidential Policy Stream," in *The Presidency and the Political System,* ed. Michael Nelson (Washington, DC: Congressional Quarterly Press, 1984), pp. 423–448.

5. Rick Harding, "NGLTF Releases Results of Candidates Survey on Gay AIDS Issues," *Advocate,* March 1, 1988.

6. Randy Shilts, *Conduct Unbecoming: Gays and Lesbians in the U.S. Military* (New York: St. Martin's Press, 1993), p. 36.

7. For more discussion of military involvement, see Jeffrey S. Davis, "Military Policy Toward Homosexuals: Scientific, Historical, and Legal Perspectives," *Military Law Review* 131 (1991), pp. 55–108; Jonathan Katz, *Gay American History: Lesbians and Gay Men in the U.S.A.* (New York: Garland Publications, 1990); Allan Berube, *Coming Out Under Fire: The History of Gay Men and Women in World War Two* (New York: Free Press, 1990).

8. Department of Defense Directive 13.32.14, January 16, 1982.

9. Max Boot, "First Monday in Office: Clinton Picks Take Over," *Christian Science Monitor,* January 25, 1993.

10. Peter Grier, "Key Senators Push Compromise on Issue of Gays in Armed Forces," *Christian Science Monitor,* May 13, 1993.

11. Melissa Healy, "74% of Military Enlistees Oppose Lifting Gay Ban," *Los Angeles Times,* February 28, 1993.

12. Craig Donegan, "New Military Culture," *Congressional Quarterly Researcher,* April 26, 1996, pp. 363–380.

13. William N. Eskridge, *GayLaw* (Cambridge, MA: Harvard University Press, 1999), Appendix C5, pp. 381–382.

14. Service Members Legal Defense Network (SLDN), "New Gay Discharge Figures Up 73 Percent Since 'Don't Ask, Don't Tell' First Implemented." Press Release to Service Members, February 1, 2000.

15. CNN.com, "Gay Ex-Military Officers Speak Out," December 11, 2003, www.cnn.com/2003/US/Northeast/12/11/cnna.gays.military/index.html.

16. Sheryl Gay Stolberg, "Persistent Conflict for Gays and G.O.P.," *New York Times,* April 23, 2003.

17. Elisabeth Beth Bumiller, "Bush Backs Ban in Constitution on Gay Marriage," *New York Times,* February 25, 2004.

18. Barry D. Adam, *The Rise of a Gay and Lesbian Movement* (New York: Twayne, 1995).

19. Donald P. Haider-Markel, "AIDS and Gay Civil Rights: Politics and Policy at the Ballot Box," *American Review of Politics* 20 (Winter 1999), pp. 349–375.

20. N. Hunter, "Identity, Speech, and Equality," *Virginia Law Review* 79 (1993), pp. 1695–1705.

21. Ibid., 1695.

22. *Congressional Record* 133 (October 14, 1987): S14216.

23. *Congressional Record* 133 (October 20, 1987): H8800.

24. *Congressional Record* 133 (October 14, 1987): S14216.

25. *Gay Men's Health Crisis v. Sullivan,* 792 F. Supp. 278 (S.D.N.Y. 1992).

26. Donald P. Haider-Markel, "Morality Policy and Individual-Level Political Behavior: The Case of Legislative Voting on Lesbian and Gay Issues," *Policy Studies Journal* 27, no. 4 (1999), pp. 735–749.

27. 74 Hawaii 530, 825 P.2d 44 (1993).

28. William N. Eskridge Jr., *Equality Practice: Civil Unions and the Future of Gay Rights* (New York: Routledge, 2002), p. 34.

29. Holly Idelson, "Panel Oks Bill to Undercut Same-Sex Marriages," *Congressional Quarterly Weekly,* June 15, 1996, pp. 1682–1683.

30. Eskridge, *Equality Practice,* p. 28. States with nonrecognition statutes as of September 2001, (with the date of enactment) are: Alabama (1998), Alaska (1996), Arizona (1996), Arkansas (1997), California (2000), Colorado (2000), Delaware (1996), Florida (1997), Georgia (1996), Idaho (1996), Illinois (1996), Indiana (1997), Iowa (1998), Kansas (1996), Kentucky (1998), Louisiana (1996), Maine (1997), Michigan (1996), Minnesota (1997), Mississippi (1997), Missouri (1997), Montana (1997), Nebraska (2000), Nevada (2002), North Carolina (1995), North Dakota (1997), Ohio (2004), Oklahoma (1996), Pennsylvania (1996), South Carolina (1996), South Dakota (1996), Tennessee (1996), Texas (2000), Utah (1995), Virginia (1997), Washington (1998), and West Virginia (2000).

31. *Lawrence v. Texas,* 02–0102 U.S. 02–102 (2003).

32. Evan Gerstmann, *Same-Sex Marriage and the Constitution* (New York: Cambridge University Press, 2004).

33. For more discussion of this topic, see Suzanne B. Goldberg, "Facing the Challenge: A Lawyer's Response to Anti-Gay Initiatives," *Ohio State Law Journal* 55 (1994), pp. 665–674, and Marcosson, "The 'Special Rights' Canard in the Debate Over Lesbian and Gay Civil Rights."

34. Find Law.com. All the cases in this section were found at this Web site. The citations and issue for each of these cases are as follows: *Bowers v. Hardwick* 478 US 186 (1986) [Georgia sodomy law]; *Romer v. Evans* 517 US 620 (1996) [Colorado Gay Rights, Amendment 2]; *Board of Regents of the University of Wisconsin System v. Southworth* (2000) [student fees]; *United States v. Playboy Entertainment Group, Inc.* (2000) [adult programming]; *Apprendi v. New Jersey* (2000) [hate crimes law]; *Boy Scouts of America v. Dale* (2000) [homosexual Boy Scouts leader ban]; *Seling v. Young* (2001) [lifetime sentence for sexually violent predators]; *Circuit City Stores, Inc. v. Adams* (2002) [employment discrimination]; *Ashcroft v. Free Speech Coalition* (2002) [child pornography]; *City of Los Angeles v. Alameda Books, Inc.* (2002) [sex-oriented businesses]; *McKune v. Lile* (2002) [sex offender punishment]; *Otte v. Doe*

(2003) [sex offender information]; *Ewing v. California* and *Lockyer v. Andrade* (2003) [three-strikes law]; *United States v. American Library Association* (2003) [Internet access]; *Lawrence v. Texas* 02–0102 US 02–102 (2003) [sodomy law]; *Stogner v. California* (2003) [child molestation statute of limitations].

35. Chuck Stewart, *Homosexuality and the Law* (Santa Barbara, CA: ABC/CLIO, 2001), pp. 53–58.

36. Find Law.com. See note 34.

37. Sheryl Gay Stolberg, "Justices, in a Reversal, Legalize Gay Sexual Conduct," *New York Times,* June 27, 2003.

38. Neil A. Lewis, "Conservatives Furious Over Court's Direction," *New York Times,* June 27, 2003.

39. Ibid.

40. The nine states that have criminal sodomy laws on their books that also apply to opposite-sex couples as of June 2003 are Alabama, Florida, Idaho, Louisiana, Mississippi, North Carolina, South Carolina, Utah, and Virginia.

41. David Dunlap, "Recognizing a Ruling, and Battles to Come," *New York Times,* May 21, 1996.

42. Linda Greenhouse, "Gay Rights Laws Can't Be Banned, High Court Rules," *New York Times,* May 21, 1996.

43. *Lawrence v. Texas,* 02-0102 (2003).

44. *Planned Parenthood of Southeast Pennsylvania v. Casey,* 505 US 833, 850 (505 US 833, 850 1994).

45. Paul A. Sabatier and Hank C. Jenkins-Smith, "The Advocacy Coalition Framework: An Assessment," in *Theories of the Policy Process,* ed. Paul E. Sabatier (Boulder, CO: Westview Press, 1999).

46. Elaine B. Sharp, "Culture Wars and City Politics: Local Government's Role in Social Conflict," *Urban Affairs Review* 31, no. 6 (June 1996); Elaine B. Sharp, "Culture Wars and the Study of Urban Politics," *Urban News: Newsletter of the Urban Politics Section/APSA* 10, no. 1 (Spring 1996), pp. 1–10.

47. Donald P. Haider-Markel and Kenneth J. Meier, "The Politics of Gay and Lesbian Rights: Expanding the Scope of Conflict," *Journal of Politics* (May 1996), pp. 332–349.

48. Eskridge, *GayLaw,* pp. 356–371. See also Ken Wald, James Button, and Barbara Rienzo, "Where Local Laws Prohibit Discrimination Based on Sexual Orientation," *PM Public Management* (April 1995), pp. 9–14.

49. Previously, other state high courts had faced this issue but did not uphold same-sex marriages. See *Singer v. Hara,* 11 Wash. App. 247, 522 P 2.d 1187 (1974); *Baker v. Nelson,* 291 Minn. 310, 191 N.W.2d 1985 (1971).

50. See 1994 Haw. Sess. Laws, Act 217, reaffirming marriage as intrinsically limited to one man and one woman and finding that "the question before the court . . . is essentially one of policy, thereby rendering it inappropriate for judicial response." See also 1994 Haw. Sess. Laws, Act 5.

51. See 1997 Haw. Sess. Laws, Act 383.

52. Donald P. Haider-Markel, "Policy Diffusion as a Geographical Expansion of the Scope of Political Conflict: Same-Sex Marriage Bans in the 1990s," *State Politics and Policy Quarterly* 1 (1), pp. 5–26.

53. 2999 Vermont Acts and Resolves, Act 91 (April 26, 2000).

54. Quoted in Lynn D. Wardle, "The Potential Impact of Homosexual Parenting on Children," *University of Illinois Law Review* 3 (1997), p. 884.

55. Philip M. Kayal, *Bearing Witness: Gay Men's Health Crisis and the Politics of AIDS* (Boulder, CO: Westview Press, 1993).

56. M. Kent Jennings and Ellen Ann Anderson, "Support for Confrontational Tactics among AIDS Activists: A Study of Intra-movement Divisions," *American Journal of Political Science* 40 (1996), pp. 311–334.

57. Mark Carl Rom, "Gays and AIDS: Democratizing Disease?" in *The Politics of Gay Rights*, ed. Craig A. Rimmerman, Kenneth D. Wald, and Clyde Wilson (Chicago: University of Chicago Press, 2000).

58. CBS News/*New York Times* poll, March 10–14, 2004. www.cbsnews.com.

59. ABC News/*Washington Post* poll, February 18–22, 2004. www.abcnews.com.

60. Clyde Wilcox and Robin Wolpert, "Gay Rights in the Public Sphere: Public Opinion on Gay and Lesbian Equality," in *The Politics of Gay Rights* (Chicago: University of Chicago Press, 2000).

Chapter 6

Thanks are due to Casey Smith, whose research assistance for this piece was invaluable, and to Ray Tatalovich for his insightful comments and guidance.

1. Garry Wills, *Under God: Religion and American Politics* (New York: Simon and Schuster, 1990).

2. Derek Davis, "Resolving Not to Resolve the Tension Between the Establishment and Free Exercise Clauses," *Journal of Church and State* 38 (1996), pp. 245–259.

3. Ted G. Jelen and Clyde Wilcox, *Public Attitudes Toward Church and State* (Armonk, NY: M.E. Sharpe, 1995).

4. Kenneth D. Wald, *Religion and Politics in the United States*, 2nd ed. (Washington, DC: Congressional Quarterly Press, 1992).

5. Leonard W. Levy, *The Establishment Clause* (New York: Macmillan, 1986).

6. A. James Reichley, *Religion in American Public Life* (Washington, DC: Brookings Institution, 1985).

7. See especially Russell Kirk, "Introduction," in *The Assault on Religion*, ed. Russell Kirk (New York: University Press of America, 1986); Robert L. Cord, *Separation of Church and State: Historical Fact and Current Fiction* (New York: Lambeth Press, 1982); and Gerard V. Bradley, *Church-State Relationships in America* (Westport, CT: Greenwood, 1987).

8. See Peter Berger, *The Sacred Canopy: Elements of a Sociological Theory of Religion* (New York: Doubleday, 1967), and Richard John Neuhaus, *The Naked Public Square* (Grand Rapids, MI: Eerdmans, 1984).

9. Ted G. Jelen, *The Political Mobilization of Religious Belief* (New York: Praeger, 1991); David C. Leege and Lyman A. Kellstedt, "Religious Worldviews and Political Philosophies: Capturing Theory in the Grand Manner Through Empirical Data," in *Rediscovering the Religious Factor in American Politics*, ed. David C. Leege and Lyman A. Kellstedt (Armonk, NY: M.E. Sharpe, 1993), pp. 216–231.

10. Alexis de Tocqueville, *Democracy in America,* ed. Phillips Bradley, 2 vols. (New York: Vintage Books, 1945), pp. 314–315 (emphasis added).

11. Wald, *Religion and Politics in the United States*.

12. Alexander Hamilton, James Madison, and John Jay, "Federalist No. 10," in *The Federalist* (New York: Modern Library, 1937).

13. Stephen J. Wayne, "Foreword," in Ted G. Jelen and Clyde Wilcox, *Public Attitudes Toward Church and State* (Armonk, NY: M.E. Sharpe, 1995), pp. xi–xii.

14. Levy, *Establishment Clause;* Leo Pfeffer, *Church, State and Freedom* (Boston: Beacon Press, 1967).

15. Pfeffer, *Church, State and Freedom;* Leonard W. Levy, *Original Intent and the Framers' Constitution* (New York: Macmillan, 1988).

16. Kirk, "Introduction."

17. See, for example, the account of the political thought of Roger Williams, James Madison, and Thomas Jefferson in *Wills, Under God.*

18. See especially Glenn Tinder, *The Political Meaning of Christianity* (Baton Rouge: Louisiana State University Press, 1989).

19. For example, some religious bodies risk losing their tax exemptions if their political advocacy becomes too direct.

20. Reichley, *Religion in American Public Life.*

21. See especially Kent Greenawalt, *Religious Convictions and Political Choice* (New York: Oxford University Press, 1988).

22. Richard A. Brisbin, "The Rehnquist Court and the Free Exercise of Religion," *Journal of Church and State* 34 (1992), pp. 57–76.

23. See especially Stephen L. Carter, *The Culture of Disbelief: How American Law and Politics Trivialize Religious Devotion* (New York: Basic Books, 1993).

24. Anne Gearan, "Divided Court Debates Church-State Case," *Las Vegas Review-Journal,* December 3, 2003.

25. Jesse H. Choper, *Securing Religious Liberty: Principles for the Judicial Interpretation of the Religion Clauses* (Chicago: University of Chicago Press, 1995).

26. It should be noted that the status of conscientious objection has historically been created by Congress and that there does not exist legal precedent for any religiously-based *right* to exemption from military service.

27. Stephen V. Monsma, *Positive Neutrality: Letting Religious Freedom Ring* (Westport, CT: Praeger, 1993).

28. Suzanna Sherry, "*Lee v. Weisman* Paradox Redux," in *1992: The Supreme Court Review,* ed. Dennis J. Hutchinson, David A. Strauss, and Geoffrey R. Stone (Chicago: University of Chicago Press, 1992), pp. 123–153.

29. Several have offered similar analyses, using the term *secularist* to describe the minimalist category. See, for example, Jose Casanova, *Public Religions in the Modern World* (Chicago: University of Chicago Press). I prefer the term *minimalist,* since there is no *necessary* connection between taking a communalist-separationist position and hostility or indifference to religion. Indeed, empirical analysis of survey data suggests that many minimalists are quite religious (and religiously orthodox) and reject public involvement of religion for primarily theological reasons. See Ted G. Jelen and Clyde Wilcox, "Conscientious Objectors in the Culture War? A Typology of Church-State Relations," *Sociology of Religion* 58 (1997), pp. 277–288.

30. This section summarizes results reported more fully in Jelen and Wilcox, *Public Attitudes Toward Church and State.*

31. Wald, *Religion and Politics in the United States.*

32. Jelen and Wilcox, *Public Attitudes Toward Church and State,* p. 59.

33. Ibid., p. 115.

34. Phillip E. Converse, "The Nature of Belief Systems in Mass Publics," in *Ideology and Discontent,* ed. David Apter (New York: Free Press), pp. 206–261; James A.

Stimson, "Belief Systems: Constraint, Complexity, and the 1972 Election," *American Journal of Political Science* 19 (1975), pp. 383–418.

35. See James Prothro and Charles Grigg, "Fundamental Principles of Democracy: Bases of Agreement and Disagreement," *Journal of Politics* 22 (1960), pp. 276–294; John R. Zaller, *The Nature and Origins of Mass Opinion* (New York: Cambridge University Press, 1992).

36. Jelen and Wilcox, *Public Attitudes Toward Church and State,* p. 152.

37. Clyde Wilcox, Ted G. Jelen, and Rachel Goldberg, "Full Pews, Musical Pulpits: The Christian Right at the Turn of the Millennium," *Public Perspective* 11 (May–June 2000): 36–39.

38. See Lyman A. Kellstedt, John C. Green, James L. Guth, and Corwin E. Smidt, "Religious Voting Blocs in the 1992 Election: The Year of the Evangelical?" *Sociology of Religion* 55 (1994): 307–326.

39. For overviews, see Allen D. Hertzke, *Representing God in Washington* (Knoxville: University of Tennessee Press, 1988); Clyde Wilcox, *Onward, Christian Soldiers: The Religious Right in American Politics* (Boulder, CO: Westview, 1996); and Robert Zwier, "Coalition Strategies of Religious Interest Groups," in *Religion and Political Behavior in the United States*, ed. Ted G. Jelen (New York: Praeger, 1989), pp. 171–186.

40. John Murley describes a number of single-issue groups formed to promote school prayer. See John A. Murley, "School Prayer: Free Exercise of Religion or Establishment of Religion?" in *Social Regulatory Policy: Moral Controversies in American Politics*, ed. Raymond Tatalovich and Byron W. Daynes (Boulder, CO: Westview, 1988), pp. 5–40.

41. Carol J.C. Maxwell, "Introduction: Beyond Polemics and Toward Healing," in *Perspectives on the Politics of Abortion*, ed. Ted G. Jelen (Westport, CT: Praeger, 1995), pp. 1–20.

42. Murley, "School Prayer," p. 7.

43. Rob Boston, "Making Amends," *Church and State* 50 (May 1997), pp. 4–8.

44. See Wilcox, *Onward, Christian Soldiers* and Matthew C. Moen, *The Christian Right in Congress* (Tuscaloosa: University of Alabama Press, 1989).

45. Matthew C. Moen, *The Transformation of the Christian Right* (Tuscaloosa: University of Alabama Press, 1992).

46. Jerry Falwell, *Listen, America!* (Garden City, NY: Doubleday, 1980).

47. Ralph Reed, *Politically Incorrect: The Emerging Faith Factor in American Politics* (Dallas: Word, 1994).

48. Carter, *The Culture of Disbelief.*

49. Hubert Morken, "Compromise: The Thinking Behind Colorado's Amendment #2 Strategy," paper presented at the annual meeting of the American Political Science Association, New York, September 1994.

50. Alfred R. Martin and Ted G. Jelen, "Knowledge and Attitudes of Catholic College Students Regarding the Creation/Evolution Controversy," in *Religion and Political Behavior in the United States*, ed. Ted Jelen (New York: Praeger, 1989), pp. 83–92.

51. Michael Hirsley, "Prisons Fear Law to Restore Religious Rights," *Chicago Tribune,* August 1, 1993.

52. Frank Way and Barbara Burt, "Religious Marginality and the Free Exercise Clause," *American Political Science Review* 77 (1983), pp. 654–665.

53. Levy, *The Establishment Clause;* Fred W. Friendly and Martha J.H. Elliot, *The Constitution: That Delicate Balance* (New York: Random House, 1984).

54. Jelen and Wilcox, *Public Attitudes Toward Church and State.*

55. See, for example, George Anastaplo, "The Religion Clauses of the First Amendment," *Memphis State University Law Review* 11 (1981), pp. 189–190. For a contrasting view, see Reichley, *Religion in American Public Life.* Reichley argues that the free exercise clause, as a right held by individuals, should be incorporated under the Fourteenth Amendment. However, Reichley argues that the establishment clause, which is not a "privilege" or "immunity" held by individual citizens, should not be applied to the actions of subnational governments.

56. Murley, "School Prayer," pp. 23–25; Kirk W. Elifson and C. Kirk Hadaway, "Prayer in Public Schools: When Church and State Collide," *Public Opinion Quarterly* 49 (1985), pp. 317–329.

57. Jelen, *Political Mobilization of Religious Belief;* Kenneth D. Wald, Dennis Owen, and Samuel S. Hill, "Churches as Political Communities," *American Political Science Review* 82 (1988), pp. 531–549.

58. Elifson and Hadaway, "Prayer in Public Schools"; Kenneth D. Wald, Dennis Owen, and Samuel S. Hill, "Political Cohesion in Churches," *Journal of Politics* 52 (1990), pp. 197–212.

59. See Elisabeth Noelle-Neumann, *The Spiral of Silence: Public Opinion: Our Social Skin* (Chicago: University of Chicago Press, 1984).

60. William K. Piotrowski, "The Kansas Compromise," *Religion in the News* 2, no. 3 (Fall 1999), pp. 10–12.

61. "The Ten Commandments Judge," *New York Times,* July 2, 2003.

62. Diana Jean Schemo, "After a Surge, Limits Return to School Prayer," *New York Times*, October 23, 2001.

63. As will be described later in this chapter, the U.S. Supreme Court upheld this practice in the 2002 case *Zelman v. Simmons-Harris.*

64. See Christi Parsons, "Constitution, Shmonstitution," *Chicago Tribune*, June 8, 1997.

65. See Celia W. Dugger, "Tug of Taboos: African Genital Rite vs. U.S. Law," *New York Times,* December 28, 1996.

66. It should be noted that in *Everson* the Court upheld a local ordinance permitting reimbursement of transportation costs to parents whose children attended parochial schools. Nevertheless, Black's opinion contains language that is quite explicitly separationist.

67. Jelen and Wilcox, *Public Attitudes Toward Church and State,* p. 18; Wald, *Religion and Politics in the United States.*

68. See, generally, Murley, "School Prayer."

69. See, generally, Thomas Robbins, "The Intensification of Church-State Conflict in the United States," *Social Compass* 40 (1993), pp. 505–527.

70. See also James J. Kilpatrick, "One More Look at a Famous Wall," *Indianapolis Star,* July 10, 1993.

71. It is perhaps instructive to read Stewart's dissent in *Engel v. Vitale,* as well as Scalia's dissent in *Kiryas Joel Village School District v. Grument.* Both of these opinions defend religious accommodationism from the standpoint of religious free exercise. See Joan Biskupic, "Special School District Ruled Unconstitutional," *Washington Post,* June 28, 1994; Linda Greenhouse, "High Court Bars School District Created to Benefit Hasidic Jews," *New York Times*, June 28, 1994.

72. Linda Greenhouse, "Court Eases Curb on Aid to Schools with Church Ties," *New York Times,* June 24, 1997.

73. Brisbin, "The Rehnquist Court and the Free Exercise of Religion"; Way and Burt, "Religious Marginality and the Free Exercise Clause."

74. See *Reynolds v. U.S.*, 98 U.S. 145 (1879).

75. Robbins, "The Intensification of Church-State Conflict in the United States"; Wald, *Religion and Politics in the United States*.

76. Leo Pfeffer, "The Current State of Law in the United States and the Separationist Agenda," *The Annals* 446 (December 1979), pp. 1–9.

77. See Wald's *Religion and Politics in the United States* for illustrations of the Sherbert-Yoder test.

78. David G. Savage, *Turning Right: The Making of the Rehnquist Supreme Court* (New York: Wiley, 1993).

79. Brisbin, "The Rehnquist Court and the Free Exercise of Religion."

80. Linda Greenhouse, "High Court Voids a Law Expanding Religious Rights," *New York Times,* June 26, 1997.

81. Michael McDonald, "Redistricting, Dealignment, and the Political Homogenization of the House of Representatives," paper presented at the annual meeting of the American Political Science Association, Boston, September 1998.

82. Ted G. Jelen and Clyde Wilcox, "Causes and Consequences of Public Attitudes Toward Abortion: A Review and Research Agenda," *Political Research Quarterly* 56 (2003): 489–500.

83. Edward G. Carmines and James A. Stimson, "The Two Faces of Issue Voting," *American Political Science Review* 74 (1980), pp. 78–91.

84. Murley, "School Prayer."

85. For a more complete overview of the legislative history of the school prayer issue, see Murley, "School Prayer."

86. Katherine Q. Seelye, "House Republicans Back Judge on Display of Ten Commandments," *New York Times,* March 5, 1997.

87. David W. Dunlap, "Church v. State: A Landmark Case," *New York Times,* February 2, 1997. Subsequently, Congress passed a much more limited measure, entitled the Religious Liberty Preservation Act, which restored the Sherbert-Yoder standard for prisons and for government decisions involving zoning regulations.

88. Boston, "Making Amends," p. 4.

89. Robert Bellah, "Civil Religion in America," *Daedalus* (Winter 1967), pp. 1–21.

90. Hamilton, Madison, Jay, "Federalist No. 10."

91. Murley, "School Prayer."

92. Ibid.

93. Ibid.

94. James L. Guth and John C. Green, "God and the GOP: Religion Among Republican Activists," in *Religion and Political Behavior in the United States*, ed. Ted G. Jelen (New York: Praeger, 1989), pp. 223–242.

95. Murley, "School Prayer."

96. Phillip E. Converse, "Religion and Politics: The 1960 Election," in *Elections and the Political Order*, ed. Angus Campbell et al. (New York: Wiley, 1966).

97. Murley, "School Prayer."

98. Most observers would agree that there were important differences between the levels of personal religiousness of Presidents Kennedy and Carter. Nevertheless, both were publicly identified with particular religious traditions.

99. Matthew C. Moen, "Ronald Reagan and the Social Issues: Rhetorical Support for the Christian Right," *Social Science Journal* 27 (1990), pp. 199–207.

100. Murley, "School Prayer."

101. James MacGregor Burns, *The Deadlock of Democracy: Four Party Politics in America* (Englewood Cliffs, NJ: Prentice-Hall, 1967). See also Joan Del Fattore, *The Fourth R: Conflicts over Religion in America's Public Schools* (New Haven, CT: Yale Press, 2004).

102. Jo Renee Formicola, Mary C. Segers, and Paul Weber, *Faith-Based Initiatives and the Bush Administration* (Lanham, MD: Rowman and Littlefield, 2003).

103. Ibid.

104. Murley, "School Prayer."

105. Ibid.

106. Jelen and Wilcox, *Public Attitudes Toward Church and State.*

107. Patricia Fauser, Jeanne Lewis, Joel A. Setzen, Finian Taylor, and Ted G. Jelen, "Conclusion: Perspectives on the Politics of Abortion," in *Perspectives on the Politics of Abortion*, ed. Ted G. Jelen (Westport, CT: Praeger, 1995), pp. 177–199.

108. Formicola, Segers, and Weber, *Faith-Based Initiatives and the Bush Administration,* p. 128.

109. Helen Rose Ebaugh, Paula F. Pipes, Janet Saltzman Chafetz, and Martha Daniels, "Where's the Religion? Distinguishing Faith-Based from Secular Service Agencies," *Journal for the Scientific Study of Religion* 42 (2003), pp. 411–426.

110. Robert Wuthnow, Conrad Hackett, and Becky Yang Hsu, "The Effectiveness and Trustworthiness of Faith-Based and Other Service Organizations," *Journal for the Scientific Study of Religion* 43 (2004), pp. 1–17.

111. See Roger Finke and Rodney Stark, *The Churching of America, 1776–1990* (New Brunswick, NJ: Rutgers University Press, 1992).

112 Ted G. Jelen, *The Political World of the Clergy* (Westport, CT: Praeger, 1993).

113. For an excellent discussion of this issue, see Choper, *Securing Religious Liberty.*

Chapter 7

My special and most sincere thanks to Grant Podelco, David Solar, and Mark Eichin for their important and valuable assistance. My thanks also to Deborah Dintino, Loretta Padavona, Marcia Carlson, and the Cornell University Law Library.

1. Merrill Jensen, *The New Nation* (New York: Random House, 1962), p. 29.

2. Bernard Bailyn, *The Ideological Origins of the American Revolution* (Cambridge, MA: Belknap Press, 1967), p. 119.

3. Peter B. Feller and Karl L. Gotting, "The Second Amendment: A Second Look," *Northwestern University Law Review* 61 (March–April 1966), p. 51.

4. John Levin, "The Right to Bear Arms: The Development of the American Experience," *Chicago Kent Law Review* 48 (Fall–Winter 1971), p. 155.

5. Harold W. Chase and Craig R. Ducat, eds., *Corwin's* The Constitution *and What It Means Today* (Princeton, NJ: Princeton University Press, 1973), p. 87.

6. Legislative Reference Service, *The Second Amendment as a Limitation on Federal Firearms Legislation* (Washington, DC: Library of Congress, 1968), p. 6.

7. Ibid., pp. 6–7. See also Robert J. Spitzer, *The Right to Bear Arms* (Santa Barbara, CA: ABC-CLIO, 2001).

8. John K. Mahon, *The American Militia, Decade of Decisions, 1789–1800.* University of Florida Monographs, Social Science, no. 6 (Gainesville: University of Florida Press, 1960), pp. 20–21.

9. For examples, see Howard I. Bass, "*Quilici v. Village of Morton Grove:* Ammunition for a National Handgun Ban," *DePaul Law Review* 32 (Winter 1983), pp. 371–398; Lucilius A. Emery, "The Constitutional Right to Keep and Bear Arms," *Harvard Law Review* 28 (1914–1915), pp. 473–477; Eric S. Freibrun, "Banning Handguns: *Quilici v. Village of Morton Grove* and the Second Amendment," *Washington University Law Quarterly* 60 (Fall 1982), pp. 1087–1118; Ralph J. Rohner, "The Right to Bear Arms: A Phenomenon of Constitutional History," *Catholic University Law Review* 16 (September 1966), pp. 53–80; Roy G. Weatherup, "Standing Armies and Armed Citizens," *Hastings Constitutional Law Quarterly* 2 (1975), pp. 961–1001; "Symposium on the Second Amendment," *Chicago-Kent Law Review* 76 (2000). For lower federal court rulings, see Spitzer, *Right to Bear Arms,* pp. 43–44, 110.

10. For examples, see David I. Caplan, "Restoring the Balance: The Second Amendment Revisited," *Fordham Urban Law Journal* 5 (Fall 1976), pp. 31–53; David T. Hardy and John Stompoly, "Of Arms and the Law," *Chicago-Kent Law Review* 51 (Summer 1974), pp. 62–114; Sandford Levinson, "The Embarrassing Second Amendment," *Yale Law Journal* 99 (December 1989): 637–659; Brandon P. Denning, "Can the Simple Cite Be Trusted? Lower Court Interpretations of *United States v. Miller* and the Second Amendment," *Cumberland Law Review* 26 (1995–1996): 961–1004.

11. Jill Smolowe, "Go Ahead, Make Our Day," *Time,* May 29, 1995, p. 19.

12. Walter Isaacson, "Leading the Call to Arms," *Time,* April 20, 1981, p. 27; Barbara Vobejda, "NRA Is Said to Lay Off Dozens," *Washington Post,* September 23, 1996; Robert Dreyfuss, "Good Morning, Gun Lobby!" *Mother Jones* (July–August, 1996), p. 45.

13. Bill Keller, "Powerful Reputation Makes National Rifle Association a Top Gun in Washington," *Congressional Quarterly Weekly Report,* May 9, 1981, p. 799.

14. Robert J. Spitzer, *The Politics of Gun Control* (New York: Chatham House, 1998), pp. 100–103.

15. Quoted in Osha Gray Davidson, *Under Fire: The NRA and the Battle for Gun Control* (New York: Holt, 1993), p. 39.

16. Spitzer, *Politics of Gun Control,* pp. 105–106.

17. Sam Howe Verhovek, "An Angry Bush Ends His Ties to Rifle Group," *New York Times,* May 11, 1995.

18. Dreyfuss, "Good Morning, Gun Lobby!" pp. 44–45, 47; Spitzer, *Politics of Gun Control,* p. 106.

19. Jan Hoffman, "Fund Linked to N.R.A. Gave $20,000 for Goetz's Defense," *New York Times,* April 16, 1996.

20. Isaacson, "Leading the Call to Arms," p. 27; Alan M. Gottlieb, *The Rights of Gun Owners* (Ottawa, IL: Green Hill Publishers, 1981).

21. Raymond S. Rodgers, "The Rhetoric of the NRA," *Vital Speeches of the Day* (October 1, 1983), pp. 758–761. On June 3, 1982, the NRA ran a full-page ad in the *New York Times* in the aftermath of the imposition of martial law in Poland. After noting that all firearms in Poland had been confiscated under the Communist regime, the ad observed that "so long as the Second Amendment is not infringed, what is happening in Poland can never happen in these United States."

22. Wayne King, "Target: The Gun Lobby," *New York Times Magazine,* December 9, 1990, p. 82. The update was obtained from HCI.

23. Tom Goldstein, "Straight Talk About Handguns," *Rolling Stone,* October 28, 1982, p. 23; Spitzer, *Politics of Gun Control,* pp. 66–69; "One Victim Every Minute," *Economist.com,* July 23, 2003, www.economist.com/agenda/PrinterFriendly.cfm?Story_ID=1936029.

24. Richard Hofstadter, "America as a Gun Culture," *American Heritage,* October 1970, p. 4.

25. Lois A. Fingerhut, et al., "International Comparative Analysis of Injury Mortality," *Advance Data from Vital and Health Statistics* 303 (October 7, 1998): 1–20.

26. James D. Wright, Peter H. Rossi, and Kathleen Daly, *Under the Gun: Weapons, Crime, and Violence in America* (New York: Aldine, 1983), p. 221.

27. Ibid. See also Spitzer, *Politics of Gun Control,* pp. 93–96.

28. Howard Schuman and Stanley Presser, "The Attitude-Action Connection and the Issue of Gun Control," in *Gun Control,* ed. Philip J. Cook, special issue of *Annals of the American Academy of Political and Social Science,* 455 (May 1981), pp. 40–47.

29. Spitzer, *Politics of Gun Control,* p. 119.

30. *Gallup Report,* no. 232–233, January–February 1985, pp. 12–14; *Public Perspective,* February–March 1997, p. 27.

31. James Wycoff, *Famous Guns That Won the West* (New York: Arco, 1968), pp. 5–6. See also Harold F. Williamson, *Winchester: The Gun That Won the West* (Washington, DC: Combat Forces Press, 1952).

32. Bob Nichols, "Should a Boy Have a Gun?" *Parents' Magazine,* October 1934, pp. 26, 77.

33. David Lester, *Gun Control: Issues and Answers* (Springfield, IL: Charles C. Thomas, 1984), pp. 98–99, 104. See also David Lester, "Which States Have Stricter Handgun Control Statutes?" *Psychological Reports* 57 (August 1985), p. 170.

34. Lee Kennett and James L. Anderson, *The Gun in America* (Westport, CT: Greenwood Press, 1975), pp. 197, 204, 211, 227, 238, 243.

35. Steven R. Weisman, "Reagan Tells of Initial Pain and Panic After Being Shot," *New York Times,* April 23, 1981.

36. Robert J. Spitzer, "Gun Rights for Terrorists? Gun Control and the Bush Presidency," a paper presented at the Conference on "A Presidency Transformed by Crises, The George W. Bush Administration," State University of New York, Fredonia, NY, October 17–18, 2002.

37. All references to party platforms are drawn from copies supplied by the national committees.

38. This pattern, as predicted by Lowi's scheme, is observed for the Omnibus Act in Robert J. Spitzer, *The Presidency and Public Policy* (University: University of Alabama Press, 1983), pp. 65–70.

39. "Gun Controls Extended to Long Guns, Ammunition," *Congressional Quarterly Almanac 1968* (Washington, DC: Congressional Quarterly, 1969), p. 552. The discussion to follow is based on pp. 555–556, 558, 560.

40. Ibid., p. 558.

41. Ibid., p. 560.

42. "Equalization Tax, Ammunition," *Congressional Quarterly Almanac 1969* (Washington, DC: Congressional Quarterly, 1970), pp. 334–336; "Bills on Bullets, 'Designer Drugs' Advance," *Congressional Quarterly Weekly Report,* December 28, 1985, p. 2755.

43. "Federal Gun Law," *Congressional Quarterly Almanac 1985* (Washington, DC: Congressional Quarterly, 1986), pp. 228–230.

44. See also John Herbers, "Police Groups Reverse Stand and Back Controls on Pistols," *New York Times,* January 31, 1986; Richard Corrigan, "NRA, Using Members, Ads and Money, Hits Police Line in Lobbying Drive," *National Journal,* January 1,

1986, pp. 8–14; Howard Kurtz, "NRA Urging Repeal of Ban on Sale of New Machine Guns," *Washington Post,* August 28, 1986.

45. "NRA, Police Organizations in Tug of War on Gun Bills," *Congressional Quarterly Weekly Report,* March 1, 1986, pp. 502–504.

46. Ibid.; "House Committee Votes 35–0 for Controversial Gun Bill," *Congressional Quarterly Weekly Report,* March 15, 1986, p. 598.

47. Linda Greenhouse, "House Passes Bill Easing Controls on Sale of Guns," *New York Times*, April 11, 1986.

48. "House Votes to Weaken U.S. Gun Control Law," *Congressional Quarterly Weekly Report,* April 12, 1986, p. 783.

49. This change can be taken as evidence of the NRA's increasingly hard line on any and all gun controls. An NRA pamphlet from the mid-1970s said that a waiting period "could help in reducing crimes of passion and in preventing people with criminal records or dangerous mental illness from acquiring guns." Quoted in Davidson, *Under Fire,* p. 194.

50. Holly Idelson, "Brady Bill Goes to House Floor," *Congressional Quarterly Weekly Report,* November 6, 1993, p. 3048; Holly Idelson, "Congress Responds to Violence; Tackles Guns, Criminals," *Congressional Quarterly Weekly Report,* November 13, 1993, pp. 3127–3130.

51. "Gun Control's Limits," *U.S. News and World Report,* December 6, 1993, p. 25.

52. Clifford Krauss, "Gun Bill Freed From a Logjam; Passage More Likely," *New York Times,* October 28, 1993. The *Times* dubbed the bill's revival "political CPR." Sarah Brady compared it to the Dewey-Truman story, when predictions of Truman's political demise in the 1948 elections proved to be premature. Adam Clymer, "How Jockeying Brought Brady Bill Back to Life," *New York Times,* November 22, 1993; Karen DeWitt, "Five Years of Struggle by Bradys Pays Off," *New York Times,* November 22, 1993.

53. P.L. 103–159. Phil Kuntz, "Tough-Minded Senate Adopts Crime Crackdown Package," *Congressional Quarterly Weekly Report,* November 20, 1993, pp. 3199–3201; Holly Idelson, "Brady Bill Goes to the Brink, But Senate Finally Clears It," *Congressional Quarterly Weekly Report,* November 27, 1993, pp. 3271–3272.

54. Richard Lacayo, "Beyond the Brady Bill," *Time,* December 20, 1993, p. 29. Data drawn from a 1991 Justice Department survey.

55. "Brady Declares Victory with Namesake Gun-Control Law," *Syracuse Post-Standard,* March 31, 1994.

56. Spitzer, *Right to Keep and Bear Arms,* p. 95.

57. Gwen Ifill, "House Passes Bill to Set 7-Day Wait to Buy Handguns," *New York Times,* May 9, 1991. Prominent defectors from the NRA included Reps. Les AuCoin (D-OR) and Susan Molinari (R-NY). See Steven A. Holmes, "Rifle Lobby Torn by Dissidents and Capitol Defectors," *New York Times,* March 27, 1991.

58. Voting patterns were similar in the Senate, but regional analysis is more statistically variable for Senate votes because of the smaller number of senators. The eleven southern states send only twenty-two senators.

59. Clifford Krauss, "House Votes a 5-Day Pistol Wait but Sets the Measure's Expiration," *New York Times,* November 11, 1993.

60. "President's Jump in Favor of Gun Control Startles Aides," *Syracuse Post-Standard,* December 10, 1993.

61. Nancy Herndon, "Moves to Make Assault Guns Illegal Matched by New Wave of Buying," *Christian Science Monitor,* February 27, 1989; "Deadly Decision on Assault

Rifles," *New York Times,* July 26, 1990. The most common of these assault weapons are (in order of popularity) the TEC-9, the AR-15, the Uzi, the MAC-11, the MINI-14, the AK-47, the MAC-10, the SPAS-12, the HK-91, and the HK-93. About fifty types of weapon fall under the assault weapon category, but these ten account for nine-tenths of all assault weapon crime. Jim Stewart and Andrew Alexander, "Assault Weapons Muscling In on the Front Lines of Crime," *Atlanta Journal and Constitution,* May 21, 1989.

62. Robert Reinhold, "Effort to Ban Assault Rifles Gains Momentum," *New York Times,* January 28, 1989; "Bush, a Lifetime NRA Member, Opposes Semiautomatic-Gun Ban," *Syracuse Post-Standard,* February 17, 1989.

63. Clifford Krauss, "Senate Approves Ban on Manufacture of Military-Style Weapons," *New York Times,* November 18, 1993.

64. Katharine Q. Seelye, "In Gun Vote, an Odd Hero for Liberals," *New York Times,* May 7, 1994.

65. Katharine Q. Seelye, "House Approves Bill to Prohibit 19 Assault Arms," *New York Times,* May 6, 1994.

66. For more on the details of this bill, see Spitzer, *Politics of Gun Control,* ch. 5.

67. Neil A. Lewis, "President Foresees Safer U.S.," *New York Times,* August 27, 1994; David Masci, "$30 Billion Anti-Crime Bill Heads to Clinton's Desk," *Congressional Quarterly Weekly Report,* August 27, 1994, p. 2490.

68. *U.S. Government Manual, 1983/84* (Washington, DC: U.S. Government Printing Office, 1983), pp. 437–438; *Federal Regulatory Director, 1981–82* (Washington, DC: Congressional Quarterly Press, 1981), pp. 753–755; Eunice Moscoso, "ATF's Move to Justice Department Worries Both Sides of Gun Debate," Cox News Service, January 10, 2003, www.coxnews.com/cox; www.atf.gov/about/snap2003.htm; "U.S. Aides Find Gun Smuggling Is a Low Priority," *New York Times,* September 26, 1985.

69. Keller, "Powerful Reputation Makes National Rifle Association a Top Gun in Washington," p. 801.

70. Mary McGrory, "Pity the Poor, Suffering Gun Owners," *Ithaca Journal,* July 15, 1985.

71. B. Drummond Ayres Jr., "U.S. to Seek Rise in Fee for Gun Dealers," *New York Times,* January 4, 1994.

72. Stephen Labaton, "Firearms Agency Struggles to Rise from the Ashes of the Waco Disaster," *New York Times,* November 5, 1993. The agency was also rocked by repeated charges of sexual harassment and racial discrimination.

73. "Firearms Agency Bans Armor-Piercing Bullets," *New York Times,* February 6, 1994; Steven A. Holmes, "Treasury Imposes New Regulations on Some Shotguns," *New York Times,* March 1, 1994; "Another Blow to the N.R.A.," *New York Times,* March 2, 1994.

74. Irving Brant, *The Bill of Rights* (Indianapolis: Bobbs-Merrill, 1965), p. 486.

75. J.W. Peltason, *Corwin and Peltason's Understanding the Constitution* (Hinsdale, IL: Dryden Press, 1976), p. 144.

76. National Commission on the Causes and Prevention of Violence, *Firearms and Violence in American Life* (Washington, DC: U.S. Government Printing Office, 1969), pp. 260–262.

77. In *Robertson,* the Court said that "the right of the people to keep and bear arms (article 2) is not infringed by laws prohibiting the carrying of concealed weapons."

78. Spitzer, *Right to Bear Arms,* pp. 43–44, 110; Robert J. Spitzer, "The Second

Amendment 'Right to Bear Arms' and *United States v. Emerson," St. John's Law Review* 77 (Winter 2003): pp. 1–27.

Chapter 8

1. T. Alexander Smith and Raymond Tatalovich, *Cultures at War: Moral Conflicts In Western Democracies* (Toronto: Broadview Press, 2003), 25.

2. *Chaplinsky v. New Hampshire,* 315 U.S. 571.

3. *Texas v. Johnson,* 491 U.S.406.

4. *R.A.V. v. St. Paul,* 505 U.S. 380.

5. *R.A.V. v. St. Paul,* 505 U.S. 394, 396 (1992).

6. *Virginia v. Black,* 538 U.S., http://laws.findlaw.com/us/000/01–1107.html (2002).

7. *Wisconsin v. Mitchell,* 508 U.S. 487 (1993).

8. *Wisconsin v. Mitchell,* U.S. 485.

9. *Barclay v. Florida* 463, U.S. 949 (1983).

10. James B. Jacobs and Kimberly Potter, *Hate Crimes: Criminal Law and Identity Politics* (New York: Oxford University Press, 2000), 46.

11. Jacobs and Potter, *Hate Crimes,* 2000, 46–55; chronicles the relationship between advocacy groups, their media campaign, and the academy.

12. Joseph M. Fernandez, "Bringing Hate Crime into Focus: The Hate Crime Statistics Act of 1990," *Harvard Civil Rights-Civil Liberties Law Review* 26 (1991): p. xx.

13. The five representatives included their objections in a minority report. Representatives Gekas (R-PA), McCollum (R-FL), Coble (R-NC), Dannemeyer (R-CA), and Smith (R-TX) argued that the collection of statistics laid "the foundation for a subsequent Federal response." Jacobs and Potter, *Hate Crimes,* 2000, 70 fn 29; Fernandez, "Bringing Hate Crime into Focus," 1991, p. 274.

14. Jacobs and Potter, *Hate Crimes,* 70–71.

15. Robert Novak, "Ted Kennedy's Senate," *Chicago Sun Times,* August 28, 2003.

16. *Congressional Record,* S4525.15

17. George H.W. Bush, *Public Papers of the Presidents of the United States* (Washington, DC: Office of the Federal Register, National Archives and Records Service, 1989), 1989 VL 2, 1562.

18. Bush, *Public Papers of the Presidents,* 1990 VL 1, 548.

19. Clinton, *Public Papers of the Presidents,* 1997 VL 1, 709–710.

20. Clinton, *Public Papers of the Presidents,* 1997 VL 2, 1533–1535.

21. Clinton, *Public Papers of the Presidents,* 1998 VL 2, 1777.

22. Clinton, *Public Papers of the Presidents,* 2000 VL 2, 1882–1885.

23. Clinton, *Public Papers of the Presidents,* 2000 VL 2, 1807–1809.

24. www.c-span.org/campaign2000/transcript/index.asp.

25. www.hrc.org.

26. Frank Newport, "One in Four Whites Worried About Hate Crimes," *Gallup.com: Gallup Poll Analysis,* February 23, 1999.

27. These were supported at the rates of 85 percent, 83 percent, and 84 percent, respectively.

28. Frank Newport, "Homosexuality," *Gallup.com: Gallup Special Reports,* September 2002. In September 2002, Gallup found that on average Americans believe that 21.4 percent of all men are gay and 22 percent of all women are lesbian. One-

quarter of all Americans believe that more than 25 percent of Americans are gay or lesbian. These numbers suggest widespread confusion on this issue.

29. Mark Gillespse, "Public Says Farrow Should Receive Death Penalty If Convicted," *Gallup.com: Gallup Poll Analysis,* August 21, 1999.

30. Wendy Simmons and Frank Newport, "Issue Referendum Reveals Mix of Liberal and Conservative Views in America Today," *Gallup.com: Gallup Poll Analysis,* November 1, 2000.

31. Simmons and Newport, "Issue Referendum Reveals Mix of Liberal and Conservative Views in America Today."

32. David W. Moore, "Poll Suggests Close Race in 2004," *Gallup.com: Gallup Poll Analysis,* November 25, 2003. The closest issue to hate crimes named in the poll, "abortion/pro-choice issues," was named by 2 percent of the public. One percent named "Christian values/beliefs" and "judicial issues," which could conceivably be connected to hate crimes in some way.

33. Hate Crime Statistics Act, Public Law 101–275, Section 2.33.

34. Haider-Markel, "Implementing Controversal Policy," p. 34.

35. Donald P. Haider-Markel, "Implementing Controversial Policy: Results from a National Survey of Law Enforcement Department Activity on Hate Crime," *Justice Research and Policy* 3 (2001), p. 33.

36. *Hate Crime Data Collection Guidelines* (1999), U.S. Department of Justice, FBI, Criminal Justice Information Services Division, 5.

37. *Training Guide for Hate Crime Data Collection* (1996), U.S. Department of Justice, FBI, Criminal Justice Information Services Division. p. 20; Jacobs and Potter, (*Hate Crimes,* p. 41) seem to argue that this is the only stage envisioned by the *Training Guide.*

38. *Training Guide for Hate Crime Data Collection,* p. 21.

39. *Hate Crime Data Collection Guidelines,* p. 6–7.

40. Haider-Markel, "The Politics of Social Regulatory Policy: State and Federal Hate Crime Policy and Implementation Effort," *Political Research Quarterly* 51 (1998) p. 82.

41. Haider-Markel, "The Politics of Social Regulatory Policy," p. 82.

42. Tatalovich and Smith, *Cultures at War,* p. 34.

43. Valerie Jennes and Ryken Grattet, *Making a Hate Crime: From Social Movement To Law Enforcement* (New York: Russell Sage Foundation, 2001), 28.

44. The eastern states were Connecticut, Massachusetts, Maryland, New Hampshire, New Jersey, New York, Pennsylvania, Rhode Island, Vermont, and West Virginia. The Midwest States were Iowa, Illinois, Michigan, Minnesota, Missouri, Ohio, and Wisconsin. In the West the states were Alaska, California, Colorado, Idaho, Montana, Nevada, Oregon, and Washington.

45. Jennes and Grattet, *Making a Hate Crime,* pp. 96–97.

46. Those with comprehensive protection are Arizona, California, Connecticut, District of Columbia, Florida, Iowa, Illinois, Louisiana, Massachusetts, New Mexico, Pennsylvania, Rhode Island, Texas, and Washington. Those with sparse protection are Arizona, Indiana, South Carolina, and Wyoming.

47. Jennes and Grattet, *Making a Hate Crime,* pp. 87–88 (emphasis added).

48. Jennes and Grattet, *Making a Hate Crime,* p. 87.

Chapter 9

I want to thank my research assistants, Kristin Baughman, Mitch Park, and Seth Whitaker, for their help in gathering the material for this new edition.

1. It has been estimated that the paid adult Internet sites number approximately 100,000 in the United States alone and 400,000 worldwide. Jennifer Burris and Cory Arberg, "No Single Solution for Protecting Kids from Internet Pornography," *National Academies,* May 2, 2002, www4.nationalacademics.org/news.nsf/isbn/0309082749? OpenDocument.

2. Mark C. Alexander, "The First Amendment and Problems of Political Viability: The Case of Internet Pornography," *Harvard Journal of Law & Public Policy,* 25 (Spring 2002), p. 988.

3. Richard C. Morais, "Porn Goes Public," *Forbes,* June 14, 1999, p. 214. This observation was supported by Frank Rich, who suggested, "Porn is not just well within the American mainstream but overdue to be outstripped by its plain brown wrapper in prime time." Frank Rich, "Finally, Porn Does Prime Time," *New York Times,* July 27, 2003.

4. "Happening Today," *Salt Lake Tribune,* June 2, 2003.

5. See Dan Ackman, "How Big Is Porn?" *Management & Trends,* May 25, 2001, www.forbes.com/2001/05/25/0524porn.html; see also criticism of the high estimates from the adult industries in "Caslon Analytics Profile: Adult Content Industries," www.caslon.com.au/xcontentprofile.htm.

6. Whenever the term *Court* is used alone and capitalized, it refers to the Supreme Court. If the word is not capitalized when appearing alone, it refers to some lower court.

7. *Miller v. California,* 413 U.S. 15 (1973).

8. *Jacobellis v. Ohio,* 378 U.S. 476 (1964).

9. See James S. Tyre, "Legal Definition of Obscenity; Pornography,"http://internet.ggu.edu/university_library/if/legal_obscene.html.

10. According to Kenneth V. Lanning's definition, "child porn" includes all materials that are "the sexually explicit reproduction of a child's image—including sexually explicit photographs, negatives, slides, magazines, movies, videotapes, and computer disks. In essence, it is the permanent record of the sexual abuse or exploitation of an actual child." See Kenneth V. Lanning, *Child Molesters: A Behavioral Analysis* 3rd ed. (Quantico, VA: Behavioral Science Unit, Federal Bureau of Investigation, FBI Academy, 1992), p. 24.

11. Jennifer 8. Lee, "High Tech Helps Child Pornographers and Their Pursuers," *New York Times,* February 9, 2003, p. 18. www.criminology.fsu.edu/book/Cybercriminology/High%20Tech%20Helps%20Child%20Pornographers%20and%20Their%20Pursuers.htm.

12. ASACP, "About Us," www.asacp.org.

13. Louis Fisher, *American Constitutional Law,* vol. 2, *Constitutional Rights: Civil Rights and Civil Liberties,* 5th ed. (Durham, NC: Carolina Academic Press, 2003), p. 559.

14. *Roth v. United States,* 354 U.S. 476 (1957).

15. *Manual Enterprises v. Day,* 370 U.S. 478 (1962).

16. *Miller v. California* (1973).

17. Here *indecent* is defined as "a description or depiction of sexual or excretory activities or organs in a patently offensive manner as measured by contemporary community standards for the telephone medium" (see 47 U.S.C.§ 223), while *cyberspace* is defined as "the nonphysical 'place' where electronic communications happen and digital data are located." See Michael Adler, "Cyberspace, General Searches, and Digital Contraband: The Fourth Amendment and the Net-wide Search," *Yale Law Journal,* 105 (January 1996), pp. 1093–1120.

18. Communications Decency Act (CDA), 110 Stat. 133 (1996).

19. "Syllabus" to *Ashcroft v. American Civil Liberties Union*, 122 S. Ct. 1389 (2002), http://supct.law.cornell.edu/supct/html/00–1293.ZO.html.

20. *Reno v. American Civil Liberties Union*, 521 U.S. 844 (1997).

21. *City of Erie et al. v. PAP's A.M., tdba "Kandyland,"* 529 U.S. 277 (2000).

22. See Linda Greenhouse, "Justices Uphold Laws Banning Nude Dancing," *New York Times*, March 30, 2000, http://query.nytimes.com/search/restricted/article?res=F00E16FA3E580C738FDDAA0894D8404482.

23. *United States v. Playboy Entertainment Group*, 529 U.S. 803 (2000).

24. *Ashcroft v. American Civil Liberties Union*, 122 S. Ct. 1700 (2002).

25. *Ashcroft v. Free Speech Coalition*, 122 S. Ct. 1389 (2002); The Court was undoubtedly encouraged to rule as it did due to some extreme examples that occurred in at least one state. In Ohio, for example, Brian Dalton in 2001 was sentenced to seven years for having perverse thoughts about children and writing them in his private journal, a book that was not supposed to circulate. So even the written word involving "fictional children" was a possible reason for incarceration in Ohio. Bob Herbert, "In America; The Thought Police," *New York Times*, July 19, 2001, http://squawk.ca/lbo-talk/0107/1253.html.

26. *City of Los Angeles v. Alemeda Books*, 122 S. Ct. 1728 (2002).

27. *United States et al. v. American Library Association, Inc., et al.*, No. 02–361 (2003); Toni Locy and Joan Biskupic, "Anti-porn Filters in Libraries Upheld," *USA Today*, June 23, 2003, www.usatoday.com/tech/news/techpolicy/2003–06–23-scotus-filters-ok_x.htm.

28. *Paris Adult Theatre I. v. Slaton*, 413 U.S. 49 (1973).

29. For example, a 1973 statute gave a very specific definition of obscenity as "an explicit representation, or detailed written or verbal description of an act of sexual intercourse, including genital-genital, anal-genital, or oral-genital intercourse, whether between human beings or between a human being and an animal, or of flagellation, torture, or other violence indicating a sado-masochistic sexual relationship." See S. 1400, 93rd Cong., 1st sess., § 1851(b)(2)(1973). But in 1990, Congress decided to go with a general "standard of decency" when funding went to purchase art rather than attempting to list specific "organs and activities." Kim Masters, "Arts Fund a Minefield for Clinton: New Struggles Appear Likely," *Chicago Sun-Times*, January 2, 1993.

30. "Amendment Offered by Mr. Smith of New Jersey," *Congressional Record (House)*, April 20, 1994, pp. H2536-H2539.

31. See "One 'Porn' Law Too Many," *Washington Post*, May 23, 1989.

32. "Syllabus" to *Ashcroft v. American Civil Liberties Union*.

33. See 47 U.S.C. § 223(d)(1).

34. "Final Vote Results for Roll Call 25," February 1, 1996, http://clerk.house.gov/evs/1995/roll025.xml.

35. "U.S. Senate: Legislation & Records," February 1, 1996, www.senate.gov/legislative/LIS/roll_call_lists//roll_call_vote_cfm?congress=104&session=1&vote=00268.1.

36. Robert Cannon, "Free Speech Issues: The Communications Decency Act." *On The Internet*, September/October 1997, www.cybertelecom.org/eda/sct-cda4.htm.

37. 521 U.S. 844 (1997).

38. Robert MacMillan, "Primer: Children, The Internet and Pornography," *Washingtonpost.com*, June 29, 2004, www.washingtonpost.com/ac2/wp-dyn/A39748–2002May31?lanugage=printer.

39. Gareth Grainger, ABA Deputy Chairman, "Freedom of Expression and Regu-

lation of Information in Cyberspace: Issues Concerning Potential International Cooperation Principles for Cyberspace," UNESCO International Congress, Infoethics '98: Ethical, Legal and Societal Challenges of Cyberspace and Expert Meeting on Cyberspace Law, Monte Carlo, Monaco, September 1, 1998, np.

40. Robert MacMillan, "Primer: Children, the Internet and Pornography."

41. House of Representatives, 107th Congress, 2d sess., H. Con. Res. 445, "Expressing the Sense of Congress Supporting Vigorous Enforcement of the Federal Obscenity Laws," July 23, 2002.

42. MacMillan, "Primer: Children, the Internet and Pornography."

43. P.L. 107–317, December 4, 2002.

44. MacMillan, "Primer: Children, the Internet and Pornography."

45. Child Obscenity and Pornography Prevention Act of 2003, 108th Congress, 1st sess., H.R. 1161, March 6, 2003.

46. Protecting Children Against Crime Act of 2003, 108th Congress, 1st sess., S. 810, April 8, 2003.

47. Truth in Domain Names Act of 2003, 108th Congress, 1st sess., S. 800, April 7, 2002.

48. George W. Bush, "Remarks on Signing the Prosecutorial Remedies and Other Tools to End the Exploitation of Children Today Act of 2003." *Public Papers of the Presidents of the United States* (Washington, DC: Office of the Federal Register, National Archives and Records Service, 2003), pp. 502–504.

49. Floyd Abrams, "Clinton vs. the First Amendment," *New York Times,* March 30, 1997.

50. "Text of President's Message on Obscenity," *Congressional Quarterly Weekly Report,* May 9, 1969, p. 702.

51. "Statement about the Report of the Commission on Obscenity and Pornography," October 24, 1970, *Public Papers of the Presidents of the United States* (Washington, DC: Office of the Federal Register, National Archives and Records Service. Richard M. Nixon, 1970, 381.

52. "Resolution Declaring That the Senate Reject the Findings and Recommendations of the Commission on Obscenity and Pornography," *Congressional Record,* 91st Cong., 2nd sess., December 17, 1970, p. 42318.

53. In 1996 the Republican Party platform endorsed Bob Dole's efforts to bring "federal penalties for child pornography in line with far tougher state penalties" while the Republican Party platform of 2000 endorsed congressional legislation requiring "schools and libraries to secure their computers against on-line porn and predators." For the 1996 platform, see Republican National Committee, "Republican Platform 1996," www.claytongop.org/platform.htm; for the 2000 platform, see Republican National Committee, "Republican Platform 2000," www.rnc.org/gopinfo/platform.

54. *Congressional Quarterly Almanac, 1984,* 49 (Washington, DC: Congressional Quarterly, 1985), p. 51B.

55. Ronald Reagan "Child Protection Act of 1984: Remarks on Signing H.R. 3635 into Law," May 21, 1984, *Public Papers of the Presidents of the United States* 2: 721–722.

56. Attorney General's Commission on Pornography, *Final Report* (Washington, DC: U.S. Government Printing Office, 1986), 1:326.

57. George Bush "Remarks to the Religious Alliance Against Pornography," *Public Papers of the Presidents of the United States,* 1991, 1280–1281.

58. Jacqueline Trescott, "Bush on Art vs. 'Filth,'" *Washington Post,* June 7, 1993.

59. Linda Greenhouse, "Supreme Court Roundup: Child Smut Conviction Vacated After U. S. Shift," *New York Times,* November 2, 1993.

60. *Knox v. United States,* 510 U.S. 939 (1993).

61. William Clinton, "Executive Order 13133–Working Group on Unlawful Conduct on the Internet," August 5, 1999, *Public Papers of the Presidents of the United States,* 1999, pp. 1566–1567.

62. William J. Clinton, "Remarks by the President at Even on the E-Chip for the Internet," July 16, 1997, www.ed.gov/PressReleases/07-1997/970716c.html.

63. William J. Clinton, "Message to the Senate Transmitting Optional Protocols to the Convention on the Rights of the Child With Documentation," *Public Papers of the Presidents of the United States,* 2000, pp. 1680–1681.

64. For the Optional Protocol to the Convention on the Rights of the Child on the Sale of Children, child prostitution and child pornography, see *Office of the High Commissioner for Human Rights*, Geneva, Switzerland, January 18, 2002, www.unhchr.ch/html/menu2/6/crc/treaties/opac.htm.

65. Clinton, "Remarks on Signing the United Nations Optional Protocols on the Rights of Children," *Public Papers of the Presidents of the United States,* 2000, pp. 1588–1590.

66. See Nicholas Confessore, "Porn and Politics in a Digital Age," *Frontline: American Porn: Special Report,"* www.pbs.org/wgbh/pages/frontline/shows/porn/special/politics.html.

67. See *Frontline,* "American Porn," 2002, www.pbs.org/wgbh/pages/frontline/shows/porn/etc/synopsis.html.

68. George W. Bush, "Remarks," White House Conference on Missing, Exploited, and Runaway Children," Washington, DC, October 2, 2002, www.whitehouse. gov/news/releases/2002/10/2002/10/20021002-4.html.

69. White House Press Release, "Increasing Online Safety for America's Children," October 23, 2002, www.whitehouse.gov/news/releases/2002/10/print/20021023.html.

70. George W. Bush. "Remarks on Children's Online Safety," *Public Papers of the Presidents of the United States,* 2002, pp. 1836–1839.

71. John Ashcroft, "Remarks" to the Federal Prosecutors' Symposium on Obscenity, National Advocacy Center, Columbia, SC, June 6, 2002, www.obscenity crimes.org/AshcroftSpeech.cfm.

72. White House Press Release, "Increasing Online Safety for America's Children."

73. George W. Bush, "Increasing Online Safety for America's Children," The White House Release, October 2002, www.whitehouse.gov/news/releases/2002/10/20021023.html.

74. Mark Helm, "Texas Firm at Hub of Kid-Porn Empire; Sting Shuts Huge Operation," *San Antonio (Texas) Express-News,* August 9, 2001.

75. Federal Communications Commission (FCC 01–90), "Policy Statement: Industry Guidance on the Commission's Case Law Interpreting 18 USC § 1464 and Enforcement Policies Regarding Broadcast Indecency," File no. EB-00-IH-0089, March 14, 2001.

76. *Miller v. California* (1973); FCC v. Pacifica Foundation; *Enforcement of Prohibitions Against Broadcast Indecency* in 18 USC § 1464, 8 FCC Rcd 704, n. 10 (1993).

77. Federal Communications Commission (FCC 01–90), "Policy Statement."

78. Associated Press, "U.S. Sets Specific Guidelines on Indecent Programming,"

St. Louis Post-Dispatch, April 7, 2001, http://web.lexis-nexis.com/universe/document?_m=e265338c31a3c94ea4ae69b0c97a07e6&_docnum=1&wchp=dGLbVzb-zSkVb&_md5=8da082780eb1884a38fa0114ec877456.

79. Tim Golden, "16 Indicted on Charges of Internet Pornography: Allegations of Molestation Are Also Filed," *New York Times,* July 17, 1996.

80. "Child Porn Crackdown," *USA Today,* December 12, 1996.

81. White House Press Release, "Increasing Online Safety for America's Children." The "Parent's Guide to Internet Safety" is available at www.fbi.gov/publications/pguide/pguide.htm.

82. "Remarks of Attorney General Janet Reno to the Online Summit," www.usdoj.gov/criminal/cybercrime/reno-sp.htm.

83. See 18 U.S.C. § 552.

84. See 18 U.S.C. § 1462, 1465; 19 U.S.C. § 1305; 18 U.S.C. § 1699.

85. ABC News, "Child Porn Site Shut Down," March 27, 2001, http://abcnews.go.com/sections/world/DailyNews/childpornbust_010326.html 7/2/2003; see also *U.S. Customs Today,* "U.S. Customs, Moscow City Police Team Up Against Child Pornography," April 2001, www.customs.gov/xp/CustomsToday/2001/April/custoday_bluorchid.xml.

86. U.S. Customs Service"45 Children Rescued, 20 Arrests in U.S. Customs, Danish Police Investigation of Global Child-Molesting, Pornography Ring," August 9, 2002, www.usdoj.gov/ciminal/ceos/hamletre.pdf.

87. ABC News, "Child Porn Site Shut Down."

88. "14 Nations Join to Bust Huge Internet Child Porn Ring," September 2, 1998, www.cnn.com./WORLD/europe/9809/02/internet.porn.02.

89. Ibid.

90. See 18 U.S.C. § 1341.

91. Julia Preston, "Acapulco's Smut Ring: The Children Remember," *New York Times,* August 9, 1996.

92. See the U.S. Postal Service Web site: www.usps.com/postalinspectors/avalanch.htm.

93. Harrell R. Rodgers Jr., "Censorship Campaigns in Eighteen Cities: An Impact Analysis," *American Politics Quarterly* 2 (October 1974), especially pp. 375, 380–381, and 389.

94. Louise Sweeney, "The Arts and U.S. Tax Dollars: Federal Endowment for Arts Shaky," *Christian Science Monitor,* April 23, 1990, p. 8; Sam Walker, "Arts Agency Still in the Hot Seat: The National Endowment for the Arts Struggles to Reclaim Its Stature and Quiet Critics," *Christian Science Monitor,* August 6, 1993.

95. See "Bush Hits 'Horror' of Pornography," *Boston Globe,* October 11, 1991, retrieved from DIALOG File 631.

96. National Coalition for the Protection of Children & Families, "Sign the Fight Corporate Porn Petition and Encourage Attorney General Ashcroft to Prosecute Illegal Pornography Distributed by General Motors and Others," http://php.eos.net/nationalcoalition/ashcroftpetition.phtml.

97. National Coalition for the Protection of Children & Families, "What You Can Do for Pornography Awareness Week–October 27 through November 3, 2002" http://php.eos.net/nationalcoaltion/pornawarenessweek.phtml.

98. This definition of pornography was later expanded in the model antipornography law to include "the graphic sexually explicit subordination of women through pictures and/or words that also includes one or more of the following: (i) women are

presented dehumanized as sexual objects, things, or commodities; or (ii) women are presented as sexual objects who enjoy pain or humiliation; or (iii) women are presented as sexual objects who experience sexual pleasure in being raped; or (iv) women are presented as sexual objects tied up or cut up or mutilated or bruised or physically hurt; or (v) women are presented in postures or positions of sexual submission, servility, or display; or (vi) women's body parts—including but not limited to vaginas, breasts, or buttocks—are exhibited such that women are reduced to those parts; or (vii) women are presented being penetrated by objects or animals; or (viii) women are presented in scenarios of degradation, injury, torture, shown as filthy or inferior, bleeding, bruised, or hurt in a context that makes these conditions sexual."

99. See "Model Antipornography Law," *Ms.,* April 1985, p. 46.

100. See *American Booksellers Association Inc. v. William H. Hudnut,* 771 F. 2d 323 (1985). *Hudnut, Mayor of City of Indianapolis, Indiana et al. v. American Booksellers Assn.,* 475 U.S. 1001, 1132 (1986).

101. "Pornography Limit Voted in Albany," *New York Times,* June 2, 1985, p. 23.

102. Matthew L. Wald, "In Maine, Obscenity Vote Brings Warnings of Purges and Plans for Prayer," *New York Times,* June 10, 1986; Matthew L. Wald, "Maine's Anti-Obscenity Plan Is Soundly Defeated," *New York Times,* June 12, 1986.

103. *Osborne v. Ohio,* 495 U.S. 103 (1990); *FW/PBS v. Dallas,* 493 U.S. 215 (1990).

104. Dirk Johnson, "Colorado Vote Will Test Law on Obscenity," *New York Times,* October 9, 1994.

105. Utah Code Ann. § 76-5a-1. p. 230. 2003 Replacement.

106. Douglas H. Wallace, "Obscenity and Contemporary Community Standards: A Survey," *Journal of Social Issues* 29 (November 3, 1973), p. 66.

107. Coke Brown, Joan Anderson, Linda Burggraf, and Neal Thompson, "Community Standards, Conservatism, and Judgments of Pornography," *Journal of Sex and Research* 14 (May 1978), p. 94.

108. See Julie Cart, "Her Job Isn't an Open-and-Smut Case: Utah's 'Porn Czar' Struggles to Define Her Role in Fight Against Indecency," *Washington Post Archives,* April 15, 2001, http://pqasb.pqarchiver.com/washingonpost/71315815. html? did=71315815&FMT=ABS&FMTS=FT&date=Apr+15%C+2001&Author= Julie+Cart&desc=Her+Job+Isn%27t+an+Open-and-Smut+Case%3B+Utah %27s+%27Porn+Czar%27+Struggles+to+Define++Her+Role+in+Fight+Against+ Indecency;1.newsbank.com/nl-search/we/Archives?p_action=doc&p_docid= OEB9BEOF260C51. . . . Accessed 5/17/2003; and Michael Janofsky, "Utah Law Creates First 'Pornography Czar,'" *New York Times,* March 16, 2000.

109. Michael Janofsky, "Bountiful Journal; Defining Pornography Proves Tricky, Even in a Utah Town," *New York Times,* February 2, 2003, www.pagefusion.com/ parse.php?site_id=zvumR11aGU&page=new_york_times1.html. See also Candus Thomson, "Utah Closes Porn Czar Office Citing Budget Contraints," *The Detroit News/Nation/World*, March 24, 2003, www.detnews.com/2003/nation/0303/24/a11-116859.htm.

110. "Public Concerned About Porn, but Divided over Court Decision," *Gallup Opinion Index* 142 (May 1977), pp. 5–6.

111. Princeton Survey Research Associates, "Tracking Online Life Survey," April 2, 2001, http://web.lexis-nexis.com./universe/document?_m= lce8b429daa38 af042al4bf6681d6761&_docnum=52&wchp= dGLbVlzzSkVb&_md5=ce2071594 b43b4f759aab98937fad8ea. August 2004.

112. R. Morgan, "Theory and Practice: Pornography and Rape," in *Take Back the Night*, ed. L. Lederer (New York: William Morrow, 1980), pp. 134–140.

113. In 1988, 56 percent of the people surveyed by National Opinion Research Center Felt that Sexual materials did lead people to commit rape. In 1991, 53 percent of those surveyed felt sexual materials did lead people to commit rape, whereas in 1993, 56 percent of the people felt this way.

114. The question asked was: Pornography on the Internet: Please tell me whether you think this is a major cause, minor cause or not a cause of moral decline." Forty-seven percent thought it was a "very major cause" and 15 percent thought it a "fairly major cause"; 21 percent thought it was a minor cause and only 10 percent thought it was not a cause of the decline in morality. Peter D. Hart Research Associates, poll released May 3, 1999, http://web.lexis-nexis.com./universe/document?_m= 8d50682102773cd100938ald7827aa79&_docnum=1&wchp=dGLbVzbzSkVA&_ md5= 21f2b024e41d4adacd00db8112472467. August 21, 2004.

115. *Public Opinion,* "Opinion Roundup: A Pornography Report," September–October, 1986, p. 31.

116. *Time/*Yankelovich, Clancy, Shulman poll, July 7–9, 1986, in *Public Opinion,* "Opinion Roundup: A Pornography Report."

117. International Communications Research, "NPR, Kaiser, Kennedy School Attitude Toward Government Survey," Roper Poll, conducted in July 2000, sampling a base of 1,557 persons, http://web.lexis-nexis.com./universe/document?_m=1 1560d0989cf92372d378c8260986a87&_docnum=1&wchp=dGLbVtbzSkVA&_md5= 8a3 ae659c7ae163b28662225778b175b. August 21, 2004.

118. Both the 1970 pornography commission report and a 1985 Canadian survey found that adolescents were more often exposed to pornography than adults were. Attorney General's Commission on Pornography, *Final Report,* 1: 916 and 921.

119. *Public Opinion,* "Opinion Roundup: A Pornography Report," p. 33.

___ About the Editors and Contributors

Raymond Tatalovich (PhD, University of Chicago) is a professor of political science at Loyola University of Chicago, where he specializes in American politics and the study of moral conflicts in public policy. Among the most recent publications are his coauthored *Cultures at War: Moral Conflicts in Western Democracies* (2003) and *The Presidency and Political Science: Two Hundred Years of Constitutional Debate* (2003).

Byron W. Daynes (PhD, University of Chicago) is a professor of political science at Brigham Young University. He has coauthored or edited twelve books, notably *The American Presidency and the Social Agenda* (2001) and *American Politics and the Environment* (2002), and written over fifty articles on the American presidency, public policy, and the Supreme Court.

Theodore J. Lowi (PhD, Yale University) is the John L. Senior Professor of American Institutions at Cornell University. He is the only American to have served as president of the American Political Science Association, International Political Science Association, and Policy Studies Organization and, in 1981, became the first political scientist appointed to the French-American Foundation Chair of American Civilization in Paris. His book *The Personal President* (1985) won the Neustadt Prize for the best book on the American presidency.

Gary C. Bryner (PhD, Cornell University) is professor in the Public Policy Program at Brigham Young University and the Department of Political Science. He is a research associate in the Natural Resources Law Center at the University of Colorado School of Law and a lawyer. He is the author of *The Politics of Public Morality: The Great American Welfare Reform Debate* (1998) and other books on environmental and natural resource policy.

Margaret E. Ellis (PhD, University of Texas at Dallas) is an assistant professor of political science at the University of Oklahoma, specializing in American politics, judicial process, and constitutional law. She has been a member of the executive council of the Southwestern Political Science Association and served on the faculties of James Madison University, Wichita State University, and Western Kentucky University.

Ted G. Jelen (PhD, Ohio State University) is a professor of political science at the University of Nevada–Las Vegas. The former editor of *Journal for the Scientific Study of Religion,* his focused research on religion and politics has resulted in several books, including his *To Serve God and Mammon: Church-State Relations in the United States* (2000) and the coauthored *Public Attitudes Toward Church and State* (M.E. Sharpe, 1995).

Jon Schaff (PhD, Loyola University of Chicago) is an assistant professor of political science at Northern State University in Aberdeen, South Dakota, where he teaches courses on the presidency, religion and politics, and American political thought. He has published on the presidency in *White House Studies* and *Political Research Quarterly,* and is currently working on a revisionist study of the Lincoln presidency.

Stephanie A. Slocum-Schaffer (PhD, The American University) is an assistant professor of political science at Shepherd University, where she specializes in American politics, political institutions, and public policy. Among her most recent publications are "Morality Policy" in *Federalism in America* (2004) and *America in the Seventies* (2003).

Robert J. Spitzer (PhD, Cornell University) is Distinguished Service Professor of Political Science at the State University of New York, College at Cortland. Formerly president of the Presidency Research Group of the American Political Science Association, he has authored over 200 articles, essays, and papers on American politics. Among his most recent books are *The Politics of Gun Control* (2004) and *The Right to Bear Arms* (2001).

Mary Ann E. Steger (PhD, Southern Illinois University) is chair and professor of political science at Northern Arizona University, specializing in public administration and public policy. Currently her research emphasis is welfare policy, and she has authored research reports on Medicaid, welfare policy, and food stamps for the Nelson Rockefeller Institute of Government in Albany, New York.

Brent S. Steel (PhD, Washington State University) is a professor of political science and director of the Master of Public Policy Program at Oregon State University. His recent coauthored and edited books include *Oregon Politics and Government: Progressive versus Conservative Populism* (2004) and *Political Culture and Public Policy in Canada and the United States: Only a Border Apart?* (2000).

Ruth Ann Strickland (PhD, University of South Carolina) is professor of political science and criminal justice at Appalachian State University, where she specializes in American politics, public policy analysis, and judicial politics. Her most recent book is entitled *Restorative Justice* (2004).

Scott Yenor (PhD, Loyola University of Chicago) is an assistant professor of political science at Boise State University, where he specializes in political philosophy and contemporary political ideologies. He has published scholarly articles on diverse topics, including David Hume, Alexis de Tocqueville, F.A. Hayek, and John Locke, as well as publications on the American presidency.

Index